Legislating Together

Legislating Together

The White House and Capitol Hill
from Eisenhower to Reagan

Mark A. Peterson

Harvard University Press
Cambridge, Massachusetts
London, England

Copyright © 1990 by the President and Fellows of Harvard College
All rights reserved
Printed in the United States of America
10 9 8 7 6 5 4 3 2

First Harvard University Press paperback edition, 1993

Library of Congress Cataloging-in-Publication Data

Peterson, Mark A., 1955-
   Legislating together : the White House and Capitol Hill from
   Eisenhower to Reagan / Mark A. Peterson.
      p. cm.
   Includes bibliographical references.
   ISBN 0-674-52415-2 (alk. paper) (cloth)
   ISBN 0-674-52416-0 (pbk.)
   1. Presidents—United States.   2. United States. Congress.
3. Legislation—United States.   4. United States—Politics and
government—1945-   I. Title.
JK585.P48   1990   89-71618
320.4'04'0973—dc20   CIP

For my parents

Contents

Preface

As long ago as 1977, in a report entitled *Studying the Presidency* (New York: Ford Foundation), Hugh Heclo commented that "at graduate schools across the country there is a ceaseless, disorganized, and non-cumulative flow of dissertations studying particular cases of Presidential/Congressional interaction" (p. 17). Over the past decade the situation has not improved. Nor is there a sense within the discipline as a whole that real progress has been made in articulating new approaches to the study of the presidency and its relations with other national political institutions. In spite of an abundance of writing on the subject, this area simply has not achieved the intellectual maturity exhibited in other fields of political analysis. Having completed my own study of the legislative interactions between the White House and Capitol Hill, I am hardly surprised at Heclo's lament. It is not easy to craft analyses that are broader in scope and more comprehensive in orientation than those that have already been performed.

I share the prevalent concern about the utility of some of the research designs, the quality of the empirical data, the seemingly small gains in useful generalizations produced by the years of scholarship on America's national representative institutions and the public policies they create. This book addresses many of those concerns. But it too has been years in the making and falls far short of my original goals. While I am satisfied that I furnish here original empirical support for the theoretical issues I raise, that both the concepts and the methods of my research suggest new directions for fruitful investigation of the presidential-congressional relationship, and that my overall assessment will invite both practitioners and observers to view the institutions somewhat differently, a thorough resolution of all the analytical ambiguities remains a distant dream.

Why is it so difficult to engage in truly innovative analysis? In the very process of trying to avoid the plague of noncumulative research, the student of the presidency, Congress, and public policy stumbles into a world of immense complexity. For me, the initial questions were easy. It struck me that the president and Congress need each other, that decisions on legislative issues are made by the president and members of Congress in a variety of identifiable ways, and that one can characterize the diverse styles of legislative action fairly simply without doing too much of an injustice to the real world. Even in the personality-ridden arena of presidential politics, the interactions between the two branches and the legislative decisions they produce are neither random nor dominated by the idiosyncratic. Moreover, the broad patterns of interaction seem to apply to all presidents and their dealings with Capitol Hill, so that it may be possible to generalize about the relationship between the two institutions.

The questions from that point on proved more difficult. As I pressed to identify the forces that influenced how the president and Congress together made choices about legislation, it became apparent that neither conceptual nor empirical parsimony would be easily attained. It was also obvious that good humor constituted a primary investigative resource. Consider the following sample of factors that the extant literature and my interviews with the practitioners themselves revealed to be of importance.

An unusual menagerie—whales, boll weevils, gypsy moths, and lame ducks, not to mention lions and foxes.

Assorted instruments of persuasion—whips, ships, telephones, tickets, planes, and (most infamous) "the Treatment."

Diverse forms of exercise—elbow bending, often "lifting a glass to liberty," arm twisting, coalition building, and the taxing gymnastic maneuver of going over the heads of Congress.

Utilitarian accounting conventions—political resources, currency, capital, and credits, all to be invested, expended, or squandered.

A variety of social gatherings—parties, interest groups, voting groups, study groups, chowder and marching societies, constituencies, and the last tuition-free institution, the electoral college.

Several inflatable objects—egos, rhetoric, positions, and consumer prices, though no ducks.

Plotted "ayes" and crossed "tees," especially committees, subcommittees, committees of the whole, committees on com-
mittees, committees to reelect, rules committees, special
committees, select committees, and standing committees,
since everyone is too busy to be sitting.

Programs approved for many audiences—to be moved or lost,
major releases and minor dramas, new innovations and old
reruns, and much type casting.

Finally, an assortment of letters to challenge even Johannes
Gutenberg—from LAs, AAs, CBO, EOP, WHO, OMB, DC,
OPD, PRMs, and the CEA, to OPL and OCL, the "liaison"
d'être of the presidential-congressional relationship.

And James Sundquist, tongue only partially in cheek, suggested to
me an explanation of congressional responses to the president
reminiscent of the tit-for-tat strategy for playing Prisoners'
Dilemma: instead of voting in accordance with the give-and-take
of assorted political forces, members of Congress may merely do
to the president this time what the chief executive did to them
last time.

Just as I was striving to bring some order to these issues, one of
my informants related the following story to me:

The process is so complex, it's impossible to . . . Well, your
job is impossible. You can't generalize or even do a detailed
analysis of how things happen . . . You see, on everything
there are a million zillion things that can come up. There's no
way you can get a fix on it . . . In the whip's office, we had a
guy working for us who was doing a book. He had written
some books on the process, and he came up and said he was
revising one of the books. And he asked whether he could
come to the office for a week and just watch. The head of the
office said, "Let me read the book." Well, he took it home
that night and read it. The next day he said to him, "I'll tell
you what, you come work here for six months. I'll treat you
like everyone else, and you will work on the staff—if you
promise me that after that six months, you will go write a
letter of apology to every student you have taught with that
book." Well, he grumbled a few things and was quite upset.
The boss said he'd hire him, not pay him much, just enough
to cover his living in Washington, and he was a whip assistant
or something. After the six months, he came back and said, "I

can't write the book about how the process works. I just can't
do it." He had been at those things for some time, but he
couldn't write it. He saw the thousands of people we talk to.
He decided to write about one bill, one that he had been
assigned. He could write about that, describing the forces that
went into shaping that bill as it went along, but that one was
different from fifty others. There's just no way to generalize.

At times, it did seem as though there was no way to generalize
about the interactions between the president and Congress, especially for the range of domestic issues and the several administrations I was examining. At times it seemed there was no way to
avoid aggravating Heclo's complaint.

The fundamental message of my research, however, is that
despite the obstacles, one *can* identify patterns in the way the
White House and Congress interact. Presidents, regardless of
their individual skills and character, are advantaged and disadvantaged in their dealings with congressional opponents by the particular configurations of the institutional, political, and economic
settings in which they must operate. These have fairly predictable
consequences for how the issues will be decided. Furthermore,
different kinds of policy proposals trigger fairly predictable types
of congressional action. Although the circumstances surrounding
each legislative issue are in some ways unique, and probably no
situation precisely fits the dictates of any one identified pattern,
generalizations are possible. Indeed, without them we cannot discover what is distinctive about each situation.

One prominent member of the White House press pool suggested
to me that it is possible to identify patterns across administrations.
The patterns, however, are not what is interesting; the differences
are interesting. But how do we know what is different without
knowing what is the same? We need to be able to judge the distance
between a generalized baseline and what actually happens in a particular case in order to assess the contributions to the process that
lie beyond the forces that affect all cases. The results of this research
indicate that the distance is not great for most issues and most
administrations. Still, having formulated a baseline of sorts, we are
in a better position to evaluate the significance and sources of the
differences that do exist, and therefore to judge both institutional
conflict and presidential performance through a less subjective eye.
These issues are the subject of the chapters that follow.

*   *   *

On the surface, few of life's experiences would seem to be as solitary as the process of researching and authoring a book. The gestation of ideas, the various forms of information gathering, the methods of analysis, the honing of interpretations, and the writing are all seemingly the province of the author alone. On quick reflection, of course, it is obvious that the completion of almost any scholarly work is possible only as a result of the contributions made by many others. This project, like most, would not have progressed very far without a wide range of financial, institutional, and individual encouragement.

The Earhart Foundation twice funded my research, first in the form of a graduate fellowship and later as a faculty fellowship research grant. Additional financial assistance came from the Horace H. Rackham School of Graduate Studies at the University of Michigan, the National Science Foundation (grant no. SES-8216865), as well as the Harvard Graduate Society Fund and the Faculty Aide Program at Harvard University. John Dolfin and the Universities Service Centre in Hong Kong provided an uncommonly captivating place to begin thinking in earnest about the presidency and Congress. Martha Derthick, Diane Hodges, Paul Peterson, and the Brookings Institution furnished a hospitable and gracious base of operations each time my research took me to Washington, D.C. The Gerald R. Ford Presidential Library, the Department of Political Science, and the Institute of Public Policy Studies at the University of Michigan afforded the use of their facilities and the good humor of their staffs. Since my arrival at Harvard University, I have benefited greatly from the resources and able staff of the Department of Government and the Center for American Political Studies.

From the beginning, I profited from the advice and guidance of several unusually helpful individuals at the University of Michigan. John Kingdon provided invaluable direction and assistance; he has always set the high standard by which to judge both scholarship and teaching. Each conversation with Joel Aberbach was a learning experience and improved my thinking about all aspects of American politics. George Grassmuck made the seemingly impossible become possible. And economist Paul Courant willingly subjected himself to a great deal of ponderous discourse. Special thanks are owed each one of them.

Another member of the Michigan community had an influence on me that I shall always cherish and the dimensions of which I cannot even begin to express. In addition to posing tough questions and furnishing a solid backboard for my sometimes less than penetrating ideas, Jack Walker touched all aspects of my life. He began as my teacher and supervisor, then soon became a lively collaborator, a valued colleague, and a deeply respected friend. As I was reviewing the page proofs of this book, his spirited life was tragically cut short in an automobile accident. I, and all who knew Jack, will sorely miss him.

My warmest appreciation is extended to former Presidents Jimmy Carter and Gerald Ford and to the scores of journalists and executive and congressional officials all of whom granted interviews, gave generously of their time, and shared their perspectives with me.

Many other individuals lent their ideas and raised important issues as the research progressed. I am grateful to Thomas Anton, Lawrence Baum, Jon Bond, Roger Davidson, Louis Fisher, Richard Fleisher, Thomas Gais, James Garrand, Stephen Hess, Cathy Johnson, John Kessel, Susan Lawrence, Paul Light, Thomas Mann, Norman Ornstein, Eric Peterson, James Pfiffner, Bert Rockman, Austin Sarat, Deborah Snow, and James Sundquist.

Colleagues in the Department of Government at Harvard had an enormous influence on the book, often just by creating a pervasive atmosphere of intellectual liveliness. H. W. Perry, Jr., originally a fellow graduate student at Michigan, read in its entirety everything that emanated from this project; the manuscript and I would have suffered greatly without his contributions. Richard Neustadt, in addition to reading and probing one version of the text after another, was an invaluable source of support and inspiration. One could not hope for a better teacher or a more genial friend. Morris Fiorina, Nelson Polsby (who visited for a year), Robert Putnam, and Judith Shklar perused one or more complete drafts and offered much-appreciated suggestions. Thanks are also due Henry Brady, Gary King, Douglas Price, Kenneth Shepsle, and Margaret Weir for the advice, perspectives, and fellowship they offered.

Many students at Harvard made it possible for me to enhance the empirical analysis and introduce other improvements in the manuscript. Marc Bodnick, Andrew Clubok, Carolyn Duffy, Robert Gustafson, Thomas Joo, Elizabeth Knapp, Chan U Lee, and Jeffrey McGuire were admirable research assistants. Much of the data collection, management, and analysis depended on the talents of Stephen Ansolabehere and Erik Corwin. Matthew Dickinson assisted with the coding, and students in various undergraduate and graduate seminars supplied pointed critiques and volunteered important ideas.

My two editors at Harvard University Press deserve a special note of appreciation. Aida Donald, patient as always, cheerfully stayed with me as the project took longer to complete than either of us had anticipated. Vivian Wheeler, with professional care and imagination, gently moved the prose in the direction of the standards I profess but did not always practice. And I am grateful for the thoughtful comments of two anonymous reviewers, who provided encouragement as well as insightful guidance in improving the manuscript.

Each of these institutions and individuals has my enduring gratitude. But it is to my parents, Elbert and Mabel Peterson, that I owe the most. If there is an American ethos articulating the virtues of education, they embody it. Without their years of support, encouragement, and patience, this book would not have been possible.

Legislating Together

1. Introduction

"Mr. Speaker, the President of the United States!" With that proclamation from the sergeant-at-arms of the House of Representatives, the assembled members of Congress and other dignitaries in the House chamber rise each January to greet the president for the annual State of the Union address. Millions of citizens view the spectacle on television. For here are gathered virtually all the major officials of the American national government. The executive branch, of course, is represented by the president, accompanied by the vice president and members of the Cabinet. The bicameral legislature is for this one event joined, representatives and senators together. The judiciary is embodied in the robed justices of the Supreme Court. It is in this setting that we see our national government as one enterprise, but with all eyes fixed on the president at center stage.

The address itself has myriad audiences. The president speaks to our allies and adversaries abroad, indirectly via media coverage and directly via the invited foreign diplomats who are present. The president also addresses the American public, indeed often more with an eye to the television sets in innumerable family rooms across the country than to the politicians seated in close proximity just beyond the rostrum. At the core of the State of the Union address, by virtue of its origins in Article II, Section 3, of the United States Constitution and by evolving tradition, is the delineation of the president's policy priorities and what they require, either implicitly or explicitly, in terms of congressionally enacted legislation. Congress is an audience of special significance: little of import desired by the president and proffered in the State of the Union can be accomplished in any enduring fashion without the support of a majority of its members.

The visual imagery surrounding the delivery offers a metaphor for the most pervasive interpretation of American politics and executive-legislative relations, what I term the *presidency-centered perspective.* The president, standing at the heart of the House chamber, dominates the room and the camera. The message is the president's, the agenda is the president's. Legislators seated throughout the chamber expect and to a considerable degree self-consciously require this projection of leadership from the chief executive, cast here as chief legislator. Whether the president succeeds or fails—in this oration and later in the policy domain—depends upon the skill with which the president fashions influence, which itself is derived from the national expectation that the unifying force of political leadership resides in the Oval Office. All too often the president does fail, by reason of either the incumbent's own shortcomings or the insurmountable barriers erected by the contemporary American political system.

The presidency-centered perspective represented in this State of the Union metaphor is firmly rooted in the popular imagination and in our civic culture. It constitutes a basic theme of textbooks at all levels and finds reinforcement in the media coverage of the Washington political scene. It is also, though not exclusively, the intellectual tradition within which scholarly work on the president and Congress has been accomplished. While this perspective has in its origins many truths about American politics in the modern era, it is also severely limited, both conceptually and empirically.

This book offers an alternative to the presidency-centered perspective. The *tandem-institutions perspective* is constructed from a more realistic prescriptive and descriptive appraisal of the symbiotic relationship of the president and Congress in the legislative arena and of the elaborate contexts in which the institutional interactions are played out. I examine these competing perspectives in some detail in this introductory chapter and give concrete illustrations of how they lead to contrasting interpretations of presidential-congressional exchanges on legislative issues. I also present an overview of the book, reporting on an empirical study conducted within the tandem-institutions framework. The focus is on the domestic issues associated with the legislative programs introduced from 1953 to 1984 by presidents from Dwight Eisenhower to Ronald Reagan. My conclusions are derived from interviews with the practitioners themselves, including two of the former presidents, and a detailed analysis of 299 presidential legislative initiatives drawn from this period and afforded congressional action between 1953 and June 1986.

From the argument and analysis built progressively in the subsequent chapters I demonstrate the advantages of the tandem-institutions approach, along with the concepts and methodology that logically evolve from it. I identify the numerous ways in which congressional coalitions respond to presidential initiatives and show how they reflect the varying degrees of conflict and cooperation in legislative deliberations. By integration of the interviews with quantitative analysis of the sample, I evaluate how congressional responses are shaped by the diverse factors that make up the institutional, political, economic, and policy contexts of legislative action on the president's program. Establishing that contextual baseline, which explains much of the variation in executive-legislative interactions, yields a unique opportunity to assess more systematically than before the performance in the legislative arena of each president from Eisenhower to Reagan. Their experiences, viewed through the lens of this analysis, provide insight into the generic role of presidents in the realm of legislative leadership.

Competing Perspectives

Given the complex and politically formidable issues confronting modern societies, along with the threat to unified leadership embodied in the potentially parochial concerns of a collective body such as Congress, it is not surprising that most evaluations of the American system have sought to identify a single institutional repository of coherent political leadership. Nor is it astonishing that due to the centrality of the modern presidency in the policy-making structure, the presidency has become the prescriptive cynosure for regenerated leadership. Studies of presidential-congressional interactions on legislation, then, often assimilate the attributes of the presidency-centered perspective, which incorporates a particular set of perceptions about the historical and contemporary institutional relationship. This perspective dramatizes interbranch autonomy and power, typically linking notions of presidential policy "success" with the interests of the nation as a whole.

The presidency-centered perspective has five main facets.[1] Foremost is the heated battle between the executive and legislative

1. I derived the "presidency-centered perspective" by reading widely on the president and Congress. The relevant sources include James Mac-Gregor Burns, *The Deadlock of Democracy: Four-Party Politics in*

branches of the American national government as they struggle to formulate the political agenda and define the goals of the contemporary state. This aspect of the presidency-centered perspective stresses the significance of the American constitutional order and its provision for the formal separation of powers between the executive and legislative branches, a structure that "legitimizes conflict between Congress and the President" by issuing, in Edward S. Corwin's famous phrase, "an invitation to struggle."[2] The institutions are seen as inherently confrontational, driven by contradictory and often irreconcilable interests, perspectives, and goals, producing a political dissonance that reached its modern zenith during the Nixon administration. Congress is evaluated solely in terms of whether it has catered to or been defeated by the president and, by implication, whether the myopia of the legislature has been overwhelmed by the national interest. Commenting on the legislature's effort to realize both legitimacy and effectiveness, Samuel Huntington asserts: "If Congress legislates, it subordinates itself to the President; if it refuses to legislate, it alienates itself from public opinion. Congress can assert its power or it can pass laws; but it cannot do both."[3]

America (Englewood Cliffs, N.J.: Prentice-Hall, 1963), and Presidential Government: The Crucible of Leadership (Boston: Houghton Mifflin, 1973); Edward S. Corwin, The President: Office and Powers, 4th ed. (New York: New York University Press, 1957); Lloyd N. Cutler, "To Form a Government," Foreign Affairs 59 (Fall 1980): 126–143; Herman Finer, The Presidency: Crisis and Regeneration (Chicago: University of Chicago Press, 1960); Charles M. Hardin, Presidential Power and Accountability: Toward a New Constitution (Chicago: University of Chicago Press, 1974); Samuel P. Huntington, "Congressional Responses to the Twentieth Century," in The Congress and America's Future, ed. David B. Truman (Englewood Cliffs, N.J.: Prentice-Hall, 1965); Harold J. Laski, The American Presidency: An Interpretation (New York: Harper and Brothers, 1940); Richard E. Neustadt, Presidential Power: The Politics of Leadership from FDR to Carter (New York: Macmillan, 1980); Clinton Rossiter, The American Presidency, 2nd ed. (New York: New American Library, 1960); and Woodrow Wilson, Constitutional Government in the United States (New York: Columbia University Press, 1908). Of special importance is Thomas E. Cronin, The State of the Presidency, 2nd ed. (Boston: Little, Brown, 1980), chap. 3.

2. Edward S. Corwin, The President: Office and Powers (New York: New York University Press, 1940), p. 200; and Nelson W. Polsby, Congress and the Presidency (Englewood Cliffs, N.J.: Prentice-Hall, 1971), p. 171.

3. Huntington, "Congressional Responses," p. 6.

Linked to the idea of clashing institutions is the second basic proposition governing analysis of the two branches, what Thomas Cronin refers to as the "cycle theory of presidential-congressional relations."[4] The institutional conflict is not just an unpatterned series of confrontations between combatants of equal potency. Rather, the president and Congress are placed, at least implicitly, in the domain of a zero-sum game of power in which the ascendancy of one institution must come at the expense of the other. During one period, the president displays the energy and wields the power necessary to dominate the relationship and therefore the major issues of governance; during the next period, Congress reasserts its authority and assumes the position of leading institution.

In the modern era, however, the cycle exhibits a peculiar twist. Both as a portrayal of the contemporary nature of executive-legislative relations and as a normative position, the third basic element of the presidency-centered perspective grants permanent ascendancy to the presidency. There have been periods of unusual aggressiveness on the part of Congress, as when it instituted the War Powers Act, installed trade embargoes, limited executive agreements, restricted covert actions of the Central Intelligence Agency, and investigated the Reagan administration's Iran contra scandal. But these spurts of assertiveness during the 1970s and 1980s are viewed, in fact or in hope, as short-lived. More important, an emboldened Capitol Hill is seen by some as detrimental to the long-run interests of the polity as the country struggles to meet the demands of an increasingly intricate and challenging world.[5] The president consequently has become a magnet attracting all manner of leadership issues. Corwin offers a concise summary of the factors leading to this convergence on the president:

The nationalization of American industry, the necessity of curbing monopolistic practices resulting from this development, the conservation movement of the first Roosevelt, the rise and consolidation of the labor movement, the altered outlook on the proper scope of governmental function that the Great Depression produced, and finally two great wars and their aftermath have all conspired to thrust into the fore-

4. Cronin, *The State of the Presidency*, p. 139.
5. Cutler, "To Form a Government"; Hardin, *Presidential Power and Accountability*; and Huntington, "Congressional Responses," pp. 5–31.

ground of our constitutional system the dual role of the President as catalyst of public opinion and as legislative leader.[6]

This reading of events in the twentieth century leads logically to the fourth characteristic of the presidency-centered perspective, that the president *should* serve as the fundamental guiding spirit within the government, a clear first without equals or empowered skeptics. In the tradition of Theodore Roosevelt and Woodrow Wilson, the president is the personification of the *national* interest, as the method of election concedes the president but one constituency: the entire nation, the people as a whole.[7] The concern is palpable, therefore, when presidents find their policy initiatives stymied by a Congress receptive to the interests of a nation disaggregated—a representational contradiction found mostly in the domestic arena, but also increasingly in the field of foreign affairs. Disquiet yields to indignation when even more presidential mastery is squandered as the result of an incumbent's ineptitude in handling the reins of power, thereby relinquishing excessive discretion to the legislative branch.

The final attribute of the presidency-centered perspective, perhaps the only logical conclusion to be derived from the first four, is the call for institutional reform. Two directions are involved: a reformulation of the means by which presidents are selected so as to ensure the election of truly competent individuals,[8] and a restructuring of the architecture of the national government, whether by minor rearrangement or by introduction of a whole new foundation. Each approach seeks reintroduction into the policy-making process of a coherence that can be achieved only by reinforcing the role of the president as leader and manager of the national government.

The perspective I have just outlined obviously has its roots in the real world. There *are* times of intense institutional conflict,

6. Corwin, *The President*, 4th ed., p. 264.

7. Jeffrey K. Tulis, "The Interpretable Presidency," in *The Presidency and the Political System*, 2nd ed., ed. Michael Nelson (Washington, D.C.: CQ Press, 1988), pp. 101–104. Corwin notes that "the present-day role of the President as policy determiner in the legislative field is largely the creation of the two Roosevelts and Woodrow Wilson." *The President*, 4th ed., p. 265.

8. Nelson W. Polsby, *Consequences of Party Reform* (New York: Oxford University Press, 1983), esp. pp. 105–114 on Jimmy Carter's problematic relations with Congress.

and the constitutional separation of the executive and legislative branches furnishes the staging for potential confrontation. Congress has never been an institution well suited to independently developing coherent or comprehensive legislative remedies for major economic or social ills, especially in the years since the committee and subcommittee reforms of the early 1970s. Further, the character of individual presidents matters; their ideologies, temperaments, and skills contribute to the nature of their policy agendas, the means by which their goals are pursued, and the politics of their reception.

As a framework for evaluation of American government, however, the presidency-centered perspective is incomplete and risks distorting our understanding of how the presidency and Congress function together as policy-making bodies. These problems can be avoided by viewing the presidency and Congress as *tandem institutions* constituting the major components of the American national legislative *decision-making system*.

The term "system" communicates that the White House and Capitol Hill operate within a legislative arena whose boundary ultimately encompasses both institutions. While the Constitution may have planted the seeds of conflict, it more precisely, as Richard Neustadt aptly states, "created a government of separated institutions *sharing* powers."[9] The legislative process cannot be understood with reference to only one branch of government. Neither institution can legislate domestic policy on its own, but must do so with the cooperation or at least acquiescence of the other.[10] The "system" itself may be interpreted as a quasi-institution in which decisions are jointly reached, with "a framework of rules, procedures, and arrangements . . . [that] prescribes and constrains . . . generally the way in which business is conducted."[11] Because of their independent constitutional authority and their separate physical locations, we tend to emphasize the discrete nature of the executive and legislature. In the legislative

9. Neustadt, *Presidential Power*, p. 26. Italics in original.
10. Ibid., p. 29; and Richard Rose, "Government against Sub-Governments: A European Perspective on Washington," in *Presidents and Prime Ministers*, ed. Richard Rose and Ezra Suleiman (Washington, D.C.: American Enterprise Institute, 1980), p. 340.
11. Kenneth A. Shepsle, "Institutional Equilibrium and Equilibrium Institutions," in *Political Science: The Science of Politics*, ed. Herbert F. Weisberg (New York: Agathon Press, 1986), p. 52.

process, however, the rules, practices, and politics of statutory policy making bind them into a single enterprise. And while the postwar proclivity for divided government has reinforced the potential for disharmony within the legislative system, the increasingly formalized activities of the congressional and public liaison offices in the Executive Office of the President, linking executive and legislative domains, suggest the "institutionalization" of this system by clarifying its boundaries and enhancing its internal structural complexity.[12]

Introducing the modifier *decision-making* to the system reveals its primary activity: making collective decisions about what issues will be considered for legislative remedy and what forms the legislative solutions will take. Even in more conventionally conceived institutions or organizations, decision making constitutes their defining attribute and "may well characterize the essence of organizational behavior."[13] Further, the decision-making orientation recognizes that the interactions among the relevant actors—the ways in which specific collective choices are made—vary enormously, evincing different levels of conflict or cooperation and leading to diverse outcomes. These attributes of decisions also depend on the circumstances of their resolution.[14]

Finally, the phrase *tandem institutions* gives definition to the role of each branch in the decision-making system. In a strict legal sense, the chief executive and Capitol Hill are a partnership to the degree that they must jointly engage in the activity of the legislative process if there are to be statutory responses to policy issues. In short, the two must act in tandem. The word "tandem" also

12. Nelson W. Polsby describes the characteristics of institutionalization in "The Institutionalization of the U.S. House of Representatives," *American Political Science Review* 62 (March 1968): 145. For discussions of the evolution of the congressional liaison and public liaison offices and staffs, see Eric L. Davis, "Congressional Liaison: The People and the Institutions," in *Both Ends of the Avenue*, ed. Anthony King (Washington, D.C.: American Enterprise Institute, 1983), pp. 59–78; and Joseph A. Pika, "Interest Groups and the Executive: Presidential Intervention," in *Interest Group Politics*, ed. Allan J. Cigler and Burdett A. Loomis (Washington, D.C.: CQ Press, 1983), pp. 298–323.

13. Lawrence B. Mohr, "Organizations, Decisions, and Courts," *Law and Society Review* 10 (Summer 1976): 627. See also Terry M. Moe, "The New Economics of Organization," *American Journal of Political Science* 28 (November 1984): 744.

14. Mohr, "Organizations," pp. 628–637.

generally includes in its meaning the placement of one member behind the other, as on a tandem bicycle. Applying that interpretation here does not violate the spirit of this analytical perspective. On matters of domestic policy, the president may sit at the "front" of the process, providing direction by influencing the policy agenda—using devices such as the State of the Union address—but the choice of direction lacks significance without a synchronized response from the "rear."

This alternative analytical framework paves the way for changing our interpretations of presidential-congressional interactions. It modifies, for instance, how we evaluate the presence of conflict in the system. While there have been numerous occasions in which the president and the dominant interests in Congress have been at loggerheads, the clash has not necessarily been strictly institutional. Many of the battles have reflected partisan conflicts.[15] Whether these wrangles have involved nineteenth-century disagreements about the procedural role of each institution or the more recent substantive divisions pertaining to the appropriate functions of government, the separation of powers allows partisan confrontations to become "institutional" when electoral results have put each party in control of one branch of government. Even when so-called institutional clashes have occurred over issues on which presidents from both parties have been in agreement (presidential appointments, war powers, and legislative incursions into policy implementation, for example), these confrontations have often come to a head when control of the presidency and Congress was divided between the Democrats and the Republicans. One can only speculate on how differently Congress might have responded to presidential actions linked to the Watergate and Iran-contra affairs, for example, if the government had not been split along party lines at the time of those disputes.

To the extent that presidential-congressional conflict exists on an institutional level, more than the separation of powers is involved. As James Madison suggested in *Federalist Paper* number 51, what infuses the separation with meaning beyond partisan terms is the intentionally engineered incongruity between the perspectives brought to Washington by each representative and senator, and by the president. The underlying

15. Joseph P. Harris, *Congressional Control of Administration* (Washington, D.C.: Brookings Institution, 1964), p. 311.

source of the disparity is the tradition of federalism in the United States, reinforced by the divergent constituencies and election procedures attached to each level of office. The association of members of Congress with regional, state, and local interests is the product of the way in which the United States developed, first as a cluster of colonies and then as a unified nation. As long as federalism remains a feature of American politics, there is the potential for legislators and the executive establishment to be at odds, even in the absence of a constitutional separation of powers.

The implicit formulation in the presidency-centered perspective of the president and Congress operating in a zero-sum game of power is also inadequate. While the presidency of the modern era is certainly a different and vastly more powerful institution than the presidency of the last century, the same is true of Congress.[16] Both have extended their range of political and policy involvement beyond the wildest imaginations of even so strong an advocate of the nation-state as Alexander Hamilton. Presidential leadership may have directed federal involvement in areas previously beyond the national domain, but the power of Congress has also been magnified by its participation, and sometimes leadership, in formulating programs that offer federal assistance in areas such as health and education, and in creating the vast body of regulations that now contribute to the societal configuration of political, social, and economic interactions. Both institutions, in a sense, simultaneously enjoyed an expanding scope of authority. In addition, the concentration on confrontational institutional power ignores the representative, policy-making, and oversight roles performed by Congress as it both formulates its own legislative responses to policy issues and deliberates those suggested by the president.[17]

Although there have been institutional battles over concerns of

16. The inappropriateness of the cycle theory of institutional power, or the notion of a power pendulum, is noted by Gary King and Lyn Ragsdale, *The Elusive Executive: Discovering Statistical Patterns in the Presidency* (Washington, D.C.: CQ Press, 1988), p. 47. Gary Orfield provides an analysis of the independent role of Congress even in the midst of the presumed ascendancy of presidential power; see his *Congressional Power: Congress and Social Change* (New York: Harcourt, Brace, Jovanovich, 1975).

17. Orfield, *Congressional Power;* and John S. Saloma III, *Congress and the New Politics* (Boston: Little, Brown, 1969).

war and diplomacy, the image of presidential ascendancy in this century probably is largely the product of American involvement in international affairs, often with an emphasis on East-West frictions and a bipartisan policy of containment of the Soviet Union. In the domestic realm, the relationship between the White House and Capitol Hill has been more balanced. To some, that balance represents an unfortunate thwarting of presidential direction; to others, it reflects the responsiveness of the government to the diverse interests populating the society. Those who begrudge less-than-overwhelming congressional acceptance of presidential policy initiatives see congressional resistance as a direct challenge to the "national interest" embodied in the president. But while the president encompasses a national constituency, gaining office is accomplished by building far more limited coalitions. Drawn from an electorate that is *geographically* national, those coalitions are in a sense as restricted as the coalitions formed by any winning politician. Some people are represented, others are not. It would be difficult to argue, for instance, that the bulk of poor people, blacks, environmentalists, and political liberals in general considered themselves represented in the "national" interest as it was articulated by Ronald Reagan—or that businesspeople, the affluent, Christian fundamentalists, and political conservatives felt any more comfortable with Reagan's Democratic predecessors. Such interests in opposition, however, can have an impact on the overall policy-making process as their perspectives are vocalized by various members of Congress.[18]

In the end, the concentration on presidential leadership and policy achievement distills into a focus on presidential power. The problem of governance is seen as the president sees it. At issue is the means for securing power in the hands of a chief executive capable of engaging in what James MacGregor Burns has called transactional leadership; in other words, employing skillfully the resources of the presidency to overcome the disparate impediments to instrumental policy making imposed by the American political system.[19] By any measure, Neustadt's classic

18. Patricia A. Hurley, "Collective Representation Reappraised," *Legislative Studies Quarterly* 7 (February 1982): 119–136; and Robert Weissberg, "Collective vs. Dyadic Representation in Congress," *American Political Science Review* 72 (June 1978): 535–547.

19. James MacGregor Burns, *Leadership* (New York: Harper Colophon Books, 1978), pp. 19–20 and passim.

injunction to incumbents on the appropriate practice of presidential power serves two vital functions. It highlights the systemic
constraints that limit effective application of the formal powers
assigned the presidency and it articulates the need for presidents
to employ their formal and informal resources strategically in
order to achieve their long-term ends. *Presidential Power* is,
indeed, a cogent depiction of the essence of politics wherever alliances and coalitions are required. But the focus on presidents and
their individual attributes limits opportunities to define the significance of the fluctuating context in which presidents, and members of Congress, must act. It places inordinate emphasis on the
political skills attributable to a single participant in the system,
the president, at the same time failing to recognize the legitimate
claims of other actors in the system or to provide a baseline for
evaluating presidential performance. Viewing the political process from the tandem-institutions perspective, on the other hand,
reveals a presidency that is neither prescriptively nor descrip-
tively emasculated, but one that is both less preeminent and less
justified in arrogating claims to unbridled leadership.

Evaluating Interactions

As the leaves began to fall in the autumn of 1981, the presidency,
like the poltergeist in a Spielberg movie, was back. After four
failed administrations broken across the shoals of Vietnam, constitutional violations, economic disorder, and political naivete, a
president of the United States had finally mastered the media,
dominated the policy agenda, vanquished the opposition, won the
hearts of the public, reordered American priorities, and in the
process demonstrated the resurgent vitality of the institution of
the presidency.[20] It all began with the election of 1980, with the

20. Norman J. Ornstein, "Introduction," in *President and Congress:
Assessing Reagan's First Year*, ed. Norman J. Ornstein (Washington,
D.C.: American Enterprise Institute, 1982), p. 1; Richard P. Nathan, "The
Reagan Presidency and Domestic Affairs," and Fred I. Greenstein,
"Reagan and the Lore of the Modern Presidency: What Have We
Learned?" both in *The Reagan Presidency: An Early Assessment*, ed. Fred
I. Greenstein (Baltimore: Johns Hopkins University Press, 1983), pp. 78,
167; John Orman, *Comparing Presidential Behavior: Carter, Reagan, and
the Macho Presidential Style* (New York: Greenwood Press, 1987), p. 3;
and Aaron Wildavsky, "President Reagan as a Political Strategist," in *The*

ouster of Jimmy Carter in an electoral college landslide that elevated to the Oval Office the most conservative major party presidential nominee since the Goldwater candidacy of 1964.

Sixteen days after his inauguration in 1981 President Ronald Reagan took to the national airwaves and reported to the American people that "we are in the worst economic mess since the Great Depression."[21] The solution, the President argued, could be found only in tax cuts to stimulate productivity, reductions in federal regulations, stable monetary policy, and budgetary cutbacks in programs administered throughout the government. On February 18 Reagan made his first televised appearance before a joint session of Congress and began to define the outlines of his "Program for Economic Recovery."[22] With his message to Congress on March 10 Reagan transmitted a plan for an additional two hundred programmatic reductions in the fiscal year 1982 budget, including, for example, elimination of the federal program that extended unemployment benefits to all states when the national rate of unemployment reached 4.5%.

In accordance with procedures established by the Budget and Impoundment Control Act of 1974, Congress on May 20, by a vote of 244–155, approved the first concurrent budget resolution for fiscal year 1982. Though not legally binding, this resolution incorporated President Reagan's proposals in the budget targets that would guide the activity of Congress over the next several months. The congressional agenda was being specifically shaped by Reagan, who triumphantly returned to Congress to deliver another televised address on April 28, a month after John Hinckley's assassination attempt. By the end of June, repeating the pattern established in the Republican-controlled Senate, the House of Representatives approved its version of the reconciliation legislation needed to implement the President's budget cuts. House action came after a close 217–211 procedural vote to take up the Gramm-Latta II substitute, the Republican version of the

---

Reagan Legacy: Promise and Performance, ed. Charles O. Jones (Chatham, N.J.: Chatham House, 1988), pp. 289–290, 302.

21. "President Reagan's Report to the Nation on the Economy," *Congressional Quarterly Almanac, 1981* (Washington, D.C.: Congressional Quarterly, 1982), p. 13-E.

22. Robert Dallek, *Ronald Reagan: The Politics of Symbolism* (Cambridge, Mass.: Harvard University Press, 1984), p. 66; and *Congressional Quarterly Almanac, 1981,* p. 18-E.

reconciliation bill that mandated a single up-or-down vote on the budget package. On July 31 the heated battle was over. The House and Senate accepted the conference committee version of the reconciliation bill, the Omnibus Reconciliation Act of 1981 (OBRA). President Reagan did not get everything he wanted in the reductions of $35.2 billion for fiscal year 1982 and $130.6 billion for fiscal 1982 to 1984, but most of his legislative objectives were handsomely fulfilled, including elimination of the extended unemployment program. With the passage of OBRA days after congressional approval of the President's tax program, the Democratic opposition was demoralized and Reagan rode a wave of apparent invincibility. That image created the parameters of media and public perception that aided Ronald Reagan throughout his administration, even during more trying times after August 1981.

To many the Reagan legislative victory of 1981 was very much a personal one, the harvest of a chief executive who applied an admirable blend of cogent ideological vision with political cunning, Hollywood training, and personal persuasiveness to regenerate power in the White House. The presidency had not been weak; presidents had been weak. Ronald Reagan displayed strength of conviction and decisiveness. He and his assistants made careful use of his skills as the "Great Communicator," putting him on television repeatedly with one message and one theme, and his avuncular mastery of the one-on-one. One technique brought the public to Congress, by way of Western Union and AT&T; the other redeemed the power of insider politics, so misunderstood by the previous administration. Rather than squandering these resources, the executive office directed them with precision to the limited, controlled agenda of the economic recovery program.

Not that the entire federal budget or tax code constitutes a narrow set of policy issues, for one could hardly think of anything more comprehensive than the budget and taxation, but the simple locution of "Economic Recovery Program" gave the appearance of measured leadership.[23] In the words of Allen Schick, "Ronald

---

23. Charles O. Jones, "Ronald Reagan and the U.S. Congress: Visible-Hand Politics," in *The Reagan Legacy: Promise and Performance,* ed. Charles O. Jones (Chatham, N.J.: Chatham House, 1988), p. 40. See also Hugh Heclo and Rudolph G. Penner, "Fiscal and Political Strategy in the

Reagan asked a lot of Congress in 1981, but he asked it to do little."[24] It was through this skillful orchestration of the influential players in Washington, from this presidency-centered perspective, that Reagan scared the Democrats already terrorized by the 1980 presidential and congressional elections, disciplined the relatively moderate Republican gypsy moths of the industrial North, and fashioned alliances with the conservative southern Democratic boll weevils. Among other things, this effort nailed down the six-vote victory on Gramm-Latta II, which set the stage for presidential domination of Capitol Hill.

Unquestionably Ronald Reagan as a political leader contributed to his own success. But that achievement was constructed on a foundation of opportunity partially effected by Reagan prior to entering office but largely beyond his direct influence. Even the basic agenda issues themselves, the tax and budget cuts, while decidedly the President's, had their origins in the previously failed efforts of his congressional allies. Whatever acumen was displayed by Reagan, his legislative victories in 1981 probably would not have been possible without the confluence of many advantageous features of the political environment that defined those first months of the administration. *Structurally*, the Budget Act of 1974 furnished the means—the reconciliation procedures—to defeat the politics of incrementalism that otherwise would have stalled Reagan's efforts to cut the budget.[25] *Politically*, the election of 1980—more a rejection of Carter than an affirmation of the Reagan vision—rearranged the Washington landscape. The congressional elections, by giving the Republicans twelve new seats in the Senate and thirty-three new members in the House, allowed Reagan to work with a Republican-controlled Senate and a conservative working majority in the House.[26] Because so much

---

Reagan Administration," in Greenstein, *The Reagan Presidency*, p. 40; and Allen Schick, "How the Budget Was Won and Lost," in *President and Congress: Assessing Reagan's First Year*, ed. Norman J. Ornstein (Washington, D.C.: American Enterprise Institute, 1982), p. 15.

24. Schick, "How the Budget Was Won and Lost," p. 28.

25. Ibid., p. 26.

26. Greenstein, "Reagan and the Lore of the Modern Presidency," p. 184; and Jones, "Visible-Hand Politics," p. 32. Ornstein highlights the symbolic significance of the Senate victory, noting that without it Reagan's election could more easily be interpreted as merely a rejection of Carter. Norman J. Ornstein, "Assessing Reagan's First Year," in *Presi-*

of the Reagan legislative juggernaut began in the Senate, perhaps no other feature of the political context was as significant.[27] *Economically*, Reagan entered office when the leading economic indicators created the desire for change, from whatever direction. As summarized by Robert Dallek:

> In January 1981 inflation, interest rates, and the projected federal deficit stood at nearly record highs, and unemployment was 7.4 percent. A 13 percent increase in the cost of living during 1980, a 20 percent prime rate for borrowing money, a predicted $56 billion deficit, and an unacceptably high rate of joblessness presented the new administration with a formidable challenge.[28]

Finally, as a *matter of policy*, the Reagan administration chose to meet that challenge by offering a program that was supposed to rectify all wrongs by dramatically cutting taxes, stimulating a business boom, reducing the deficits, and building America's defense capabilities with apparently little cost to anyone, an idea that quickly won the support of two-thirds of the public.[29]

The events of 1981, therefore, are most accurately interpreted as the consequence of a president working together with an allied congressional coalition of significant size, whose momentous task was facilitated by the presence of rules, political resources, economic circumstances, and policy choices that could be exploited and mobilized to their advantage. Like Lyndon Johnson sixteen years earlier, Reagan's claim to leadership was his ability to recognize and manipulate this auspicious constellation of forces as a form of "strategic management."[30] The context of the times provided the opportunity for the administration to craft the illusion of presidential leadership forged in the person of Ronald Reagan, even though his successes would be more correctly portrayed as resulting from the strategic interaction of the President and his allies with the favorable prevailing forces of the political system. Especially after the Republican midterm losses in the 1982 election that reestablished an effective Democratic majority in the

dent and Congress: Assessing Reagan's First Year, ed. Norman J. Ornstein (Washington, D.C.: American Enterprise Institute, 1982), p. 91.

27. Ornstein, "Assessing Reagan's First Year," p. 91.

28. Dallek, *Ronald Reagan*, p. 63.

29. Ibid., p. 67.

30. Heclo and Penner, "Fiscal and Political Strategy," p. 36.

House, the conditional quality of Reagan's presidential leadership became more obvious.[31]

If President Reagan in those early months embodied in the popular perception the quintessence of presidential command of American government, President Carter before him personified the nightmare of failed political leadership. In 1977, not long into his administration, pundits and the public alike began to question whether the office of the presidency was more than the quondam Georgia governor could handle, a concern buttressed by media interpretation of his activities.[32] Carter was generally perceived to be antipolitical and either unable or unwilling to adjust to the realities of maneuvering in the policy communities of Washington. He was an engineer, a technocrat, a person lacking a unifying philosophical vision. When he developed substantively comprehensive policy solutions, they were presented moralistically as "the right thing to do," to be accepted on that basis alone.[33] Nothing was more revealing of his political naivete than his commitment to fulfill each of his campaign promises, a commitment that required the introduction of a legislative agenda too controversial, too comprehensive, and too big to win approval from Congress. Given the huge Democratic majorities in the House and Senate, there would seem to be little to explain the legislative difficulties of the Carter administration beyond the deficient style with which he himself handled the presidency.

This stark interpretation of Carter as president has been refined and amended in important ways by the analysis of Charles Jones. Jones argues that Jimmy Carter, rather than being apolitical, simply practiced politics of a different sort. Carter viewed the president, in the tradition of Edmund Burke, as a trustee of the public interest, where " 'doing what's right, not what's political' is . . . *doing the political in the right way.*"[34] This personal

31. Greenstein, "Reagan and the Lore of the Modern Presidency," p. 176; and Jones, "Visible-Hand Politics," pp. 44–47.

32. Orman, *Comparing Presidential Behavior,* pp. 94, 106.

33. Betty Glad, *Jimmy Carter: In Search of the Great White House* (New York: W. W. Norton, 1980), chaps. 25 and 26; Laurence E. Lynn, Jr., and David deF. Whitman, *The President as Policymaker: Jimmy Carter and Welfare Reform* (Philadelphia: Temple University Press, 1981), pp. 90–91, 258–259, 261–280; and Orman, *Comparing Presidential Behavior,* pp. 3–5, 77–106.

34. Charles O. Jones, *The Trusteeship Presidency: Jimmy Carter and*

understanding of politics was consistently reinforced throughout Carter's political career, from his service as a Georgia legislator to his successful campaign for the presidency.[35] In a way, Carter became the victim of his own institutional analysis, since the tenets of the trusteeship presidency—concern about the parochial interests of members of Congress and the role of special interests, the view of the president as the representative of the whole public and the national interest, and the need for leadership to emanate from the Oval Office—constitute the main outlines of the presidency-centered perspective.[36] Carter did not see himself as a tandem-institutions president.

Nevertheless, he had to operate in a tandem-institutions world, and it is from that perspective that his presidency is most effectively understood. Consider one of Jimmy Carter's most discouraging defeats, his inability to get Congress to enact his hospital cost containment program, which mandated annual ceilings in the rise of hospital costs, but permitted some discretionary adjustments for individual hospitals. This legislative program was vintage Carter. It tackled a tough issue, and with hospital costs skyrocketing the situation appeared to require urgent redress, all the elements of a policy that "attracts the trustee president."[37] Carter announced the program about a month into office, and within another couple of months legislation was sent to the Hill. Then, except for hearings, nothing happened. Finally, in 1978, although the Senate in a partisan vote accepted a compromise version, the bill died in the House when it was narrowly defeated (22–21) in the Interstate and Foreign Commerce Committee. The Ways and Means Committee, which also had jurisdiction, decided to take no further action. The full House by a vote of 234–166 formally rejected the legislation resubmitted by the administration in 1979. This was unmistakably legislation of the highest priority to the President, but despite the Democratic dominance of each chamber, the White House was unable to muster majority coalitions in both the House and the Senate.

Certainly there were problems with the way Carter approached

---

the United States Congress (Baton Rouge: Louisiana State University Press, 1988), pp. 2, 7. Italics in original.
    35. Ibid., pp. 11–39.
    36. Ibid., p. 6.
    37. Ibid., p. 155.

this issue, overloading the agenda and not involving members of Congress early enough in the process, and with the generally developing perception that Carter was politically weak.[38] It would not be until 1978 that the White House developed more effective lobbying techniques built on the establishment of coordinating task forces.[39] Other factors shaping the political environment of Carter's interactions with Congress, however, cannot be ignored.

Although the Democrats maintained the control of Congress they had established in 1955, the institution itself was vastly different from the one known to Kennedy and Johnson.[40] Just as Carter was about to enter office,

> the Ninety-fifth Congress was preparing itself to assume an expanded and more effective role in governance. Many of the changes were designed to make Congress more directly competitive with the executive . . . Thus a more pretentious, confident, and aggressive Congress awaited the new president when he was inaugurated on January 20, 1977 . . .
>
> Members of Congress thought differently about themselves and about the presidency. Several complementary developments contributed to their being more interventionist in the policy process: Republican control of the executive branch, the decline in status of the White House during Watergate, conflict over foreign and domestic issues, media attention to Congress during Watergate and as a consequence of policy battles, and the expansion of analytical capabilities on Capitol Hill.[41]

Among the changes were the committee and subcommittee reforms that expanded power to so many members of Congress that the Carter White House had to get to know an unprecedented

38. Joseph A. Califano, Jr., *Governing America: An Insider's Report from the White House and the Cabinet* (New York: Simon and Schuster, 1981), p. 148.

39. Jones, *Trusteeship Presidency*, p. 164.

40. Norman J. Ornstein, "The Open Congress Meets the President," in *Both Ends of the Avenue: The Presidency, the Executive Branch and Congress in the 1980s*, ed. Anthony King (Washington, D.C.: American Enterprise Institute, 1983), pp. 185–211; and Barbara Sinclair, *Majority Leadership in the U.S. House* (Baltimore: Johns Hopkins University Press, 1983).

41. Jones, *Trusteeship Presidency*, pp. 47, 59.

number of new congressional leaders. Advice offered by participants in previous administrations proved to be dated.[42]

For legislation aimed at containing hospital costs, this fragmentation of congressional authority required success in eleven jurisdictions: four health subcommittees, five full committees, and the
House and Senate floors.[43] The existence of so many potential
veto points was highly beneficial to the interests organized in
opposition to the program, an assemblage of some of the most
respected groups with a presence in just about every congressional
district.[44] Like hundreds of other interest groups, unions, and cor-
porations, by the time of the Carter administration these groups
packed the added punch of political action committees (PACs).
During the previous decade, there had been extensive mobilization of entirely new interests in the society and countermobilization of their opponents, resulting in both a larger number of
organized interest groups and a reemphasis by established interests on securing political influence. These patterns, for hospital
cost containment and other issues, only complicated the task of
cultivating legislative coalitions allied with the President's policy
positions.

Other than the Democratic majorities, there was little to link
President Carter politically with Congress. He won an extremely
narrow victory in the 1976 election, garnering 80% of his votes in
just two regions of the country, the Northeast and the South, and
running behind the vast majority of successful Democratic congressional candidates.[45] With the sizable Democratic majorities in
Congress generated by the 1974 post-Watergate midterm election,
Carter had little incentive to run a campaign closely tied to his
fellow partisans. The net gain of one seat in the House and none
in the Senate did nothing to suggest that Carter led the ticket.[46]
While he took office with reasonably high levels of public support
as reported by the Gallup poll, by the time the House defeated
hospital cost containment in 1979, less than a third of the public
approved of his handling of the presidency.

Nor did the policy context of hospital cost containment bode
well for its passage by Congress. A regulatory proposal of this

42. Ibid., pp. 61–62.
43. Califano, *Governing America*, p. 147.
44. Ibid., p. 144.
45. Jones, *Trusteeship Presidency*, p. 45.
46. Ibid., pp. 43, 45.

type, introduced in a well-established policy community and posing obvious and concentrated costs for a small sector—the health care industry—and more amorphous and widely distributed benefits among consumers, leads to controversy and vigorous opposition.[47] Because the public was protected by third-party insurance coverage from the direct ramifications of medical inflation, it was not possible to organize a broad-based coalition of groups in favor of the legislation.

Not all presidential initiatives have as much significance as Reagan's 1981 budget cuts and Carter's effort to control medical inflation. Three additional examples of presidential proposals, drawn from the Nixon, Eisenhower, and Ford administrations, illustrate the diversity of contexts and congressional actions that characterize the legislative relationship of the president and Congress.

Lost in the turmoil of the impoundment battles and the Watergate scandal, before President Nixon shifted to the strategy designed "to *take over* the bureaucracy and *take on* the Congress," it is almost forgotten that on some issues the legislation submitted by Richard Nixon attracted majority coalitions in Congress.[48] On August 6, 1970, Congress approved with some amendments Nixon's plan for reorganizing the U.S. Postal Department into the Postal Service. Included in that legislation was the related issue of pay increases for postal employees; the general 8% increase that the administration had negotiated with the postal employees' union was ratified. The pay increase, however, was made retroactive to April 16, 1970, a deviation from the arrangement negotiated with the postal unions to have the pay increase become effective with the passage of the legislation. Postmaster General Winton Blount considered this change severe enough to contemplate requesting a presidential veto, but the administration decided to accept the congressional compromise. Richard Nixon was in no position to dominate Congress, having been elected in 1968 with only 43% of the vote and with

47. James Q. Wilson, "The Politics of Regulation," in *The Politics of Regulation*, ed. James Q. Wilson (New York: Basic Books, 1980), p. 370. These issues are apparent in Joseph Califano's discussion of what happened to hospital cost containment. *Governing America*, p. 144.

48. Quote from Richard P. Nathan, *The Plot That Failed: Nixon and the Administrative Presidency* (New York: John Wiley, 1975), p. 8. Italics in original.

Republicans holding barely more than four in ten seats in the House and Senate. Congress passed this initiative, however, while the President's popularity remained relatively high and prior to the onslaught of stagflation and increasing budget deficits that would have limited the economic viability of such pay increases. In addition, both Congress and the administration were responding to the force of events: the pressure generated by the walkout of federal postal workers, the first major strike against the United States government.[49] Nixon's later confrontations with the Democratic majority in Congress revealed that he did not possess any special ability to move the controlling opposition party in directions favorable to his policy initiatives; but compromise on the postal pay increase, as well as the postal reorganization, demonstrated that there were opportunities for cooperation between the White House and a majority on the Hill.

Cooperation was also frequently manifested in the relationship between Republican Dwight Eisenhower and the Democratic congresses of the 1950s, sometimes to the point of consensus. Deep-seated confrontation between Eisenhower and the majority in Congress was generally avoided by virtue of the fact that the President wanted little from Congress and demanded even less. A previous career rooted almost entirely in national security issues and an approach to government that was incrementalist at the height of his activism, more intent on thwarting unwanted policies than prosecuting innovations, yielded a president with few intense legislative priorities, especially in the domestic realm.[50] Federal support for education, however, emerged as a major issue for both the President and Congress, leading to years of discord between Eisenhower, who sought federal aid for school construction, and both liberals and conservatives on Capitol Hill, who, respectively, desired far more or far less intervention.

When the Soviet Union on October 4, 1957, launched the first Sputnik orbiting craft, the politics of education changed dramatically as Americans began to question the quality of scientific

49. "Postal Workers' Strike Muddies Pay Raise–Postal Reform Compromise," *National Journal*, March 28, 1970, p. 658.

50. Fred I. Greenstein, *The Hidden-Hand Presidency: Eisenhower as Leader* (New York: Basic Books, 1982), pp. 229, 232; James L. Sundquist, *Politics and Policy: The Eisenhower, Kennedy, and Johnson Years* (Washington, D.C.: Brookings Institution, 1968), p. 419.

instruction in their schools and universities.[51] In August of the following year Congress passed the National Defense Education Act of 1958. The statute included—along with funds for student loans, grants for improved science and mathematics instructional facilities, and graduate fellowships—a matching-grant program to states for improving counseling and guidance services in high schools and colleges. Although some provisions of the initial legislation, such as student scholarships, proved to be controversial, the original administration and Democratic education bills were in almost complete agreement on the counseling matching-grant program.[52]

Recent analyses of President Eisenhower derived from previously undisclosed documents, notably Fred Greenstein's book on Eisenhower's "hidden-hand politics," dispel the earlier assessments of the President as an unwilling and ill-equipped practitioner of the art of politics and personal persuasion.[53] The success of the education program and other legislative efforts by the administration undoubtedly derived more from Eisenhower's leadership skills than originally believed. It is unlikely, however, that those skills account for the enactment of the education legislation. The shock of the Soviet achievements in space compelled action and cultivated a broad-based consensus on the need for federal intervention. Few members of Congress wanted to return home for the fall congressional elections without some evidence of accomplishment on this front. Once included as part of the overall education package, the guidance counseling provision was aided by its relatively small magnitude and the general attractiveness of distributive policies that allow federal dollars to flow to innumerable states and House districts.

Limited in size and scope, the agenda politics of the guidance counseling proposal introduced by Eisenhower was largely determined by its association with a major piece of legislation. By my estimates, only about half of all legislative initiatives suggested by Presidents Eisenhower to Reagan were linked to major bills or programs. President Ford, for example, in March 1975 transmitted to Congress his request that thirty-seven new areas be added to the National Wilderness Preservation System, including

51. Sundquist, *Politics and Policy*, p. 174.
52. Ibid., pp. 176–177.
53. Greenstein, *Hidden-Hand Presidency*.

the nearly one million acres of the Kenai Wilderness in the Alaskan Kenai National Moose Range. Congress ignored Ford's proposal, never taking any noticeable action. One could attribute this failure to a lack of political leadership by the President. One could perhaps argue more effectively that the circumstances of 1975, with an unelected president suffering low public approval, facing a generally hostile Congress and a severe recession, conspired to deprive Ford of many potential allies. Since almost every modern president, however, experienced congressional inaction on similar kinds of proposals no matter how successful he was with other legislation, more was involved here than leadership abilities and contextual constraints. The reality is that considerably more gets proposed by presidents and by members of Congress than can be processed, or decided upon, within the tandem-institutions legislative arena. Many relatively inconsequential proposals merely fall by the wayside.

For each of the cases I have presented, there is no ready procedure for distilling out the independent influences of presidential leadership capabilities and contextual factors that help to structure the politics of congressional decision making. Lyndon Johnson, particularly with regard to the halcyon days of the Eighty-ninth Congress, endures as the exemplar of gifted legislative leadership directed from the Oval Office. But how much was Johnson and how much was political setting? How different was his influence from that of Kennedy, or of Carter? Jeff Fishel puts it this way:

> Since we can never know whether another Democratic president would have been equally successful, it is impossible to calculate accurately what proportion is attributable to the "Johnson factor," and what proportion to all the favorable circumstances surrounding the dynamics of legislative achievement in 1964 and 1965. Neither Carter nor Kennedy, however, enjoyed what Johnson momentarily possessed: a structural responsiveness in the policy-making system that was ripe for effective presidential leadership in helping forge agenda breakthroughs.[54]

The central objectives of this book, then, emerge as establishing

54. Jeff Fishel, *Presidents and Promises* (Washington, D.C.: CQ Press, 1985), pp. 200–201.

the conceptual tools and empirical basis for (1) moving beyond case studies to assess at a more general level the range of congressional responses to presidential initiatives, (2) identifying the coalitional alignments reflected by those responses, (3) ascertaining the degree to which they reveal cooperation or conflict in the tandem-institutions setting, and (4) calculating the latitude for presidential leadership in the modern era.

In the chapters that follow, I continue to use the president as referent and the president's program as point of departure. There are, of course, innumerable ways in which the president interacts with individuals on Capitol Hill. Legislation is discussed, some of that discussion stimulated by the president, much of it by members of Congress. Some bills are signed by the president, others are vetoed, a few vetoes are overturned. All bills approved by Congress are reviewed by the president's administration in some manner. Presidential appointments, both judicial and executive, are routinely studied and ratified by the Senate, although some that ignite controversy are rejected. Treaties negotiated by the administration are introduced for Senate ratification. The specter of combat and war involving American forces triggers either consultation or confrontation between executive and legislature. To draw a complete picture of these interactions would require a comprehensive examination of each facet of the relationship.

The scope of this book is more limited. It examines the domestic legislative programs introduced by presidents from Eisenhower to Reagan, through the end of Reagan's first term. For my purposes this approach is quite appropriate. First, although legislative action is only one way of generating public policy decisions at the national level, it is the most important and most enduring method by which the government addresses policy issues.[55] My emphasis on the legislative product of executive-legislative interaction acknowledges the significance of bill passage or defeat to governmental problem solving and the potential influence of the president in shaping formal policy responses to national concerns.

55. John W. Kingdon, *Agendas, Alternatives, and Public Policies* (Boston: Little, Brown, 1984), p. 39; and Paul C. Light, *The President's Agenda: Domestic Policy Choice from Kennedy to Carter* (Baltimore: Johns Hopkins University Press, 1982), pp. 114–118.

Second, legislation enjoying presidential sponsorship is by definition of concern to both the president and Congress, necessarily calling into play the role of each institution. That is not true of *all* legislation considered by Congress, much of it of little concern to the administration and of even less consequence to the occupant of the White House.

Third, the administrations under consideration furnish a period of study well suited to any analysis intended to inform interpretations applicable to the present and near future. Certainly any study of the contemporary presidency must begin after FDR's administration, which initiated a "revolution" in public policy and institutional arrangements.[56] Our period of analysis needs to be both short enough to remain relevant to presidential-congressional government as it is currently experienced, and long enough to allow consideration of legislative situations that span numerous administrations and diverse political settings. Fred Greenstein assesses the situation this way: "The transformation of the office [of the presidency] has been so profound that the modern presidencies have more in common with one another in the opportunities they provide and the demands they place on their incumbents than they have with the entire sweep of traditional presidencies from Washington's to Hoover's."[57] Along with

56. Terry Moe places the beginning of the institutional presidency with the Budget and Accounting Act of 1921, which established the Bureau of the Budget in the Department of the Treasury. See "The Politicized Presidency," in *The New Directions in American Politics*, ed. John E. Chubb and Paul E. Peterson (Washington, D.C.: Brookings Institution, 1985), pp. 246–247. It was FDR's Reorganization Plan Number 1, authorized by the Reorganization Act of 1939, however, that created the Executive Office of the President (EOP) in the president's domain and moved the Bureau of the Budget to the EOP, solidifying the administrative apparatus of the chief executive. See Richard Polenberg, *Reorganizing Roosevelt's Government: The Controversy over Executive Reorganization, 1936–1939* (Cambridge, Mass.: Harvard University Press, 1966); and John Hart, *The Presidential Branch* (New York: Pergamon Press, 1987), pp. 29–48. The institutionalization of the presidency in the EOP begun and revealed during the administrations of Franklin Roosevelt and Harry Truman became "controlling" during the Eisenhower administration, according to Corwin, *The President*, p. 301.

57. Fred I. Greenstein, "The Need for an Early Appraisal of the Reagan Presidency," in *The Reagan Presidency: An Early Assessment*, ed. Fred I. Greenstein (Baltimore: Johns Hopkins University Press, 1983), p. 3.

the rudimentary similarity of the executive experience in the modern era, there has been enough variation in institutional structures, political forces, economic indicators, and policy choices to have presented members of Congress and Eisenhower, Kennedy, Nixon, Ford, Carter, and Reagan with divergent challenges and opportunities.

Finally, there is the focus on domestic policy. Ideally, we might prefer to examine an unabridged collection of legislative interactions between the president and Congress in both the domestic and foreign spheres, including military affairs and the international economy. Some foreign policy issues, such as foreign aid, trade, and defense procurement, have never been immune from extensive congressional involvement. Others have emerged on the congressional agenda more recently, from questions of military intervention in the Third World to the regulation of covert action. Not all of these issues have had legislative ramifications, but many important ones have. Consider the Marshall Plan during the Truman administration, and the significance of defense appropriations during the Vietnam War and the Cambodian incursion. In addition, the president is the one participant in the tandem-institutions setting who must integrate government involvement and judgment across both domestic and foreign policy domains. No president practicing the art of governance in the modern era has been able to bifurcate the world of politics and policy as neatly as scholarship sometimes does.[58]

Nevertheless, I have restricted this book to the world of domestic policy. The analytical issues involved are already enormously complex, entailing more than three decades, seven administrations, innumerable legislative contexts, and a tremendous diversity of domestic issues. By concentrating on domestic policy, I am able to reduce the intricacy of the subject to manageable levels, as well as to avoid the more restricted access to information associated with foreign affairs.[59] Further, without suggesting that the real world can be pristinely compartmentalized, I believe that the domestic arena deserves more attention than it has sometimes received. John F. Kennedy frequently noted, with some

58. I am grateful to Morris Fiorina and Richard Neustadt for highlighting the significance of these issues.

59. Paul Light argues that the differences in the "policy processes" associated with domestic and foreign affairs justifies their separate treatment. *The President's Agenda*, p. 7.

hyperbole, that the distinction between domestic and foreign policy can be found in the consequences of mistakes: domestic errors in judgment may lead to defeated bills, but foreign policy mistakes have the potential of destroying the country. All modern presidents have shared this concern for international affairs, both in the time committed to those issues during their incumbency and in the reflections offered in their memoirs.[60] Events abroad, military action, and the president's role on the world stage naturally draw our attention. Most Americans, however, have been affected more consistently and more directly by Roosevelt's New Deal, Truman's Fair Deal, Kennedy's New Frontier, Johnson's Great Society, and Carter's domestic agenda—and by the efforts of Eisenhower, Nixon, Ford and Reagan to transfix and to transform their effects—than by issues of foreign policy. Domestic issues also more typically require legislation and congressional action. While international issues monopolize the president's time, "the White House must allocate most of the total resources to domestic affairs."[61]

Justification for use of the president's domestic legislative program also hinges on a fundamental assumption that is rarely questioned, or even explicitly considered, in popular or scholarly appraisals of executive-legislative interactions. The assumption is best identified by raising the question, What if the president's program does not reflect true presidential preferences, but rather is an amalgamation of the president's desires mixed with preemptive, perhaps strategic, substantive concessions to powerful interests in Congress? The executive and legislative branches are closely linked because of the tandem-institutions arrangements, even before the president makes policy announcements. Perhaps the meat of legislative interaction is concluded at that stage, not when Congress formally responds to initiatives. From interviews with the participants in the process (see Appendix A), however, I conclude in Chapter 2 that the consultative process and the impact of White House anticipations of congressional actions are not so influential that they contaminate the president's legislative program with a congressional perspective that erodes the utility of the program as a baseline for analysis.

60. Cronin reports that presidents devote from one-half to two-thirds of their time to foreign policy matters. *The State of the Presidency*, p. 146.

61. Light, *The President's Agenda*, p. 7.

Three related topics are addressed in Chapter 3. The first is a thorough explication of the concepts guiding the study, followed by an explanation of the research design and, finally, an empirical depiction of congressional action on presidential initiatives from 1953 to 1986 derived from the integration of these themes and methods. Even at this stage of the analysis, the results invite a reinterpretation of the presidential-congressional relationship in the legislative arena. Outright conflict over the president's program is found to have been less prevalent than previous case studies have suggested, occurring on only about a third of the initiatives. Congress has also responded far more favorably to the domestic proposals of modern presidents than revealed in past quantitative studies. A distinct majority of initiatives, rather than about 40% as commonly cited, have been enacted. Appendix B discusses the specific deficiencies of the data used in many quantitative studies that have led to inaccurate assessments of the executive-legislative relationship.

Chapters 4 and 5 present a bivariate analysis of how congressional responses to the proposals of the Eisenhower to Reagan administrations were influenced by the contexts or settings existing at the time of legislative action. The first of these chapters examines the contextual attributes over which the president has the least control, institutional structures defining the pure context, and those over which the president exerts some but limited influence, the political and economic factors that constitute the malleable context. The decentralization of Congress after 1970, for example, inhibited the scope and success of presidentially led coalitions, resulting in fewer instances of consensual legislative action and more outright defeats of the president's allies. Electoral mandates associated with the president, on the other hand, under some circumstances allowed presidents to form winning coalitions on the Hill. The state of the economy had less importance, although declining inflation and unemployment reduced conflict to some degree.

The policy context, investigated in Chapter 5, is far more open to strategic presidential direction. Yet however free or inhibited presidents feel in shaping their agendas, not all proposals are the same. Their impact on the society varies. Presidents and their staffs can—in fact, must—assign different levels of priority to their legislative initiatives. Predictable but varied kinds of politics may also be associated with the substantive content of the selected proposals. The choices that presidents from Eisenhower to Reagan made about the scope and direction of their agendas affected the manner in which Congress acted on them. The most consequential presidential initiatives, for example, stimulated the largest proportion of conflictual situations and were the most difficult to enact. The least consequential initiatives by and large were ignored by the Hill or passed by consensus.

Chapters 4 and 5 examine separately the influence on congressional responses of each feature of the institutional, political, economic, and policy contexts. While this style of analysis permits close inspection of the politics associated with each contextual property, it does not provide the basis for assessing their independent effects by simultaneously taking into account the presence of the other contextual properties. Nor does it measure the cumulative impact of these factors on the presidential-congressional relationship in the legislative arena. Chapter 6 reexamines the roles of these attributes by using ordered probit analysis, a multivariate statistical technique uniquely suited to the conceptual and methodological approaches of this research. Two underlying dimensions of congressional action are considered. The first is the association between the contexts of congressional responses and the extent of cooperation or conflict between the president and Congress. The second is the fulfillment of presidential preferences as reflected in the various kinds of legislative responses. Many of the characteristics of the executive-legislative relationship noted in Chapters 4 and 5 are confirmed in the multivariate setting, demonstrating the resilient power of contextual politics in explaining both the extent of conflict in the legislative arena and the capacity of presidents to move their legislative initiatives through Congress.

None of these contextually derived results are meant to imply that it makes no difference who is elected president or that actions of individual incumbents are irrelevant. Chapter 7 reviews the broad array of choices available to presidents to improve the chances that their initiatives will be favorably reviewed by Congress. First, chief executives make decisions that may precipitate changes in the contextual contours of congressional action. Second, they make choices about their agendas, the organization of the Executive Office of the President, their personnel appointments, and their own relationships with the political world that have the potential to sway congressional deliberations. To measure the impact of individual presidential actions, I use the predicted probabilities of different kinds of congressional responses generated by the probit analysis of Chapter 6 to compare the legislative achievements of the seven presidents, controlling for individual circumstances. Even though the aggregate distributions of congressional responses conform quite closely to what the contextual analysis predicts, there is also evidence that some of the presidents considered were less or more adroit in exploiting the opportunities or overcoming the adversities afforded by the times in which they served.

The last chapter offers a summary assessment of presidential-congressional relations and the problems of governance in contemporary America. Presidents overall in the tandem-institutions setting have exceeded the levels of legislative success suggested by many previous studies, and there have been more opportunities for legislative harmony. Nonetheless, the trend during recent administrations has clearly been toward more legislative confrontation and increased frustration of presidential preferences. Chapter 8 examines the sources of this trend and weighs the various suggestions that scholars and practitioners have put forward to improve the process of governance as it is practiced by the president and Congress.

2. A Point of Departure

It is a scene with which we are all familiar. In the sun-drenched Rose Garden, just outside the Oval Office, the president is seated at an antique table, surrounded by various administration figures and an assortment of Senate and House members. Everyone watches as the president affixes his signature to the recently enacted legislation, a bill representing some component of the chief executive's domestic legislative program. As his pen turns legislation into law, the president vividly expresses his appreciation for Congress's responsible enactment of his program. If this is a ceremony of the Great Society, soon one of the many pens used for the signature will be ensconced in "the shrine"—a glass container in the president's outer office brimful of pens that symbolize the flood of presidential initiatives written into the statute books. Or, to advance to the 1980s, the setting is a hilltop at a rustic Western ranch, where a denim-clad president signs his name to telephone-book size pieces of legislation arcanely labeled ERTA and OBRA that represent the bulk of "his" economic program. Again there is praise for a Congress that has acceded to presidential designs.

Of course, not all presidentially inspired and congressionally approved legislation is afforded such fanfare. Many bills, though a part of the president's legislative agenda, cross the president's desk to acquire a quick signature unrecorded for the evening news. Still others enjoy a less favorable reception on Capitol Hill and never receive the imprint of the presidential pen. In all of these cases, though, the initiatives have borne the imprimatur of the president, they have constituted some facet of the chief executive's legislative program, they have been gilded by their mention in a presidential speech or message. The president has proposed, and the Congress has disposed. *Congressional Quarterly* has chronicled each case of presidential success and failure, and students of the two institutions have employed their various interpretive schemes in attempts to understand the causes of institutional conflict or cooperation, of presidential victory or defeat.

But there is a central question that is often left unanswered or simply not addressed: *Is the president's program really presidential?* By the time a proposal turns up in the State of the Union address or some other presidential speech, or at the point when it is discussed in a special presidential message, is that initiative a reasonably pristine representation of the president's desires or has the chief executive's position already been eroded by the inclusion of congressionally inspired amendments and the deletion of provisions considered to be troublesome on the Hill? In short, has the president's program been substantially given away even before it has officially gone on sale? Is the tandem-institutions web so encompassing that even the *proposed* legislation of the president has congressional fingerprints all over it? From a presidency-centered point of view, is the coherence of presidential legislative leadership sacrificed early on to the parochialism of Capitol Hill?

On the surface, there are serious conceptual ambiguities associated with the president's domestic legislative program. Much of the "presidential" agenda is composed of rejuvenated legislation borrowed from bills that have already passed through the congressional hopper. Even when initiatives are not plucked from the Hill, two general processes may be at work that distort the presentation of original presidential preferences. Prior to announcing a legislative proposal, individuals in the White House may engage members of Congress in a consultative exchange that generates modifications in the initiative designed to facilitate its passage. Some proposals may be dropped altogether. Similarly, even without direct consultation, those responsible for preparing the presidential proposals may introduce substantive alterations intended to avoid expected problems with Congress or to compensate for the effects of successful amendments anticipated on the part of the opposition. In either case, the proposals sent to the Hill may not constitute the actual preferences of the president. Consequently, the kind of response a proposal encounters in Congress, the presence of a spirit of cooperation or the politics of confrontation, and the nature of presidential "success" or "failure" could be more highly sensitive to the skills and choices of the president in the preinitiation period than to anything that happens to the proposal later on. Analyses focused solely on the postinitiation process will be inadequate, misspecified, and unlikely to yield consistent conclusions. In order to understand fully the dynamics inherent in the tandem-institutions perspective, one cannot ignore the lively interactions that take place even before the president submits legislative initiatives. In addition, it is necessary to assess the utility of focusing on the president's program as it is publicly announced.

This chapter tackles such issues, taking the president's legislative program as a point of analytical departure. Two rival scenarios are suggested, each one exploring the influence of the explicit or implicit interaction of executive officials with members of Congress and their staffs. The final congressional response to a presidential initiative is undoubtedly related to both the strategic interactions of the participants and the external, or exogenous, forces that set the context in which legislative action on the president's program is completed.

The first possible scenario I refer to as *strategic accommodation*. Presidents and their aides strategically use information derived from consultations with members of Congress or the anticipation of congressional reactions to mold policy initiatives so as to maximize the likelihood of achieving a particular legislative outcome. The alternative possibility, what I term the *fixed position and uncertainty scenario*, suggests that the complexity of goals and the potential lack and distortion of information in the complicated world of legislative policy making attenuate the significance of congressional input in presidential initiatives. I argue that most of the implications for the president's program generated by the strategic-accommodation scenario cannot be sustained sufficiently to contaminate the picture of executive preferences; the fixed position and uncertainty scenario is closer to reality. This conclusion is grounded in more than one hundred interviews with executive and legislative officials, as well as with journalists who cover one or both branches of the government.

Rival Scenarios

The strategic-accommodation scenario has a plausible foundation. To begin with, when one speaks of the president's legislative program, one recognizes immediately that very little of that program has its origins in the imagination of the individual president.[1] While presidents may provide the inspiration for a number of initiatives, their programs as a whole are an aggregation of ideas that have surfaced from a variety of sources. They may have percolated through the clearance process from a bureaucracy laden with as yet untested policy options. They may be the choices of commissions or task forces intended to tap the creative spirit of policy thinkers on campuses, in business, or among organized interests. Or they may be cultivated directly within the White House—the brain child of a Sorensen (Kennedy), the product of a highly structured Domestic Council (Nixon), or the progeny of an elaborate array of cabinet councils (Reagan). Whatever the mechanism, in the end they emerge as components of the president's program, legitimately bearing the president's name.[2]

There is an additional fertile spring for presidential initiatives, and that is Congress. Difficult as it may be to determine the origins of a policy initiative, to identify the parent of an idea, it is evident that a large bulk of what becomes "presidential" first met the legislative light of day as "congressional."[3] A Washington journalist put it this way:

If there were no presidential proposals, these things would happen anyway. They have been in the works for ten or twenty years. In the legislative process, there's a lot of continuity, inertia. Things like reauthorization bring the issues up over and over again. They provide an opportunity for making changes here, making changes there. The president sorts

1. Nelson W. Polsby, *Political Innovation in America: The Politics of Policy Initiation* (New Haven: Yale University Press, 1984), p. 5. See also Robert L. Galluci, *Neither Peace nor Honor: The Politics of American Military Policy in Viet-Nam* (Baltimore: Johns Hopkins University Press, 1975), p. 7.

2. Lawrence Chamberlain, *The President, Congress, and Legislation* (New York: Columbia University Press, 1946); Edward S. Corwin, *The President: Office and Powers,* 4th ed. (New York: New York University Press, 1957), p. 485n76; and Polsby, *Innovation,* p. 5.

3. Chamberlain, *The President, Congress, and Legislation;* and John R. Johannes, "Where Does the Buck Stop?—Congress, the President, and the Responsibility for Legislative Initiation," *Western Political Quarterly* 25 (September 1972): 396–415. Nelson Polsby discusses in particular the role of the Senate as a forum for the "incubation of new policy proposals that may at some future time find their way into legislation," including the president's program. *Innovation,* p. 162.

through the proposals to give the impression that he is leading the country. [Presidents] read the handwriting on the wall and then try to make those issues our issues. And then people go along with him, want to give the president a chance. They are not discrete administration proposals, really, they're just opinions about options that are on the Hill already.

Ever since the modern presidency had its genesis with the administration of Franklin Roosevelt, presidential agendas have often been tested in legislative waters before the ascendancy to the White House of a particular party's nominee. In evaluating the surge of legislation embodied in Kennedy's New Frontier and Johnson's Great Society, James Sundquist concludes that

the Democratic program which was presented to the country in 1960 was truly a *party* program. The platform writers and the presidential nominee contributed emphasis, style, and form, but the substance of the program had been written with unusual precision and clarity during the eight years out of power—eight years that at the time seemed endlessly frustrating but that were, it is clear in retrospect, extraordinarily fruitful.[4]

Congressional incubation in advance of presidential "initiation" is not a uniquely Democratic phenomenon. When President Reagan entered office in 1981, large segments of his program for economic recovery—the central and almost sole focus of his first year—were borrowed nearly wholesale from legislation Congress had already considered. The Economic Recovery Tax Act of 1981 (ERTA) had at its core the three-year personal income tax reductions previously known as the Kemp-Roth bill. Many of the programmatic and budgetary changes introduced in the Omnibus Budget Reconciliation Act of 1981 (OBRA) were also pulled from legislation already making the rounds on the Hill, as reported by a Republican Senate committee staff member:

When [David Stockman, Reagan's budget director] left the House, he took with him in effect what was called the Black Book. That Black Book was put together by staff members of

4. James L. Sundquist, *Policy and Party: The Eisenhower, Kennedy, and Johnson Years* (Washington, D.C.: Brookings Institution, 1968), p. 415.

key congressional committees with the knowledge and support of staff at the Congressional Budget Office . . . Those things in the Black Book were not new. They had been proposed before. Some had been discussed, some had been flatly rejected. All of them were options that had had some hearing on Capitol Hill over the previous four or five years.

Evaluating presidential ability to succeed with Congress or examining the nature of the relationship between the two institutions is therefore frequently an exercise in witnessing the president push initiatives whose success or failure may well be determined more by the extent of past legislative fertilization than by employment of present presidential leadership skills. Kennedy, for example, "was 'getting the country moving' by sending back to Congress legislation that had been debated many times, in some cases for decades."[5]

Even if the issues are being considered for the first time, congressional input on a nominally presidential proposal may be significant. The reason is simple and provides the basis for the strategic-accommodation scenario: presidents wish to avoid defeat and members of Congress hate surprises. The White House in particular and the administration in general have an incentive to consult extensively with congressional actors. An intimate of President Johnson described the process:

> You pay attention to the pre-announcement, pre-decision period. You touch all of your bases, and you can't leave anybody out. If you do, then they may say, "Hey, you didn't contact me," and then they may go screw you in the subcommittee the next week. You have to be sure when you make an appointment that you know the district the guy is from, and that you've gone to his congressman and checked, and you've gone to the two senators and checked. The reason is that on a policy decision they can shoot you down, not based on the merits of the proposal but because of what you did to them.

The White House should consult, one congressional liaison official suggested, "because it is good for your image, that you are working with Congress, and you want those suckers out there with the president so it is their proposal, too, and they

5. Harry McPherson, *A Political Education* (New York: Little, Brown, 1972), p. 189.

have some pride in it." Because the legislative process is inherently complex and unpredictable, and the administration is aware of the fact that there will always be times of trouble with legislation, there is an interest in bringing members of Congress in early for the "takeoff" so they will be around for the potential "crash landing." Stated more colorfully by an aide to the Senate Republican leadership, when "you're in cold water like that, it gets a lot warmer the more people you can get in with you." The introduction of more people into the process is not costless, however. The very act of communication and the understood desire of the White House to find allies to help shoulder the burden of politically difficult choices infuse members of Congress with the expectation that their substantive contributions will not be ignored.

White House officials are not the only administration figures having a discourse with members of the congressional establishment. Agency heads and staff engage in a continuous series of exchanges with legislators and congressional staffs who are active in an agency's area of jurisdiction. At the extreme, these relationships form a key component of "iron triangles," subgovernments, or policy communities in which programmatic decisions are collectively produced by congressional, bureaucratic, and interest-group actors who share political perspectives and interact with some regularity. To the extent that much of the presidential program percolates up from the bureaucracy, a large part of that program may already be the result of agreements reached between the Hill and "Downtown."

Finally, even though there may not be a direct dialogue between the administration and Capitol Hill on a particular policy proposal, the president's assistants do not operate in a political vacuum. They are not unaware of what was wrought in the past, nor are they ignorant of what certain members of Congress are likely to think about some ideas. A Reagan administration official commented:

> You know, consultation, it's not always such that you say, "Well, I'm going up to consult, I'm going to go see Senator So-and-So and consult with him." Another aspect is to know a senator and his position well enough that you don't have to consult with him. Now if someone suggested repeal of the investment tax credit, I know that Bob Dole and Russell Long

are not going to agree to that—and I don't have to call them
to find out.

A White House staffed with people of talent and aided by the
expertise resident in the agencies will be able to anticipate the
reactions of Congress to various policy suggestions.[6] If that
reaction is expected to be negative, it may well be that elements
of the president's legislative program, including some of more
than passing importance, will be changed or deleted from the
legislative agenda before they have even been announced. When
an administration is guided by a president with the deeply
rooted congressional experience of a Lyndon Johnson or a
Gerald Ford, some proposals of interest to the chief executive
may be scotched prior to being aired even in the White House.
Both Ford and Johnson undoubtedly possessed a better sense of
the prospects of passing a particular initiative than did their
staffs, and sometimes therefore abruptly killed ideas that had
been fermenting in their own minds without leaving a public
trace of any kind.

Anticipation of congressional reactions can distort what are
revealed as presidential preferences beyond just the addition or
deletion of desired provisions. Modifications to a proposal may
intentionally be introduced that are quite contrary to the true,
though unrevealed, preferences of the president. The application
of game theory to legislative behavior has highlighted the potential significance of "sophisticated voting," where members of
Congress cast votes in opposition to their preferences on a particular vote—on an amendment, say—if the success of *that* vote
enhances the probabilities that the ultimate outcome of the process—passage or defeat of the legislation—will conform to their
actual preferences.[7] Presidents and their aides could pursue a similar strategy in the course of formulating legislative proposals. In
order to advance the likelihood of obtaining what they actually

6. See Carl F. Friedrich, *Constitutional Government and Democracy*
(Boston: Ginn, 1950), p. 49; and John W. Kingdon, *Congressmen's Voting
Decisions*, 2nd ed. (New York: Harper and Row, 1981), pp. 136–137,
196–197, 288–289.

7. James M. Enelow and David H. Koehler, "The Amendment in Legis-
lative Strategy: Sophisticated Voting in the U.S. Congress," *Journal of
Politics* 42 (May 1980): 396–413; and Robin Farquharson, *Theory of
Voting* (New Haven: Yale University Press, 1969).

desire, presidents may craft proposals that are at odds with their preferences but that, when the anticipated reactions of Congress are calibrated and factored in, will lead to the desired policy results. To return to our initial question, How presidential is the president's program?

What I have described is a strategic process in a presidential-congressional game in which the final legislative outcome is structured to a significant degree by the preemptive choices made by presidents and their aides, where the consequences of those choices are fully calibrated by the White House based on the intelligence gathered through consultation or the seasoned judgments of anticipated reactions. We assume that presidents have as their prevailing goal the embodiment in law of their own preferences. To achieve that goal, presidents withhold their preferences from public knowledge and project only those positions that they calculate will lead to optimal outcomes. Because of this strategic game, with the ultimate product of congressional responses being determined largely by the endogenous infusion of congressional interests at the proposal initiation stage, it may be fanciful to speak of a publicly articulated "presidential" program.

The conceptual implications of this jumble for the analysis of presidential-congressional interactions could be devastating. Suppose for a moment that what is announced in the president's legislative program does represent true policy preferences. As one then compares two presidencies and finds one significantly more immersed in policy conflict or one distinctively more "successful" at getting its program passed by Congress, one could explain the variation in conflict or success by defining analytical models incorporating factors such as the nature of the issues, the number of people in the president's party on the Hill, and other elements that make up the context of the legislative and political process. If we assume reasonably good model specification and accurate measurement of the various factors involved, these models should be able to provide meaningful explanations for diverse kinds of interactions between the White House and the Hill and offer results that are consistent across similarly situated administrations.

But what happens if the strategic-accommodation scenario is the real case? In general terms, since most studies concentrate on postinitiation characteristics, as does this one, their models—whether explicit or implicit, quantitative or inductive, historical or contemporaneous—are misspecified and highly suspect.[8] The confounding results can be easily illustrated. Assume again that we are interested in explaining different levels of institutional conflict or divergent success rates for various presidents. One chief executive may appear to be highly skilled in the legislative process because—all other factors being equal—that chief executive enjoys success in getting Congress to enact "the president's" proposals. If that president, however, unlike the others, does not send up legislation that may have a risk of losing, or redrafts proposals to suit the desires of key legislators, or even secures the presidential seal to already existing legislation that has a favorable congressional future, is that president really more successful— and by implication more skilled—at passing "the president's" program? Willingness to consult and sensitivity to likely congressional responses can be legitimate indicators of successful politicians, but that is considerably different from evaluating the ability of presidents to get done programmatically what *they* want to get done. Also, understanding and explaining what occurs during the postinitiation process, what Congress does as its members formally respond to the announced presidential program, cannot be accomplished without distortion if what Congress *does* includes what it *did*, implicitly, by way of consultation or anticipated reactions, in the preinitiation period. Further, if there is enormous variation in the effects of the endogenous strategic game, across both presidencies and issue areas, how reliable will be generalizations developed from the postinitiation analysis? In fact, the consequences will be great and our analyses of presidential-congressional relations will be far less robust and meaningful than we might expect. We are thus left with the crucial question, Can the empirical foundations and implications of the strategic-accommodation scenario be challenged?

To assess this question requires careful examination of the implicit assumptions about the setting in which strategic accommodation occurs. These assumptions pertain to both the objectives of the president's initiatives and the nature of information

8. The problems being discussed here have obvious implications for quantitative studies of presidential-congressional relations, but they are also applicable to any empirical approach. In quantitative studies, misspecification results in high standard errors and mismeasured coefficients; in other types of empirical analyses, conclusions derived inductively are not responsive to all of the relevant factors.

about the legislative arena available to White House strategists. The scenario rests on a fairly simple assumption that presidents have the operational goal of maximizing their chances—in the immediate instance—of enacting legislation that may advance one of any number of basic objectives motivating their general behavior. Likely defeats are avoided by recognizing them in advance, and adverse compromises are prevented by strategically identifying initial positions that will bring bargained outcomes within range of the president's actual preferences. One assumes that in order to make these judgments the president, with the assistance of White House aides, is able to use communications with members of Congress and correct anticipations of member reactions to calculate the probabilities of various legislative outcomes, given particular versions of the president's proposals. To use the argot of the decision-making literature, presidents therefore make choices about the character of their policy initiatives in situations of "risk," where "risk" is distinguished from "uncertainty" by the fact that more than one outcome or consequence of a decision is possible, but the objective probabilities of those outcomes are known at the time that the decision is made.[9]

A strong conceptual argument may be made, however, that these simple assumptions are in many circumstances violated. Like all other political actors, presidents have multiple, sometimes conflicting, goals as they make decisions about everything from personnel selection to policy proposals. While obtaining some kind of favorable legislative response from Congress in the near term is certainly a plausible operational goal of presidents, thereby giving them some impact on policy and demonstrating their legislative acumen, a chief executive may well act on potentially competing objectives. In addition to the operational goal of enacting legislation, presidents have an interest in staking out a position or in pursuing what they define as good public policy, both of which may lead them to present "fixed" rather than accommodated positions at the initiation stage of a legislative proposal.

9. See John C. Harsanyi, *Rational Behavior and Bargaining Equilibrium in Games and Social Situations* (Cambridge: Cambridge University Press, 1977), p. 22; James G. March and Herbert A. Simon, *Organizations* (New York: John Wiley, 1958), p. 137; and John D. Steinbruner, *The Cybernetic Theory of Decision* (Princeton: Princeton University Press, 1974), p. 17.

In staking out a position, presidents may wish to announce publicly their precise legislative preferences, regardless of the near-term consequences on the Hill, in order to reap electoral benefits in the next campaign (as Truman did prior to the 1948 election) or to claim a position they feel will earn them credit in future historical retrospections.[10] It is also reasonable to posit that the individuals who get elected to the White House bring with them opinions about what constitutes good public policy. They will announce and hold fast to those positions when half a loaf at the announcement stage does not strike them as better than none, or they are willing to set a long-term agenda rather than seek immediate partial returns. Presidents, therefore, have incentives to be quite sincere in the public announcement of their initiatives and to prefer to wage a campaign for their programs after initiation rather than temper them beforehand.

Even if presidents do consistently emphasize legislative enactment of their operational goals, one needs to investigate the extent to which presidents and their assistants have the information necessary to make accurate strategic judgments about their proposals. Consultation with members of Congress and White House anticipation of congressional reactions certainly occur, but executive judgments about congressional responses happen largely under conditions of uncertainty rather than risk. Rather than knowing precisely the probabilities of different kinds of legislative responses, presidents and their aides can often only formulate loose guesses about the outcomes. Like many other types of decision makers, they experience "uncertainty about uncertainties."[11] Whatever level of knowledge about Congress presidents bring to office—and for some that knowledge has been quite limited—and

10. Paul C. Light, *The President's Agenda: Domestic Policy Choice from Kennedy to Carter* (Baltimore: Johns Hopkins University Press, 1982), pp. 62–69.

11. Hillel J. Einhorn and Robin M. Hogarth, "Decision Making under Ambiguity," in *Rational Choice: The Contrast between Economics and Psychology,* ed. Robin M. Hogarth and Melvin W. Reder (Chicago: University of Chicago Press, 1986), p. 43. See also Robert B. Duncan, "Characteristics of Organizational Environments and Perceived Environmental Uncertainty," *Administrative Science Quarterly* 17 (September 1972): 317; Harsanyi, *Rational Behavior,* p. 22; and James G. March, "Bounded Rationality, Ambiguity, and the Engineering of Choice," *Bell Journal of Economics* 9 (Autumn 1978): 589.

whatever the talents of the individuals who surround each president—and some have been embarrassingly deficient—the strategic decision makers in the White House face an enormously complex and uncertain world on Capitol Hill. While the Executive Office of the President rests squarely within the tandem-institutions legislative system, at the point in the process at which policy positions are being formulated it is a somewhat isolated organization operating in a relatively complex, unpredictable environment, especially during periods of divided government.

The environments of organizations may be characterized by two dimensions: the number and diversity of factors that constitute the environment and the amount of change over time in those factors. Decision makers perceive the most uncertainty when they operate in complex-dynamic environments.[12] While White House strategists typically are able to generate accurate vote counts prior to committee or floor action on a piece of the president's legislative program, information of that quality is not readily available before a bill has been drafted. At such an early juncture, given the enormous number of influential figures on the Hill, the vast assortment of veto points available, and the potential for change at the margin that exists with congressional elections held every two years, it is extremely difficult to predict the result of congressional deliberations.

The very efforts made to overcome the problems created by a complex and fluid environment may create distortions of their own. Every organization attempts to mitigate the effects of environmental uncertainty, and the White House is no exception. The congressional liaison staff and consultation constitute the institutional means and process by which presidents and their assistants seek to buffer the uncertainty of the legislative arena.[13] Yet several individual and group attributes relevant to White House legislative decision making can skew the information needed to make accurate strategic judgments.

The ways people cope with uncertainty may create erroneous perceptions of their environment. First, individuals may through a cognitive process impose more structure on the environment

12. Duncan, "Organizational Environments," pp. 314–317, 320. 321, 325.

13. See James D. Thompson, *Organizations in Action* (New York: McGraw-Hill, 1967), pp. 12, 21–24.

than actually exists; they may feel more comfortable with categorical beliefs about projected outcomes, however misinformed, than with the ambiguity of considering a broader range of probabilistic outcomes.[14] Second, especially when decisions must be made about issues that may not be resolved for a considerable period of time, individuals may find it difficult to project with any certainty what their own future preferences will be.[15] There is no reason to believe that presidents and White House staff members are immune to these characteristics. They often appear to see a world far simpler than the one that actually exists, or choose to make political calculations that seem contrary to a traditional cost-benefit analysis of trade-offs.[16] Presidential preferences also must be crafted in the context of the moment, with the recognition that changing circumstances, both substantive and political, may lead to revised preferences.

The means by which groups arrive at collective judgments about the world may also be flawed in ways incompatible with the strategic-accommodation scenario. Groups—especially if made up of people sharing basic values, a common attribute of White House staffs and the people with whom they interact on the Hill—may fall victim to what Irving Janis has termed "group-think." Highly inaccurate perceptions of alternative actions and their consequences are produced by "reliance on consensual validation" instead of "reality-testing."[17] If perceptions of reality are not skewed by the presence of a common conceptual lens, they can be distorted by failures in internal communication. Agents acting as the nexus between the decision makers and their environment have the beneficial function of "absorbing uncertainty," but any biases in their interpretations of the environment will lead to inaccurate calculations about the consequences of group action.[18] Even the most skilled congressional liaison staff can com-

14. Steinbruner, *Cybernetic Theory*, pp. 17–18, 66–67, 110–112.

15. March, "Bounded Rationality," pp. 589, 597.

16. Richard E. Neustadt, "Presidents, Politics, and Analysis," 1986 Brewster C. Denny Lecture, Graduate School of Public Affairs, University of Washington, May 13, 1986, esp. pp. 40–44.

17. Irving L. Janis, *Victims of Groupthink* (Boston: Houghton Mifflin, 1972), p. 38.

18. See March and Simon, *Organizations*, p. 165; and Charles Perrow, *Complex Organizations: A Critical Essay* (Glenview, Ill.: Scott, Foresman, 1972), p. 153.

municate incorrect assessments of a legislative initiative's reception in Congress. Finally, because of the need to simplify complex problems and the failure of individuals or groups to have the time or the capacity to process all the information needed to make fully optimizing calculations, group decisions often reflect the acceptance of adequate rather than optimal realization of objectives— what Herbert Simon describes as "satisficing."[19] If such processes characterize White House strategic decision making as well, then any scenario that relies on the assumptions implicit in optimization strategies is apt to miss the mark.

One can argue in the abstract, therefore, that for a variety of reasons the assumptions necessary for accepting the strategic-accommodation scenario as typical are suspect. Instead, these conditions reflect an alternative scenario that includes more fixed positions taken by the president and greater uncertainty about congressional responses. The question, then, is, Which of these scenarios has the most empirical support?

The View from the White House and the Hill

It is extremely difficult to evaluate accurately the role of consultation and anticipated reaction in the development of presidential initiatives: the processes are so complex, the participants are so varied and numerous, and executive decisions about legislative issues are often not discrete events. Ideally, one would like first to have an accurate assessment of the president's operational goals and sincere policy preferences, and then be able to examine the record of each proposal, before its submission by the president, for traces of congressionally inspired changes. So many events and maneuvers never enter the paper trail, however, and those that do are so voluminous that the task of identifying them all is probably beyond the capabilities of even the most encompassing research enterprises.

One feasible alternative is to talk with individuals who have participated in or witnessed the interaction between the agents of the

19. Herbert A. Simon, *Administrative Behavior: A Study of Decision-Making Processes in Administrative Organization*, 3rd ed. (New York: Free Press, 1976), pp. 38–41. See also Richard M. Cyert and James G. March, *A Behavioral Theory of the Firm* (Englewood Cliffs, N.J.: Prentice-Hall, 1963).

president and policy makers on the Hill. The analysis in this chapter is based on my interviews with 107 officials—65 from the Executive Office of the President (EOP), 33 from Capitol Hill, and 9 prominent journalists (see Appendix A). They are not a randomly selected sample of equally weighted respondents, impossible in this kind of study, but rather a purposively chosen group of informants or expert witnesses whose reflections on their experiences serve as analytical windows on the diversity of interactions between the Executive Office of the President and Congress. Those with service in the EOP include individuals at the highest ranks, some with experience in more than one administration. The congressional group is composed primarily of committee staff directors and aides to each party's leadership. Among the issues discussed with these informants are the process of consultation and the effect of White House anticipation of likely congressional responses. All informants were asked about the circumstances leading to consultation, the influence of that communication, and the consequences of anticipating a negative congressional reaction.

In addition to quoting extensively from these interviews, I summarize the collective responses and provide a sense of the prominence of several themes that run through the interviews by reporting the percentage of the informants who made reference to them. The results cannot and should not be mistaken for "hard data." There ought to be a correlation between the actual presidential-congressional interactions and the percentage of the informants offering a specific characterization of events, but the percentages do not indicate how often particular interactions and anticipated reactions took place. They do suggest, however, more forcefully than the simple use of quotations, what seems most important to these experienced practitioners. In the process, percentages help support and enrich with an empirical foundation the previously elucidated argument that erodes the solidity of the strategic-accommodation scenario.

The first point in our strategic-accommodation scenario was that many of the legislative proposals that form the president's domestic program originate on the Hill. Presidential ideas are often reworked versions of policy options that have already experienced a modicum of the testing of the legislative process. While this basic fact cannot be disputed, it does not take into account the transformation that occurs when a proposal rises from the profusion of legislation introduced in Congress to become an item on the presidential agenda. At any one time, there is an enormous pool of legislation on the Hill, outlining proposals in almost any policy area imaginable. Saying that presidents select ideas from among those policy antecedents does not tell us very much. What is important, though, is that initiatives adorned with the imprimatur of the president of the United States provide an example of upward mobility, at the extreme moving from obscurity to prominence. Presidents are "policy dramatists."[20] Even those issues that previously attracted considerable attention achieve greater prestige once they become presidential.[21]

As much as anything, the essence of the modern presidency can be seen in the central role played by the president's agenda in defining the bulk of the congressional agenda:

> The assumption that it was a presidential responsibility to propose legislation and try to influence its adoption was not questioned after the mid-1950s. In fact, the role of policy initiation was seen as a primary obligation of the office, one which could not be shirked without reprobation . . . When Eisenhower failed to propose a legislative program during his first year as president, he was criticized from both sides of the aisle. "Don't expect us to start from scratch on what you people want," an irate member of the House Foreign Affairs Committee told an Eisenhower official. "That's not the way we do things here. You draft the bills and we work them over". . . [What is meant by initiation?] Is it the origin of an idea, the first time it is introduced in Congress, or the point at which it becomes the center of a public or congressional debate? Clearly, the president has an advantage in getting attention for issues even if the idea did begin with him or his staff.[22]

Many of the informants I interviewed, at both ends of Pennsylvania Avenue, repeated the familiar aphorism that "the president

20. Gary King and Lyn Ragsdale, *The Elusive Executive: Discovering Statistical Patterns in the Presidency* (Washington, D.C.: CQ Press, 1988), p. 39.

21. Chamberlain, *The President, Congress, and Legislation;* Corwin, *The President,* p. 485n76; John Johannes, "Congress and the Initiation of Legislation," *Public Policy* 20 (Spring 1972): 292; and Polsby, *Innovation,* p. 5.

22. Stephen J. Wayne, *The Legislative Presidency* (New York: Harper and Row, 1978), pp. 19, 28.

proposes and Congress disposes." An initiative embodied in the president's program, whatever its source, possesses a special quality. A member of President Johnson's domestic policy staff recalled that a prominent senator "called up once about something in the president's program, on a particular proposal that was in the program, and he said, 'Hey, that's my idea.' I asked him, 'Would you rather get credit or get a bill?' And he responded, 'I would rather have the credit.' He said that with a bit of a laugh." What presidents appropriate does become their own. A proposal with the president's name at the top is different from one without it, even if the content is the same.

Consultation with Congress

Even proposals that have acquired the special aura of presidential sponsorship may begin to look more congressional if the administration consults extensively with members of Congress and incorporates their points of view into the initiatives. It is necessary, therefore, to evaluate the magnitude of the consultation and attempt to assess its contribution to the policy development process.

Although there are incentives for administration officials to engage members of Congress in dialogue about a presidential proposal, there are also reasons why the president and administration agents may fail to have this dialogue or avoid doing so in a meaningful way. Roughly eight of ten (83%) of the individuals I interviewed, in both the EOP and Hill samples, volunteered reasons why the White House might shun consultation prior to sending a proposal to the Hill. The most significant of these—suggested by 60% of the informants—are situations in which the president has a firm position on the issue, at least at the outset. A sampling of comments will illustrate the point:

> *An aide to Republican presidents:* Presidents and politicians are dominated by their own vision of what is right for the country and what needs to be done. They come in with a lot of baggage. They have to; they believe a certain course is right for the country and they see it as a leadership role to bring the country along with them on some of those issues . . . There are certain essential issues, such as Reagan on the economy, in which he has a certain set of ideas about how things should be done.

An aide to President Ford: Many of the statements made in the State of the Union address or the budget message are the president's. There's a limited amount of consultation, but most of it is after the mosaic is put into place. When the president gets up there on January 21st or 22nd, it's a political statement—this is what we have done, this is where we are going. We don't tell Congress much before that. Even the leadership of our own party doesn't see it much beforehand.

An aide to President Reagan: Usually sending up the bill is the initial step in the negotiations. And you're not going to want to negotiate away your position right from the start, since you're going to have to negotiate later.

Both the executive and the legislative informants emphasized that presidents avoid consultation when they feel that their position is "the right thing to do" from the president's perspective. While the presidential assistants often referred to this behavior in the context of leadership, of doing the correct thing or staking out a strong bargaining position, those on the Hill were more critical of the self-righteous, ideological, or partisan character of the chief executive. Comments from each kind of informant, however, emphasize that the president's program serves many purposes or reflects the pursuit of varying operational goals, thereby making the strategic-accommodation scenario less viable. Frequently a proposal is made to assuage a constituency group sympathetic to the administration or to fulfill a promise made during the campaign.[23] Consultation on these issues is less feasible than on those for which the president is seeking concerted action and is unconstrained by past commitments.

A good deal of concern about Congress was expressed by those working for the president. Forty-one percent of the EOP officials were apprehensive, at least on some occasions, about the institutional weaknesses of Congress. Complaints ran the gamut from the parochial and sievelike nature of the Hill, to its collective inability to do what is right for the country, to its tendency to transform any issue into pork-barrel politics. A Republican congressional liaison operative claimed that "the Hill does two things

23. Jeff Fishel analyzes the legislative and administrative proposals and policy pursued by presidents as a result of their campaign commitments in *Presidents and Promises* (Washington, D.C.: CQ Press, 1985).

best: nothing at all and overreaction." Further, said one assistant in the Ford White House:

> There is an underlying suspicion of Congress. You tell one of them and all the others will find out. The first thing they do is go out and tell the press . . . You want to orchestrate [a proposal] in the administration, in a way that puts it in the best possible light. You don't want them making the announcement.

Congressional informants, on the other hand, only occasionally identified leaks as a problem for the White House. In addition, while a quarter of the EOP officials mentioning problems with Capitol Hill commented that members of Congress simply are not interested in a proposal so early in the process, no one representing the Hill volunteered that sentiment.

The critical view of the Hill held by many in the White House is matched by cynicism on the part of the Capitol Hill informants in their evaluation of the motivations of the executive. Fifty-five percent of the congressional part of the sample felt that presidents and their staffs consult with Congress only when it is to their advantage. One aide to the Democratic leadership, speaking in the context of the Reagan administration but alluding to others as well, commented:

> Recently the only times they have consulted with us are when they felt that we controlled the House numbers. They didn't do any of it during the first two years, or at least there was very little of it. They've consulted with us when they've needed us, when they needed us for votes. Carter dealt with us on a regular basis, obviously because we were of his party, but also because we were controlling the timetables. When they have to consult with us, they do; and when they don't, they don't.

Only a quarter of the presidential aides expressed a similar view. Those on the Hill were also more likely to view a president's firm position on an issue as part of a plan to blame Congress for not passing a proposal after the executive had defined a course of action.

The nature of the particular issues involved may also inhibit the opportunities, or the will, of the president's people to engage members of Congress in prior consultation, as 16% of the informants suggested. On noncontroversial issues there is no need to consult—and, of course, there are so many items on the agenda that thorough consultation on each one would be impossible even if that were the interest of all the participants. Some issues, though, including prominent ones and those high on the president's wish list, are too sensitive or jurisdictionally too complex to permit extensive communication before the president's package has been formulated. The Energy Plan of 1977, proposed by President Carter, is a case in point. Its scope was sweeping, it challenged multiple interests, it ran directly into the jurisdictional overlap of the congressional committee system—and there was no consultation with Congress. As a senior official in the Carter administration argued: "On energy, if we tried to work things out with them ahead of time, we would not have gotten anything out up there, given the fractured and fragmented nature of Congress. If we were still there [in the White House], right now we would still be trying to negotiate the damn energy package."

An assistant to a member of the Democratic leadership on the Hill expressed a somewhat different view of the legislative process. Pointing out that passage of the energy package would have required leadership from skilled political operatives under the best of circumstances, he lamented that "all we got was a speech and a sweater."[24] On sensitive issues, it appears that those in the congressional establishment feel the administration needs to start negotiations early if anything is to be accomplished, whereas White House operatives fear descending into a congressional cavern in which lives a multiheaded policy-eating monster. Since it is the prerogative of the president's advisers to initiate contact, or to be receptive when the request for communication comes from the Hill, the views of the executive about the proper role and timing of consultation are likely to prevail.

A few informants mentioned the lack of time for consultation, and those who did emphasized the importance of the problem. Some made reference to the crisis atmosphere of the White House; others noted more self-imposed constraints. An aide in the Carter administration put it this way:

24. The informant is referring to President Carter's "fireside chat" to a television audience in 1977, in support of his energy program. Carter, wearing a cardigan, spoke informally and was seated in front of a glowing fire.

The deadlines were the single most important decisions we made. On energy we had this April 20th deadline. It limited our ability to consult, to make changes. The single most important thing was the deadline. I say in hindsight, I would say in foresight, it's stupid to live so much by the deadlines. Now deadlines are important, but this was crazy. Then we had the MEOW speech, you know, the moral-equivalent-of-war speech. There wasn't time to consult, to explain it.

Despite all the reasons that we might expect extensive consultation, therefore, there are many that illustrate why presidents and their administrations may choose not to communicate with Congress early in the process. Further, the example of Carter's energy program demonstrates that many of those deterrents can be present at once. In 1977 Carter had clear goals for a comprehensive energy program, he submitted a package of proposals that he felt represented correct and good public policy, the White House was concerned about the parochial tendencies of the Hill, the issues were extremely sensitive and complex, and Carter himself had imposed a nearly impossible deadline for formulating a comprehensive set of proposals shortly after he came into office.

These inhibiting factors are not always present, of course. When they do not have a bearing on the process and consultation does occur, what does that consultation look like?

The fact that administration officials and members of the congressional establishment talk to one another does not necessarily ensure that there is an authentic process of consultation, or that the information being exchanged permits accurate judgments about future congressional actions. Consultation means many things to many people, ranging from actual substantive negotiation to prior notice—merely informing members of Congress, often the night before, of the president's intentions. Officials in the two institutions may have rather different interpretations of what it means to consult, as noted by a congressional liaison aide:

> The rule of thumb on consultation to a member of Congress is spending an hour a week in the Oval Office with the president and having the president accept all he says. Consultation, well, it's really something different to Congress than to the president. Far too often, consultation to the Congress means following the wishes of key members of Congress and key members of the staff. Far too often, too, consultation to

the president means acquiescing to the president and what he wants to do, and accommodating him.

Given the array of definitions associated with consultation, it is necessary to consider more fully what consultation can signify when it does occur, how much substantive communication is involved, and what the consequences may be for evaluating congressional contributions to the president's program. This suggests a hierarchy of questions to be pursued. When the informants made reference to the occurrence of consultation, what form of consultation did they mention? More important, did they cite instances in which consultation with members of Congress did or did not directly affect the substance of the president's proposals?

Despite the constitutional wall of separation between the executive and legislative bodies and the often compelling reasons for communications to be restricted, the tandem-institutions setting affords continuing opportunities for those in the administration to converse with individuals serving on the Hill when they choose to. Letters, hearings, social gatherings, and telephone calls all provide channels for communication with members of Congress for both the White House and officials in the bureaucracy. In short, there is constant intercourse, and a recognition among presidential aides that Congress, as a human institution, must be stroked to solidify its relationship with the executive. Deeply aware of human elements involved in presidential-congressional interactions, a Johnson associate commented:

> You've got to have those things in place before you can bring them on your side. You need an atmosphere, a mood, a feeling. Otherwise there is suspicion, ill will, a gloomy forecast. You know, with a girl, before you ask to marry her, you take her out on a few dates, you bring her flowers. Then you marry her—you don't start out with marriage. I.e., you don't make a policy proposal without doing the groundwork.

This florid description portrays the White House as engaged in a continuous effort to nurture a favorable atmosphere. About half of the informants (48%), especially those on the Hill (54%), referred to a general aura of communication, a constant process of interaction. Many of those comments paralleled the theme expressed above; still more pointed out that agency officials are always communicating with the Hill. There are indeed interbranch exchanges, but that says little about their substantive content or impact.

The interviews, however, lent additional credence to the problem of congressional influence on presidential initiatives. About four-fifths of the informants, with no discrepancy between those in the EOP and those on Capitol Hill, mentioned generalized consultation about specific president proposals. A closer examination, though, reveals the meaning of this general form of consultation. The congressional informants emphasized the importance of leadership meetings and working with the president, as well as the executive's willingness to communicate with key members of Congress having an interest in the policy area. But, as a House leadership aide suggested, consultation with congressional leaders tends to be "more on the landing, not the takeoff. By the time the leadership is involved, the context is pretty well set." Both those in the Executive Office of the President and on Capitol Hill described consultation as a mechanism for running a proposal around the Hill, as a means of avoiding surprises. In the Kennedy administration, commented one staffer, "we called that touching base. There's no exact equivalent for that. It's touching base. If you touch base with a committee chairman and if he does not scream and demand to see the president, then you know that, well, 'I won't be responsible,' but he won't say, 'You idiot!! Why did you send that up?' You have not given him a veto, you have given him a comment on it." The remarks by members of Congress may provide useful intelligence, but they do not necessarily imply the active introduction of congressional perspectives into a proposal before it is announced.

Much more supportive of the strategic-accommodation scenario in which consultation seems to have such an effect is the fact that a third (but only a third) of the informants reported instances in which there was detailed consultation about the specifics of a presidential initiative. Among both the presidential aides and the congressional informants recalling such occasions, 45% described situations when the administration actually wrote legislation together with members of Congress or congressional staffs. One example was trucking deregulation during the Carter administration. A member of Carter's Domestic Policy Staff indicated that "we worked very closely with Kennedy and also with [Senator Howard] Cannon—those were the two who had been working on trucking deregulation in the Senate. We negotiated personally with him [Kennedy] and his staff. We actually negotiated that pretty much line by line. In the end, we had a joint administration-Kennedy bill." Of course, two-thirds of the informants did *not* mention occasions entailing such detailed consultation. That brand of specific negotiation unquestionably introduces a congressional element into some legislation, but it is not a pervasive form of interaction.

Approximately a fifth of the individuals interviewed indicated times when the initial consultation occurred *after* a decision about the substance of a proposal had already been made in the White House, a view expressed by nearly a third of the congressional informants. Several informants suggested that this was the norm. Two Republican presidential aides described what often happened in their respective administrations. First, in the Nixon administration:

> Many times the consultation was just a PR move. Too often it was, "Here it is, fellas." The farther the administration progresses, the more you get to that point. Then you just do it and say to hell with it . . . [Earlier in the interview:] You just send things up to shove it up the Congress. And pretty soon you get to the point where you're having buttons printed up. [He exhibited a button that said, "Up Congress."]

And in the Reagan administration:

> As a general rule, when there was consultation, it was pro forma, purely ceremonial. They [senior White House aides] would listen to what people had to say and then completely disregard it. Once they actually said, "A decision has been made, now we need to set up consultation." Set up what? They just did not have respect for the legislative process.

Frequently, then, consultation on a specific proposal followed presidential initiation rather than preceding it. A choice had been made, and the White House was either interested in giving the appearance of working with Congress, or (as was suggested more often in the interviews) in attracting allies and commencing the process of negotiation. Further, just as the EOP officials had suggested that members of Congress are not interested in a proposal at the early stages, a few informants from the Hill, such as an aide to the House Democratic leadership, observed that the "real key is what happens and whether you've had some input by the end, not whether consultation occurred in the beginning."

Having confirmed that consultation is a fairly common activity and that there is often communication about specific legislative proposals being considered by the president, we next need to try to assess more directly whether that consultation has any influence on what the president ultimately proposes. Again, discourse alone need not have any effect. Yet there are times when it does. A whopping 78% of the informants reported situations in which consultation did indeed affect the substance of a presidential initiative, and there was no disagreement between executive and congressional officials. Nevertheless, some interesting trends appear when we analyze the responses that aggregate to the 78%. First, fewer than a quarter of those informants volunteered that consultation is frequently influential; a far greater proportion said something similar to "it *can* be, but it depends." Congressional aides, perhaps naively, were more optimistic on this score. A somewhat greater percentage suggested that if a key legislator, such as a congressional leader or a vital committee chairman, expressed reservations about a proposal or some aspect of it, the White House would certainly pay attention. Second, a fifth of the informants who mentioned that proposals were influenced by consultation were referring to the inclusion of congressional initiatives in the president's program that were compatible with White House interests. In the words of a political appointee in the Office of Management and Budget, "Imitation is the most successful form of consultation." It is not so much that an executive proposal is changed, but rather that a congressional idea becomes presidential. A White House assistant remarked, for example, that at the outset of the Carter administration

> there were members of Congress who had pent-up ideas from years of the Republican administrations. We felt that we had to forward many of those with our own proposals, and they were ultimately reflected in our own program. We felt a need to accommodate Congress, and of course they had such high expectations following so many years of Republican control.

Some of these remarks lend credence to the strategic-accommodation scenario, but the story is not yet complete. Almost 40% of the informants, and half of those serving in the Executive Office of the President, spoke of consultation as affecting not the basic substance of proposals, but rather matters peripheral to what the president wanted to accomplish. The packaging—the way a proposal was to be announced—might be adjusted, or the technical details of an initiative might be fine-tuned to enhance its attractiveness, but these refinements would have minimal bearing on the core of the initiative representing the president's position. In addition, as many of the informants noted, the consultation might not affect the substance at all, but rather structure the politics of the proposal's consideration. A Democratic presidential domestic policy adviser described the process:

> A guy from Wyoming might want a road in his district; someone else might want a VA hospital. These things were dealt with at the same time. A little bit of horse-trading went on. This would go on in a sophisticated, seemingly casual way. The White House would bring something up, suggest a proposal, and a member of Congress would say, "Well, I'll give that consideration. I'd also like you to consider *my* need for a road or for a VA hospital in my district."

Consultation does have an effect on the legislative agenda, but not the sort stipulated in the strategic-accommodation scenario as I have characterized it.

Even more disruptive of the scenario is the proportion of informants who cited instances where prior consultation with Congress had no effect on the content of a presidential initiative. Fully three-quarters made at least one such reference, as did four of five congressional informants, who were more likely than their EOP counterparts to recall instances in which consultation was not very efficacious from the congressional perspective. Although meaningful consultation does occur on some occasions, it would be inaccurate to characterize it as the norm. One committee staff director commented that "members of Congress would be very disappointed that the message they had sent or the letter they had written, pointing out all of the problems, had been ignored." Sometimes there would be an appearance of executive cooperation with Congress, but the reality would be quite different, as the 1981 chairman of the House Budget Committee learned while dealing with the Reagan administration. A committee staff member reported that "Stockman was talking to people on the [Budget] Committee. They were operating the way that [Chairman

Jim] Jones thought he could cut a deal. And then they just cut, left Jones dangling. I think it is a story of the kind of consultation [that occurred] and whether or not the consultation is taken seriously."

Two final points about consultation need to be made. First, even though the individuals I interviewed were asked explicitly about consultation as it occurred *prior* to the submission of a presidential initiative, many of their comments pertained more to the postinitiation stage of the process. Because executive-legislative interactions are so complex and amorphous, it is difficult to think and speak about distinct stages in the process of formulating a policy initiative. What is sharply focused in the textbook is nonexistent in legislative affairs. As a result, the amount and influence of consultation suggested above may well be overstated with respect to what occurs *before presidents announce elements of their legislative programs*. Second, while I have been careful to refer to individuals rather than institutions when discussing communication between the White House and Congress, there is the ambiguity of what is meant by "consulting with Congress." Obviously one does not consult with Congress, but with the particular individuals who work in or for Congress. If "consulting with Congress" signifies talking only to members of the president's own party, then the implications of consultation are far more limited than would be the case with an exchange that includes legislators of diverse philosophical orientations. For example, Ronald Reagan's initial proposals for social security in 1981 might have been rather different had the consultation with Congress been other than what actually occurred. According to an aide to President Reagan:

[Health and Human Services] Secretary Richard Schweiker announced that plan to a Republican leadership meeting and no one said anything, no one voiced anything. Everyone thought it was an incredibly painless way to work out of a difficult problem . . . Everyone thought, "It sounds good to me." Well, time worked in some problems and the Democrats got hold of it. If it had been a bipartisan meeting, maybe that wouldn't have happened.

Much communication is restricted to those members of Congress who share the president's party identification. Administration lobbyists often behave in ways similar to lobbyists for interest groups, spending most of their time with known or likely allies rather than with the opposition.[25] By staying close to those of like mind on the Hill, "consultation with Congress" may only serve to reinforce whatever groupthink has developed in the White House itself. That perspective was stated quite forcibly by Democrats on the Hill in reference to the Reagan administration, which they not uncommonly accused of being the most partisan in history. Referring to the budget battles of 1981, an aide to the Democratic leadership in the Senate declared with some bitterness that "talking to Phil Gramm is not consultation." Gramm, of course, is the Texas Democrat (now Republican) on the House Budget Committee who in 1981 fed intelligence about Democratic strategies directly to David Stockman and the White House, and who provided President Reagan with the patina of bipartisanship in the Gramm-Latta substitute, the foundation of the Omnibus Budget Reconciliation Act of 1981.

The Anticipation of Congressional Reactions

Consultation is not the only activity that may introduce congressional themes into presidential policy proposals. Whether or not the White House communicates with individuals on the Hill, and regardless of the range of perspectives tapped there, the substance of what presidents propose may be influenced by the congressional responses that are anticipated by chief executives and their aides. Unfortunately, attempting to discover evidence of the effect of such "anticipated reactions" is tricky indeed. The concept is real; its manifestation is more nebulous. A senior Democratic adviser with considerable experience in government, referring to White House anticipation of congressional reactions, offered the following comment:

> I suspect it happens a lot, but you're going to have a hard time trying to get anecdotes. It's just so ingrained in the way things are done. It's more subtle. It may be something where you just don't do it, and not with a big discussion.

An official in the Reagan administration fulfilled this prediction:

25. Raymond A. Bauer, Ithiel de Sola Pool, and Lewis Anthony Dexter, *American Business and Public Policy: The Politics of Foreign Trade* (New York: Atherton Press, 1963), pp. 350–357.

Gosh, I think that happens all the time, but you are going to ask me for an example, and I . . . Mostly they're small things. I draw a blank on anything specific, but I know that it has happened. I know that in the early stages, when something draws a number, when it's going to go to the cabinet councils, and someone will say, "Hey, that's just not going to happen." There's a sense of why waste the time working on that. But that happens so early, before much work has been done on them, that I forget what the examples are.

Also, trying to predict reactions may be more a matter of mapping strategy than of adjusting substance. The Legislative Strategy Group organized in the first term of the Reagan White House, chaired by then Chief of Staff James Baker and composed of other senior presidential advisers, spent much of its time trying to anticipate hurdles and strategies of the opposition. Said one participant, the members would ask each other, "How would you screw things up if you were against it?" In such cases reevaluating the content of the proposal is less significant than searching for weak spots in the ramparts of the other side.

Undaunted by the difficulties of evaluating anticipated reactions, I asked those I interviewed whether there were occasions when a presidential proposal was changed or completely dropped as the result of the expectation of a negative response on the Hill. The officials in the EOP were able to respond much more directly, of course; those on Capitol Hill were asked to speculate based on what they had witnessed. One component of the strategic-accommodation scenario is reinforced by this query. Overwhelming majorities of the informants (89% of the EOP and 73% of the Hill samples) agreed that predictions of likely congressional action could or did influence the content of executive proposals. Reflecting on some of the Reagan administration's budgetary initiatives, a career OMB official revealed that on some occasions, "there are proposals in the budget that fall into that category that I find to be mystifying. They look like real losers. I wonder how they get in. They're going to look draconian to somebody, and you know it's not going to go in an organization like Congress. And then along the way, after a lot of sighing, the decision is made to just forget it."

Once again it is necessary to look below the surface and consider in greater detail the meaning of many of the comments that fall in this general category. The bulk of the informants who noted the effect of anticipated reactions, 58%, remarked that presidential policy proposals are not formulated in a darkened closet, but rather with some sensitivity toward Congress. Members of any president's congressional liaison staff view as part of their responsibilities the transmittal of congressional sentiment to the White House so that the president is aware of the likely problems. Several of the comments, especially from the Hill sample, suggested that those in the White House felt fairly confident that they knew what the reaction would be.

Also included among these responses were statements that presidential proposals would incorporate a certain amount of flexibility to make them more attractive, without altering the direction of the proposal. Legislation considered on the Hill during the Reagan administration offers an illustration, as described by a domestic policy adviser:

> To the extent that something is politically possible, that will have an effect on a proposal and the decision on whether or not to send something over. The enterprise-zone proposal had a laundry list of tax incentives. There may be tax incentives that key members just won't buy, so they might be left out. Now something that was not a tax incentive was to provide for a subminimum wage in the enterprise-zone proposal. It was left out because, while it might be good public policy, it might have gotten opposition from people who might otherwise be supporters.

So an anticipation of possible congressional reactions can have an effect ranging from minimal to significant, though not often to the point of having a substantial influence on major proposals. When examples were offered of instances when either consultation or anticipated reactions led to the dropping of a proposal *almost all of those examples were cases where the proposal had in fact been announced in a presidential statement of some kind, but then efforts to push the initiative had been terminated because a congressional snub was expected.* Recent examples include Carter's natural resources reorganization and his National Energy Board, and in the Reagan administration the proposed dismantling of the departments of Energy and Education, the initial social security reforms, and the various proposals linked to "social issues." All of these items were announced—they entered the president's program—but they were not pressed. These kinds of issues are represented in the sample of presidential proposals used for this study.

What about the more strategic kinds of policy formulation, the use of "sophisticated" proposal selection in which presidential initiatives include items the president does not really want but that should combine with a predicted congressional response to produce a desired overall result? The age-old practice of incorporating bargaining chips in a proposal certainly continues, as a journalist described:

> That year they had the farm bill, I called [a member of President Reagan's congressional liaison staff]—this was when they were trying to get the boll weevils on the budget—I called and said that there were some funny proposals in their farm bill for peanut farmers and sugar. I asked if these were to buy votes, and he started laughing. These are probably put in because that's what they wanted to do, but they also knew they were useful, and they were expendable parts of the proposal. They were talking policy on the one hand, but also what they had to buy to look around for winners. They could use them as bargaining chips. A lot of times it is that crass.

This addition of attractive provisions to a proposal can become extreme. A Carter administration official complained about the augmenting of the bill for a windfall profits tax on oil with a provision to give credits for wood-burning stoves, an action driven by the desire to gain votes: "It's really so naive to think that that is how one puts together legislation. It's like reading Machiavelli in *Readers' Digest.*" These alluring bargaining chips generally include items that are not unwanted by the president and that are often expected to be retained in the final bill. They do not really confound the effort to identify presidential preferences, nor do they challenge presidential discretion over the agenda.

The real concern is when, for strategic purposes, the president's program includes provisions that run counter to presidential preferences. Several episodes during the Reagan administration give reason to believe such situations occur. For the fiscal year 1983 budget President Reagan, while rejecting pressures for new taxes, suggested a series of contingency taxes to take effect in fiscal year 1986 if the deficit problem loomed larger. The $50 billion in revenue to be derived from those taxes was included in the budget figures, yielding a paper improvement of the deficit picture.[26] A Democratic committee staff member on the Hill speculated that Reagan had no real interest in the contingency taxes and had no intention of pursuing them. That speculation was confirmed by an OMB official.[27] Another congressional Democratic aide expressed the feeling that many of the program cuts proposed by the administration were suggested with the full expectation that Congress would bail them out. The administration could publicly state its apparent preferences, then be saved from the political fallout by Capitol Hill. Finally, a congressional staff member on the Republican side commented:

> I think that Stockman, for example, is very adept at predicting the course of events and throwing up straw men which are ruthlessly to be torn apart, and we do exactly what he wants us to do. I do spend some of my time trying to ignore Stockman and not wanting to know what he's thinking. Then I don't have to worry about what he wants us to do.

This remark suggests that sophisticated choice on the part of the administration may fundamentally distort presidential preferences as expressed in various facets of the president's program, such as the budget. On the other hand, an individual with senior-level experience in Democratic administrations volunteered his skepticism of such behavior:

> As a general proposition, but obviously with exceptions, it was fairly difficult for the White House to do a standard form of bargaining requiring you to put in things that you really didn't want. You can't develop a strategy when you know you're not going to use it. As a case in point, people sometimes say that Stockman knew that the tax cut was too big, but he thought that they would cut it back. My impression is that that is too devious by half. You can't play the system that way. I've been at a lot of these meetings, and you may develop legislation with all kinds of bargaining chips, but you

26. David A. Stockman, *The Triumph of Politics: Why the Reagan Revolution Failed* (New York: Harper and Row, 1986), pp. 363–365.

27. Reagan's opposition to the contingency taxes is also made clear in Stockman's book, *Triumph*, p. 355.

don't put in bargaining chips or provisions that you don't want to keep or which would terrify you if they stayed.

While there will be exceptions, there are compelling reasons why the policy preferences articulated in the president's program are not likely to stray far from true preferences. Under the best of circumstances the legislative process is too unpredictable for the administration to risk having to live with a provision that is anathema to its position. Presidents are also not fond of having to veto their own legislation.

I have developed in some detail the various aspects of anticipated reactions as they occur during the course of formulating the president's program, but it is also the case that two-thirds of the informants recalled situations in which expectations of a negative congressional response did *not* have any effect. The proposals were sent up anyway. Real-wage insurance, a scheme the Carter administration developed to ease wage-based pressures on inflation, is one example. At a meeting of the Economic Policy Group in the dining room of the secretary of the treasury, the liaison staff expressed its lack of enthusiasm for the real-wage insurance initiative:

> Another guy on the liaison staff and I said, "Now, that's the dumbest idea we have ever heard. If it works, there's no net gain; and if it doesn't work, it's going to cost billions and we can't afford to pay for it." It was an issue that was hard to sell; it was hard to explain—*to me!* But I went up and marketed it, asked what they thought, told them it was not going to pass, and it went into a speech anyway.

As Carter did on this occasion, presidents often ignore advice about political problems and strategy because they believe the long process toward passage needs to be started at some point, or they feel that what they are proposing is the right thing and adjustments cannot be made.[28] A staff director on the Hill put it this way:

> Now, Carter might have had his congressional liaison people say that something wouldn't pass, but he would think, "I

28. Committee chairmen sometimes arrive at similar conclusions when their committees are working up legislation for floor consideration. See Kingdon, *Congressmen's Voting Decisions*, p. 137.

have a responsibility to go ahead with this. It might take ten years to pass, but it's something that needs to be done." Every president must send up some stuff that is not going to get enacted. And they'll do it because it's the right thing to do, or it's something that's important to them, or they want to cut short Ted Kennedy on health insurance. As a result, I tend to be very broad-minded about why presidents send things up.

Not all of this informant's colleagues on the Hill are as magnanimous. As before, while many on the Hill recognize that presidents are often directed by what is "right," that attitude is frequently interpreted as a sign of self-righteousness and partisanship, not leadership. In addition, the congressional informants were four times as likely (39%) to think that the people in the White House just were not very skilled at reading Congress and calculating what would happen with a particular proposal.

After this leisurely consideration of the intricacies of the consultative process and reflection on the issue of anticipated reactions, it seems fairly certain that the strategic-accommodation scenario—leading to the notion that the president's program is a hopeless muddle—can be pretty well laid to rest. The realities of the political process do not allow us to cast that scenario aside entirely, however. There will be times when the president's program is diluted as a result of consultation and executive estimates of congressional action. They will primarily be those situations when the prevailing operational goal of the administration is to pass legislation, and when the issues or the setting facilitate the collection and accurate interpretation of information about how Congress is likely to respond to the president's initiative. I have made the argument that such conditions represent the exception rather than the rule. A series of points have been established that give credence to the alternative argument, one more consistent with the fixed position and uncertainty scenario, that there are many reasons why the president's program will remain unaffected. As several of the informants commented, what goes into a presidential speech, often the definition of the president's program, is pretty much what the president wants. In the end, remarked an aide to the Speaker of the House, "the President of the United States only has to convince one person, and he's the guy he sees in the mirror each morning." One question remains to be addressed, however. Are all presidents the same, or do some invite special problems?

Special Problems: Johnson and Carter

While prior consultation and sensitivity toward the Hill may not be a source of conceptual problems in general, difficulties could still arise if there were wide variation from one president to another. Any comparison of the executive-legislative relations for different presidencies could produce erroneous conclusions if the source of variation involved the preinitiation period. Two presidents are especially suspect. The first is Lyndon Johnson, universally described as being the modern president who lived and breathed the Congress, who worked every fabric of that institution as no other president has. The second is Jimmy Carter. More than anyone else, Carter was criticized for not consulting in advance on legislation and for self-righteous policy stands that ignored practical realities. Yet after their first two years people in the Carter White House seem to have overreacted to earlier complaints, becoming *too* sensitive to congressional perspectives.

In an effort to evaluate these issues, let us look at the Johnson and Carter administrations separately in a little more detail.

Lyndon Johnson loved to say, "I passed 83% of what I proposed." He would claim victory on something even if they had struck out everything after the initiating clause. We had a scoreboard of all the proposals, and they had an even bigger scoreboard over in the White House. If there was some problem with child illness, but Johnson couldn't get anything to pass except some statement about how it's awful that children are ill, then that's all right, he would pass that. I don't think any president since then has been like that.[29]

Johnson did love victory. But did that mean his own legislative program represented just a quick finger to the wind, or did he at least start the legislative process with what he actually desired? There is no question that LBJ understood Congress and knew its operations.

There is also little doubt that he was the most consultative pres-

29. Interview with a congressional staff member who also had executive-branch experience in the Johnson administration.

ident in recent decades. His technique for dealing with the Hill, as may informants remarked, was to wear out the telephone. Recalled one Johnson adviser:

> You didn't hear things about people who should have been consulted and were left out. Sure it happened. There were times when someone's nose would get out of joint, but Johnson was such a one-man full-court press that it seemed he was always consulting. A more likely response would be, "By God, consult? If only he would leave me alone!" . . . Johnson was the all-time champion in telephoning members. No one else has ever done as much. Sometimes at seven o'clock in the morning he'd be calling people. There's a wonderful story about Johnson calling a senator at two-thirty in the morning. "How are you doing?" Johnson asked, as if it were the middle of the day. The senator responded, "I was just lying here waiting for you to call me, Mr. President."

Johnson and his people were talking to members of Congress and important staff people all the time, constantly cultivating and fertilizing the legislative domain. Johnson would also work closely with key members of Congress, as he did with Wilbur Mills, chairman of the Ways and Means Committee, when he sought to trim the budget to keep it below the $100 billion mark.[30]

Much of that ongoing communication involved touching base, making contact with all of those who would be upset—and lethal—if left out. Often touching base meant a specialized form of consultation in which rough outlines of proposals would be run around the Hill to test congressional reactions. According to a Bureau of the Budget official, these outlines would be shown to members, but not surrendered, and their content would be general in tone, not detailed. What did this kind of consultation mean for the president's program? Generally, it did not instigate a wholesale recrafting of the proposals and restructuring of the executive's legislative agenda. Nonetheless, a participant in that process who later worked on the Hill argued that "you've got to understand that that allowed a subcommittee chairman to shoot [a proposal] down. It allowed him to say, looking at the sheet, 'Well, on this point I can accept it; these two points I don't like, but maybe we can work something out. And on these items there's just no

30. Interview with a congressional staff member.

way.' They would take those things back and lot of things would get dropped or changed. That's really affecting the substance of things."

It could influence the substance, but perhaps not as dramatically as this comment suggests. There were some policy areas in which President Johnson had strong convictions, and acted on those convictions. He had firm ideas about what he wished to accomplish in the field of civil rights and in health and education. Those policy domains constituted a significant portion of the Great Society agenda. Keenly aware of political realities, Johnson still was not afraid to move ahead. One of his advisers explained this dimension of the President:

> Johnson said when he was majority leader that his major task in life was to keep [southern conservative Democrat] Dick Russell from crossing the aisle and embracing [minority leader] Everett Dirksen. At the same time, when he was elected along with a big majority in the Senate and the House, he was no opponent to setting about trying to do it [taking the initiative and pressing the issue]. He didn't hang back.

Further, Johnson was quite personal about what was sent to the Hill. It was "his" program, mostly built in "his" White House, said a Budget Bureau official. Even during less than advantageous times, after the huge loss of Democratic seats in the 1966 election and in the midst of the inflamed passions of Vietnam, Johnson continued to push his program, "serving up his menu," in the words of a White House assistant.

Second, the consequences of Johnson's mode of operation with Congress must be considered in the context of the times. Except for the polarization over the conduct of the war in Vietnam, which did cast a pall over executive-legislative relations in general, Johnson's legislative program was given congressional consideration during a period of remarkable unanimity. Compared to today, commented a congressional committee staff member, "there was considerably more consensus . . . as to what you wanted to do and closer agreement as to how you were going to do it." The distances between the president and Congress, in a relative sense, were telescoped, the divisions muted. A member of LBJ's domestic policy staff remarked that "the separation of powers is a phrase we have all heard. Well, at that time some of the separation got collapsed. It seemed we were all working on the same thing; we were all mobilized together." The president and Congress were tandem institutions in political theme as well as authority.

In addition, the Johnson administration predated the enormous expansion of congressional staffs and the recent development of independent congressional technical capabilities as symbolized by the Congressional Budget Office and other informational arms of the legislature. As a result, the White House and the executive branch were in a much more advantageous position vis-à-vis the Hill, and were, in the assessment of a Johnson domestic adviser, more able to dominate the development of legislation. Although this president and his assistants were more sensitive politicians than those who came before or after them, and although they flooded the lines of communication between the Hill and the White House, the magnitude of dissension they greeted was reasonably constrained, at least in the domestic arena. There is a considerable difference between talking with and accommodating members of Congress in the context of a policy-making consensus and doing the same things when the political establishment is more polarized. The nature of the Johnson administration and its effect on the President's program can be summarized in a Johnson aide's comments about whether anticipation of a negative reaction on the Hill would lead the White House to drop a proposal.

> Let me say, it would have to be an awfully negative reaction and not something that was live or die for us. If it's important, I would be awfully concerned if we were to give up too early . . . You know, by 1969 I don't think we had an awful lot left over that we had wanted to do.

To find the antithesis of Lyndon Johnson, one need to look no farther than Jimmy Carter. Where Johnson relished Washington politics, Carter was disgusted by it.[31] One man who came to appreciate the contrast was Joseph Califano, LBJ's chief domestic policy adviser and Carter's first secretary of health, education, and welfare. Reflecting on the initial meetings of the Cabinet prior to Carter's inauguration, Califano recalled that "the odor of naivete perfumed those two days off the coast of Georgia. The new Presi-

31. For an analysis of Carter's brand of politics, see Charles O. Jones, *The Trusteeship Presidency: Jimmy Carter and the United States Congress* (Baton Rouge: Louisiana State University Press, 1988).

dent evidenced little sense of what Washington was like or of the complexities of governing. Except for Stuart Eizenstat . . . and Jack Watson, . . . Carter's staff seemed naive to a fault and appeared to believe the anti-Washington rhetoric that had carried Carter to the White House."[32] A congressional staffer, also with experience in both administrations, made a similar observation: "Carter was characterized most aptly, I think, by two brief paragraphs in an interview-book review a couple of years ago. In one little paragraph he said, 'Yes, I miss being president. No, I don't miss Washington.' That really said everything about Carter, I think. Carter basically never understood that Washington is a part of the presidency and Congress is a part of Washington."

Combined with that anti-Washington naivete was a misperception among Carter's staff of the amount of influence they were to have. A member of the Domestic Policy Staff remarked that "in the beginning, when we thought we were very powerful, we thought we really had influence with Congress." An aide serving in the congressional liaison office was a bit more blunt: "I think it is fair to say that our domestic policy staff, in the development of policy initiatives, did not have an adequate recognition of the fact that Jimmy Carter was elected president, not crowned king."

In addition, of course, Carter himself developed very set ideas about what he felt was appropriate and meritoriously correct public policy. When his orientation toward producing good public policy ran into a Congress governed first and foremost by the political rules of accommodation, neither partner in the relationship was exactly bowled over by the other. A journalist recounted an illustrative scene:

> One member of Congress told me that he was in a meeting with Carter; they were all sitting around, and Carter just sat there as they talked. And at the end he told them all that they didn't know what they were doing, that they didn't know what they were talking about. He could tell Carter was just seething. A story like that is probably true. He just told them off. He never understood, respected, or appreciated the relationship with Congress.

32. Joseph A. Califano, Jr., *Governing America: An Insider's Report from the White House and the Cabinet* (New York: Simon and Schuster, 1981), p. 25.

Carter's distaste for congressional politics would sometimes carry over into his meetings with individual members of Congress. One aide explained that "on occasion, I would go to the president and say that we need to sit down with Senator X and talk to him, and the president would say, 'I don't know why I should spend my time kissing that fellow's ass when he's playing politics and what I want to do is right. Why should I have to compromise when he is using only a political view? I don't understand.' " The informant reported that Carter would reconsider and meet with the senator, but it is unlikely that the exchange would be especially fruitful, given the attitudes of the participants.

Finally, of course, there were vociferous complaints about Carter's congressional liaison operation, which was under the direction of a Washington novice, Frank Moore. Many of the individuals I interviewed in the Carter administration protested the exaggerated nature of many of these complaints; nevertheless, there are enough stories of miscues to suggest difficulties in consulting with Congress about policy initiatives. As one correspondent recapitulates:

The major thing about the Carter years was the rampant incompetence. They made those excuses, but they didn't know what they were doing. The hospital cost containment issue was a big example. They didn't check to see what kind of reception it was going to get. They just handled it terribly. They would do all kinds of dumb things. Someone called up the speaker's office to find out what his first name is. They wouldn't find out who was sponsoring a bill, so they'd call up that guy and ask him to vote against it. They did none of the easy things, the things you do to keep members of Congress happy.

All of these elements—the anti-Washington attitudes, the focus on "correct" public policy, the mistakes in dealing with Congress—bred a situation in which there was not much consultation with members of Congress about the initiatives in the President's program. The extreme was the 1977 energy program, on which there was no advance consultation. In short, what Carter sent up to the Hill was what Carter wanted. Why, then, is Carter a potential problem for this analysis? It would appear that the presidential program of the Carter years suffers the least from congressional contamination.

The problem is that by late 1978 the Carter staff had learned some lessons from their two years of experience with the Hill. Perhaps they learned the lessons too well. Evidently thinking about the second and not the first half of the Carter administration, an OMB official told me that "the Carter administration would go up [to the Hill] and just give everything away. They'd ask, 'What do you think?' and the member of Congress would say, 'Oh, no, no, this would never go,' and they were forced to make changes too early. This really won the contempt of people in Congress. The Carter people would come up, and you'd just blow and they'd fall over."

Republicans, such as a Senate committee staff member, were highly critical of Carter for compromising "all over the place with a group of people before submitting a legislative initiative," or for "weakening the presidency by sitting down with members of Congress and selecting water projects to stop or preserve." Protesting that such situations were rare, an assistant in Carter's White House agreed that there may have been times then the White House staff, having been burned, would go to the Hill and be too forthcoming: "I remember a time when I was negotiating with a strong, powerful member of Congress, and I called in a White House staff member. I knew what I wanted from that member, and I had a sense of what he would accept. I found I almost had to gag the White House staffer—he was ready to give away more than we needed to." Another senior aide to the President also noted his regret that the White House had become overly sensitive to Congress.

This leaves a feeling of schizophrenia about President Carter's legislative program and the impact of exchanges with the Hill. Given Carter's basic orientation and views about the formulation of public policy, and the friction that remained between Congress and the White House throughout the term, it is difficult to believe that the last two years of his administration really constituted a complete about-face from the first two. As in any administration there were issues, such as trucking and airline deregulation, on which the Carter White House worked hand in glove with members of the congressional establishment. On numerous others, the presidential perspective held sway. Perhaps the stark contrast between the complete lack of prior consultation on the early energy issues and the later willingness to occasionally negotiate in detail on a proposal has lent a degree of exaggeration to the stories of Carter aides being "blown over" by members of Congress. Or perhaps one of the more respected of Carter's assistants offers the best perspective:

> Under Carter consultation had its greatest impact on the fine-tuning. The president and the staff knew what direction we wanted to go. Consultation may affect the way a proposal is announced or packaged; it's just not going to have all that great an impact. Sometimes when an issue is not so major, all of the good people in the White House, and the good staff members from the committees, and the good people from the agencies, when there's no publicity, can sit down together and work things out early. In our White House and others, there's a great temptation to jam things through.

In the end, owing to factors unique to each administration, there is probably no reason to conclude that the Johnson and Carter presidencies pose special problems for interpreting the meaning of the president's program. Johnson knew how to play the Congress and did, but he started with some strong convictions, had the political capital to move ahead, and served at a time when disagreements on domestic issues were not sharp. Carter began by closing out the Congress from policy deliberation. His administration eventually became more sensitive to congressional reactions and the need for priorities, yet Carter's presidency continued to reflect his basic desire to construct rational policies and his disdain for pragmatic politics. Just as the validity of the strategic-accommodation scenario falters upon analysis across all administrations, so too it can be viewed with equanimity from the perspective of the Johnson and Carter years.

We are now in a position to identify those situations when consultation is most likely to occur and have an impact on the substance of the president submits. The likelihood of meaningful consultation is greatest when specific factors are present: a need for action, which can occur when the issues involved are of considerable importance and the president desires a fairly rapid legislative resolution; a strong willingness to cooperate on the part of those in each institution, reflected in the fact that the White House does not have the resources to go it alone and prominent figures on the

Hill evince an interest in reaching some agreement; the lack of prior campaign or constituency commitments; and a presidential disposition to work with members of Congress. Such situations do exist—a nice example being offered by the compromises on social security achieved in the early 1980s—but they hardly define the context in which most presidential proposals are formulated.[33] And they may, as in the case of social security, follow episodes when presidents have already been rebuffed after suggesting their own proposals.

The president's domestic legislative program, then, provides an appropriate and fruitful point of departure for assessing presidential-congressional relations and the domestic policy choices made by the two institutions, but only if the analysis is built upon appropriate theoretical constructs examined with the aid of the most suitable methodologies. In the next chapter I elucidate the guiding conceptual and methodological principles of this study and suggest one approach for using the president's program to assess the interbranch relationship within a tandem-institutions perspective.

33. See Paul C. Light, *Artful Work: The Art of Social Security Reform* (New York: Random House, 1985).

3. Conflict, Cooperation, and Context

With the legislative program of the president formulated and publicly announced, attention shifts from the offices and conference rooms of the White House west wing and the executive buildings of downtown Washington to the warren of hallways, hideaway offices, committee rooms, and chambers that constitute Capitol Hill. In the uninterrupted flow of policy making, there is not necessarily a fundamental transition in the players or activity levels at the opposite ends of Pennsylvania Avenue, but the fate and ultimate shape of the executive's programmatic initiatives now rest in the hands of the legislature.

Congress, for presidency-centered assessments of policy making, emerges as a legislative labyrinth in which the presidential policy battle is either won or lost. The institutional relationship is characterized according to the legislative *outcomes*, as defined by presidents and their administrations. From this perspective the dominant questions typically are, When presidents initiate policy measures requiring legislative enactment, are they "successful," and if so, why? What aspects of the president's political maneuvering and White House strategy yield achievement or failure with respect to Congress? Why does the legislative branch either acquiesce to presidential dictates or thwart presidential leadership?

The concentration on outcomes, however, and whether they represent successes or failures for the president distorts some important features of legislative policy making. These are the nature of Congress as a collective institution and the process by which Congress acts on programmatic issues. The emphasis on presidential success and failure oversimplifies the coalitional complexity of Congress. While it is easy and not entirely illegitimate to treat a single individual, the president, as the personification of an institution, the presidency and the presidential administration, it is entirely inappropriate to view the Congress as a unified enterprise.[1] To the extent that there is a legislative struggle, "it is rarely the presidency with or against the Congress as an institutionally coherent force. It is the presidency and some of the Congress, often a majority, against the rest of the Congress."[2]

To speak of presidential-congressional interactions on issues of statutory policy, therefore, is to address the challenge of coalition formation, the crux of all collective politics. The positive legislative action required of both institutions is achieved by bringing together a coalition whose domain encompasses a majority of those on the Hill with the initial and frequently catalytic inclusion of the president. When a president is "successful," numerous members of Congress participate in the coalition and share in that legislative victory.

The plain language of presidential success and failure suggests little about the many legislative roads that lead to them, from inertia to concerted action, from acclaim to flat rejection. Each style of congressional response is unique, representing a divergent form of politics and having different implications for assessing the institutional relationship. Each type of congressional action is accomplished within a context that is defined by more than presidential initiation and lobbying of legislation. The structure of American political institutions, the play of political forces, the condition of the economy, and the issues themselves all influence the building of coalitions on the Hill.

To incorporate the tandem-institutions theme of a legislative decision-making system thus requires a somewhat different set of concepts that give theoretical definition to the legislative interactions between the president and Congress. The conceptual and methodological perspective offered here recognizes the duality of

1. The unitary individualism of even the presidency can be easily exaggerated. Alfred de Grazia has commented that "the President is a Congress with a skin thrown over him," giving only the appearance of unitary simplicity. "The Myth of the President," in *The Presidency*, ed. Aaron Wildavsky (Boston: Little, Brown, 1969), p. 51. That theme is emphasized in Gary King and Lyn Ragsdale, *The Elusive Executive: Discovering Statistical Patterns in the Presidency* (Washington, D.C.: CQ Press, 1988), pp. 185–186, 483–487.

2. Joseph A. Califano, Jr., *A Presidential Nation* (New York: Norton, 1975), p. 56.

conflict and cooperation in the system, and identifies the varied processes by which Congress responds to or makes collective choices about presidential initiatives. It then provides the basis for introducing the ways in which the institutional, political, economic, and policy contexts of congressional decisions contribute to the nature of the legislature's responses to the president's initiatives. These contextual factors, joined ultimately with the attributes of individual presidents, are sets of properties of the congressional decision environment that range from those almost entirely beyond presidential control to those over which presidents have considerable influence.

The Legislative Decision-Making System

When Richard Neustadt speaks of separate institutions sharing power, or when one of my informants comments that the president and Congress together get things done because that is the only way to do things, they are both alluding to the fact that members of Congress and the president are all formal participants in an authority structure that requires their concerted effort in order for action to be taken. The relationship between business and government suggested by Charles Lindblom offers a useful analogy:

> Inevitably two separate yet cooperating groups of leaders will show hostility to each other. They will also invest some of their energies in outwitting each other, each trying to gain the upper hand. *Conflict will always lie, however, within a range of dispute constrained by their understanding that they together constitute the necessary leadership for the system. They do not wish to destroy or seriously undermine the function of each other.*[3]

Within the constitutional structure, the president and members of Congress possess even more formal bonds. Because of the dictates of law and tradition, and the requirements of state sovereignty, the government cannot conduct its affairs without their mutual accommodation. They constitute a legislative decision-making system.

3. Charles E. Lindblom, *Politics and Markets: The World's Political-Economic Systems* (New York: Basic Books, 1977), p. 179. Emphasis added.

Portraying the president and Congress as a decision-making system introduces a degree of neutrality to the analysis. Instead of a presumption of conflict between the constitutionally discrete institutions, there is recognition that these constituent parts of the system, when brought into direct interaction, can experience both conflict and cooperation depending on the occasion. Let me emphasize a crucial point: without question conflict occurs, but so does cooperation. The central question then becomes, what engenders conflict or cooperation? More specifically, what stimulates patterns of conflictive or cooperative legislative responses involving the president and Congress on issues related to the president's program?

The potential for both conflict and cooperation in the same decision-making system leads to a second essential feature of this conceptual perspective. While success and failure depict outcomes, the terms "conflict" and "cooperation" allude to the existence of several *processes* that lead to what previous studies have identified as either presidential success or presidential failure. An outcome that is successful from the president's perspective, for example, may be the product of agreement by virtually every participant in the legislative arena to go along with the proposal. Or it may be the result of the president's heading or stimulating a coalition of enough scope and political resiliency to defeat outright one or more opposing factions in Congress. Or it may be the yield of compromise, of adjustments in the proposal acceptable to both administration and congressional negotiators. Similarly, failure for a presidential initiative may be due to active defeat. Or it may be that members of Congress simply ignore the proposal. Each of these responses of Congress—each path to an outcome—represents a distinct kind of decision-making process within the legislative arena.

Treating the president and Congress as a decision-making system, furthermore, opens up new opportunities for understanding their collective decisions. Not all decision-making systems are the same with regard to mission and design, but they do share the necessity of making group choices under diverse conditions. Much has been learned about how organizations, primarily private ones, function as decision-making systems. These lessons can be appropriately applied to explaining the ways decisions are made in public or governmental settings. In an analysis of the court system, Lawrence Mohr demonstrates the utility of incorporating decision-making concepts from organization theory into the study of government enterprises.[4] Without question the White House, Congress, or the two taken together are not organizations in the sense that one applies the term to business firms or other typically hierarchical enterprises. Their objectives, the relationship between them and their environments, the motivations and perhaps longevity of the participants, and their internal management are often quite dissimilar. But governmental units frequently confront problems, develop routines, and display behaviors reminiscent of those that characterize traditional organizations. Borrowing and building from these themes, we can elaborate on a set of ideas about the various ways in which members of Congress collectively respond to presidential initiatives.

Five Decision-Making Processes

To isolate and categorize unique decision-making processes, one must first be able to demarcate the temporal and procedural boundaries of each process. The introduction of a presidential initiative is treated here as the formal starting point of a decision process in the legislative arena. The process ends with either final congressional action on the initiative or the termination of the administration.

In the real world, of course, these boundaries are not so easily drawn. The continuous web of interactions between members of the congressional and presidential establishments does not fit neatly into a well-defined schedule. When White House aides, departmental personnel, members of Congress, and Capitol Hill staffs constantly exchange ideas about active and latent issues in a plethora of formal and informal forums, from committee hearings to lunches in the White House mess, there is among these participants no clear sense of when the policy development phase has begun or when the deliberation and action phase has ended.

Most policy proposals entail ill-defined periods of incubation and active consideration.[5] The concept of a national Medicare

4. Lawrence B. Mohr, "Organizations, Decisions, and Courts," *Law and Society Review* 10 (Summer 1973). See also Charles Walcott and Karen M. Hult, "Organizing the White House: Structure, Environment, and Organizational Governance," *American Journal of Political Science* 31 (February 1987): 109–125.

5. John W. Kingdon, *Agendas, Alternatives, and Public Policies*

program originally received formal attention in the deliberations of the Committee on Economic Security appointed by FDR to develop what became the Social Security Act of 1935.[6] The interest in a national health insurance program linked to social security remained alive from that time on, with President Harry Truman proposing the relevant legislation in 1945. Democrats during the Eisenhower administration, and later John Kennedy as president, pursued the idea. It finally passed with LBJ's leadership in 1965. The American polity engaged in a decision process on Medicare that encompassed three decades. (Some might argue that the process continues.) Nevertheless, there were distinct segments of this process within numerous administrations.

Marking the length of the decision process even within the confines of a single administration can pose conceptual and practical problems.[7] On the one hand, a favorable congressional response to a president's initiative anytime during the administration represents the fulfillment of a policy commitment and the completion of part of the programmatic agenda offered by that particular president. The chief executive leaves office with that specific task consummated, and the record should disclose that fact. On the other hand, because a president's reputation and image link actions on disparate legislative issues, "victories" early in the administration have important implications for how the president is perceived, and thus how Congress responds to subsequent requests. The entire domestic program of Jimmy Carter might well have benefited from quick, positive action by the Ninety-fifth Congress on his National Energy Plan introduced in April 1977. Certainly the significant twin victories on the tax and budget cuts in 1981 were instrumental in defining the tone of President Reagan's relationship with Congress in the months and even years that followed.

In the end, regardless of the origin of the ideas, the evolution of policy alternatives, the amorphousness of the communication pat-

---

(Boston: Little, Brown, 1984), esp. chaps. 6, 8; and Nelson W. Polsby, *Political Innovation in America: The Politics of Policy Initiation* (New Haven: Yale University Press, 1984), esp. chap. 5.

6. Herman M. Somers and Anne R. Somers, *Medicare and Hospitals: Issues and Prospects* (Washington, D.C.: Brookings Institution, 1967), pp. 3–4.

7. Thanks are due Lawrence Baum, Jon Bond, and Richard Fleisher for raising this issue.

terns, and the interdependence of the issues, much of what transpires in the legislative arena has relatively concrete manifestations. Reasonably nonambiguous events serve as "tags" for identifying and defining the attributes of each legislative decision process. Presidents submit fairly specific requests for legislation in recognizable messages and statements issued on known dates. Congress, in committees and on the floor of each chamber, displays behaviors linked explicitly to consideration of presidential programs. Issues are or are not brought to a vote and the results are recorded. Legislation supplements or amends the existing body of law or it does not. Administrations, due to assassination, electoral defeat, the Twenty-second Amendment, or voluntary retirement, end and are replaced. In short, a series of events marks the evolution of each proposal, denoting the beginning, end, and consequences of each decision-making process. The range of congressional responses to the president's initiatives can be captured by five kinds of decision processes, which constitute a set of mutually exclusive alternative means for making legislative decisions.

Inaction

In any given year Congress is swamped under a flood of pending legislation, some of it suggested by the president, more of it at the behest of the bureacracy, most of it generated by the members themselves. The preponderance of draft bills placed in the legislative hopper never proceed beyond their assignment to relevant committees. The initiatives are denied any kind of meaningful attention. While presidential proposals play a significant role in determining what appears on the active congressional agenda, even the proposals of the president may drop to the bottom of the pile. A president may identify an issue for decision, but either house may choose, for a variety of reasons, not to decide. One response always available to Congress, therefore, is *inaction*—simply ignoring a presidential proposal, and by ignoring I mean not engaging in any activity that reveals serious consideration. A hearing by a committee or subcommittee may be held, but in cases of inaction votes are not taken in committee and the measure never reaches the floor of the parent body.[8] The proposal is not actively defeated, it is just

8. For purposes of this study, in discussions of the decision making of the entire Congress, *inaction* includes instances when at least one house

not afforded space on the congressional agenda. At another time, during a future administration, the president's proposal may eventually be considered and even enacted; but from the perspective of the current incumbent, no action is obtained, and none of what the chief executive has submitted passes into law.

Over the last thirty-five years numerous presidential proposals for expanding specific areas of the national wilderness system have received such a reception—for example, President Ford's proposal to include the Kenai Wilderness area in Alaska. Sometimes, as with Jimmy Carter's Oil Pricing Act of 1977 and Ronald Reagan's plan for a new Department of International Trade and Industry, inaction is encouraged by presidents when they either change their minds about the need for legislative action (the former case) or let up the pressure because of the early anticipation of obvious defeat (the latter instance).

Opposition Dominance and Presidential Dominance

Melville Dalton describes organizational decision-making systems as political enterprises, rife with factions and participants engaged in a battle for advantage.[9] Interactions within the organization involve "contention, struggle, and the attempt to overpower with superior force."[10] Even in organizational settings that exhibit routine or managerial means for making decisions, instances can arise in which the absence of a consensus leads to more politicized efforts by various factions to dominate the decision-making process.[11] Resolution is accomplished not by producing agreement, and not by providing mutually satisfying adjustments, but rather by one coalition's overpowering another. The victorious faction enjoys the full fruits of its policy preferences, the defeated group suffers complete programmatic defeat on the particular issue being decided.

---

of the Congress took no action, even if the other did. Because the inaction of one house prevents acceptance of the president's initiative, that lack of action becomes the defining event.

9. Melville Dalton, *Men Who Manage* (New York: John Wiley, 1959); and Mohr, "Organizations," p. 632.

10. Mohr, "Organizations," p. 632.

11. Walcott and Hult, "Organizing the White House," p. 119. See also Michel Crozier, *The Bureaucratic Phenomenon* (Chicago: University of Chicago Press, 1964), chap. 6.

There are times when presidential proposals and the bills of which they are a part enter such an arena on the Hill. Clear lines, often marking partisan, ideological, or regional divisions, are drawn between those who support the programs and those who do not. Bargaining to reach compromise may be attempted but fails, and eventually presidents are left with either all that they wanted, *presidential dominance*, or none of what they requested in that particular proposal, *opposition dominance*. In the case of opposition dominance, others parts of the encompassing bill may be enacted, but the specific proposal under review goes down to defeat. In either instance a legislative coalition secures victory for its programmatic position by overpowering its known opponents. The policy rift is public and recorded.

Dominance becomes presidential when the president, on action dealing with the chief executive's proposal, is victorious in such settings. That happened with some civil rights initiatives and various facets of model cities legislation during the Johnson administration, and with several of the Reagan budget-cutting provisions in 1981. When the opposition dominates, the ultimate results are equivalent to those produced by inaction—none of the initiative is enacted—but the failure stems from the forthright rejection of the president's position. The successful blocking action occurs in any number of settings, from a majority vote on the floor to a failed effort to obtain cloture on a Senate filibuster, from defeat in the committee of substantive jurisdiction to denial of a rule from the House Rules Committee. President Carter's hospital cost control legislation was defeated outright by Congress, for example. Parliamentary maneuvering by House Republicans in 1968, on the other hand, stopped Johnson's proposal for public disclosure of gifts to members of Congress, and a filibuster by southern Democrats in 1970 killed Nixon's proposed constitutional amendment calling for direct popular election of the president.

Compromise

If there is one word that epitomizes the workings of government, it is the word "compromise." Compromise represents the palette from which the art of politics emerges. The idea of accepting less than one wants, hardly unique to politics or government, may be the most universal mechanism of collective decision making in and out of the public sector.[12] Even those enterprises directed by the highest apparent degree of goal consensus, profit-motivated private industries, demonstrate the need for mechanisms to alleviate internal conflict and satisfy diverse demands.[13] For this analysis of legislative decision making, however, I give "compromise" a specific meaning. Using the artifact of outcomes to draw conclusions about the antecedent processes, *compromise* occurs when Congress acts on a presidential proposal, but without granting the full dimensions of the president's request. One assumes that the president would prefer the unamended request, or would prefer some of it to none, and that a process of compromise emerges to arrive at the ultimate result. Opportunities for compromise are facilitated when the substantive nature of the proposal permits relatively easy adjustments. It is far simpler, for instance, to split differences of opinion on a tax measure than on the provision of abortion services. Many presidential budget requests undergo compromise before being enacted in one of the thirteen annual appropriations bills; authorization levels are adjusted; or the proposed statutory duration of a program is changed, as occurred with the postal wage hike negotiated during the Nixon administration.

Vital to this application is recognition of the fact that compromise is limited to adjustments in the specific proposal itself. It does not include logrolling or bargaining across a series of proposals, where one measure may be sacrificed, added, or traded in order to retain another. Bargaining of that sort is pervasive in the American system and in congressional politics.[14] It was frequently mentioned by my informants. When one considers entire legislative packages, or the activities of whole policy communities, logrolling and bargaining are frequently the order of the day. The interpretation of compromise used here, however, is most suited

12. Charles E. Lindblom, "The Science of 'Muddling Through,'" *Public Administration Review* 19 (Spring 1959): 79–88; and Aaron Wildavsky, *The Politics of the Budgetary Process*, 4th ed. (Boston: Little, Brown, 1984).

13. Richard M. Cyert and James G. March, *Behavioral Theory of the Firm* (Englewood Cliffs, N.J.: Prentice-Hall, 1963); and Mohr, "Organizations," p. 630.

14. John Ferejohn, *Pork Barrel Politics* (Stanford: Stanford University Press, 1974).

to the kinds of initiatives that serve as the units of analysis: specific presidential proposals that sometimes are the building blocks from which entire bills are constructed.

Consensus

The final form of congressional response to a presidential initiative involves one of two kinds of issues. Employing the distinction drawn by Barbara Nelson, the proposals are either those for which the potential opposition is unorganized or tempered by a logrolling exchange, or "valence" proposals on which there is no real disagreement.[15] Either way, there is little apparent conflict or organized opposition and the proposal passes intact. The measure finds space on the congressional agenda, comes to a vote, and is enacted overwhelmingly with "hurrah" votes. The issue is decided by *consensus*. As in the case of presidential dominance, the president achieves all that was desired from the proposal, but is able to do so without a battle. Sputnik propelled some of Eisenhower's education proposals along this path late in his administration. Although much of John Kennedy's legislative program experienced trouble on the Hill, proposals to expand research on maternal and child health, to study air and water pollution, and to conduct a transportation census enjoyed consensual congressional action.

The two circumstances leading up to a consensual response are obviously rather different. Valence issues may have little substantive significance for the political system, whereas consensus derived from the inadequate representation of latent interests reflects an artificial harmony at the expense of government responsiveness. Any empirical study of decision-making processes, to be complete, should retain the distinction. Unfortunately, consensus created by submerging voices of discord is no easier to identify than nondecisions on policy issues of the sort described by Peter Bachrach and Morton Baratz—what one White House official characterized as "the babies that were never born."[16] It is difficult to see that which leaves no explicit

15. Barbara J. Nelson, *Making an Issue of Child Abuse: Political Agenda Setting for Social Problems* (Chicago: University of Chicago Press, 1984), pp. 27–29.
16. Peter Bachrach and Morton S. Baratz, "The Two Faces of Power,"

record.[17] For the purposes of this study, therefore, consensus has to be viewed as consensus only in terms of the prevailing array of interests that are represented by the president and members of Congress at the time the legislature is responding to the president's program.

It is important to note, however, that the system of interest representation is not static. A policy determined by consensus at one time may give way in subsequent years to more conflictive modes of social choice as the number and diversity of interests are elaborated. New groups projecting a broader range of values and willing to widen the arena of decision making can introduce conflict where only harmony reigned before.[18]

Finally, an unfavorable congressional response to a presidential proposal does not necessarily spell complete policy defeat for the administration. Presidents are often in a position to use existing statutory authority in order to implement at least part of what they had originally intended in the legislative initiative. When defeat on the Hill occurs (or is anticipated), the president may use administrative or other means to fulfill at least partially the administration's objectives. According to Harry McPherson, LBJ felt that "the main argument for issuing an executive order was the difficulty of getting Congress to pass a law."[19]

Easily recognizable examples of unilateral action by the executive are relatively few in number but they are not insignificant. The

American Political Science Review 56 (December 1962): 947–952, and "Decisions and Nondecisions: An Analytical Framework," American Political Science Review 57 (September 1963): 632–642.

17. The problem of identifying nondecisions is discussed in Geoffrey Debnam, "Nondecisions and Power: The Two Faces of Bachrach and Baratz," American Political Science Review 69 (September 1975): 889–899.

18. Christopher J. Bosso, Pesticides and Politics: The Life Cycle of a Public Issue (Pittsburgh: University of Pittsburgh Press, 1987), esp. chaps. 2, 6, and pp. 255–263; Thomas L. Gais, Mark A. Peterson, and Jack L. Walker, "Interest Groups, Iron Triangles, and Representative Institutions in American National Government," British Journal of Political Science 14 (April 1984): 161–185; and Kay Lehman Schlozman and John T. Tierney, Organized Interests and American Democracy (New York: Harper and Row, 1986), esp. chap. 4.

19. Harry McPherson, A Political Education (New York: Little, Brown, 1972), p. 288.

Crude Oil Pricing Act of 1977 was originally included as part of Carter's National Energy Plan. Immediately after announcing the program, however, Carter chose to pursue the goal of the act—gradually increasing oil prices—with the executive authority he already enjoyed under the Energy Policy and Conservation Act of 1975.[20] He ultimately decided that seeking legislative action was not necessary and would complicate the problem of persuading Congress to accept the rest of the energy program. The threat of this kind of unilateral administrative action can also help in negotiations with Congress. President Nixon, frustrated by congressional resistance to his efforts to decentralize manpower training programs, set in motion plans to implement administratively manpower revenue sharing; a legislative compromise was finally struck in 1973.[21] Congress, too, is cognizant of such maneuvering. Legislation regulating the special milk program in 1966 expressly forbade President Johnson to attempt administration action to redirect the program more toward the poor, and when Nixon threatened executive action to initiate manpower revenue sharing, the House moved to prohibit it.[22]

These examples demonstrate that the potential of unilateral action of this kind is limited. Presidents require at least some vestige of legal authority to proceed with a purely administrative approach once the legislation has been submitted to the Hill. Congress can always intervene. And while the president as chief executive may be uniquely situated to engage in this brand of policy making, where motivations and authority permit, the tandem-institutions arrangement of American government gives members of Congress the instruments of budget control and oversight to engage in their own forms of relatively unilateral policy making.[23] Nevertheless, administrative action by the president means that

20. Richard Corrigan, "Oil Pricing Act, 1977 (R.I.P)," *National Journal* (May 7, 1977): 726.

21. *Congressional Quarterly Almanac, 1973* (Washington, D.C.: Congressional Quarterly, 1974), p. 349.

22. "School Milk, Lunch Programs Merged in Nutrition Act," *Congressional Quarterly Almanac, 1966* (Washington, D.C.: Congressional Quarterly, 1967), p. 328; "Compromise Manpower Training and Jobs Bill Cleared," *Congressional Quarterly Almanac, 1973* (Washington, D.C.: Congressional Quarterly, 1974), p. 347.

23. The significance of unilateral action on the part of Congress was highlighted for me by Deborah Snow.

congressional inaction or defeat need not produce complete failure in implementation of the objectives pursued in presidential proposals.

The Contexts of Congressional Decision Making

The submission of each presidential legislative proposal results in one of the five types of congressional responses or decision-making processes, but the specific way Congress will act on the executive's program at any given moment or for any particular issue is never totally predictable. Nothing about the politics of presidential-congressional interactions is determinative. Rather, the occurrence of each process has an implicit conditional probability distribution. For any single presidential initiative, it is possible that Congress will respond in any of the five ways. Because they are mutually exclusive and collectively inclusive of all possible responses, for any given initiative the probabilities for all sum to one. The individual probabilities vary from one presidential proposal to the next. Sometimes consensus is highly likely, other times it is not expected. But just as it may rain on a day when the weather service has predicted only a 10% chance of precipitation, a congressional response of minimal likelihood may ultimately be what concludes legislative consideration of a presidential proposal.

What gives rise to variation in the probabilities associated with the occurrence of congressional responses? Presidential proposals are not considered in a political or institutional vacuum; the actions of both the president and members of Congress as a whole are influenced, one may presume, by a diversity of factors that establish the specific contexts in which the decisions are concluded. The characteristics of the decision setting for each proposal shape the incentives of each participant in the process by adjusting around the margins the costs and benefits of particular courses of action, as they are perceived by the participants.[24] Richard Fenno contends, with respect to our understanding of individual politicians:

24. Samuel Kernell notes that contexts involve "two realities: objective conditions and politicians' responses to those conditions." *Going Public: New Strategies of Presidential Leadership* (Washington, D.C.: CQ Press, 1986), p. 128.

You face an individual who is pursuing certain goals, holding certain personal attitudes and values, carrying a residue of personal experience. But you also face an individual who is perceiving, interpreting, and acting in a complex set of circumstances. And you cannot know what you want to know about that individual until you have knowledge of these "circumstances," or this "situation," or this "context."[25]

The same conclusion holds true when addressing the collective behavior of individuals. Contexts help us to understand decisions at all levels but, in the legislative arena at least, contexts undergo enormous and continuous change. Although some factors that define the circumstances in which each legislative proposal is decided are relatively static phenomena, many exhibit rapid and potentially dramatic fluctuations.

Of concern here is how these various contextual features, both individually and in combination, structure the politics of congressional action on presidential initiatives and contribute to the likelihood of each kind of response. At the base of the analysis is an implicit interpretation of legislative coalition formation. When presidents introduce legislation, they search for a coalition of supporters. These supporters emerge from two broad categories of legislators. One is made up of "natural allies," those who by virtue of affiliation with the president's party or ideological compatibility are most likely to be sympathetic to the president's objectives. The other consists of "persuadables," individual legislators who, though not inherently predisposed to support the president, for whatever reasons can be enticed to act favorably on this particular request. The success of the resulting presidential coalition is determined by both the relative size of the coalition, composed of natural allies and persuadables, and its capacity to dominate the numerous points of decision in the legislative arena. If opponents are able to lock up the House Rules Committee, or to prevent a cloture vote in the Senate, for example, then the strength of the presidentially led coalition in other parts of the legislative arena is largely irrelevant.

Presidents and their administrations, therefore, face the same kind of coalition-building problems as other lobbyists in Congress. Like interest groups with political action committees, they

25. Richard F. Fenno, Jr., "Observation, Context, and Sequence in the Study of Politics," *American Political Science Review* 80 (March 1986): 4.

confront the dual task of generating supporting coalitions by attempting to increase or maintain the number of natural allies (accomplished through the electoral process) and by supplementing them with persuadables (brought on board by either positive or negative inducements).[26] Presidents, though, may actually enjoy less influence in aiding the electoral success of their allies than do interest groups. They cannot provide direct financial support for election campaigns, and the moral suasion of their office in congressional elections has not been shown to be particularly effective. FDR proved unable to influence the selection of more ideologically compatible southern Democrats in the 1936 election. In the 1970 election Richard Nixon launched a decidedly ineffective challenge to the Democratic control of Congress. Despite extensive campaigning by the President himself, Ronald Reagan watched as Democrats recaptured the Senate in 1986.

What does the process of coalition formation mean specifically? For any particular piece of legislation submitted by the executive, the core strength of the president's coalition, the natural allies, is a product of the outcome of each congressional election, which determines the number of the president's fellow partisans and ideological soul mates in Congress for two sessions. There may also be issue-specific natural allies that cross partisan and ideological lines. Persuadables are encouraged to join the core supporters by their perception or interpretation of inducements, which can be characterized along two dimensions. First, the inducements may be either positive or negative, moving members of Congress to the president's position because of the benefits of that position or the costs of opposition. Second, they may be experienced collectively by many legislators or targeted individually to particular senators or representatives.

Four broad categories of inducements thus can be identified:

(1) Collective benefits, such as favorable economic conditions, are powerful motivations.
(2) Individual benefits, such as supporting a senator's suggestion for a judicial nomination, can persuade legislators to join the president's position.

26. Gary C. Jacobson, *Money in Congressional Elections* (New Haven: Yale University Press, 1980), esp. chap. 3; and Larry J. Sabato, *PAC Power: Inside the World of Political Action Committees* (New York: W. W. Norton, 1984), esp. chaps. 3, 4.

(3) Collective fear, perhaps created by strong popular support for the president in their constituencies, may lead otherwise skeptical legislators to think twice before challenging the president's initiative.

(4) Individually based threats from the White House, however rare, may also be influential.

The aggregation of all of these factors establishes the size of the coalitions supporting and opposing the president's position. In conjunction with the institutionally determined existence of decision and veto points in the legislative process, they affect the probabilities of different kinds of congressional responses to the president's program.

The source of natural allies and the inducements perceived by both presidential allies and persuadables find empirical definition in a broad assortment of factors, ranging from constitutionally mandated institutional arrangements to specific manifestations of a particular president's ability to work with individual legislators. These coalition-building factors vary enormously in the degree to which their presence and effects can be influenced by presidents and therefore there is considerable variation in the ability of presidents to affect the contexts of congressional action on their programs. In the course of this book these coalition-building factors are treated as "properties" of the political process and are examined with respect to a four-level hierarchy representing the extent to which they can be manipulated by individual presidents.

(1) The "pure context" includes the institutional properties of American national government over which presidents have at best marginal influence and certainly no control. These factors involve modifications in the institutions or the rules that govern them. While political and governmental institutions can be dramatically transformed, their structures and rules neither fluctuate wildly from one extreme to another nor do so within narrowly defined periods of time. Three changing features of the institutional setting—Congress, political parties, and interest groups—and their impact on congressional deliberations are evaluated in detail in Chapter 4.

(2) The "malleable context" consists of two sets of properties impinging on the political process over which the president has greater but unpredictable influence, and still no control. One set

includes dynamic political properties, typically associated with election cycles. They contribute significantly to the substance of the president's political capital, "defined as the number of votes the President can generate in Congress at any one time on any given issue."[27] The second category of factors contributing to the malleable context are measures of the condition of the economy, indications of the resources available to the society and the government. The state of the economy can have significant implications for what is possible to accomplish through government policy, and indeed, for what is demanded of government in general.

Not only are dramatic oscillations possible in these features of the malleable context, but the changes occur frequently and are often proximate in time. Underlying cycles may be present, but they may fail to reveal any discernible patterns. While the sources of the fluctuations in these political and economic properties can be identified and explained, their presence lends a degree of irregularity to the practice of presidential-congressional interaction. While the implications of the institutional setting can be known well in advance, the final disposition of the president's program depends to some extent on circumstances that have not yet developed, that can readily change, and over which no one has real control. These features of the malleable context are also investigated in Chapter 4.

(3) The "policy context" represents the constrained strategic choices that presidents make with regard to the legislative agenda. Three basic dimensions are involved. First, all policy proposals do not share the same level of consequence for the political system; they vary in their social and budgetary impact. Second, presidents and their administrations give their initiatives different levels of lobbying effort depending, among other things, on their significance for fulfilling presidential policy goals. Third, presidential agendas comprise issues tied to inherently divergent politics. Some are rooted in controversy, whereas others support the received wisdom or distribute universal benefits. Each of these dimensions, analyzed in Chapter 5, helps to shape congressional action.

27. Paul C. Light, *The President's Agenda: Domestic Policy Choice from Kennedy to Carter* (Baltimore: Johns Hopkins University Press, 1982), p. 26.

(4) The "individual context" includes the idiosyncratic attributes of the presidents themselves and of their administrations. Incumbents bring individual skills to the job and make quite personal choices about the organization of the executive branch and the means for exerting personal influence in the Washington community. These qualities produce the distinguishing identity of each presidency and provide the basis for evaluating the performance and competency of each president in the realm of legislative leadership. They are the subject of Chapter 7.

The Methodological Design

Devising the appropriate means for gathering empirical evidence about the legislative facet of presidential-congressional relations is as challenging as crafting a suitable conceptual basis. That challenge has not always been adequately met in previous quantitative work on the presidency and Congress, as is discussed in Appendix B. Standard data-gathering practices simply do not fulfill the needs of research concentrating on the president's legislative program.

For a precise empirical examination of the themes raised by this study, three objectives must be fulfilled by the methodological design of the research. First, enough detailed information about congressional activities has to be acquired to enable us to make relatively refined judgments. To be more precise, for each proposal offered by the president we require specifics about what actually transpired in Congress, so that legislative responses can be classified according to the kinds of decision processes they entailed. Second, sufficient information has to be collected to characterize the four classes of contexts of congressional action, ranging from the institutional setting to the extent of presidential lobbying effort. To the degree that congressional behavior is influenced by the temporal context—the constellation of factors present at the very moment of legislative action—these contextual properties, as I have termed them, must be portrayed as individually as is possible. Broad aggregations of contextual measures, where more proximate measures are available, do not suffice. Third, a reasonably large representative sample of presidential initiatives from the period under investigation is essential if meaningful generalizations are to be drawn about the interactions between the White House and Capitol Hill on legislative matters and the influence of various attributes defining the four contexts of congressional action. These objectives can be fulfilled only by wedding the richness of the case study approach to the breadth of analysis offered by quantitative designs.

The procedures developed and followed to meet these objectives are reviewed in detail in Appendix C and need not be described here. They resulted in the identification of 5,069 specific presidential domestic legislative initiatives submitted by Presidents Eisenhower, Kennedy, Johnson, Nixon, Ford, Carter, and Reagan from 1953 to 1984. While Democrats were domiciled in the White House for less than 40% of this time, they accounted for almost 60% of the domestic proposals submitted to the Congress. On average, Democratic presidents proposed 244 new initiatives a year, compared to 107 for the Republicans. Johnson alone was responsible for 27% of the proposals made during the period. To a significant degree, to speak of a domestic presidential program is to speak of a Democratic program. Democratic presidents, by ideology, temperament, and situation, have been the architects of most of the domestic establishment existing today at the national level.[28]

From the population of presidential initiatives, a sample of 299 proposals was selected randomly, stratified by year to reflect the shape of the overall domestic legislative process generated by presidential action. The stratified sample reflects the greater legislative prolificacy of Democratic administrations. But since all presidents have presented a domestic legislative agenda, each administration, and a diverse array of issues and circumstances, is represented in the sample. For each of the proposals in the sample, legislative histories were derived and contextual data were collected for 1953 through June 1986, the last date for which information was available on congressional responses to initiatives submitted as late as 1984.

Three Decades of Congressional Response

Our sample of presidential legislative proposals offers considerable insight into the nature of presidential-congressional relations in the modern era. Contrary to both the executive preeminence

28. Bert A. Rockman, *The Leadership Question: The Presidency and the American System* (New York: Praeger, 1984), p. 31.

normatively associated with the presidency-centered perspective and the congressional intractability embedded in its descriptive view, Congress has responded to the submission of presidential initiatives in a relatively balanced way. As one would anticipate in light of the tandem-institutions arrangement, neither conflict nor cooperation alone has characterized the relationship between the two branches. Outright conflict, in the form of presidential and opposition dominance, constituted less than a third of the legislature's responses, as shown in Table 3.1. Cooperative legislative action, involving either consensus or compromise, was not the rule at 43%, but it obviously outweighed open hostility. Indeed, consensus was the result in almost a quarter of the cases, a congressional action more prominent than public defeat of the president's proposals (20%). While Congress ignored through inaction 25% of the executive's initiatives, the vast majority of presidential legislation was subjected to serious legislative attention. No political player other than the chief executive has such an impact on the legislative agenda. In the end, by whatever means, Presidents Eisenhower through Reagan witnessed something favorable happen to 54% of their proposals (compromise, presidential dominance, and consensus), with more than a third being passed exactly as introduced (presidential dominance and consensus). Nothing could be more indicative of a system of tandem institutions in the legislative arena.

Table 3.1 Congressional decision-making processes in response to presidential domestic initiatives

Legislative body		Congressional decision-making process			
	Inaction	Opposition dominance	Compromise	Presidential dominance	Consensus
Congress	25%	20%	19%	11%	24%
(N)	(76)	(61)	(58)	(33)	(71)
House of Representatives	25%	18%	20%	13%	25%
(N)	(74)	(53)	(59)	(38)	(75)
Senate	24%	13%	21%	10%	31%
(N)	(73)	(40)	(62)	(31)	(93)

The proposals in the sample are relatively specific legislative requests made by the president. They are typically not whole programs or bills, which frequently are made up of anywhere from a couple to dozens of separate initiatives. It should not be surprising, therefore, that for these specific proposals, compromise is not the most likely result. On the other hand, while a fifth of the proposals were decided by compromise, approximately half of the bills or programs of which the 299 proposals were a part ultimately passed in a compromised form. Sixty-seven percent of the bills associated with the proposals decided by presidential dominance were enacted in an overall legislative compromise, as were 63% of the bills involving consensus on the specific proposal and 26% of the bills that initially included initiatives defeated by opposition dominance. Compromise is the most prevalent form of legislative decision making in evidence on Capitol Hill for entire bills or programs that are a part of the president's program, but not for the more specific components of each bill. Again, one would not expect anything different from institutions with tandem authority.[29]

In general, the patterns evident for the entire Congress are essentially repeated for both the House and the Senate, with one interesting exception. Compared to the House and Congress as a whole, the Senate during the 1953–1986 period demonstrated a greater tendency to accept presidential proposals in their entirety, and to do so with less dissension. Almost one-third of the proposals were decided by consensus in the Senate; only 13% were actively defeated by the opposition.

Several explanations are possible. First, resulting from the 1980 election and maintained by two subsequent congressional elections, the Senate has been controlled by the party of the president somewhat more often than the House. That fact alone need not lead to consensus, but for this sample of proposals there was a higher percentage of consensual responses and more presidential initiatives were passed in the Senate when the president's party was

29. As tandem institutions, the president and Congress can be viewed as members of what Mancur Olson refers to as an "exclusive" group in which the participation of each member is required for action. Since each member is needed by the group as a whole, each can force bargaining as the means for buying inclusion in the process. *The Logic of Collective Action: Public Goods and the Theory of Groups* (Cambridge, Mass.: Harvard University Press, 1971), p. 41.

in the majority. A similar pattern held in the House. Second, though the two-per-state allocation of senators contributes to a rural bias, a potential source of conflict with the president,[30] there are other grounds for speculating that senators may be open to a more "national" perspective on public policy than their colleagues in the lower house. It is often argued that the president plays a predominant role in defining that national perspective. By virtue of Section 1 of the Seventeenth Amendment to the Constitution, the six-year electoral term relieves senators of the continuous pressure to respond to local interests in order to maintain their immediate electoral standing. Perhaps this allows them to concentrate on public policy now and then in splendid isolation.[31] In addition, although both houses of Congress have been affected by the localization of electoral campaigns and, at least during the 1970s, the fragmentation of their internal structures, these potential deterrents to accommodation with the president seem to have been less pronounced in the Senate.[32] The movement toward "subcommittee government" and all it may imply for national policy making proceeded farther in the House than in the Senate.[33]

Finally, we should note the additional challenge to the president's program engendered by a factor that extends the tandem-institutions theme, the bicameralism of the American national legislature. Compared to the 54% measure overall, the House passed 58% of the president's proposals and the Senate approved even more, 62%. Altogether, 66% of the presidential initiatives received favorable treatment in at least one chamber of Congress, but some of these initiatives failed because of the requirement to pass in

30. Wilfred E. Binkley, *The Man in the White House: His Powers and Duties*, rev. ed. (New York: Harper Colophon Books, 1964), pp. 119–121.

31. John H. Kessel, *Presidential Parties* (Homewood, Ill.: Dorsey Press, 1984), p. 195.

32. Thomas E. Mann, "Elections and Change in Congress," in *The New Congress*, ed. Thomas E. Mann and Norman J. Ornstein (Washington, D.C.: American Enterprise Institute, 1981), pp. 32–54; Samuel C. Patterson, "The Semi-Sovereign Congress," in *The New American Political System*, ed. Anthony King (Washington, D.C.: American Enterprise Institute, 1978), p. 161; and Steven S. Smith and Christopher J. Deering, *Committees in Congress* (Washington, D.C.: CQ Press, 1984), pp. 149–152.

33. Lawrence C. Dodd, "Congress and the Quest for Power," in *Congress Reconsidered*, ed. Lawrence C. Dodd and Bruce I. Oppenheimer (New York: Praeger, 1977), pp. 269–307; and Smith and Deering, *Committees in Congress*, pp. 150–151.

both houses. For individual presidents, the one-house passage rate ranged from a low of 53% for Nixon to a high of 78% for Johnson. The two presidents most hurt by the bicameral structure of Congress were Ford and Carter, whose legislative success was reduced by 31 and 21 percentage points respectively, compared to about 8 percentage points for Johnson and Nixon and 4 for Reagan. Of the 13% of the proposals in the sample that were ultimately defeated by having to survive in both forums, most were the product of a dominating opposition coalition (55%), usually in the House of Representatives. The defeats resulting from inaction in one of the chambers also occurred most frequently in the House. It is not so much the constitutional authority of Congress as a whole that has stymied some executives and fed presidency-centered concerns, but rather the modern residue of the Connecticut Compromise accepted in 1787 by the delegates to the constitutional convention in Philadelphia that gave us a bicameral legislature.

The distribution of congressional action that emerges from the 1953 to 1986 period belies the presidency-centered view of the executive-legislative relationship. During the presidencies of Eisenhower to Reagan, neither cooperation nor conflict has been the norm. Rather, both have characterized the institutional relationship, with instances of cooperation actually more common than instances of conflict. The task before us now is to develop a more detailed understanding of what has led to patterns of cooperation or conflict, and to presidential achievement or frustration in the legislative arena. The next four chapters test the proposition that the executive-legislative relationship can be explained with reference to the contexts of congressional action.

4. The Pure Context and the Malleable Context

When Jimmy Carter announced his National Energy Plan in April 1977, he set in motion one of the most complex policy-making apparatuses in the world—the American national political system, replete with an institutional labyrinth, an array of cultural biases, and an overlay of political pressures likely to stun even the most sophisticated imagination. In response, the gears of this governmental machine whirled and sometimes sputtered, meshed and often clashed. In the end, however, energy policy was produced; perhaps not *an* energy policy, and certainly not *the* energy policy that Carter desired, but policy nonetheless. The statutory provisions of the act that passed a year and a half later would alter the behavior of both suppliers and consumers of coal, natural gas, petroleum, and other forms of energy.

Reflection on the results of congressional deliberations on the multifaceted Carter energy program evokes several questions. How do we explain the ways in which Congress responded to the proposals? More specifically, how was legislative action influenced by the myriad institutional changes that have swept the national political structure of the United States in recent decades: the reforms of Congress that complicated committee and subcommittee politics; the transformed and perhaps weakened party system; and the extensive mobilization of commercial, environmental, and consumer interests? To what extent was final action by Congress the product of the 1976 election returns and other sources of changing political fortunes? In what manner were legislative decisions about energy policy governed by concerns about inflation, unemployment, and economic growth? Finally, to what extent were the politics of Carter's energy program consistent with or different from previous and subsequent encounters between the president and Congress, both during the Carter administration and in the course of other presidencies?

Such issues are the subject of this chapter—not in response to a particular program or with respect to an individual president, but rather within the domain of domestic legislation writ large. At a fairly abstract level Stephen Skowronek argues the need to conduct analyses that incorporate more than assessments of the individual incumbents in the Oval Office:

> Although the significance of the particular person in office cannot be doubted, this perspective on leadership presents a rather one-sided view of the interplay between the presidency and the political system. It is highly sensitive to differences among individual incumbents, but it tends to obscure differences in the political situation in which they act. If presidential leadership is indeed something of a struggle between the individual and the system, it must be recognized that the system changes as well as the incumbent. The changing universe of political action is an oft-noted but seldom explored dimension of the leadership problem.[1]

To understand presidents, and therefore their relation with other governmental institutions including Congress, one must understand the "political time" in which they serve.[2] Skowronek suggests that presidents find their opportunities for leadership strongly affected by their temporal placement in the cycle of evolving and decaying political regimes identified by the enduring, dominant partisan coalitions of the era. Presidents of different regimes who share approximately the same political time or location in the regime cycle confront similar forces shaping the fortunes of their administrations.[3]

The shifting settings of executive-legislative interactions from the 1950s to the 1980s might well be understood with reference to political time, except that all presidents in the postwar period have held office in the party system that emerged from the New Deal. Despite substantial evidence of an ongoing transformation

1. Stephen Skowronek, "Presidential Leadership in Political Time," in *The Presidency and the Political System*, 2nd ed., ed. Michael Nelson (Washington, D.C.: CQ Press, 1988), p. 154; see also Jeff Fishel, *Presidents and Promises* (Washington, D.C.: CQ Press, 1985), p. 7.

2. Skowronek, "Political Time," p. 115.

3. Ibid., p. 128.

of the current party system, mapping political time in the current regime with concrete moments is extremely difficult. While we may reasonably peg its beginning in the years of Franklin Roosevelt's administration, there is no certainty about its end. Penetrating the abstract visage of regimes, however, one can tap characteristics of the politically relevant world that imbue political time with its meaning and that differentiate the variegated contexts of congressional responses to the president's initiatives. Considered here are two facets of these contexts that lie farthest beyond the reach of individual presidents to craft or transform to their liking. First is the institutionally based "pure context," then the properties of the American political-economic system that establish the "malleable context" of congressional action. The derivation of each of these factors is given in Appendix D.

The analysis presented here is a simple one that offers an empirical story without the kinds of statistical controls necessary for arriving at firm judgments about the independent effects of each contextual property or the cumulative impact of the attributes taken together. Those issues are pursued with the use of multivariate techniques in Chapter 6. My purpose now is to delve into the nooks and crannies of the executive-legislative relationship as it has been influenced by various attributes of the American political system over the past three decades. What emerges is a portrait of the president as a major player in American legislative policy making, but one who is effectively joined by a legislative partner, the Congress, which provides political access to an increasing array of representational interests.

The Pure Context

Institutions constitute a major part of the context of legislative policy making because they provide the scattered forums in which competing coalitions gain authority and confront one another with the legitimate possession of political power. In any polity, the way that institutions are designed biases legislative deliberations and actions either for or against particular coalitions competing on specific policy issues. My focus here is those coalitions stimulated and led by the president and those formed in opposition. As each new president enters the White House, he or she learns (or confirms) that the possibilities for leadership during the new term are contingent on precisely the institutional factors that few presidents—or anybody else—have ever been able to affect strategically. These institutional arrangements thus establish the pure context of presidential-congressional interactions and the politics of coalition formation that drives the interbranch relationship. The institutional arrangements of any particular period may facilitate policy *cooperation* by reinforcing the development of shared policy perspectives among the relevant players, by limiting the points of access available to the opposition, and by providing leaders at each stage of the legislative process with the means for coordinating action. *Conflict* is nurtured, even in the presence of skilled political leadership, when access is unregulated and institutionally proffered veto points afford competing factions the leverage to thwart action.

In his assessment of the emerging Washington community of the new American republic, James Sterling Young highlights the institutional feature of the federal government that lies at the heart of American national policy making and that dictates all other institutional concerns. It is the constitutionally mandated web of separated but overlapping powers vested in the president and Congress that gives the two branches what I have called tandem authority over legislation.[4] Certainly executive-legislative relations cannot be assessed without keeping that institutional constant in mind; indeed, it defines much of the uniqueness resident in the American system of government. It also embodies the normative frustrations expressed by those concerned with presidency-centered government while furnishing the initial analytical platform of tandem-institutions analyses.

Although each individual elected to serve in the White House or on Capitol Hill has encountered essentially the same constitutional structure of American government, the dynamics of political culture, tradition, organizational responsiveness, and law have functioned to give varied shape to these institutional arrangements. Some of the changes in Congress, the party system, and the interest-group community have accentuated the decentralization that has always permeated the American federal system; others have reinforced the centralizing tendency of modern political states. Still others, arguably, have reflected a disintegration of political institutions. As points of access to governing institutions are expanded, potentially more divergent factions can gain a foothold in debates and decisions involving

4. James Sterling Young, *The Washington Community, 1800–1828* (New York: Harcourt, Brace and World, 1966), pp. 157–158.

legislated policy. When political parties weaken and divergent interests proliferate, the politics of consensus and accommodation may be replaced by a system of policy development in which coherent policy leadership is difficult for anyone to demonstrate.

No evolutionary feature of the institutional arrangements in this country has received more concerned attention than the apparently continuous fragmentation of the political structure, creating what a practitioner calls "a world of molecular politics" and paralleling Anthony King's claim of an "atomization" of the political system.[5] Consider one part of the policy world supposedly managed by Joseph Califano, President Carter's first secretary of health, education, and welfare:

> Twelve of the thirteen Cabinet departments and at least seven agencies administer income security programs, and 119 of the more than 300 congressional committees and subcommittees oversee their operations. In addition, these programs are shaped in part by 50 state legislatures, 54 state and territorial welfare agencies, and more than 1,500 county and city welfare departments, and by the Supreme Court and scores of lower courts.[6]

Every time a president, or a member of Congress, announces a new domestic initiative, a veritable institutional gauntlet must be run.

While this complex of institutional entities exists throughout the government, it has taken on symbolic proportions in Congress itself as a result of the democratizing reforms of the 1970s.[7] Old

5. Joseph A. Califano, Jr., *Governing America: An Insider's Report from the White House and the Cabinet* (New York: Simon and Schuster, 1981), p. 23; and Anthony King, "The American Polity in the Late 1970s: Building Coalitions in the Sand," in *The New American Political System*, ed. Anthony King (Washington, D.C.: American Enterprise Institute, 1978), p. 391.

6. Califano, *Governing America*, p. 365.

7. Roger H. Davidson, "Subcommittee Government: New Channels for Policy Making," in *The New Congress*, ed. Thomas E. Mann and Norman J. Ornstein (Washington, D.C.: American Enterprise Institute, 1981), pp. 99–133; Lawrence C. Dodd and Richard L. Schott, *Congress and the Administrative State* (New York: John Wiley, 1979), p. 280; Norman J. Ornstein, "Causes and Consequences of Congressional Change: Subcommittee Reforms in the House of Representatives, 1970–1973," in *Congress in Change: Evolution and Reform*, ed. Norman

Washington hands, such as one long-time adviser to Democratic presidents whom I interviewed, enjoy sharing tales of the good old days, when party discipline could move votes and bipartisan deals could be struck at the moment that Speaker Sam Rayburn, Senate Majority Leader Lyndon Johnson, and President Dwight Eisenhower would "lift a glass to liberty" at their intimate, after-hours get-togethers in the President's private quarters. As one member of the Ford White House lamented:

> I remember a time . . . when Speaker [Carl] Albert said [something like], "Mr. President, in the old days, the speaker could say, 'We're going to do this,' and the party would go along. But I'm only one vote and there's a lot of independence. Now we have to snag the votes one by one". . . and I remember Ford agreeing.

Of course, it was not so easy "in the old days," either. John Kennedy complained that the complexities of Congress made it easier to defeat legislation than to pass it, at a time long before the onslaught of reforms. And while the past power of the committee chairmen narrowed the range of individuals needed to reach an agreement, the most influential and entrenched of them, such as Ways and Means Chairman Wilbur Mills, were in a position of considerable strength when bargaining about the future of the president's program.[8]

The changes in Congress, especially the subcommittee reforms, mean that more people have to be involved in decisions. As a result, a senior adviser to Jimmy Carter commented, it becomes "harder and harder to have an intimate interaction between the president and Congress." Votes for roll calls are collected in small blocks at best, and now, as a Reagan liaison official revealed, the White House—a Republican White House—even had to contact *freshman Republicans*, at the lowest end of the minority totem pole in the House. He continued: "If you're studying the early

J. Ornstein (New York: Praeger, 1975), pp. 88–114; and Steven S. Smith and Christopher J. Deering, *Committees in Congress* (Washington, D.C.: CQ Press, 1984), chaps. 5, 9.

8. Thomas E. Cronin, *The State of the Presidency*, 2nd ed. (Boston: Little, Brown, 1980), pp. 169, 213; Paul C. Light, *The President's Agenda: Domestic Policy Choice from Kennedy to Carter* (Baltimore: Johns Hopkins University Press, 1982), p. 54; and Theodore C. Sorensen, *Kennedy* (New York: Bantam, 1966), p. 426.

'80s, you know you had to work with the boll weevils, the gypsy moths, the honey bees [conservative House Republicans who proposed a 'flat tax' in 1982]. I never realized that in this job I would get such an education in insect life." Many observers have argued that the reforms, including the proliferation of subcommittees, have granted a huge proportion of Congress the capacity to claim preeminence over narrow slices of policy turf, aggravating the splintering of national policy into single issues.[9] When proposed legislation requires comprehensive changes in existing policy, addressing a variety of issue areas simultaneously, the decentralization of congressional authority makes it especially difficult to maintain the substantive coherence of the program.[10] Even the reemergence of large-scale floor activity in both the House and Senate during the 1980s, which has granted the leadership more opportunities to exercise its power, frequently cannot overcome the resilient independence of the subcommittee system.[11]

What have these changes meant for congressional action on the president's program? The essence of decentralization in the structure of Congress, the dispersion of authoritative power, can be illustrated by examining the empirical manifestations of factors that contribute to increased autonomy for various legislative

9. Barbara J. Nelson, *Making an Issue of Child Abuse: Political Agenda Setting for Social Problems* (Chicago: University of Chicago Press, 1984), pp. 96–97. See also Steven H. Haeberle, "The Institutionalization of the Subcommittee in the United States House of Representatives," *Journal of Politics* 40 (November 1978): 1054–65; and Smith and Deering, *Committees in Congress*, pp. 50–55, 125–162, 219–226. Richard Hall cautions against assuming that the expansion of subcommittees necessarily translates into autonomous power for each of them, noting that there is a distinction between decentralization of activity and fragmentation of authority. But his research demonstrates that at least one committee, the House Education and Labor Committee, exhibits the kind of behavioral patterns associated with "subcommittee government." "Participation and Purpose in Committee Decision Making," *American Political Science Review* 81 (March 1987): 105–128.

10. Bruce I. Oppenheimer, "Policy Effects of U.S. House Reform: Decentralization and the Capacity to Resolve Energy Issues," *Legislative Studies Quarterly* 5 (February 1980): 5–30.

11. See Roger H. Davidson, "The New Centralization on Capitol Hill," *Review of Politics* (Summer 1988): 345–364; and Steven S. Smith, *Call to Order: Floor Politics in the House and Senate* (Washington, D.C.: Brookings Institution, 1989).

arenas and even individual members. They include the total number of committees and subcommittees for the entire Congress, and the number of committee staff members.[12] In addition, one may include in the assessment the lack of membership tenure, which reflects the decay of institutional memory and links to the old internal party structure. Individually, each of these attributes may be of marginal consequence. None standing alone fully captures the thrust of the decentralization and autonomy argument. Large staffs, for example, do not necessarily translate into the independent power of committees and subcommittees; but they furnish the requisite resources for crafting independent judgments on legislation. Together these factors lay the foundation that provides members with the incentives and capacity for independent action to be taken against legislative competitors, potentially including the president.

The complexities introduced into legislative deliberation by congressional decentralization, especially since the early 1970s and despite recent growth in the importance of floor activity, have complicated the business of coalition building for recent presidents and their allies. The difficulties are evident in Table 4.1. When over the past three decades the structural fragmentation of Congress was at its lowest ebb, with fewer subcommittees, smaller professional staffs, and a more pervasive institutional memory, a third of presidential initiatives passed by consensus and there were the fewest occasions of public conflict in the form of presidential or opposition dominance. When legislative confrontation occurred, the president's coalition was the more likely winner. High levels of decentralization, however, led to much greater inaction on the part of Congress in response to presidential initiatives (35%), more discord (a 44% increase), and a very strong likelihood that the president's allies would lose when conflict erupted. These patterns are essentially repeated when one examines the effects of decentralization within the House and the Senate individually. Quite simply, institutional fragmentation of power bases in Congress enhanced the opportunities for well-placed opponents to defeat presidential initiatives. Opposing fact-

12. Samuel C. Patterson, "The Semi-Sovereign Congress," in *The New American Political System*, ed. Anthony King (Washington, D.C.: American Enterprise Institute, 1978), pp. 164–166. Patterson suggests that the expanded staffs increase fragmentation by strengthening the committees.

Table 4.1   Congressional responses to presidential proposals and level
of congressional decentralization of power

Level of decentralization	N	Congressional response				
		Inaction	Opposition dominance	Compromise	Presidential dominance	Consensus
Lowest	76	21%	10%	21%	14%	33%
Intermediate	119	20%	21%	18%	11%	29%
Highest	104	35%	27%	19%	9%	11%

Note: N = 299; chi square = 24.54; $p < .005$.
Source: See Appendixes C and D.

ions, perhaps relatively tiny ones, needed only to dominate the
expanded number of congressional bottlenecks to stymie proposals.

There have been, of course, other institutional changes in Congress. Some, such as the modification in the House rules permitting split and joint referral of bills to committees, further exa-
cerbate the problem of fragmentation.[13] Another rule change,
instituted in 1971, forbade members of the House to chair more
than one subcommittee; as an aide to the speaker noted, this
restraint caused "power to go zip," dispersing in all directions at
once. Not only were there more subcommittees, but this new rule
constituted them as the major bastions of influence for scores of
members. If these factors could be systematically included, they
would probably sharpen the effects of decentralization already
discussed.

Other institutional transformations in Congress may have the
benefit of counteracting the dispersion of power by centralizing
authority in the legislative party leadership or in other potentially
unifying centers of activity.[14] That was certainly the wish of the
Kennedy administration and Speaker Rayburn when they moved
at the beginning of Kennedy's term to enlarge the House Rules
Committee in order to bring it under the control of the leader-

13. Light, *The President's Agenda*, p. 210.
14. Oppenheimer, however, argues that changes reinforcing the influence of the House leadership have not been potent enough to overcome
the effects of the decentralization reforms of the 1970s. "Policy Effects,"
p. 12.

ship. In the 1950s conservatives, especially southern Democrats, demonstrated too ready an ability to bottle up legislation in the Rules Committee to give much hope for the success of the new president's legislative agenda. For obvious reasons of protocol, the Kennedy administration could neither mandate nor even publicly initiate the movement to tame the recalcitrant Rules Committee—but the administration's resources were effectively used to help the reformists succeed.[15] Assessing the impact of the change, however, is problematic. The planned expansion of the committee from twelve to fifteen members was achieved; still, it had little effect on the behavior of the committee until changes in its makeup and leadership occurred much later, in the 1970s.[16]

Another potentially centralizing institutional reform in Congress is more easy to evaluate. In 1974 Congress enacted the Budget and Impoundment Control Act, creating budget committees in each house, the Congressional Budget Office to generate economic analysis independent of the executive's, and a calendar and rules for creating something resembling a unified congressional budget. Even though this budget process was laid over the existing system of appropriation and revenue committees and the requirement that thirteen separate appropriations bills be passed each year, the full implementation of the act in 1976 disrupted the old patterns of business. At least on some occasions, it transformed the traditional distributive politics and logrolling procedures on program expenditures into direct redistributive confrontations.[17] In short, it forced more conflict. Before the implementation of the act, 36% of the presidential proposals in the sample involving budgetary, appropriations, or revenue requests enjoyed a consensual response; afterward, none did. Leg-

15. Lawrence F. O'Brien, *No Final Victories: A Life in Politics from John F. Kennedy to Watergate* (New York: Ballantine Books, 1974), pp. 106–109.

16. Bruce I. Oppenheimer, "The Rules Committee: New Arm of Leadership in a Decentralized House," in *Congress Reconsidered*, ed. Lawrence C. Dodd and Bruce I. Oppenheimer (New York: Praeger, 1977), pp. 98–101.

17. John W. Ellwood, "Budget Control in a Redistributive Environment," in *Making Economic Policy in Congress*, ed. Allen Schick (Washington, D.C.: American Enterprise Institute, 1983), p. 88. See also Allen Schick, *Congress and Money: Budgeting, Spending, and Taxing* (Washington, D.C.: Urban Institute, 1980), pp. 577–579.

islative action involving explicit conflict (dominance) rose from 19% to 52%, and significantly more presidential initiatives were rejected. For budget and appropriations matters alone, the story is much the same.[18] Before the act, 48% of such proposals were compromised, 40% passed by consensus, and all received some kind of action. After its implementation, there was no consensus, much less compromise, and congressional action involving conflict rose from 12% to 57% of the legislative responses. Presidential dominance occurred, however, in 43% of the cases. The Budget Act includes a provision that can be manipulated to break almost entirely the hold that the fragmented system can have on Congress. I speak, of course, of reconciliation—used by Democrats allied with Carter in 1980, and the primary instrument for achieving the Reagan budget successes of 1981.

Modifications in other institutional characteristics of the American political system have also had a bearing on congressional reactions to the initiatives of the president. First among these are changes in the political parties. Although not given formal recognition in the Constitution, the party system has been instrumental in the successful application of constitutional government in the United States. The dominant political parties have helped to bridge the formal strait separating the executive and legislative branches. That bridge has several parts.[19] There are parties as organizations, composed of staffs, activists, buildings, and money-raising facilities. These corporate aspects of parties have been notoriously amorphous in the United States, except for the past reign of the tightly run political machines in many urban areas. There are parties of the public, the psychological affiliations of the electorate with primarily the Democratic and Republican parties. These ties do not bring the loyalty associated with actual membership; nonetheless, they represent the core of each

18. Some caution is required when interpreting the figures for budget and appropriations proposals alone. The sample includes only 25 cases prior to implementation of the Budget and Impoundment Control Act, and only 14 afterward.

19. See Frank J. Sorauf, *Party Politics in America*, 4th ed. (Boston: Little, Brown, 1980), chaps. 2, 3, 5. Also valuable are Samuel J. Eldersveld, *Political Parties in American Society* (New York: Basic Books, 1982), esp. chaps. 4, 5, 16; and James A. Schlesinger, "The New American Political Party," *American Political Science Review* 79 (December 1985): 1152–69.

party's electoral coalition. And finally there are parties of elected officials, furnishing a sense of shared electoral fate that links officials throughout the political system. Whether in the White House, Congress, or state and local preserves, individuals who have sought and won office on the same ticket, under the same party emblem, feel a congruence of interest cultivated by the common reactions of voters to their party.

Much of the concern about systemic fragmentation has to do with the decline of parties as organizing devices for people and politics, especially over the past two decades.[20] The structural decentralization of Congress would be much less significant if representatives and senators were tightly joined by shared partisanship. American parties have never been particularly robust at any level, but throughout the 1960s and 1970s partisan ties among the mass public slackened as more individuals denied an identification with either of the major parties.[21] As the partisanship of the public diminishes, with party affiliation losing its appeal as a decision tool in elections and voters splitting their ballots to vote more frequently for candidates of mixed partisan orientation, the small amount of party-based "glue" binding the Hill and the White House loses its adhesion. Congressional elections become more isolated from the presidential contest.[22]

This process has been accentuated since 1968 by the opening up of the presidential nominating process, which has deprived party leaders (including members of Congress) of a meaningful role in the selection of each party's nominee and largely eliminated the coalition-building functions of the electoral process.[23] Presidents rely more on personal networks than on party organizations. In

20. See, for example, David S. Broder, *The Party's Over: The Failure of Politics in America* (New York: Harper Torchbooks, 1971).

21. Martin P. Wattenberg, *The Decline of American Political Parties, 1952–1980* (Cambridge, Mass.: Harvard University Press, 1984).

22. Walter Dean Burnham, "Insulation and Responsiveness in Congressional Elections," *Political Science Quarterly* 90 (Fall 1975): 411–435; and Erwin C. Hargrove, *The Power of the Modern Presidency* (New York: Knopf, 1974), p. 203.

23. Theodore J. Lowi, *The Personal President: Power Invested, Promise Unfulfilled* (Ithaca, N.Y.: Cornell University Press, 1985), p. 112. Lowi also argues that while the nominating reforms implemented in the 1970s accelerated the weakening of parties, the decline *"was already in train."* Parties were "already too weak to resist the reforms" (p. 111; italics in original).

many ways Jimmy Carter became president as a result of these changes in the political parties, his nomination facilitated by the rule reforms in the Democratic party.[24] But according to one Carter aide, his administration found that these changes, further removing presidential politics from other aspects of the party, would return to haunt them:

> On energy . . . this became really clear to me when the Democratic National Committee, the DNC, was having its platform-drafting session right here at the Mayflower [Hotel]. I was working up on the Hill then. And it really described the Democratic party, which we had to deal with simultaneously. On the Hill, those guys [Democrats] were telling us that what we were trying to do made us akin to a raving, wide-eyed radical. But before the [Democratic] platform session, we were placed somewhere to the right of Ghengis Khan, like we were Attila the Hun. That was really a dramatic shift in focus.

With such ideological divisions, there would appear to be little congruence of interest produced by shared party labels, and little about either the presidential selection process or congressional elections that would bring the party's elected officials together.

If the partisan ties of the public and those of elected officials facilitate the development of natural coalitions linking the president and Congress—especially, of course, when the two institutions are controlled by the same party—then greater institutional congruence on legislation tends to occur during periods when the party links are strongest.[25] As those links disintegrate and weaken the bonds reinforcing the core presidential coalition, getting any legislative action at all proves more difficult and factions in opposition to the president enjoy an increased capacity to dominate legislative decision making. If there is no common constituency, then elected officials find little incentive to be bound to one

24. Nelson W. Polsby, *The Consequences of Party Reform* (New York: Oxford University Press, 1983), pp. 128–130.

25. One could pose the alternative argument that during periods of divided government, when the White House and Congress are controlled by different parties, more rigid electoral partisan cohesion would diminish the ability of members from the opposition party to join in ad hoc alliance with the president, frustrating the executive's coalition-building strategies. Yet greater partisan consistency in voting for offices throughout the ballot would reduce the incidence of divided control.

another either by the partisan tendencies of the electorate or by the votes actually cast in elections for executive and legislative offices. There is some evidence that these patterns have been reflected in the presidential-congressional relations of the modern era. As participants in tandem institutions, the president and members of Congress are compelled to work together. But reduced partisan ties aggravate the burden of identifying the necessary common ground.

At those times after 1953 when public attachment to the two major parties was most tenuous, opponents of the president in Congress were more successful in defeating presidential initiatives outright. The most numerous occasions of presidential dominance (15%) and consensus (29%) occurred when public partisan attachments were strongest. Enacting any part of the president's program proved most difficult when the partisan attachments evidenced the greatest strain. The effect of institutional change in the parties is even more pronounced when examined in the context of direct partisan linkages among elected officials, understood as the consistency demonstrated by voters in selecting candidates from the same party for different offices. When these linkages were weakest, inaction (35% of the cases) and opposition dominance (27%) were much in evidence, and only 38% of the president's initiatives passed Congress. On the other hand, 59% of presidential proposals were accepted by the legislature when, during the past three decades, the bonds were strongest. These presidential successes derived from more instances of consensus and from fewer occasions of dominance by the opposition than was true during the periods of partisan decline.

Interest groups also constitute a significant nongovernmental set of institutional forces in American national politics that impinge upon the tandem institutions of the presidency and Congress. For example, President Carter commented in my interview with him that Reagan's tax program in 1981 (the Economic Recovery Tax Act) "was looked on by the press as a great achievement, but what he did was just lie down and let the congressional special-interest representatives run over him." Carter continued:

One thing that I can think of that's caused me the most concern—I mentioned it in my farewell speech—is that there's a growing importance of lobbying groups and their legal payoffs to members of Congress, through threats, like from NCPAC [the National Conservative Political Action Committee] and so forth, campaign contributions, honoraria. Those kinds of things can be quite persuasive, particularly within a subcommittee or committee . . . I think it's becoming much more serious now than before. And the chairmen of committees, like Ways and Means in the House and Finance in the Senate (just to use two examples, not exclusively), can get enormous campaign contributions even though they don't have any opposition. And this kind of thing . . . I think is the single greatest threat to the proper functioning of our democratic system.

While Carter's focus here is on the role of campaign financing, he is fundamentally concerned about the ability of "special interests" to fracture the national purpose. It is a view shared by many. But what has actually happened to the structure of the interest-group community? How has that influenced the legislative coalitions in support of and in opposition to presidential initiatives?

The significance of interest representation is not a new development. Wilfred Binkley argues that throughout our history, the prominence of the president or Congress has been largely determined by which one has been controlled by the "dominant interests of the nation." Presidents are always constrained by the extent to which there is agreement or dissension among the elite groups in a given policy area.[26] Indeed, a popular conception among academics has long been that major interest groups join forces with agency personnel and congressional committee members and staff to form "subgovernments" or "iron triangles" that are relatively impervious to outside intervention, even from the president.[27] In recent decades, however, these subgovernments have been increasingly challenged by the appearance of more

26. Wilfred E. Binkley, *The Man in the White House: His Powers and Duties*, rev. ed. (New York: Harper and Row, 1964), p. 122.

27. J. Leiper Freeman, *The Political Process: Executive Bureau-Legislative Committee Relations* (New York: Random House, 1955); Dorothy Buckton James, *The Contemporary Presidency* (New York: Pegasus, 1969); Theodore J. Lowi, *The End of Liberalism: Ideology, Policy, and the Crisis of Public Authority* (New York: W. W. Norton, 1969); and Grant McConnell, *Private Power and American Democracy* (New York: Vintage Books, 1966).

amorphous, conflictive, and dynamic policy communities, what Hugh Heclo refers to as issue networks.[28] This change has arisen partially from the mobilization of previously unrepresented and less consensual groups and from the reactive proliferation of the old-order commercial interests.[29] The result has been not only the potential demise of subgovernments, but also the exponential expansion of the organizational representation of interests.

The dramatic transformation of the structure of interest representation obviously challenges the nature of legislative interactions in the tandem-institutions setting. One school of thought, resonating most closely with presidency-centered analyses, would now view the old subgovernments as not being so detrimental, arguing that they at least introduced order into the political system and served on occasion as the building blocks of larger policy coalitions. Without them political chaos is far more pronounced and presidential control of policy making is even more elusive. As Samuel Kernell asserts, increasing numbers of specialized interests represented by political action committees, national organizations, and caucuses in Congress do not contribute to brokering the broad range of interests and positions extant in the society. Rather, they may, from the perspective of the White House, "balkanize the political process" by disaggregating even further the articulation of interests.[30]

Assessments more compatible with the tandem-institutions perspective recognize the increased institutional complexity engendered by the elaboration of the interest-group system, but view the current situation with less alarm. First, a vigorous com-

28. Hugh Heclo, "Issue Networks and the Executive Establishment," in *The New American Political System*, ed. Anthony King (Washington, D.C.: American Enterprise Institute, 1978), pp. 87–124.

29. Thomas L. Gais, Mark A. Peterson, and Jack L. Walker, "Interest Groups, Iron Triangles and Representative Institutions in American National Government," *British Journal of Political Science* (April 1984): 170–176; and Jack L. Walker, "The Origins and Maintenance of Interest Groups in America," *American Political Science Review* 77 (June 1983): 397–401. The countermobilization is discussed in Kay Lehman Schlozman and John T. Tierney, *Organized Interests and American Democracy* (New York: Harper and Row, 1986), chap. 4.

30. Samuel Kernell, *Going Public: New Strategies of Presidential Leadership* (Washington, D.C.: CQ Press, 1986), p. 35. The quote is from Stuart Eizenstat, chief domestic aide to President Carter.

munity of interest representation is consistent with a constitutional structure that denies a monopoly of political power and that encourages the gestation of ideas and marshalling of information in a variety of political quarters. Second, members of Congress and the president have always braved a multitude of political forces, and the very number of pressures permits them latitude in decision making by giving no single interest a monopoly on access.[31] Special-interest pressure on Congress in particular need not mean special-interest dictation. Third, despite the implicit notion in the linkage group literature that viable parties and a vigorous interest-group system are mutually exclusive, the two can actually reinforce each other.[32] The present array of interest organizations operating in Washington is not devoid of ideological cleavages and groupings that can be skillfully exploited on some issues by the president, or other policy leaders, to generate victorious legislative coalitions.[33]

These efforts to find coherence in the interest-group community and to organize group activity, nevertheless, recognize the increased challenge to legislative coalition building imposed by the presence of ever more interest representatives. The number of registered Washington lobbyists and national voluntary membership organizations has grown, and the number of political action committees, the organizations through which interest groups seek to have direct influence on the selection of elected officials, has exploded. Even in combination these attributes do not fully

31. Louis Anthony Dexter, "The Representative and His District," in *New Perspectives on the House of Representatives,* ed. Robert L. Peabody and Nelson W. Polsby (Chicago: Rand McNally, 1969), pp. 9–14.

32. For the conflict between political parties and interest groups, see Robert A. Dahl, *Dilemmas of Pluralist Democracy: Autonomy vs. Control* (New Haven: Yale University Press, 1982), p. 190; and E. E. Schattschneider, *Party Government* (New York: Farrar and Rinehart, 1942), p. 182. The opposite point is made in Mark A. Peterson and Jack L. Walker, "Interest Group Responses to Partisan Change: The Impact of the Reagan Administration upon the National Interest Group System," in *Interest Group Politics,* 2nd ed., ed. Allan J. Cigler and Burdett A. Loomis (Washington, D.C.: CQ Press, 1986), pp. 177–179.

33. Gais, Peterson, and Walker, "Interest Groups, Iron Triangles and Representative Institutions," pp. 170–171; and Mark A. Peterson, "Interest Groups and the Reagan White House: For Whom the Doorbell Tolls," paper presented at the annual meeting of the American Political Science Association, Washington, D.C., August 1986, pp. 35–36.

account for the numerical and substantive elaboration of interests represented in Washington, but joining these factors affords a more accurate view of the interest-group community than evolves from a focus on any one of these characteristics.

Table 4.2 shows that before the growth occurred along each of these dimensions, when the interest-group community was simpler and less numerically extended, consensus and presidential dominance were more prevalent congressional responses to presidential initiatives. As the interest-group community grew more elaborate, there was much less in the way of consensus and presidential dominance (both down to 8%). They were replaced by more frequent occasions of inaction and opposition dominance. The presence of more interest groups, with more active lobbyists and increased direct electoral involvement representing a broader array of policy perspectives, simply means that coalition building became more complicated, at least for some kinds of issues. Members of Congress now have to pay attention to both an expanded number of issues and increasingly diverse positions on questions of public policy. Further, the number and range of interest representatives increased at precisely the same time that the structural reforms in Congress created more points of access to be exploited and weakened party affiliations enhanced the potential role of groups. It is not likely that even the most effective public liaison operation in the White House can overcome these forces on the entire collection of issues constituting the president's domestic agenda.

Table 4.2   Congressional responses to presidential proposals and elaboration of the interest-group system

Level of elaboration	N	Congressional response				
		Inaction	Opposition dominance	Compromise	Presidential dominance	Consensus
Less complex	99	24%	17%	14%	15%	29%
Intermediate	102	17%	17%	24%	10%	33%
More complex	98	36%	28%	20%	8%	8%

Note: N = 299; chi square = 30.88; $p < .001$.
Source: See Appendixes C and D.

The Malleable Context

For all the importance of institutional arrangements, research on the presidency and Congress demonstrates the analytical limitations of trying to understand politics as solely the practice of executing enumerated powers and exercising formal authority. Legislative policy making depends as well on a politics in which the public, through elections and other devices of representative democracy, confers on specific individuals additional political resources and the condition of the economy establishes the relative opportunity costs of various policies to different groups in the society. These together provide both the means for building coalitions to span the institutional gaps and the opportunity for opponents to stimulate efficacious dissent. Unlike institutional structures, however, these political and economic attributes are often subject to rapid and unpredictable variation (see Appendix D).

While all players in the policy-making process are affected by and can seek to exploit political and economic resources, presidents are uniquely situated. Chief executives and their administrations influence the contours of the political and economic world. Presidential campaigns, however crude the art of electioneering, undoubtedly have some effect on creating the perceived mandates that presidents enjoy. Whatever the weaknesses of macroeconomic prediction and advice, presidential actions have some impact on the course of the economy. Political and economic attributes are therefore malleable with respect to presidential action, and more so for the president than for any other member of the government. Few presidents have succeeded, however, in actively and consistently manipulating electoral outcomes, public support, and economic performance. This relative presidential advantage is fully consistent with a tandem-institutions analysis, precisely because it is constrained by the opportunities of others to capitalize on the same resources, the inherent inability of presidents to command good fortune, and the complex institutional setting in which the resources must be employed.

Dynamic Political Properties

The properties that define the dynamic political environment of presidential-congressional relations may be the most important of those included in the malleable context. Their dynamism is first apparent in the simple rhythm that characterizes every presidential term. Each year of the four-year term is different. The very process of conducting electoral campaigns, the effects of time, and the increasing practical experience of participants in the White House join to produce relatively standard and patterned fluctuations in every administration.[34] First, because of the electoral calendar, the "qualitative" length of a president's term is rather different from the actual four years; there is little time, perhaps only two years, for policy making and reasonably undisrupted relations with the Hill.[35] Second, elections have both numerical and atmospheric consequences. A journalist pointed out to me, for example, that although the Republicans did not lose any Senate seats in 1982, the Republican incumbents certainly came back to Washington with a message that "they can't always go along with the President." One of Reagan's assistants confirmed that sentiment. Third, during the course of the term, people acquire skills, experience, judgment, and personal networks. They get better at their jobs.[36] This pattern was particularly pronounced in the Carter administration, with the staff coalescing into a more skilled operation after the first several months of legislative chaos and a few painful mistakes.[37] All of these forces combine to create what Paul Light labels a *cycle of decreasing influence* and an opposite *cycle of increasing effectiveness.* As time passes in a presidential term, political capital is expended and resources decline, reducing political influence; but expertise, skills, and awareness rise, enhancing effectiveness.[38]

Finally, the substantive flexibility available to a president changes as well, with implications for how deals can be struck and coalitions formed. A Reagan official described the general process:

This administration, any administration, starts off with a fairly clean slate. Even during the campaign with the bucket-shop people sending letters off to the various groups, you're not that committed. When you walk in the door as president,

34. John H. Kessel, *Presidential Parties* (Homewood, Ill.: Dorsey Press, 1984), pp. 47–72.
35. Light, *The President's Agenda*, pp. 17–18.
36. Ibid., p. 37.
37. Interviews with aides to President Carter.
38. Light, *The President's Agenda*, pp. 36–37.

on the first day, you are committed to about 20 or 30 things. But there are about 5,000 policy opportunities, and as time goes on, you make decisions on those 4,970 which are remaining. After a couple of years you have made a decision about almost everything at least once, and you just fill in the box. In the early days, you can propose lots of things because you're not tied in. But at this stage [later in the term] you have made a commitment to everybody about something, so it's much more difficult to make adjustments. It becomes zero sum.

As a result of these factors, *when* issues get proposed in an administration and *when* they receive final consideration affect *how* they are resolved.

From the perspective of legislative accomplishment, the most important time for action in an administration is the first year in office. The initial year—with the political equanimity of the "honeymoon" spirit joining the president with Congress, the media, and the people—offers the opportunity for policy innovation, driven by the new ideas and optimism of the successful campaign along with the freedom and coherence of the nascent administration.[39] All is fresh, expectations are high, and for at least the first several months the public appears willing to grant the new administration the benefit of a reflective pause before casting judgment. Few people have understood better than President Johnson the significance of the honeymoon and the tarnished perceptions of subsequent years:

> You've got to give it all you can, that first year. Doesn't matter what kind of majority you come in with. You've got just one year when they treat you right, and before they start worrying about themselves. The third year you lose votes; if this war goes on, I'll lose a lot of 'em. A lot of people don't belong here, they're in Republican seats, and the Republicans will get them back. The fourth year's all politics. You can't put anything through when half of the Congress is thinking how to beat you. So you've got one year.[40]

39. Valerie Bunce, *Do New Leaders Make a Difference? Executive Succession and Public Policy under Capitalism and Socialism* (Princeton: Princeton University Press, 1981), pp. 25–26.

40. Quoted in Harry McPherson, *A Political Education* (New York: Little, Brown, 1972), p. 268.

So Johnson, declared a senior adviser, sent up a "tidal wave of stuff" and "just stuffed it right down the damn gullet." The Reagan administration, also recognizing the significance of the honeymoon of perceptions, used that period to push through the bulk of the president's economic agenda, dispelling the sense of institutional stalemate that had existed previously and mitigating the concerns of presidency-centered commentators.

Early legislative involvement by modern presidents has generally been rewarded. Of the domestic proposals submitted by Presidents Eisenhower to Reagan (his first term) that received final congressional action in the first year of the term, consensus occurred with some frequency (23%), and presidential dominance (16%) was more likely than in other years. These trends are much more pronounced when one examines proposals considered in just the honeymoon year of the first term without including the post-reelection year of the second term. For the initial year of the first term, consensus occurred in 29% of the cases, presidential dominance was more prevalent than opposition dominance (19% to 14%), and there were fewer instances of inaction compared to other years. The first year of the second term simply does not carry the same glow. The president is too well known for the allure of new acquaintance to be retrieved.

To follow up on Light's suggestion that presidents should move their domestic agendas quickly, for proposals that were *introduced* during the first-term honeymoon year, only 13% ended with inaction and 68% received some kind of favorable response.[41] About one in five was actively defeated, the same proportion as for the entire sample. The agendas moved, however, and the initiatives introduced in the first year of the first term received more action, and more favorable action, than those in any other year. In addition, the nature of the legislation initiated in the first-year period fits the pattern of programmatic innovation reported by Valerie Bunce.[42] Based on analyses of both Western democratic systems and nations in the socialist bloc, she concludes that policy innovation is most likely to follow the inauguration of new leaders, especially those heading parties different from those of their predecessors. Of the twelve proposals in the sample initiated in the first year of the second term of a reelected

41. Light, *The President's Agenda*, chap. 2.
42. Bunce, *Do New Leaders Make a Difference?* p. 10.

president, only one represented a "large" departure from existing policy, and it was enacted. For the seventy-five measures introduced in the first year of a new presidency, however, twenty-four involved such innovative policies, and two-thirds of those received favorable congressional action.

As President Johnson indicated, the advent of election years proves more strategically troublesome for executive-legislative policy making. Elections alter the behavior of the two branches. Members of Congress, especially those in the House, begin to pay more attention to their own political situations. Seeking to protect their electoral fortunes, they prefer to avoid commitments on controversial issues, as Carter discovered in 1978 on energy legislation.[43] When the election is one that includes the presidential campaign, accommodation, especially between a president and members of the other party, proves more elusive. According to a Republican White House official:

> As you get closer to an election period or a presidential election, it's more likely that people become partisan, and it makes it harder to work with people. When you're doing things, if anyone is seen as winning more, it's going to be the president. He's the one the country turns to. And the opposition party doesn't want to get involved in something that looks like the president is going to get the credit. So it's hard in the election year to get the opposition party to go along.

An election year also affects the orientation of those in the White House. If an incumbent is seeking reelection, policy choices are made with that in mind.[44] The timing may also influence decisions about whether a veto is a productive instrument for attempting to reshape legislation.[45] More generally, an election year disrupts the established patterns of the policy-making process. There is, said a Republican official, "a movement from government to campaigning," restricting the time available for serious legislating. During election years, proposals may be announced by the president as a form of "position taking," staking out a politically advantageous posture for the election that

43. Jimmy Carter, *Keeping Faith: Memoirs of a President* (New York: Bantam Books, 1982), p. 106.

44. Light, *The President's Agenda*, p. 72.

45. McPherson, *A Political Education*, p. 279.

may be less relevant to the actual practice of governance.[46] And with the reforms that have occurred in the nominating process and the tendency for incumbent presidents in the modern era to be challenged for the nomination within their own parties, this reelection stage of the term has lengthened.[47] Of course, if an incumbent is not running for reelection, then that president's influence in the legislative process is diminished by acquiring the status of a lame duck. The tandem-institutions balance shifts unfavorably for the president and administration allies on the Hill.

The challenges imposed by electoral politics, however, have not entirely disrupted the opportunities for cooperation in the tandem-institutions setting. Nor have they thwarted the potential for achieving presidential success in the legislative arena. While the number of presidential proposals submitted in election years after 1953 that resulted in opposition dominance (roughly one of four) is what one would expect, final action in the midterm election years involved consensus almost 30% of the time. Compromise also was not hindered by electoral politics. Even consensus rose regularly in the presidential election years (28%), imbuing election years with a greater spirit of acclamation than any other period in the presidential term.

There are several explanations for this performance in the face of electoral demands. First, each of the election years included action not only on proposals submitted during that particular "campaign period," but also on measures initiated earlier that came to final resolution in that year. When the election year arrived, the political structure of those issues was already firmly established. Many of the matters raised in the campaign, on the other hand, are not likely to be settled until a later year.

Second, while electoral partisanship can trigger interinstitutional animosities, no legislative faction generally desires a record of total defeat. Contrary to the concerns reported earlier about giving the president the image of success, members of Congress and the president may choose to reach agreement on issues that are not controversial and that permit relatively speedy, conflict-

46. For a discussion of position taking by members of Congress, see David Mayhew, *The Electoral Connection* (New Haven: Yale University Press, 1974), p. 61.

47. Kessel, *Presidential Parties*, p. 65

free resolution in order to go into the campaign with some accomplishments that they can advertise. As an aide to President Nixon recollected:

> In an election year . . . we felt it was better to give the easy shots to the Congress because of their political appeal, such as a tax cut. We always came forward with a tax cut in an election year. Or, say, a larger appropriation for a popular program so that we could give them a goody. In the first year which was not an election year, we would push the tougher issues so that if members had to make some difficult votes, they could survive them, since they would not be up for reelection that year. In the honeymoon year, . . . that is clearly the best time to move the tough issues.

Only 42% of the proposals in the sample receiving final action in an election year were associated with major legislation, compared to 53% for the years in which no elections were scheduled. Furthermore, in election years presidents from Eisenhower to Reagan introduced fewer proposals linked to major bills.

Third, in election years involving the incumbent seeking reelection (1956, 1964, 1972, 1976, 1980, and 1984), the president's public approval generally rose, perhaps reducing the incentives to challenge the chief executive.[48]

Finally, while the entire election year may not facilitate accommodative decision making, the legislative crunch that occurs at the end of a sitting Congress, sometimes after the election itself, provides an opportunity that can be manipulated to secure rapid action on legislation, without the time or the occasion for organized opposition. Measures that can be passed during this legislative flurry are likely to be those that enjoyed substantial, perhaps consensual, support because many are enacted in the House under suspension of the rules procedures and require a two-thirds majority.[49]

If the first year favors the president, and institutional accommodation is possible in election years, the post-midterm election year of an administration is hardest on the president. Even though most administrations by then have developed improved political and policy skills, the nearly inevitable decline in seats for the pres-

48. Kernell, *Going Public*, p. 187.
49. Kessel, *Presidential Parties*, p. 186.

ident's party on the Hill and the change in "atmospherics" mean
that the White House often finds itself, in the words of a Reagan
staff member, "having a tougher time getting the decisions at all,
or getting the decisions to fall in our favor." As noted by an assistant to LBJ, building successful legislative coalitions is more difficult to accomplish and may require compromising more with
members of Congress. There is even a greater likelihood that presidential vetoes will be successfully challenged in the third year of
the term.[50] In the worst of situations, one particularly colorful
aide to Richard Nixon asserted, presidents "go international" and
"screw the domestic side." For Eisenhower to Reagan, on the proposals in the sample, there was little in the way of legislative consensus (15%) or compromise (16%) in the post-midterm years.
Rather, there were more oppositional defeats of initiatives (18%)
and a good deal more inaction (38%) than in other years. The
fortunes for the president's program in the third year of the first
term were even worse, with fully 43% of the proposals being
ignored by Congress. Part of the problem is that it takes time to
consider legislation, and it may not be possible before the end of
the administration to seriously consider initiatives proposed in
the third year. Legislative measures resulting in inaction were
proposed an average of twenty-seven months prior to the termination of the administration, while those producing presidential
dominance came considerably earlier in the administration (forty-
nine months, on average).

From the variations witnessed in the different periods of the
presidential term, it is evident that elections have some impact on
setting the context of congressional decision making. These effects
need to be investigated in greater detail with reference to two products of elections. The first has to do with the message of electoral
outcomes, the perceived mandates that they convey to the president and the president's party. These electoral messages may be
helpful to presidents and their allies by increasing the number of
persuadables among the ranks of legislators at any particular time.
The second effect is more direct. Elections determine which individuals, with specific partisan and ideological orientations, will sit

50. David W. Rohde and Dennis M. Simon, "Presidential Vetoes and
Congressional Response: A Study of Institutional Conflict," *American
Journal of Political Science* 29 (August 1985): 423; and Dean Keith
Simonton, *Why Presidents Succeed: A Political Psychology of Leadership*
(New Haven: Yale University Press, 1987), p. 255.

in Congress and provide the foundation for coalition building by the president. The larger the number of natural allies for the president, presumably the more responsive Congress as a collective institution will be to the president's legislative interests.

All presidents do not enter office able to claim the same size mandate from the electorate. During the election night coverage of the 1984 Reagan landslide, Walter Mondale's home state of Minnesota (the only state he carried) looked very lonely on the network maps of the United States—a sharp contrast with the tapestry of color seen in 1976. But do these numerical mandates—large, small, or nonexistent—make a difference? Some observers think not, noting that the opposition party in Congress almost always retains enough political resources to challenge the president.[51] On the other hand, Harry McPherson, a long-time aide to Lyndon Johnson, describes the 1964 election as "Senator Goldwater's contribution to the welfare state," implying that his trouncing at the hands of Johnson paved the way for enactment of the Great Society.[52] Other presidents have been less fortunate. John Kennedy's aides note that, as a student of history, Kennedy often repeated Jefferson's dictum that "great innovations should not be forced on slender majorities"; Kennedy had been elected by only 118,574 votes—and less than a majority of popular votes, white votes, and states.[53] He looked forward to what he anticipated would be a convincing reelection victory, thereby elevating his leadership role from "the stage of public education to one of accomplishment."[54] Carter enjoyed a similarly narrow mandate but forged ahead anyway with a loaded agenda, meeting a less than responsive Congress. Suffering the worst fate, an appointed presidency, Ford had *no* mandate, shaky legitimacy, and an oppo-

51. Douglas Rivers and Nancy L. Rose, "Passing the President's Program: Public Opinion and Presidential Influence in Congress," *American Journal of Political Science* 29 (May 1985): 186.

52. McPherson, *A Political Education*, p. 247.

53. Ibid., p. 182; see also Sorensen, *Kennedy*, pp. 245–251. By one method of counting the presidential vote in Alabama (the results of which were confused by direct voting for electors and the presence of uncommitted electors on the ballot) Kennedy actually lost the popular-vote contest to Nixon by 58,181 votes. Neil R. Pierce, *The People's President: The Electoral College in American History and the Direct-Vote Alternative* (New York: Simon and Schuster, 1968), pp. 101–103.

54. Hargrove, *The Power of the Modern Presidency*, p. 192.

sition party enjoying extraordinary majorities in Congress, leading
Ford to what one of his aides called the political equivalent of
"driving from the back of the bus." What makes these varied experiences important is the extent to which the perception of a mandate translates the electoral numbers into measures of political
strength linking the president to the fortunes of members of Congress, particularly those with the same partisan affiliation.

Perceived presidential mandates—their dimensions, not their
substantive direction—can be constructed from election returns
in a variety ways. Their influence, as a result, can be construed to
have both indirect and direct manifestations. There is, first, the
sheer size of the president's share of the popular vote cast in the
presidential balloting. The 60% range garnered by Eisenhower,
Johnson, Nixon, and Reagan in 1956, 1964, 1972, and 1984
respectively suggests a greater consonance with the popular will
than the minority wins of Kennedy in 1960 or Nixon in 1968. At
least the incumbent can cite the landslide as a political and very
public resource, a signal that others in the Washington community must notice. The influences may be indirect, but the apparent
expression of popular will is known to all but the most unin-
formed. The numbers, too, may be summed in a couple of ways.
The electoral college can dramatically exaggerate the dimensions
of a victory apparent in the popular vote, as it did in both 1980
and 1984.[55] This magnifying effect was most pronounced in 1980,
when Ronald Reagan secured a bare majority of the popular vote,
51%, but ran away with 489 electoral college votes, 91%.

The extent of the president's mandate can also be interpreted
according to the relationship between the vote received by the president and the vote attained by congressional candidates of the president's party. Traditionally, the potency of the presidential mandate
depends to a large extent on the length of the president's coattails.
A first-term president, suggests Richard Born, "can appeal to mem-

55. With the nationalization of the mass base of the Republican and
Democratic parties eliminating to a large degree the previous regional
voting patterns, especially in the South, it may be that any future presidential candidates able to secure much more than 50% of the popular
vote will essentially sweep the electoral college. At that point the magnifying effect of the electoral votes will be meaningless, and it would be
conceivable for such sweeps to alternate between the parties with some
frequency if the Democratic party is able to break the current Republican
lock on the White House.

bers' self-interest, emphasizing that any improvement in his own reelection chances accruing from policy accomplishments will likely rebound to their electoral advantage as well."[56]

Although coattail effects in the past have been significant, there is some debate about whether they have lessened or even disappeared since the 1960s.[57] Randall Calvert and John Ferejohn, based on National Election Study surveys, calculate that the 1964 Johnson thrashing of Goldwater produced the largest coattail potential of presidential elections from 1956 to 1980, and that Nixon's landslide over McGovern in 1972 added seven percentage points to the two-party support for Republicans in the House of Representatives. There was essentially no coattail effect in 1976.[58] If these results actually translated into voter decisions that explicitly linked the fates of presidents and House members of their parties, the electoral message could be quite meaningful. Even Calvert and Ferejohn note recent declines, however, in the "efficiency" of coattail effects, the extent to which "citizens . . . [make use] of their evaluations of presidential candidates in making decisions about how (and whether) to vote in the congressional contest."[59] According to James Campbell, one must also take into account the potential for generating coattails. If the president's party already possesses an unusually high percentage of the seats in the House of Representatives, then even a presidential landslide may produce relatively few new seats at the margin.[60] Further, since subsequent midterm elections almost

56. Richard Born, "Reassessing the Decline of Presidential Coattails: U.S. House Elections from 1952–1980," *Journal of Politics* 46 (February 1984): 77.

57. George Edwards argues that coattails had a marginal impact in the 1964 Johnson landslide and little effect thereafter, whereas Randall Calvert and John Ferejohn find a significant coattail effect in 1964 and subsequent elections, as does Richard Born. George C. Edwards III, *Presidential Influence in Congress* (San Francisco: W. H. Freeman, 1980), pp. 73–76; Randall L. Calvert and John A. Ferejohn, "Coattail Voting in Recent Presidential Elections," *American Political Science Review* 77 (June 1983): 407–419; and Born, "Reassessing the Decline of Presidential Coattails." See also James E. Campbell, "Predicting Seats Gains from Presidential Coattails," *American Journal of Political Science* 30 (February 1986): 165–183.

58. Calvert and Ferejohn, "Coattail Voting," pp. 414–415.

59. Ibid., p. 417.

60. Campbell, "Presidential Coattails," pp. 167, 173.

always bring about a loss of seats for the president's party in the House, the direct influence of coattails lasts only two years.[61]

In the absence of coattail effects, the combination of presidential and congressional election returns may carry an alternative message of use to the president. The amount by which presidents lead or trail congressional candidates from their own parties can communicate indirect signals about the strength of the president among the electorate.[62] Representatives and senators of the president's party, already linked to the chief executive by a generally shared philosophical position, may remain cautious about challenging a president, the standard-bearer of their own party, who enjoys demonstrable popularity among those constituting their own electoral base.[63]

The indirect and direct influences of presidential mandates are difficult to measure. We are most interested in their impact within the individual constituencies of each representative and senator, information that to date is unobtainable. Nevertheless, it is worth examining what happened in Congress to the presidential proposals of Eisenhower to Reagan when these presidents enjoyed mandates of various proportions, as reflected in different ways of viewing national electoral outcomes.

The occurrence of conflictive outcomes, involving opposition or presidential dominance, was most infrequent when the president received more than 60% of the two-party popular vote in the previous election. Presidents securing less than a majority of the vote in the preceding election saw 58% of their proposals fail to pass, compared to only 38% for presidents with the largest share of the two-party vote. The patterns for the electoral college vote

61. Ibid., p. 172.

62. This measure of presidential strength is obviously different from that of coattails, although the two are related. If coattails were in fact strong, one would expect the president's party to do about as well as the president in the popular vote since fewer voters would be splitting their tickets. See Born, "Reassessing the Decline of Presidential Coattails," pp. 63–64; and Warren E. Miller, "Presidential Coattails: A Study in Political Myth and Methodology," *Public Opinion Quarterly* 19 (Winter 1955–56): 356–357. But running ahead of fellow partisans in the House is undoubtedly better for presidents, despite the lack of coattails, than suffering the ignominy of no coattails *and* falling behind the rest of the party.

63. Edwards, *Presidential Influence*, p. 103.

are similar, although they are not amplified by any magnifying influence of electoral college returns. Differences in the electoral college do count when there is legislative conflict, however. Presidents who won public legislative battles had received on average 403 electoral college votes in the previous election; presidents who lost outright in Congress had garnered an average of only 345 electoral votes.

Electoral mandates, of course, are unlikely to have uniform effects throughout the four years of a president's term, and perhaps no effect at all by the end of the term. Perceived mandates apparently contribute to determining whether any part of the initial year of the first term is indeed a honeymoon period for the president. Beginning in 1953, presidents who received over 60% of the two-party vote saw Congress give some consideration to 95% of their proposals in the first year, compared to only 65% for those with less than a majority of the vote. In addition, 58% of their initial-year proposals were decided in Congress by consensus; the figure was 20% for plurality presidents. In subsequent midterm election years, landslide presidents apparently challenged Congress, leading to a high incidence of inaction (31%) and conflict (44%), and they often lost the struggles over their programmatic initiatives. As late as the third year of the terms, mandates in the previous presidential election still contributed to the atmospherics of presidential-congressional relations. Presidents with the largest popular-vote mandates experienced the most consensus (35%), plurality presidents experienced the most inaction (61%), and those in between saw almost half of their proposals decided in public fights, most of which they won. Even in the fourth year, the year of the presidential election, plurality presidents were plagued. They lost 44% of their initiatives to opposition dominance, whereas presidents with some kind of majority vote in the earlier election saw more of their proposals enacted, even with some measure of consensus.

Whatever perceptual mandates are derived from the election returns, therefore, shape the politics of each year differently. When presidents have garnered the highest returns in the two-party vote, they have almost always been more successful in enacting their programs than those elected with less than a majority, except when their vote-getting capacity led them to challenge Congress, or more specifically the opposition in Congress, during the midterm elections. Depending on the circumstances, electoral mandates can either reinforce coalitions that bind the tandem institutions, or offer incentives for the president to challenge the role of the opposition party when it is in the legislative majority. The latter strategy, however, does not breed legislative success.

These mandate effects are generally, though weakly, reinforced by the link between the voting in presidential and congressional elections. When presidents ran behind the House members of their own party and generated no coattails (or created "negative" coattails), their proposals in the subsequent years were more likely to be ignored in Congress (about a third of the time) or actively defeated. There were also, generally speaking, more consensual responses to the president's initiatives, and more outright victories, when the president could claim the advantage in the previous election. One problem for such presidents was that if they ran well ahead of their own partisans, it typically meant that candidates of their party had not done well in the congressional elections, leading to control of fewer House seats by the presidential party. It is hard to lead one's party in the election and also have one's party control Congress after the election. Both contribute to the coalition-building power of the president, but they tend to be negatively related to each other.[64] On those occasions when presidents did lead their party and their party had firm control of Congress, presidential proposals encountered relatively low levels of conflict, with only 30% of the initiatives being decided by dominance of one form or another. For those relatively few proposals considered when the president ran behind the party's House candidates and the opposition controlled Congress, there were no instances of consensus and public fights occurred on half of the initiatives.

Because elections every two years determine the number of seats held by the president's party in the House and Senate, those elections should be directly related to how Congress responds to

64. While the president's proportion of the two-party vote and the electoral college vote, the strength of the coattail effects, and the amount by which the presidents have run ahead of House candidates of their own party are all positively correlated with each other (Pearson's r ranging from .35 to .81), the coattail effects and difference between the House and presidential vote variables have a mild negative correlation with the number of House seats controlled by the president's party (−.02 and −.35 respectively).

presidential initiatives. Light argues, for example, that when it comes to the accumulation of political capital—a president's vote-getting ability in Congress—electoral margins enjoyed by the chief executive do not amount to much if the president's party does not also have the necessary seats in Congress. These tools of the political trade, in short, must go together.[65] Studies of presidential-congressional relations typically find the number of seats controlled by the president's party to be of considerable importance in assessing the chief executive's legislative success.[66]

Deficiencies in electoral mandates and congressional seats can also reinforce each other. When Kennedy was barely elected in 1960, the Democrats lost one Senate seat and twenty-nine House seats. Without those seats "no amount of expertise or charm can make a difference."[67] At the very least, without a strong party presence in Congress, the White House is forced to consider more negative legislative strategies, such as the veto campaigns pursued late in the Eisenhower administration and all through Ford's tenure.[68] Coalition building becomes an ad hoc, search-anywhere-for-votes kind of operation. As President Ford volunteered in an interview:

> Any time a president [faces a] Congress, in both houses, where the opposition holds two-thirds of the seats, he's got problems . . . We exploited every single angle we could conjure up, and it ended up where we would have a floating coalition—a floating coalition to get something done, and an equally floating coalition to sustain vetoes. When you're that much outnumbered, you don't really have any choice!

65. Light, *The President's Agenda*, pp. 16–28.

66. See Edwards, *Presidential Influence*, p. 81; Richard Fleisher and Jon R. Bond, "Assessing Presidential Support in the House: Lessons from Reagan and Carter," *Journal of Politics* 45 (August 1983): 750–753; John W. Kingdon, *Congressmen's Voting Decisions*, 2nd ed. (New York: Harper and Row, 1981), pp. 180–187; Paul C. Light, "Passing Nonincremental Policy: Presidential Influence in Congress, Kennedy to Carter," *Congress and the Presidency* 9 (Winter 1981–82): 69; Rivers and Rose, "Passing the President's Program," p. 193; and Rohde and Simon, "Presidential Vetoes," pp. 408–412, 415–423.

67. Light, *The President's Agenda*, p. 26

68. Rowland Evans and Robert Novak, *Nixon in the White House: The Frustration of Power* (New York: Vintage Books, 1972), p. 128; and interviews with Ford administration officials.

It may seem to border on a truism that the president's position will fare better when there is a greater number of compatible partisans in Congress,[69] but the connection is not automatic. For one thing, in the American context a party can be a rather large umbrella stretched over a wide diversity of viewpoints. Given a Senate Democratic party that counted Wayne Morse, Strom Thurmond, and Harry Byrd among its members, President Kennedy fully anticipated losing the support of about a fourth of the Democratic senators on each domestic issue.[70] An interview with one of Carter's assistants dramatized the problem of a president and a congressional party who shared a party label but not a political philosophy:

> Jimmy Carter, at least in the Senate, never had a working philosophical majority. He had a *numerical* Democratic majority, but not a working philosophical majority. He did not have a working philosophical majority in the House either. People have never understood that. They would say, "You have sixty-two goddamn Democrats, you should be able to get anything that you want!" [One of the Carter staff people had a member say to him about an upcoming vote,] "I'm going to hold my nose on this one and go along with the President, but I'm doing that for three reasons. One, he's a Democrat; two, he's from the South; and three, you used to work for me."

That is hardly an effective way to build coalitions, unless one has an exceedingly large White House staff with prior Capitol Hill experience.

So partisan majorities on the Hill may not translate directly into agreement or large coalitions in support of presidential initiatives. At this point, not controlling for any other influences on congressional action, it is obvious that from 1953 to 1986 the number of party seats in Congress alone was not determinative in either establishing cooperation between the White House and Capitol Hill or ensuring the success of the president's program. In the

69. George C. Edwards III, "Quantitative Analysis," in *Studying the Presidency*, ed. George C. Edwards III and Stephen J. Wayne (Knoxville: University of Tennessee Press, 1983), p. 114.

70. Carrol Kilpatrick, "The Kennedy Style and Congress," in *John F. Kennedy and the New Frontier*, ed. Aida DiPace Donald (New York: Hill and Wang, 1966), p. 52.

House of Representatives, the institutional relationship and the president's initiatives fared better (greater consensus, less conflict, fewer outright defeats for the president) when the president's party was in the majority, but not in possession of a supermajority of the seats (61% of more). Given the political characteristics of the past three decades, of course, only Democrats have simultaneously held the White House and controlled an enormous majority in the House. Because of the demographic heterogeneity of the party, and the North-South split, it has not been easy for Democratic presidents to hold an expanding party-based coalition together. Lyndon Johnson was known to comment that he would rather the Democrats have more narrow control of Congress than try to keep so many people "on the reservation." Party unity is much harder to enforce in these situations. The Senate, with its fewer members, followed a little more closely the standard assumptions about control of seats by the president's party. Supermajorities of the president's party produced somewhat more responsiveness to the chief executive's program and somewhat less conflict. Confrontations and problems for the president's legislative proposals ensued precisely when the partisan lines were more closely drawn. Under such circumstances fewer than half of the initiatives introduced by presidents from Eisenhower to Reagan survived the Senate in any form.

The weakness of the party-seats component may have to do with the ideological as well as the partisan composition of each chamber. In their study of the individual-level behavior of House members during the Carter and Reagan administrations, Richard Fleisher and Jon Bond found ideological influences that cut across the partisan divisions. Carter and Reagan each lost support from representatives of both their own and the opposition party as the ideological distance between the president and the members of Congress increased. They were also supported more than expected by House members of the opposing party when there was greater ideological compatibility.[71] Policy congruence can create natural allies just as surely as, and in some cases more consistently than, a shared party label. President Johnson's achievements in the Eighty-ninth Congress, the Congress of the Great Society, were certainly aided by the myriad Democrats elected

71. Fleisher and Bond, "Assessing Presidential Support," pp. 748–750, 751–753.

in the 1964 election. But those Democrats included many southerners opposed to civil rights and a number of the social welfare provisions of Johnson's programs. He needed moderate Republicans. And while Jimmy Carter faced a Senate that was 62% Democratic during his first two years in office, at least from the administration's point of view it was not always clear that the ideological perspectives of the two entities were consonant on the issues presented by the president. Carter frequently had to work with Republicans, often because aspects of the policy agenda he was pursuing ran counter to the traditional liberalism captured in measures such as the legislative support scores produced by the Americans for Democratic Action. Interviews with Carter aides and with President Carter himself underscored the administration's frustrations derived from working with Democrats in Congress, as well as liberals in the Washington community as a whole. Ideology is therefore a far more complicated concept than shared partisan affiliation, but at least sometimes it is just as consequential.

A final form of political capital for the president, a well-regarded asset for influencing the pool of persuadables among members of Congress, is the president's standing with the public. It is usually interpreted as the proportion of the public expressing satisfaction with the chief executive's job performance. As Richard Neustadt has long argued, in a president's efforts to build coalitions and generally strengthen the administration's position among other actors in the Washington community, a president's "public standing is a source of influence for him, another factor bearing on their willingness to give him what he wants."[72] Still, individual members of Congress know that even a popular president cannot ensure the defeat at the polls of congressional candidates with opinions that differ from those of the chief executive. The link between approval and influence, therefore,

> rests not on any calculation by the congressman of how his constituents will judge his support of or opposition to the president's program, but on a sense of "common fate" among congressmen based on their understanding of how the public holds government accountable for policy failures.[73]

72. Richard E. Neustadt, *Presidential Power: The Politics of Leadership from FDR to Carter* (New York: Macmillan, 1980), p. 64.
73. Rivers and Rose, "Passing the President's Program," p. 187.

Moreover, lack of popularity with the American people diminishes a president's policy-making stature. One of the senior-level advisers to President Jimmy Carter explained what he perceived to be the salience of public approval in the American system:

> The biggest difference between our system and a parliamentary system is that in a parliamentary system, even if public opinion gets less favorable, the prime minister still can act. Margaret Thatcher, even before the Falklands war, was still able to act. That's not true in our system. The president can get only as much as Congress perceives the president has support for. When the president's popularity goes down, his ability to get things from Congress dissipates.

A domestic policy aide in the Johnson White House noted a particularly concrete ramification of diminished presidential popularity. He suggested that "when a president is less popular, he loses control over a department and its secretary. They will not help him on the Hill as much, and they have more of their own power." Those presidents who have attempted to lead in the absence of public support have seldom been perceived as successful.

Popular support as a political resource is really the president's alone, and given what would appear to be the highly personal tie between presidents and their popularity, the expectations about influence are more commensurate with a presidency-centered perspective than a tandem-institutions analysis. Here is where we have an unambiguous opportunity to see the president qua dominant political player. Presidents cultivate respect and support among the public, and the utility of that resource for forging presidentially led coalitions depends on the ability of individual incumbents to harness and exploit it. President Reagan, for example, possessed communicative skills not normally associated with presidents. He was able to apply those skills to gain the greatest return from high levels of support among the public, even though his approval ratings were not always uniquely high throughout his administration.

But the story is not quite so simple or straightforward. The level of presidential popularity is affected by both the legislative activism of the president and the administration's past successes, in addition to events completely beyond the president's control.

Less active chief executives, legislatively speaking—such as Eisenhower—enjoyed greater stability in their public support than did more energetic presidents. Taking, announcing, and pursuing controversial stands breeds opponents, and it is presidential involvement in legislative affairs that does the most to capture public attention.[74] So levels of support and influence are interactive, probably incorporating a lagged response to each other, and to some extent independent of presidential action. They are also defined through whatever complex lens happens to inform popular perceptions. Early on, Carter was perceived by the public as ill suited to the demands of national leadership, whereas Reagan struck the popular imagination. To one Carter official, these disparate perceptions seem to ignore the fundamental issue of what each was trying to accomplish:

> I could not help but laugh when [President Reagan] got credited with great legislative victories when he succeeded in getting a 25% reduction in taxes over a three-year period. Contrast that with what we had to do, with the windfall profits tax, the largest tax increase in the history of the republic until the tax increase last year. And we got it through. The public perception was that when we did it, it was because we did not screw up; when they did it, it was because of their legislative brilliance. Well, this is not sour grapes, . . . [but] I'm saying that the *image* that the president has in the public and with Congress is absolutely the key, *the key.*

Another Carter aide lamented that the public probably would not even believe that Carter actually increased defense spending, concluding that "perception is reality and reality isn't in this town."

There are also limits on how much presidents can exploit their popularity, particularly by employing the explicit strategy of influencing the Washington community by what Samuel Kernell characterizes as "going public."[75] Presidents are not likely to be successful in using the weight of their public support if their job performance is approved of by less than half the public, as was the case when Congress acted on 41% of the presidential initiatives

74. Binkley, *The Man in the White House,* p. 132; and Cronin, *The State of the Presidency,* p. 330.

75. Kernell, *Going Public.* This strategy will be examined in detail in Chapter 5.

included in this study. Sometimes even high levels of public support cannot be readily tapped. With his narrow mandate and the slim Democratic majority in Congress, John Kennedy chose to be restrained in turning to the public for support on major issues, fearing that such efforts might be divisive, alienating, and wasteful of his political capital.[76] Dwight Eisenhower believed he could go to the well only occasionally and still be effective, so he restricted his appeals to the public to the most essential administration priorities, such as labor law reform.[77]

There is the added danger that such efforts can reinforce the responsibility of the president in what may turn out to be a failed effort, thus leaving the president falling short of public expectations and undermining the already brittle public trust.[78] In addition, no matter how popular the president, the chief executive's ability to forge winning alliances on Capitol Hill depends on public attitudes about the particular issues at hand. Sixty-eight percent of the presidential proposals submitted between 1953 and 1984 did not involve policy areas mentioned by any of the public as being related to the nation's most important problem, according to the Gallup poll. Even when the issues are publicly salient, proposals of the president do not always benefit from the level of public interest. Civil rights and consumerism were aided by the emergence of an at least momentary national consensus; proposed tax hikes in 1967 encountered a skeptical Congress aware of the widespread public opposition.[79]

Finally, institutional changes in the media have provided new opportunities as well as perils for chief executives. During the period from the early 1950s to the 1980s, the structure and role of the media were dramatically transformed. The centrality of television grew as set ownership by the public rose from 47% to 98% of households and the reliance on television as the primary source of

76. Sorensen, *Kennedy*, p. 329.

77. Interview with an Eisenhower administration official. President Eisenhower was also very protective of his public support, by and large not wishing to engage in activities that would diminish it. See Fred I. Greenstein, *The Hidden-Hand Presidency: Eisenhower as Leader* (New York: Basic Books, 1982), pp. 95–99.

78. Cronin, *The State of the Presidency*, p. 102.

79. Sorensen, *Kennedy*, p. 494; Joseph A. Califano, Jr., *A Presidential Nation* (New York: Norton, 1975), p. 131; and Arthur M. Okun, *The Political Economy of Prosperity* (New York: W. W. Norton, 1969), p. 87.

news increased from 40% to 65% of the public.[80] The broadcast media in general have became more nationally oriented, with both the national networks and the local stations placing enhanced emphasis, and allocating more personnel, to the coverage of national institutions and events.[81] All of these changes permit a president to command more forcefully and effectively the attention of the entire nation and stimulate public appeals to Congress in support of the administration's programs. They also, however, put the president—and presidential weaknesses and failures—in a continual spotlight, on a national stage. The role of public support for the president in helping to define the tandem-institutions relationship, therefore, cannot be evaluated without some reflection on how the public interprets leadership, the public salience of the issues involved, the evolution of the media as a collective national institution, and the various interactions of these factors.

Given the complexities associated with the role of public approval in the overall legislative process, there is considerable ambiguity about its influence on domestic policy making by the president and Congress. Some studies of presidential legislative success have found a positive but relatively limited association between presidential popularity and achievement.[82] Harvey

80. Television ownership statistics are from U.S. Department of Commerce, Bureau of the Census, *Statistical Abstract of the United States, 1984*, 104th ed. (Washington, D.C.: G.P.O., 1984), p. 558. The figures on reliance on television news are from the Roper polls for 1953 and 1982, reported in Nelson W. Polsby and Aaron Wildavsky, *Presidential Elections*, 6th ed. (New York: Charles Scribners and Sons, 1984), p. 307; and Evans Witt, "Here, There, and Everywhere: Where Americans Get Their News," *Public Opinion* (August–September 1983): 46.

81. Kernell, *Going Public*, p. 67. For later years, television and radio correspondents were counted from several years of the *Congressional Directory* (Washington, D.C.: G.P.O.), sections on radio and television gallery memberships.

82. George Edwards considers public support to be quite important. Bond and Fleisher, controlling for factors such as party control of Congress, find that public support of the president explains only a small amount of the variation in levels of presidential influence with Congress. Rivers and Rose, controlling for party and for aggressiveness of the president's legislation agenda, find that a 1% increase in popularity translates into a 1% increase in presidential success with passing the program. Edwards, *Presidential Influence*, pp. 92–110; Jon R. Bond and Richard Fleisher, "Presidential Popularity and Congressional Voters: A Reexamination of Public Opinion as a Source of Influence in Congress," *Western*

Zeidenstein suggests that investigations of this sort are relegated to "a futile search for patterns."[83] His attempt to pin down useful generalizations proved to be fruitless. Public support has even been found on occasion to have a negative effect on presidential influence, especially on members of Congress who are from the opposition party. Controlling for the ideological differences between the president and individual members of the House, Jon Bond and Richard Fleisher find that enhanced presidential popularity helped with members of the president's own party, but actually triggered greater resistance among those in the opposition.[84]

Each of these studies involves the use of aggregate data—the *mean level* of public approval of the president for *each year.* While it is unlikely that members of Congress respond to every fluctuation in the presidential support polls,[85] it also seems unlikely that political actors are so insensitive that annual means capture the significance of public approval as a political resource or constraint, or as a defining feature of the tandem-institutions relationship. If presidential popularity is to have an effect, it is likely to be apparent only when observed at the time that congressional action on initiatives is actually being taken. One way to examine this issue is to consider the percentage of the public approving of the president's job performance, as reported by the Gallup poll in the most recent month available prior to final action by Congress on the president's initiatives.

To judge by my sample of initiatives, from Eisenhower to Reagan instances of coalitional conflict were marginally associated with this measure of presidential approval. Levels of presidential legislative success have varied even more as the president's public fortunes have changed. The highest levels of conflict (37% of the cases), involving opposition or presidential dominance, occurred when no more than 40% of the public approved

Political Quarterly 37 (1984): 291–306; and Rivers and Rose, "Passing the President's Program," p. 193.

83. Harvey G. Zeidenstein, "Varying Relationships between Presidents' Popularity and Their Legislative Success: A Futile Search for Patterns," *Presidential Studies Quarterly* 8 (Fall 1983): 530.

84. Jon R. Bond and Richard Fleisher, "The Limits of Presidential Popularity as a Source of Influence in the U.S. House," *Legislative Studies Quarterly* 5 (February 1980): 75.

85. Edwards, *Presidential Influence*, p. 91.

of the president's job performance. Consensus took place twice as often when at least 61% of the public supported the president rather than when fewer than 40% did (30% compared to 16% of the cases). More important for the president, when public support was under 41%, only four of ten presidential initiatives passed in some form. When more than 60% of the public liked how the president was handling his job, better than six of ten initiatives were enacted.

These tendencies remain when a dynamic element is introduced by combining the level of public approval of the president with the trend in public support over the three months leading up to congressional consideration. Congressional inaction and outright defeats plagued modern presidents whose popularity was low and either declining or constant for the three months prior to legislative review. Somewhat greater consensus and presidential dominance occurred when the president's popularity was high and either constant or rising over the previous quarter. These patterns were particularly pronounced when viewing action by the House of Representatives alone on presidential initiatives. The new data suggest that there are reasons for incumbents not to squander their public support. At the same time, despite the increasingly plebiscitary nature of the presidency, to use Theodore Lowi's terminology,[86] there is no panacea for presidential leadership to be unearthed in the chief executive's relationship with the public. The constraints inherent in a system of tandem institutions are simply too pervasive to permit such freedom of action.

Economic Properties

Especially in the context of the past twenty years, there has been a growing awareness of the connection between the choices made by political institutions and the performance of the economy. Specifically, of interest here is the political economy of the tandem-institutions setting, the effects of economic conditions on the ways in which Congress takes action on presidential legislative initiatives. Even policy choices that have no direct economic implications must be considered with reference to one issue that plagues all societies, the problem of scarcity. All resources are limited; the less plentiful they are, the greater the propensity for

86. Lowi, *The Personal President*, chap. 5.

heated struggles over their allocation. The expansion of resources lessens these pressures. Former Chairman of the Council of Economic Advisers Walter Heller, a principal architect of the economic growth of the 1960s, argues that the "growing horn of plenty" overcomes ideological barriers to programs and "consensus replaces conflict."[87]

An economic squeeze generates the opposite effect. When Lyndon Johnson attempted to pursue a policy of both guns and butter, implementing the Great Society and fighting the Vietnam War, the fiscal increment of additional revenues that had flowed automatically into the federal coffers and had been instrumental in reducing conflict began to disappear. With the ensuing period of "stagflation," the fiscal increment evolved into a fiscal decrement and the means for securing policy consensus dissipated.[88] The resulting economic transformation of politics from a distributive to a redistributive basis, from logrolling to conflict, was further accentuated by the political decision to implement the Budget and Impoundment Control Act of 1974.[89] These economic and political transformations spelled trouble, especially for the passage and maintenance of human services legislation.[90] They also made economic costs extremely important when presidents and their staffs formulated their legislative agendas.[91] Indeed, they prompted President Ford to declare a "no new starts" approach to domestic policy, with the exception of energy programs.[92] Stuart Eizenstat, Carter's chief domestic policy adviser, emphasized the significance of contrasting economic settings:

> I first worked in the White House under President Johnson. He launched the Great Society in 1965 with an inflation rate of 1.9% and a budget deficit of about $1.6 billion. I ask whether the Great Society would have been launched with a $50 billion deficit and inflation averaging 8% for three years before we took office—which is what we inherited.[93]

87. Quoted in Michael H. Best and William E. Connolly, *The Politicized Economy*, 2nd ed. (Lexington, Mass.: D. C. Heath, 1982), p. 221.

88. Schick, *Congress and Money*, pp. 20–30.

89. Ellwood, "Budget Control," p. 88.

90. Nelson, *Making an Issue of Child Abuse*, p. 136.

91. Light, *The President's Agenda*, p. 141.

92. Interviews with aides to President Ford.

93. Quoted in David S. Broder, *Changing of the Guard: Power and Leadership in America* (New York: Penguin Books, 1981), p. 119.

In addition, since FDR presidents have acquired in the popular perception the principal responsibility for ensuring economic prosperity. Kennedy and Johnson benefited from that formula; every subsequent president, if we exclude the first years of the Reagan administration, has suffered its consequences.[94] With respect to economics, chief executives are treated as presidency-centered players, even though they reside in the realities of a tandem-institutions world. Or perhaps it is now a tripartite-institutions world, since the Federal Reserve has considerable autonomy in shaping monetary policy and thus economic performance.[95] All of these institutions are caught in the web of an increasingly integrated world economy, which offers diminished opportunity for independent action.

Two measures of the nation's economic condition speak directly to the issue of plenty versus scarcity, and therefore to the potential politics of accommodation in presidential-congressional relations. The first pertains to the health of the economy itself, as indicated by the gains in the Gross National Product (GNP) calculated on a quarterly basis. Surprisingly, an examination of congressional responses to presidential initiatives for different levels of economic growth seems to offer little support for the notion that an expanding economy reduces conflict and aids the president's legislative agenda. During the Eisenhower to Reagan administrations, the president's program was somewhat more likely to get action when the economy experienced the greatest growth. Under those conditions there was also a higher percentage of instances in which the president's coalition dominated legislative decision making than was otherwise the case. When conflict occurred, the president was victorious more often than when the economy was stagnant. But these patterns are indistinct, and conflict (the two forms of dominance taken together) actually occurred slightly more frequently when the economy was booming (35% of the cases compared to 29% for periods of no growth or decline).

94. Alan Wolfe, "Presidential Power and the Crisis of Modernization," in *Rethinking the Presidency*, ed. Thomas E. Cronin (Boston: Little, Brown, 1982), p. 147.

95. Paul E. Peterson and Mark Rom, "Macroeconomic Policymaking: Who Is in Control?" in *Can the Government Govern?* ed. John E. Chubb and Paul E. Peterson (Washington, D.C.: Brookings Institution, 1989), pp. 139–182.

This initial analysis, of course, ignores the fact that while economic conditions are likely to affect policy proposals in all policy areas, they should not be expected to have the same impact on initiatives of varying size and scope. Some policy initiatives place greater demands on the country's resources than do others. For presidential proposals involving large policy departures, of which there are 67 in this sample, all received some kind of congressional action when GNP expansion as calculated in the previous quarter was more than 5%. About a fifth of the large initiatives considered under less robust economic conditions were ignored by Congress. In addition, a fifth of the proposals taken up during high-growth periods involved public victories for the president when conflict ensued—which is again more than usual. But many more proposals lost as a result of opposing coalitions (45%), and almost two-thirds of the proposals generated legislative conflict. For small proposals, involving little budgetary or social impact, the situation is somewhat clearer. When the economy was rapidly expanding, more of the initiatives were enacted, conflict was lower, and the president was more likely to win what public struggles developed.

Let us refine this size distinction a bit more. If one considers the 103 proposals in the sample that were the least consequential— small policy departures, associated with minor bills, and of lowest priority to the president (see Chapter 5)—the issue of economic growth or decline becomes more pronounced. For the nine of these proposals considered when the economy was in decline or stagnant, five were ignored by Congress and the other four were settled by factional battles. When the economy was growing at a rate greater than 5% annually, there was little conflict; 76% of the proposals received some kind of action, 65% were enacted, and of those, six of ten passed by consensus. Because the demand on resources of these fairly insignificant proposals was small, they encountered little legislative trouble during periods without major economic constraints.

A similar pattern emerges from an examination of the impact of the federal budget deficit. The deficit, of course, provides a more explicit picture of resource scarcity, especially with respect to what can be expended on governmental activities.[96] That is per-

96. To measure the size of the federal deficit within a calendar year, I calculate the deficit as a percentage of GNP, using the GNP and federal

haps why the size of the federal deficit offers a more discernible pattern of relationships with congressional action than was true of changes in the GNP. When the federal budget was balanced or in surplus during the Eisenhower to Reagan years, conflict was lowest (21%), consensus was highest (30%), and over 60% of the president's initiatives were enacted. Conflictive congressional responses were much more common (40%) and less of the president's overall program passed (49%) when the deficit climbed to 2% or more of the GNP. These effects were most pronounced when the resource demands of policy proposals were the greatest. When the deficits were highest, a fifth of the large presidential initiatives were not acted upon, only 4% enjoyed a consensual reception on the Hill, and almost half led to some kind of public conflict between presidential allies and opponents. Moreover, the president lost those fights two-thirds of the time. Even for large proposals, the deficit may ironically provide the basis for producing less conflict and more presidential legislative success than one might expect. As Allen Schick points out, the acceptance of deficits in lieu of tax increases tempers the conflict associated with cuts into the budgetary base.[97] Perhaps they reduce it enough to permit the building of legislative coalitions with the president in the majority.

Two additional economic indicators do not reflect resource conditions as sharply as changes in the GNP and in the size of the deficit, but they do address the relevant atmospherics associated with the health and performance of the economy. The first is the monthly unemployment rate reported for the month prior to congressional action. Whenever an unemployment rate of less than 5% prevailed during the preceding three decades, suggesting good economic times, presidential initiatives encountered the fewest instances of conflict (25%), the most consensus (32%), and relatively high levels of success (65%). Greater conflict (42%) and a lower passage rate (48%) were associated with presidential proposals considered when 7% or more of the work force was unemployed. Quarterly trends in unemployment have mattered too. Over 90% of the president's initiatives were acted upon when unemployment was on the decline over the previous quarter;

---

deficit figures from the National Income and Product Accounts (NIPA) provided by the Department of Commerce. See Appendix D.

97. Schick, *Congress and Money*, p. 30.

Table 4.3   Congressional responses to presidential proposals and level of monthly inflation

Level of inflation	N	Inaction	Opposition dominance	Compromise	Presidential dominance	Consensus
			Congressional decision-making process			
Less than 2%	106	20%	17%	16%	14%	33%
Between 2% and 5%	95	26%	17%	21%	10%	26%
5% or more	98	31%	28%	21%	9%	11%

Note: N = 299; chi square = 19.01; $p < .02$.
Source: See Appendixes C and D.

almost half were completely ignored when introduced during periods of rising joblessness.

We come finally to inflation, treated in Table 4.3. In Keynesian macroeconomic analysis, which has dominated the postwar period, inflation is the product of an overheated economy in which demand should be constricted by reducing, among other things, public-sector contributions to aggregate demand. With that perspective prevailing, one would expect less action to be taken on presidential initiatives when inflation is running high, especially since the vast bulk of initiatives involve either program authorization or reauthorizations. When inflationary effects are less of a concern, there should be smoother sailing for all kinds of policy initiatives, other things being equal. Indeed, that is what we find when we examine congressional action through the lens of variations in the annual inflation rate measured in the month prior to congressional action. Under conditions of low inflation (a less than 2% annual rate) 80% of the president's proposals in the sample received some kind of formal attention, there was relatively less conflict, consensus occurred a third of the time, and 63% of the initiatives were enacted. When inflation was high, almost a third of the proposals were ignored by Congress, most never passed (59%), and there was far less opportunity for consensus. When conflict occurred, the president's coalition was defeated three times more than it won, rather than enjoying the even odds of the low-inflation periods. The effects of inflation pose special problems for Democratic administrations, in that they tend to emphasize reducing unemployment at the expense of some inflation.[98] That kind of policy emphasis may cause inherent difficulty in winning approval of Democratic presidential programs. Perhaps, however, that problem for Democrats involves levels of inflation rather than trends. Unlike the case of unemployment, the trends in inflation made less of a difference in distinguishing types of congressional responses.

The pure context and the malleable context of the political system are certainly not the only factors that explain the nuances of presidential-congressional relations. It makes a difference what kinds of proposals a president sends to Capitol Hill. The substantive nature of the proposals themselves, and how much effort the president puts behind them, affect the composition of coalitions allied with the administration and therefore the probabilities of how initiatives will be treated once they reach Capitol Hill. This strategic policy context of congressional decision making is the subject of the next chapter.

98. Douglas A. Hibbs, Jr., "Political Parties and Macroeconomic Policy," *American Political Science Review* 71 (December 1977): 1467–87.

5. Strategic Choices and the Policy Context

A few months after taking office in 1977, President Carter submitted to Congress a series of proposals designed to bring under control the high level of inflation in hospital costs. Among his legislative proposals offered four years later was a plan to rename and reorganize the National Petroleum Reserve in Alaska. These two disparate initiatives illustrate Paul Light's maxim that "all presidential proposals are not created equal."[1] Presidential programs comprise a wide variety of measures, some that loom large in either the contemporary or the historical context, others that seem more the routine business of administration. How individuals, including members of Congress, interpret these initiatives and make decisions about them depends in some measure on the "issue-context" in which they are observed and experienced.[2] Each proposal presented by a president may have its politics shaped by the history of similar initiatives, actions previously taken, or the general distribution of opinions that has already crystallized in a particular policy area.[3]

The previous chapter addressed those features of the setting of congressional responses over which the president has little control and sometimes even little influence. The policy context of congressional responses, on the other hand, is more sensitive to the

1. Paul C. Light, "Passing Nonincremental Policy: Presidential Influence in Congress, Kennedy to Carter," *Congress and the Presidency* 9 (Winter 1981–82): 61.

2. Aaron Wildavsky, "The Analysis of Issue-Contexts in the Study of Decision-Making," *Journal of Politics* 24 (November 1962): 717.

3. Ibid., pp. 720, 730. See also Aage R. Clausen, *How Congressmen Decide: A Policy Focus* (New York: St. Martin's Press, 1973), for an examination of how initial decisions structure future choices when the policy context remains the same.

strategic choices made by presidents as they define the scope, character, and timeliness of their legislative proposals. Indeed, when we think of presidential leadership, we often envision direct presidential involvement and action on the issues of the day. When the stock market suffered the October crash of 1987, among the first issues raised on news reports were how President Reagan would respond and what the White House would do to meet the sudden financial crisis. A direct manifestation of the presidency-centered perspective, the theme had a formulation applicable to any policy concern: problem, president, action.

Even in the domain of strategic choices on policy, however, chief executives do not enjoy unlimited flexibility. If inflation of medical costs is a serious problem, it is hard to offer any solutions without turning to relatively major regulatory alternatives of one kind or another. A president who won the White House by obtaining the nomination of the Democratic party would find it politically uncomfortable to tout the virtues of small, inactive government. An administration that perceived its mandate to include a refinement or even a turning back of the New Deal or the Great Society inevitably would have to craft proposals that challenged existing programs and their clienteles. Presidents get to choose their own initiatives and to follow their own policy preferences to a considerable degree, but not without limitations. They can manipulate the policy context, but they cannot write it on a clean slate. The tandem-institutions setting presents too many constraints, even though those constraints vary enormously from one policy domain to the next.

In this chapter I examine the policy context of congressional responses by exploring the significant ways in which presidential legislative proposals differ from one another, and by considering the implications of those differences for the manner in which the president's program is received on Capitol Hill.[4] There are three

4. Some previous research has assessed the role played by the substantive content and significance of particular presidential policies. See, for example, Lance T. LeLoup and Steven A. Shull, "Dimensions of Presidential Policy Making," in *The Presidency: Studies in Public Policy*, ed. Steven A. Shull and Lance T. LeLoup (Brunswick, Ohio: King's Court Communications, 1979); Light, "Passing Nonincremental Policy"; David M. Olson, "Success and Content in Presidential Roll Calls: The First Three Years of the Reagan Administration," *Presidential Studies Quarterly* 15 (Summer 1985): 602–610; Robert J. Spitzer, *The Presidency and*

primary means for distinguishing among presidential initiatives. First, some proposals, if enacted, have greater consequences for groups within the population, for particular areas of public policy, or for the polity as a whole. They differ in their *impact.* Consider the two proposals from the Carter administration mentioned above. If hospital cost containment had become law, it would have fundamentally altered the procedures by which hospitals throughout the nation calibrate their prices and administer their services. The administration claimed that hospital cost containment should be viewed as part of the overall effort to vanquish the inflation bugaboo and secure the conditions needed to introduce national health insurance. Providing new management for an oil reserve in Alaska, on the other hand, offered at best modest returns from expedited extraction of petroleum on one area of federal land. Presidents cannot command Congress to take up either type of issue, but they have commanded more attention on the big issues. Less significant proposals have had to compete with the agendas pursued by other players in the tandem-institutions setting.

Second, unlike the National Petroleum Reserve, the plan to regulate hospital costs lay at the core of Carter's legislative interests. An enormous amount of *effort* was expended by the administration to pass the legislation. It was a campaign pledge, ensconced in *Promises, Promises,* the White House document outlining the commitments made on the 1976 campaign trail.[5] Carter's critics charged him with presenting too subdued a presidential profile on hospital cost containment, yet he made at least general reference to the program in fifty-two statements, messages, or appearances during the four years of his administration. Thirteen presidential mentions a year contrasts sharply with the two associated with the petroleum reserve. The hospital cost control legislation enjoyed a higher priority and considerably more administration attention—or, more precisely, more White House attention— than the other measure. But for hospital cost containment, like all

---

Public Policy: The Four Arenas of Presidential Power (University: University of Alabama Press, 1983); Aaron Wildavsky, "The Two Presidencies," and Donald A. Peppers, "Two Presidencies: Eight Years Later," both in *Perspectives on the Presidency,* ed. Aaron Wildavsky (Boston: Little, Brown, 1975), pp. 448–471.

5. John K. Ingelhart, "And Now It's Carter's Turn to Try to Control Health Costs," *National Journal,* April 9, 1977, p. 551.

complex legislation impinging upon so many aspects of the American political system, administration lobbying influenced congressional action only at the margin. Often that margin is too small to make a difference.[6]

Finally, the introduction of the two proposals produced or initiated very different kinds of *politics*. Whereas the regulatory aspects of hospital cost containment triggered contention and controversy, and the potent opposition of various groups representing the medical establishment, the petroleum reserve legislation prompted little in the way of opposition that could not be resolved fairly easily through compromise. By their very natures, these two initiatives engendered contrasting responses on Capitol Hill. The president's role in legislative policy making, and the response to the executive's initiatives, depend on the type of policy under consideration, because the structural implications of the tandem-institutions setting differs across policy domains.

Impact

Presidential initiatives vary widely in their importance, however one defines the dimension. Standing out among the hundreds of pieces of legislation offered by presidents in the modern era are Eisenhower's successful effort to enact labor law reform; the 1964 Kennedy-Johnson tax cut contributing to years of economic growth; the myriad social welfare and civil rights programs of Johnson's Great Society; the extensive energy legislation emerging from the Carter years; and the Omnibus Budget and Reconciliation Act of 1981, part of Reagan's economic recovery program that fundamentally altered the direction of federal commitments and expenditures. While presidents and their administrations must of necessity focus much of their time and energy on the more routine matters of government, or on nonlegislative crisis management, some portion of the legislation they propose, and some portion of that which gets enacted, represents significant policy departures.

As John Campbell suggests in his analysis of Japanese aging policy, initiatives can be distinguished along two dimensions rele-

6. The theme of the marginal impact of presidential lobbying is discussed in George C. Edwards III, *At the Margins: Presidential Leadership of Congress* (New Haven: Yale University Press, 1989), esp. chap. 10.

vant to innovation.[7] First, in simplified form, their budgetary or social impact can be either large or small. Second, they can represent either a continuation or modification of old programs or an entirely new policy departure. Presidents are most innovative when they introduce legislation that is both "large" and "new." "Small" initiatives affecting "old" or existing programs are the least innovative. This variable, and others explored in this chapter, are described in Appendix D.

The scope of presidential initiatives has implications for evaluating the performance of the presidency and Congress as tandem policy-making institutions, and from a more general view, the capacity of the overall political system to make fundamental social choices. The level and pervasiveness of conflict within the legislative system cannot be understood without ascertaining the significance of the issues on which it occurs. Coalitional struggle that translates into institutional conflict should be anticipated and accepted as the consequence of deliberations on major policy questions of the day. But if such conflict characterizes more routine interactions between the president and Congress, legitimate questions about the functioning of the political system are germane.

On another level, when one is assessing the legislative "success" of the presidency as a whole, or of particular presidents, the appraisals should be sensitive to whether success or failure occurs on significant or relatively insignificant legislation. Let us posit two hypothetical chief executives, each with a legislative success rate of 60%. One has seen 80 of his 200 proposals go down to defeat in one fashion or another, but they were all relatively inconsequential measures. The other had 40 of her 100 initiatives fail in the legislature, but each of them derived from the part of her program most committed to fundamental change. With their equivalent success rates, should the two presidents be accorded the same level of policy achievement? To answer affirmatively would be to render meaningless our assessments of presidential legislative leadership. While the two hypothetical cases may describe unrealistic extremes, the distinctions are relevant. Most conventional empirical measures of success, for instance, show that President Kennedy did not suffer too greatly; but of the pro-

7. John Creighton Campbell, "The Old People Boom and Japanese Policy Making," *Journal of Japanese Studies* 5 (Summer 1979): 329–350.

grams identified as most important to his administration, legislative enactment proved more elusive.[8] Even if one is interested only in the generic presidency across administrations, the fact or fiction of presidential leadership of the legislative agenda depends considerably on whether presidential coalitions in the Congress are able to win when significant issues are involved.

So far I have discussed the idea of impact—consequence, importance, significance—in the most general of terms. There are a variety of ways, however, in which to give definition to the concept. One approach is to return to the innovation dimension discussed earlier, and to distinguish large proposals from small ones, new departures from old ones. Of the specific initiatives in my sample, 12% involved both large and new programs. Most of the proposals (58%), however, dealt with small changes in existing programs. Such adjustments are what Bert Rockman would call incremental change, prevalent in a governmental system in an advanced state of equilibrium and with an elaborate structure of interest groups.[9]

Proposals entailing large changes in the existing structure of the public sector, either by introducing entirely new programs or by dramatically expanding existing ones, will be controversial as they challenge prevailing patterns of interaction. Proposals representing smaller substantive changes will not stimulate the same kind of politics. According to Campbell:

> Most case studies about policy-making are written about decisions which involve both a new idea and a significant commitment of national resources . . . Because such legislation perceptibly changes the relationship between the state and large segments of society, considerable publicity will be generated, and a variety of groups will attempt to participate

8. Erwin C. Hargrove, *The Power of the Modern Presidency* (New York: Knopf, 1974), p. 211.

9. Paul C. Light, "Passing Nonincremental Policy," and *The President's Agenda: Domestic Policy Choice from Kennedy to Carter* (Baltimore: Johns Hopkins University Press, 1982). See also Bert A. Rockman, *The Leadership Question: The Presidency and the American System* (New York: Praeger, 1984), pp. 22–24. Large policies divide into cases of "accelerative change," involving the more rapid expansion of existing programs (mostly large-old), and "innovative change," reflecting significant adjustments in the direction of current policies and institutions (mostly large-new).

Table 5.1   Congressional responses to presidential proposals and
innovativeness of the initiatives

Type of program	N	Inaction	Congressional response			
			Opposition dominance	Compromise	Presidential dominance	Consensus
Large/new	35	20%	40%	11%	20%	9%
Large/old	37	11%	27%	32%	16%	14%
Small/new	55	29%	18%	7%	11%	34%
Small/old	172	28%	16%	22%	8%	26%

Note: N = 299; chi square = 35.75; $p < .001$.
Source: See Appendixes C and D.

in the decision-making process . . . The outcome of decision making in the large-new arena will in some sense represent the balance of effective power in the country as a whole . . .

Since by definition . . . small-new programs either affect relatively few people in significant ways or affect somewhat larger numbers less significantly, fewer interests are engaged and participation will be narrower than in the large-new arena. Only the few administrative agencies, interest groups, and politicians already directly concerned with the narrowly defined policy area will become involved.[10]

When these patterns prevail, large presidential proposals draw active legislative attention and trigger congressional responses involving explicit conflict more often than their smaller counterparts, which elicit proportionately more occasions of consensus. Table 5.1 reports these results. Overall, small proposals led to legislative inaction twice as often as large ones, 29% to 15%. Proposals, both old and new, involving large programmatic impacts were resolved in the wake of a public struggle with a frequency roughly twice that of the small initiatives, one-half compared to one-quarter. In conflictive situations the president's position, represented by the presidential coalition on the Hill, also tended to fare rather badly, especially when the issues comprised new policy departures: 40% of the initiatives were defeated outright.

10. Campbell, "The Old People Boom," pp. 329, 339.

Presidents offering initiatives that make adjustments to existing programmatic arrangements are casting their proposals into already established policy communities consisting of participants with stakes to protect and resources to exploit. If anything resembling subgovernments do exist, they are located in policy areas where past government programs created clienteles or attracted otherwise actively interested parties. When initiatives are launched that modify those programs, organized interests are more likely to become activated, if not agitated, because established and ongoing programs become accepted as legitimate.[11] The public and private interests represented in the established policy communities often have enough political clout to thwart or at least amend proposed changes, if the challenge is great enough.[12]

As shown in Table 5.1, congressional compromises were most prevalent for proposals of any size intended to alter established programs. Often these proposals were linked to the reauthorization of expiring legislation, a fact prompting both active consideration by the Hill and the involvement of an established policy community. Several other "old" proposals were more easy to compromise because they concerned budget and appropriations issues.[13] Since funds must be allocated each year, only one of thirty-seven of these proposals (3%) suffered inaction. The dollar figures, too, allowed disagreements to be resolved by splitting the differences, an option not available for other kinds of issues.

Finally, since the perception of adverse consequences is minimal for programs with a small policy impact, they were more readily decided by consensus. In fact, about a third of "small" initiatives that challenged no existing government activity enjoyed a consensual response. They constituted two-thirds of the small initiatives that received favorable action by Congress and half of those accorded any legislative action at all.

11. Michael T. Hayes, *Lobbyists and Legislators: A Theory of Political Markets* (New Brunswick, N.J.: Rutgers University Press, 1981), p. 66; and James Q. Wilson, *Political Organizations* (New York: Basic Books, 1973), pp. 331–337.

12. Dorothy Buckton James, *The Contemporary President* (New York: Pegasus, 1969), p. 126; Theodore J. Lowi, *The End of Liberalism: Ideology, Policy, and the Crisis of Public Authority* (New York: W. W. Norton, 1969).

13. Campbell notes that for small-old decisions, "the typical process is budgeting." "The Old People Boom," p. 346.

The impact of legislation can also be thought of in terms of its perceived importance in the Washington community. Since Congressional Quarterly and the *National Journal* provide both practitioners and students of politics with an inside view of Washington affairs, the information they report can be used to divide the presidential proposals into categories of importance. As explained in Appendix D, the proposals in the sample are identified as being associated with major bills, minor bills, or bills of intermediate importance. Forty-seven percent of the initiatives were components of bills that fit the description of major legislation.[14]

The legislative workload on Capitol Hill is enormous. In *each* Congress over the last thirty years, well over ten thousand bills have been introduced in the House of Representatives, and often more than four thousand in the Senate.[15] Each bill encompasses an additional number of separate specific proposals. Given these burdens, and the time limitations confronted by members of Congress, the energies of representatives and senators must be concentrated on the issues of greater rather than lesser importance. A substantial portion of major legislation bears the imprimatur of the president. Therefore, the presidential initiatives most ignored by the Hill over the past three decades have been proposals linked to minor legislation, whereas the major initiatives have almost always enjoyed some kind of active review, as demonstrated in Table 5.2. Few proposals linked to major programs survived an entire administration without some form of congressional response, whereas 54% of the minor legislative proposals received no congressional action. Once the minor initiatives did receive full-scale attention, the bulk passed consensually. Since 81% of the least important measures ended in either congressional inaction or consensus, evidently the factor determining the fate of these initiatives was whether or not space could be found for them on the crowded agenda.

Initiatives tied to major legislation may have secured a place on the active agenda fairly easily, but they received a wider range of responses from Congress. More often than in other cases, they

14. Fewer than 10% of the specific proposals in the sample satisfied the definition of "major" legislation.

15. Norman J. Ornstein, Thomas E. Mann, and Michael J. Malbin, eds., *Vital Statistics on Congress, 1987–1988* (Washington, D.C.: American Enterprise Institute, 1987), pp. 165–167.

Table 5.2   Congressional responses to presidential proposals and
importance of the overall program of which the presidential
proposal was a part

Importance of overall program		Congressional decision-making process				
	N	Inaction	Opposition dominance	Compromise	Presidential dominance	Consensus
Major	140	14%	27%	21%	19%	20%
Intermediate	107	26%	18%	22%	7%	28%
Minor	52	54%	8%	12%	0%	27%

Note: N = 299; chi square = 50.13; $p < .001$.
Source: See Appendixes C and D.

saw resolution in which one faction defeated its opposition by
dominance (46%). While presidential coalitions were defeated a
majority of the time in these public disputes, they fared better on
major legislation than when a struggle ensued on more minor programs. Despite the fact that 27% of the proposals associated with
major bills were actively defeated, presidents actually enjoyed
greater overall legislative success on the major initiatives than on
less important legislation. For the initiatives in the major category, 60% were enacted at least in part, compared to 39% of the
most minor proposals.

Moreover, when the congressional response was not favorable,
in no case involving minor legislation was there an indication
that presidents sought out administrative or judicial means for
accomplishing at least partially their policy objectives. There
was some evidence of exploitation of nonlegislative remedies
when major legislation was involved. Indeed, with the addition
of these instances of independent executive action, a total programmatic loss to the president occurred on only 36% of the
proposals attached to major programs. Over the past three
decades presidents have proposed a considerable amount of legislation in the domestic field, much of it found in major bills.
While coalitional conflict has been most readily apparent in the
case of the most significant legislation, even those proposals
have not usually involved direct confrontations. Presidents have
not been as frustrated, nor have the two branches experienced as

much conflict, as one might believe from presidency-centered commentators.

The innovativeness and importance of the policies included in the president's domestic agenda, therefore, have significance beyond their role in shaping the politics of how the issues are resolved. Nurtured in presidency-centered politics, we have come to expect most major policy innovations and systemic reforms to spring from the executive. It is to the White House that the public turns for leadership; it is by the scope of the president's aspirations and accomplishments that it evaluates presidential performance. As Reo Christenson suggests:

> Both historians and voters judge a president partly by what he tried to achieve, and not merely by what he succeeds in doing. Our economic and political system has become so resistant to major reform that only a president's trumpet notes, sounded repeatedly and insistently, can sometimes make major reforms a possibility. If not in that president's day, then in one of his successor's.[16]

How have presidents in the modern era fared in these terms? Of the 299 proposals in the sample, 67 entailed relatively significant budgetary or social impacts, although few would be considered to represent a fundamental restructuring of the programmatic or political systems. In addition, successful enactment of the president's program became more elusive when the issues involved significant new departures in policy. On the other hand, on these toughest issues of all—large, new policy departures—Presidents Eisenhower through Reagan legislatively won some measure of what they proposed about 40% of the time; and 62% of the proposals introducing substantial changes (additions or deletions) in existing programs were at least partially accepted. When the analysis is presented from the perspective of program importance, the president's position prevailed most of the time on proposals tied to major legislation, and success was higher there than in the case of minor legislation. Certainly these presidents were more successful when their initiatives had been designed to preserve the policy status quo rather than challenge it (75% compared to 53%).

16. Reo M. Christenson, "Presidential Leadership of Congress," in *Rethinking the Presidency*, ed. Thomas E. Cronin (Boston: Little, Brown, 1978), p. 261.

This was also true when acceptance of a presidential proposal required no congressional activity instead of positive action (71% success compared to 54%). But presidents, as these figures indicate, witnessed a majority of their initiatives enacted even when they introduced change and required formal mobilization of congressional support.

Although not the norm, presidents and their congressional allies have been able to propose and enact legislation of some consequence. And when legislative passage has not proven possible, presidents have often been willing to pursue nonlegislative means to accomplish their goals. It bears repeating that presidential success with innovative proposals does not generally derive from scaling back or distorting true presidential policy preferences in order to accommodate the known or anticipated positions of members of Congress when proposals are being formulated. In short, enactment of these initiatives represents real legislative accomplishment in the face of the contextual uncertainties imposed by the tandem-institutions setting.

Effort

Not only do legislative proposals submitted by the president vary in their level of importance, they also differ according to their priority on the presidential agenda. While each initiative may be transmitted to the Hill with the chief executive's signature, of the hundreds of proposals found in the numerous presidential statements and addresses, relatively few are of central concern to the White House—or, more fundamentally, to the president. In the words of a Reagan aide, "I could tell you some 300 to 400 issues that have kicked around in the cabinet system in the last two and a half years. Clearly we have not engaged in a marketing campaign on 400 issues." Rather, administrations organize their legislative efforts in response to the diverse nature of the presidential program and the scarcity of resources available to market the individual components of that program.

Interviews with officials in the Executive Office of the President revealed what tends to be a four-level hierarchy of priority assigned to legislation. The fourth or lowest level in the ordering does not concern us here, as it pertains to those issues that may be live in the Congress but on which the administration has offered no proposals and taken no known position.[17] The next level of concern, involving agency legislation, also does not apply to this study of *presidential* proposals, for the legislative issues are handled entirely in the departments or agencies without reference to a presidential initiative. The departments may well be pursuing programmatic goals of the administration writ large, but the proposals themselves have not received specific presidential attention. The two highest levels in the hierarchy, however, are relevant to the president's program. I distinguish between those issues most central to the president and the White House, and those left to cabinet secretaries and their departments.[18]

It is essential for two reasons to differentiate levels of priority. First, these distinctions have significance for evaluating the substantive *outcomes* of the congressional deliberations engendered by the initiatives. One may well ask, Should we assess presidential performance on the basis of the hundreds of measures that constitute the president's program, including those rather distant from presidential concerns, or should our assessment be focused on what each president really wanted to accomplish, involving those issues in which the administration indicated the most interest? It is, of course, valid to consider critically the scope of a president's policy ambitions and the consonance between those aspirations and the demands of the times. We may not wish to reward with great praise a presidency that provided "successful" leadership on a meager and insignificant agenda, even if that agenda reflected the full extent of the president's interest. On the other hand, if we are to appraise accurately presidential legislative leadership in general, or individual presidents in particular, some special consideration should be given those measures that attracted higher presidential attention. In the context of this study, in other words, what kinds of congressional responses are produced when proposals are of particular interest to the initiating president?

A second imperative for distinguishing among the priorities of proposals is implicit in the discussion about assessing outcomes. Initiatives that are of higher priority to a president and the White House staff, that are the marrow of a president's policy interests,

17. Interview with a Republican official.

18. One may also wish to divide proposals at the level of White House concern into two categories: those of clear personal interest to the president, and those of White House but not presidential significance. Interview with a Carter official.

are likely to be those on which the administration, from the agency congressional liaison offices up to the president, expend the most time, energy, and resources. Again, in this *process* sense, all presidential proposals are not the same. The effort behind them is different. If legislative skills have any bearing on the manner in which policy choices are made on the Hill, their effects presumably would be on those issues for which the administration's collective talents are applied most directly and forcefully. In addition, the very nature of the political system—where fragmentation of decision structures is the norm, wide-ranging policy demands from numerous sources are continually circulating, and political resources are scarce and expendable—necessitates identification of the top priorities from the mass of proposals. Presidents have an incentive to outline their priorities. And those issues that become the main focus of congressional action have choices made about them that are influenced more by the lobbying activities of the administration's personnel than is true of lesser-priority initiatives.

In the modern era, administration lobbying has come to include a greater emphasis on strategies of legislative influence that extend beyond direct interactions between members of the executive and legislative establishments. As Samuel Kernell has put it, for some of their initiatives presidents now "go public," trying to rally popular support for the administration's position in ways that influence congressional decision making.[19] Jeffrey Tulis sees in this strategy a deeply rooted transformation of the American presidency as an institution, with a shift to an emphasis on public rhetoric.[20] He notes that "since the presidencies of Theodore Roosevelt and Woodrow Wilson, popular or mass rhetoric has become a principal tool of presidential governance. Presidents regularly 'go over the heads' of Congress to the people at large in support of legislation and other initiatives."[21] In *The Personal Presidency* Theodore Lowi arrives at similar conclusions. He discovers in Franklin Roosevelt the first peacetime "personal" president whose activities, approaches, and strategies set the stage for the "plebiscitary presidency." The weakened traditional party appa-

19. Samuel Kernell, *Going Public: New Strategies of Presidential Leadership* (Washington, D.C.: CQ Press, 1986).

20. Jeffrey K. Tulis, *The Rhetorical Presidency* (Princeton: Princeton University Press, 1987), p. 7.

21. Ibid., p. 4.

ratus was shunned in favor of direct appeals to the public, an institutional transformation that is grounded in the executive's claim that the president is the people's representative.[22]

It would be a mistake to read too much into this institutional change, especially to find the presidential-congressional inter-actions of the past couple of decades decidedly different from those of the more distant past. Presidents and their aides still talk and bargain with members of Congress and their staffs. Even though his analysis emphasized the essential elements of bar-gaining and persuasion, Richard Neustadt was careful to note in 1960 the value of the president's "public prestige" in gaining con-gressional support through a more expansive view of negotia-tions.[23] Continuing transformations of the media certainly have sharpened some elements of public-oriented strategies, but those strategies still must be integrated with more traditional occasions of exchange.

One would be wrong also to take too simplistic a view of efforts to mobilize the public. As Kernell points out, appeals to the public take many forms, as does the meaning of "public" as a target of presidential influence. National television addresses by the presi-dent represent one important and effective means for mobilizing support for the president's interests, but the technique must be used sparingly if it is not to diminish in value.[24] More specifically:

> Going public is neither premised on, nor does it promote, a perception of America as a homogeneous society. Nor does it reduce politics to a plebiscite in which the president seeks continually to bring the weight of national opinion to bear in the resolution of policy questions. Governance under individ-ualized pluralism remains largely a process of assembling temporary coalitions from among diverse constituencies. For this purpose, minor presidential addresses directed toward special constituencies are particularly well suited.[25]

22. Theodore J. Lowi, *The Personal Presidency: Power Invested, Promise Unfulfilled* (Ithaca, N.Y.: Cornell University Press, 1985), esp. p. 65.

23. Richard E. Neustadt, *Presidential Power: The Politics of Leader-ship from FDR to Carter* (New York: Macmillan, 1980), chap. 5. The original volume was published in 1960.

24. Kernell, *Going Public*, p. 145.

25. Ibid., p. 91.

The significant feature of any of these approaches is the tapping and mobilization of the public, including specialized publics as constituencies, directly at the grass-roots level instead of conducting negotiations among elected officials and group leaders without a public component.[26] Sometimes this style of lobbying through the public will include not only mobilization but education or opinion leadership as well.[27] Because of their unusual visibility and therefore centrality in the media, presidents brandishing persuasive oratory are sometimes able to stimulate the kind of public attitudes and issue salience that are the prerequisites of going public.[28]

In a fairly direct way, presidents indicate their priorities by their choice of settings in which to advertise their initiatives. They announce policy proposals in forums that range from televised appeals before a joint session of Congress to "town meetings" in small New England communities. A standard technique for identifying issues of special significance to a president is to examine the content of the State of the Union addresses.[29] As one Reagan official commented when discussing the means for identifying President Reagan's central interests, "You usually can tell pretty easily in this administration. If something is new and takes up more than one paragraph in the State of the Union Address, then it is a presidential initiative, and he really wants it. Virtually all other cases are agency-sponsored legislation."

One must also look elsewhere to recognize presidential priorities. Not all newly inaugurated chief executives give State of the Union addresses in their initial year, and some proposals delivered by other means in that crucial period of the administration may well pass prior to the next opportunity for a State of the Union address. Even when the State of the Union addresses are

26. Ibid., p. 38.

27. George C. Edwards III, *The Public Presidency: The Pursuit of Public Support* (New York: St. Martin's Press, 1983), esp. pp. 38–103; Kernell, *Going Public*, pp. 150–153; and Dean Keith Simonton, *Why Presidents Succeed: A Political Psychology of Leadership* (New Haven: Yale University Press, 1987), p. 116.

28. Benjamin I. Page and Robert Y. Shapiro, "Presidential Leadership through Public Opinion," in *The Presidency and Public Policy Making*, ed. George C. Edwards III, Steven A. Shull, and Norman C. Thomas (Pittsburgh: University of Pittsburgh Press, 1985), pp. 22–36.

29. Light, "Passing Nonincremental Policy," p. 6.

conveyed to Congress, there is no consistency in their form. Some are short, rather rhetorical assertions of philosophical principles, others are lengthy enumerations of diverse legislative requests. Sometimes, as was the case with President Carter, they are both— relatively brief messages delivered in person followed by a written compendium of presidential policy preferences. Former Carter speechwriter Hedrick Hertzberg suggests that the process of producing a State of the Union address is like "a great big family sitting around the dinner table."[30] The demands for space in the speech are regulated by presidential aides, but there are a great many topics that may get included by various members of the "family." Not everything is going to receive extensive presidential attention. Finally, issues significant to the president may arise *after* a State of the Union address and be resolved prior to the subsequent January.

Examining several different types of statements by the chief executive, however, permits identification of three levels of presidential legislative priority: highest, medium, and lowest, as explained in Appendix D. Roughly half of the presidential proposals in the sample were associated with highest-priority legislation, one-third were of medium priority, and 15% fell into the lowest-priority category. Recall that the entire sample includes only administration proposals with some kind of specific presidential endorsement.

The presidential priority of legislation, and the effort expended by the White House on its behalf, can also be seen in the frequency with which presidents furnished some kind of general public statement about the policy. A fifth of the initiatives in the sample, for example, received only one presidential mention, and that occurred in the documents announcing the proposals. Another fifth were mentioned in ten or more statements, addresses, or speeches by the president during the period that the proposals were under consideration on Capitol Hill. If we take the length of administrations into account, the number of monthly presidential references ranged from 0.01 to 20, with an average of a little over one a month.

An additional indication of the priority of legislation to the president is where the draft bill was formulated. Reports in the

30. Quoted in John H. Kessel, *Presidential Parties* (Homewood, Ill.: Dorsey Press, 1984), p. 150.

Congressional Quarterly *Almanac* and other sources indicate, for instance, that 15% of the proposals in the sample involved legislative drafts produced by the White House or special commissions and task forces, whereas 75% were apparently drafted in the agencies or departments of the bureaucracy. The remaining 10% involved cases in which the president assimilated a version of legislation already circulating on the Hill or made a proposal without including a draft of the legislation.

The White House staff may be employed to handle legislation for policy proposals that have no natural policy home in existing agencies or departments if, as often happens, the issue cuts across jurisdictional boundaries. But explicit White House participation, or the use of commissions and task forces, can suggest a higher level of presidential commitment than is the case for legislation left to the departments. There are undoubtedly exceptions to this generalization, but in combination with the other measures of presidential priority the distinction is useful for discriminating among the proposals according to their centrality to the presidential program and the lobbying effort they were afforded.

So far, I have referred to presidential priority and lobbying effort as though the two factors were intrinsically linked. The priority of an issue to the president and the administration serves as a key determinant in the White House decisions that are made about how various parts of the presidential program should be sold to Congress.[31] But one must go a step further and elaborate on the sources of the relationship between the centrality of an issue to the president and the strategies that are employed to get it enacted.

The argument is quite simple. Presidents and their staffs are generally aware of the relative importance of the various legislative proposals that make up the overall program of the president. They are also cognizant of the limits imposed by the finite amount of time, energy, and expertise that they can bring to bear on each proposal. These constraints necessitate a degree of specialization throughout the government. When it comes to the "focusing" function of lobbying—nurturing and maintaining congressional attention on the president's initiatives—decisions are required about what units in the administration are to

31. Light, *The President's Agenda*, pp. 75–76.

shoulder responsibility for pressing the program on the Hill.[32] There are simply too many issues for them all to be managed by the White House staff. According to a Republican domestic policy adviser, "The White House needs to focus on the big issues. There's a limit to the number of issues the White House can handle. On the more minor issues, the departments have to carry the water."

Just as there is a hierarchy delineating the level of priority given a policy proposal, there is also a hierarchy of responsibility for lobbying the president's program. The two structures are closely interrelated. The Reagan administration formulated its own variant of the hierarchy, yet the design it followed, as described by a senior appointed official in OMB, is not unique:

> The way we tend to do things is that we [in OMB] will get together with the cabinet secretaries and their people. If it's an agency thing, and not presidential, and if they want our advice, then we'll help. If they want to do it on their own, then we will release them to do that; or if we think there are some presidential concerns, then we'll try to constrain them. If it is a larger piece of legislation, or a precedent will be set that you want—or you want to avoid—and it's at a level of generality which does not fit neatly into any one agency area, then we run things out of the Executive Office. For the big issues, it goes through the Legislative Strategy Group, with [James] Baker and [Edwin] Meese and the boys. If it's not like that, then [David] Stockman and the associate directors in the substantive policy areas will decide what will be done.

While other presidencies have not placed as much coordinating authority in the Office of Management and Budget, and the Legislative Strategy Group (LSG) was an invention of the Reagan White House, other administrations have followed similar patterns for allocating the proposals and strategic efforts. Perhaps no other topic in my interviews produced as much consistency of response.

In each administration there appeared to be a lexicographic decision process for determining lobbying responsibilities. There need not be a formal checklist, or even a conscious set of decision rules, but my interviews make it clear that proposals that did not involve a definitive presidential or White House interest were left

32. Light, "Passing Nonincremental Policy," p. 71.

to the agencies and departments in each administration. As a White House congressional liaison aide said, the "White House is responsible for everything and at the same time nothing"; presidential staffs enjoy considerable flexibility in determining their own participation. To a considerable extent, that decision is based on the level of Executive Office interest. This link between low-level priority and agency lobbying effort may be complicated by two factors, however. First, there is no need for White House direction of the lobbying effort, even on issues of major interest to it, if victory is assured.[33] One Carter aide commented, "I can't emphasize too strongly that the White House staff is wasting its time if it works on votes that it will win 90 to 6." Second, even proposals not at the core of the agenda may move into the White House sphere of operations if trouble is anticipated on the Hill. Frustrated departmental liaison personnel often solicit the assistance of those in the White House when events take a turn for the worse.

On the next rung up the priority ladder, coordination of congressional liaison activities resides in the White House, primarily with the staff serving in the office responsible for legislative relations. Unless there is evidence of trouble or the issue involved is fundamental to the president, the congressional liaison staff performs most of the lobbying duties with little assistance from others in the Executive Office.

Some issues, because of their centrality in the presidential agenda and the intensity of the president's interest, benefit from what many dubbed "the full court press." In these situations the relevant agencies and the entire White House staff may become active participants in the effort to win enactment of the president's initiatives. During Reagan's first term, the leadership of the LSG was engaged in harnessing all of the resources available to the president. In the Carter White House, a senior presidential aide commented relative to major issues like hospital cost containment:

33. Congressional leaders employ the same decision rule in selecting the legislation with which they will get involved. As reported by Barbara Sinclair: "Expected closeness of the fight still affects the leadership's level of resource expenditure [on the programs of their party's president]. If leaders anticipate no trouble or if they think winning is completely impossible, they will not mount a massive effort." *Majority Leadership in the U.S. House* (Baltimore: Johns Hopkins University Press, 1983), p. 127.

We used the task force approach on the big stuff. There would
be a point person responsible for organizing and managing
the task force. We would have a chairman, usually on a
rotating basis . . . The task forces included all of the White
House departments that were essential. Those included the
press people, congressional liaison, public liaison, OMB, and
intergovernmental affairs—the Watson shop—if that was
appropriate, and, mostly in the early days, a representative
from Hamilton's [Jordan] office, though they tended to
wander in and out.

In the less institutionalized Johnson White House, a senior aide to
the President noted that "on the big ones we would use the whole
staff." An individual with experience in several Republican
administrations described the traditional, full-scale lobbying process:

All get together and are involved in a campaign, really. Each
group does its thing. Public liaison mobilizes groups. If it's an
issue having to do with space, they'll go out and talk to the
Aerospace Association, the National Electronics Association,
the California delegation, all of these types. Congressional
Affairs will touch all of its congressional bases. And the
Domestic Council will monitor what's going on, using the
enlightenment of the feedback. The press people will check
the papers, make sure that the major columnists are saying
nice things about the proposal, and they'll send out hundreds
of press releases to all the small-town newspapers across the
country. The Reagan people have done a good job of this.
They have set up an office that not only schedules the
speeches, but also provides what to say. They produce two- to
three-page speech inserts. So if someone's going to go and
address the orange growers in Southern California, they may
also mention the importance of the administration proposal
for a flight to Mars in 1990. This is the orthodox way, when
you have a full court press.

One facet of the full court press, of course, may be the direct
involvement of the president, either as lobbyist or as public moti-
vator. What are the informal rules that govern unleashing the
most potent political resource in each administration? First, obviously, is the matter of priority. President Carter told me, "I

would try not to get involved in that process unless the legislation was important enough to warrant my direct consideration." Nearly everyone I interviewed ratified in some way the sentiments of one congressional liaison aide who said, "I always thought that my most precious commodity was the president's time"; in other words, that time was not to be squandered on unimportant matters. The chief executive is brought in when the president's personal impact is likely to be the greatest, when the last few votes are needed, "when it came down to, as Lyndon Johnson used to say, 'the short strokes' "—perhaps "when all else fails."[34]

While one avoids wasting the president on less significant issues, or those for which success is not in doubt, several aides indicated some hesitancy about employing the president as lobbyist when outright defeat is likely. In short, the decision to use the president may reflect an assessment of "winnability" that avoids either extreme.

Finally, decisions to involve the president take into consideration the effects of overuse on the value of the presidential "commodity." An assistant to President Carter highlighted the problem:

> You have to be careful when you use the president. A visit with the president or a call from the president has to be an event in the life of a senator or representative, or it loses its magic. Or they say, "Why should I give you a commitment, [respondent's name]? I want to talk to the President. John has talked to the President. And George has talked to the President. Are you taking us for granted?" You've got to be sure that you don't squander him. If a call from you or [chief domestic adviser] Stuart Eizenstat or a cabinet secretary is almost as good, then you use them instead.

Almost by definition, then, for the call from Air Force One or the meeting in the Oval Office to remain effective, direct presidential involvement must be used sparingly. Even the White House establishment carries its own aura, one diminished by excessive familiarity. The president speaks to the public, or addresses specialized constituencies, with the same kind of con-

34. Interviews with President Carter and aides to Presidents Ford, Carter, and Reagan.

cern about priorities. It is therefore in the interest of the president and White House aides to reserve most of their efforts for the proposals most conducive to furthering the primary goals pursued by the administration. It is on these issues that they will work the hardest, that most of the resources of the presidency will be committed, that the most likely tests of the president's political skill and acumen will ensure. They are also likely to be the proposals on which some form of congressional action is most assured.

Now that we have considered in some detail the nature of presidential priorities and legislative effort, it is essential to note that their effects on congressional action defy simple generalizations. Two countervailing forces are at work. Proposals can pass or fail owing to the inherent contentiousness of the issues involved, or as a result of the intensity and persuasiveness of the campaign to enact them. Lowest-priority initiatives, for instance, may consist of easily resolvable issues, but they may have trouble getting positioned on the congressional agenda, a disadvantage exacerbated by the modest or nonexistent activities implemented by the administration to press the Congress into action. Highest-priority proposals, on the other hand, are most likely to reap the benefits of the full court press, but they are also apt to embrace controversial and threatening issues. Further, if the White House establishment led by the president husbands its resources for situations where the outcome is most uncertain, then extensive effort may be linked to cases in which Congress responds unfavorably to the president's initiative. It is not necessarily true that the lobbying efforts of the White House are ineffectual, only that intensive marketing activities are initiated in the most challenging of circumstances, in which a significant number of defeats are almost certain to occur.

Because proposals of low presidential priority rarely attract much in the way of administration efforts to focus congressional attention on them, and one may assume that administration lobbying efforts have some impact, it is not surprising to find many of these proposals ignored on the Hill. During the Eisenhower to Reagan presidencies, congressional inaction was the most frequent congressional response to lowest-priority issues, accounting for 43% of the cases, twice the percentage for proposals tied to highest-priority programs. Initiatives ending in inaction were also subject to executive neglect, receiving fewer monthly mentions (0.54) by the president, on average, than any other part of the president's program.

Legislation drafted in the departments and agencies was also slightly more likely to be ignored than initiatives receiving more direct White House attention (28% compared to 20%).

The greatest coalitional conflict, leading to either opposition or presidential dominance, occurred when congressional consideration was given to the issues of highest priority to the president, and the ones produced by the White House itself. The contrast between high-priority issues and low-priority issues is striking, with 43% of the former being decided by either presidential or opposition dominance, in contrast to 15% of the latter. Presidential defeat was more likely than victory in these situations; still, presidents fared better on the high-priority issues. And for the proposals that teetered between legislative success and failure for the president's coalition, presidents expended their most significant efforts in support of their program. The most extensive White House efforts were put behind those initiatives in which the president's position finally prevailed in a clash of coalitions, to judge by the average of 3.2 monthly presidential references they received, which is far higher than any other category of congressional action. In those instances when the battle lines were drawn and presidents gave dramatic emphasis to the intensity of their policy interests, they enjoyed more legislative success.

White House lobbying, of course, extends far beyond the definition of priorities and direct communication with Congress. If Samuel Kernell and other scholars are correct in their assessment of the growing importance of presidential mobilization of either the public or specialized constituencies, then we need to investigate the influence of more public-oriented activities coordinated by the White House. We need to know when, and to what effect, presidents over the past three decades have, first, reached out to the entire nation through broadcasts on television or radio; second, sought the support of segments of the public with special messages or appearances; and third, not pursued a strategy of public mobilization.

In addition, it is necessary to know something about the conditions underlying public strategies that either enhance or diminish their efficacy. In Chapter 4, for example, I suggested that efforts to build on public approval of the president's job performance to garner support for the executive's program are considerably less effective when the president is supported by less than half the public. With respect to attributes of the proposals themselves, it is difficult to employ a pure strategy of public mobilization if the public is not interested in the policy under review. In fact, we might expect both the president and Congress to react quite differently to proposals by virtue of their relative salience to the public. If we look at the public's responses to the Gallup poll's frequently repeated question about the most important problem facing the country, 203 (68%) of the proposals in the sample did not pertain to any of the policy issues raised by the public around the time that the proposals were considered in Congress. Thirty-two percent were associated with areas of policy identified by some small proportion of the public, and 14 proposals (5%) were tied to problem areas mentioned by half or more of the Gallup poll's respondents. There was far more congressional inaction (28%) on proposals of no public salience than on those tied to national problems recognized by most people (7%). The most prominent issues also engendered the greatest conflict, involving 72% of the proposals, but the president won the majority of these fights. The higher the public salience of the issue area, the more successful was the president.

We are now in a position to address when and with what result presidents in the period under study pursued a public strategy. As is true of other forms of presidential lobbying, limited resources and diminishing marginal returns mean that going public cannot be used in every instance. Television or radio broadcasts were used by Presidents Eisenhower to Reagan to address policies related to 14% of their proposals; another 26% of their proposals were linked to presidential messages to or appearances before more specialized constituencies. Twenty-two percent of the proposals representing large policy departures, however, received at least a general presidential mention on television or radio, compared to only 12% of the small initiatives. The percentages for major and minor legislation are 24% and 2% for broadcast messages, and 56% and 17% for the combination of broadcast and nonbroadcast forms of going public.

The style of public mobilization also varied with the relevant conditions faced by Presidents Eisenhower to Reagan. Conducive conditions were in effect when both the president's job performance was approved of by 50% or more of the public and the percentage of the public identifying the issue area of the president's proposal as a most important problem was greater than zero. The opposite circumstances define adverse conditions for a public strategy. For the proposals in the sample, presidents tended to use public strategies mostly at the extremes, when the conditions were either the best or the worst. The actual type of public strategy varied in appropriate ways. Broadcast strategies predominated when the president was popular and the issues salient, accounting for 38% of the relevant proposals. Only once was television or radio used when things looked more grim.[35] On the other hand, presidents used messages to specific constituencies for half of the proposals considered when conditions for a national public strategy were poor. Similar limited approaches were tied to only 16% of the initiatives given congressional consideration during the best of circumstances.

When conditions were conducive to implementing a strategy of going public, especially efforts to mobilize the public as a whole, both broadcast messages and special messages were effective. When neither approach was employed by the president, 41% of the initiatives received no action in Congress. When television or radio were incorporated into the lobbying effort, the most conflict ensued, with either presidential or opposition dominance prevailing for half of the proposals. In part this is a product of the inherently controversial nature of the large policy departures and major programs that are more likely to be given such presidential attention. But it may also be a consequence of the public strategy itself:

Public discussion requires issues to be stylized in ways that frequently reduce choices to black and white alternatives and to principles that are difficult to modify. In part this reflects

35. When they experience low levels of support among the public, presidents have to be careful about their use of the national media and how the media interpret events and presidential activities. According to Samuel Kernell, correspondents find it much easier to challenge a president with little public support, which may work against a broadcast-oriented public strategy. *Going Public*, p. 148. In addition, Cary Covington has suggested that when issues are divisive for the president's party and public campaigns in behalf of the president's program would only force ideologically distant members of the president's party into opposition, it may be better for the administration to pursue a strategy of "staying private." He finds evidence of such a strategy in the Kennedy and Johnson administrations. " 'Staying Private': Gaining Congressional Support for Unpublicized Presidential Preferences on Roll Call Votes," *Journal of Politics* 49 (August 1987): 737–755.

the rigidifying effect of declaring one's preferences publicly, but it also results from the stylization of issues required to accommodate the limited attention span of the public audience and the brief time slots available on national television. Perhaps more damaging, public discussion tends to harden negotiating positions as both sides posture as much to rally support as to impress the other side. Bargaining and compromise suffer.[36]

Despite conflict, the broadcast strategy led to the greatest presidential success. Overall, 64% of the proposals referred to in a broadcast were enacted in some form, as were 55% of those associated with special messages, compared to the success of only 47% of the initiatives denied any kind of public strategy. And in the case of proposals mentioned in broadcasts, when conflict ensued, the president's coalition prevailed two-thirds of the time.

Going public also proved effective when the president was unpopular and the issue area of little concern to the public. Overall rates of presidential legislative success were much lower, but presidential involvement with specific constituencies through special messages raised the rate of enactment from 18% to 45% and lowered inaction from 64% to 46%. In these situations presidents may have been able to identify pockets of support and attentive publics more attuned to the issues involved. Because the president was unpopular nationally and the issues of little concern to the general public, television or radio was tried only once and to no effect.

One thing that may help to stimulate a public strategy, or reinforce its effectiveness, is the presence of events related to the programmatic area of a proposal. Just as White House activity can be viewed as a focusing action, "focusing events" can take place that reinforce issues already in the congressional field of attention.[37] When events trigger a presidential initiative, or reinforce the position presented by the chief executive and provide distinct symbols for a public-oriented message, they can be used by the administration to speed congressional consideration. President Johnson was particularly adept at exploiting events as catalysts for action. One of his senior aides commented:

36. Kernell, *Going Public*, p. 218.
37. John W. Kingdon, *Agendas, Alternatives, and Public Policies* (Boston: Little, Brown, 1984), p. 265.

It's a matter of timing. After [the protests in] Selma, Johnson moved on the Voting Rights Act . . . To get the breakthroughs on Medicare, civil rights, and education he had the help of outside events. Almost every one of the civil rights bills had energy given to it by some event attached to Martin Luther King [Jr.]. He was the agent for all that legislation, including the last one, fair housing, after his assassination. But Johnson took advantage of those events.

To a large extent the events surrounding the marches in Selma made the exploitation of public pressure possible, as it contributed to making civil rights the prime public issue. When events were associated with the proposals of presidents from Eisenhower to Reagan, the initiatives they introduced were slightly more likely to secure active congressional consideration. In addition, of the 37 proposals either triggered by an event or relevant to subsequent events, 62% were at least partially enacted, compared to the 53% success rate of other initiatives. Events tied to particular parts of the presidential program, therefore, constituted an effective device to be manipulated in the lobbying efforts of administration officials.[38]

Politics

In addition to the effects of a policy proposal's impact and the efforts of administration personnel to market their initiatives, several scholars posit a more direct causal link between the substantive nature of policy initiatives and the politics they encounter. Rather than the political circumstances yielding a particular class of policy, they see certain kinds of policies triggering a predictable pattern of politics. Focusing on the domestic programs of modern presidents, Robert Spitzer argues that "policy characteristics determine the shape of the president's political universe, at least as it relates to his dealings with Congress."[39] Students of the political process are not the only observers of the

38. Some events can have adverse consequences for the president's position. The discovery of a Soviet military brigade in Cuba, for example, thwarted efforts during the Carter administration to win ratification of the SALT II arms control treaty, as one Carter administration official mentioned.

39. Spitzer, *The Presidency and Public Policy*, p. 154.

linkage. Jimmy Carter, when I asked him to reflect on the sources of his troubles with Congress, singled out the role played by *what* he sought to accomplish:

> I think the main factor that was deleterious to the relationship was the controversial nature of the proposals that I presented to the Congress. We had to face up to some long-postponed issues that I felt were in the best interests of our country to address: SALT II. The Middle East, where the Jewish lobby was aroused. Normalization with China, where the Taiwan lobby was aroused. The Panama Canal treaties . . . Energy legislation, where we roused the animosity of both consumer groups and the oil industry. The Alaska lands bill, which had been long postponed. The environmental questions, particularly concerning Corps of Engineers projects in individual congressional districts or states. Those kinds of things were very important to me and I think to the country. But there was nothing in any of those issues that I've just described to you that was politically beneficial to members of Congress . . . It was not a God, Mother, Flag, and Apple Pie sort of thing. Quite often it showed that our country had to face limits, that it had to make compromises, that it had to protect the environment in spite of opposition from some folks.

One need not deny that other factors are instrumental in shaping the politics of congressional decision making to acknowledge the potential for the substantive content of policies themselves to structure how they are collectively received by various actors in the political process. The relationship between politics and policy is undoubtedly symbiotic, with each affecting the other. Congressional responses to presidential initiatives, therefore, are likely to be influenced by, among other things, the nature of the issues involved. Perhaps the most recognized theoretical perspective treating policy as the driving force of politics is the typology introduced by Theodore Lowi.[40] He argues that the content of public policies, the means by which a given policy is to be

40. Theodore J. Lowi, "American Business, Public Policy, Case Studies and Political Theory," *World Politics* 16 (July 1964): 677–715. See also Hayes, *Lobbyists and Legislators,* esp. chap. 2; Randall B. Ripley and Grace A. Franklin, *Congress, the Bureaucracy, and Public Policy,* rev. ed. (Homewood, Ill.: Dorsey Press, 1980): and James Q. Wilson, "The Poli-

achieved, structures the method by which the political system responds to it.

The fully evolved schema employed by Lowi and later by Spitzer includes four classes of policy: distributive, regulatory, redistributive, and constituent. Distributive programs are non-confrontational, allocating goods that can be provided one at a time to individual recipients. Legal structures or rule making are used in regulatory policies to direct or modify behaviors of tar-geted groups. Resources are transferred from one class of individ-uals to another by redistributive programs. And constituent ini-tiatives create or alter governmental structures and the rules governing the political process. The politics associated with each kind of policy reflects variations in the range of participants and the location of resolution.[41]

Presidents from Eisenhower to Reagan have tended to introduce more proposals under the general rubric of redistribution than any other single policy type. Of the 299 proposals in the sample, 92 fall into this category. One could argue that presidents *ought* to concentrate on redistributive issues. Congress is fundamentally a distributive enterprise, and by its norms and structures has the capability to address that species of societal demands. As demon-strated by the safety and environmental legislation of the 1960s and 1970s, members of Congress are also able to identify regu-latory problems and to enact laws that deal with them.[42] Redis-tributive concerns, however, especially unadulterated ones, may require more extensive leadership from the executive. Presidential resources can be substituted for those otherwise unavailable to resource-poor groups.

The frequency with which presidents submitted constituent ini-tiatives is almost the same as for redistributive proposals. Why

---

tics of Regulation," in *The Politics of Regulation*, ed. James Q. Wilson (New York: Basic Books, 1980), pp. 357–394.

41. The theoretical underpinnings, the clarity of distinctions among types of policies, and the practical application of the Lowi typology are open to criticism. See Hayes, *Lobbyists and Legislators*, chap. 2; and Mark V. Nadel, "Making Regulatory Policy," in *Making Economic Policy in Congress*, ed. Alan Schick (Washington, D.C.: American Enter-prise Institute, 1982), p. 221.

42. Jack L. Walker, "Setting the Agenda in the U.S. Senate: A Theory of Problem Selection," *British Journal of Political Science* 7 (October 1977): 423–445.

should constituent issues be so prominent on presidential agendas? One explanation is that much of the presidential program, rife with the rhetoric of problem solving, actually comprises measures that only symbolically address political demands. Rather than challenging the status quo and the existing power relationships in the polity, presidents may prefer to publicize changes in rules and structures that appear to rectify problems without imposing substantive reforms likely to arouse influential opposition.[43] Proposed restrictions in campaign finance law, for example, may be used to check perceptions of inordinate influence by commercial interests in politics without fundamentally challenging the dominant or "privileged" position of business in the American political system.[44]

When we look at the entire presidential program, distributive policies submitted by presidents during the Eisenhower to Reagan administrations were the most likely to be ignored by Congress; 34% received no action. Because most of these initiatives were not associated with major bills or legislation of high priority to the president, they had difficulty securing space on the busy legislative agenda. Once given a serious airing, distributive proposals were decided with the fewest occasions of factional conflict, perhaps by what Randall Ripley and Grace Franklin term subgovernment resolution. Conflict and confrontation are not generally necessary because of "the decentralized distribution of federal largessse to a seemingly unlimited number of recipients . . . [who] do not compete directly with each other for the subsidies."[45] The costs of these programs are also diffuse, not clearly the burden of any sector of the society and therefore not the source of opposition.[46] In the place of conflict we find legislative decisions characterized by consensus and, when disagreement requires resolution, by compromise. These account for 68% of the distributive proposals that received active consideration by Congress.

The occurrence of consensus may shield a process of bargaining involving logrolling exchanges that integrate specific initiatives.

43. Murray Edelman, *The Symbolic Uses of Politics* (Urbana: University of Illinois Press, 1964), chap. 3.

44. Charles E. Lindblom, *Politics and Markets: The World's Political-Economic Systems* (New York: Basic Books, 1977), chap. 13.

45. Ripley and Franklin, *Congress, the Bureaucracy, and Public Policy*, p. 88.

46. Wilson, "The Politics of Regulation," pp. 366–372.

The harmonious acceptance of the president's proposal may come at the cost of the overall package containing provisions of little interest to the president but important to influential members of Congress, a process that one senior Democratic adviser described as being "salamied to death." Although the approach of this study does not permit clear inspection of that kind of process, its presence in the consensus category should be noted.

Factional conflicts were most pronounced for regulatory proposals submitted by the president. Forty-two percent involved dominance decision making of one sort or another, conflictual situations pitting the presidential coalition against opposing factions. When such confrontations occurred, presidents did not fare well, losing almost three times as often as they won. Regulatory issues also led to relatively few occasions of compromise. In short, regulatory proposals introduced a configuration of political forces that was the most disadvantageous to the president's position. Congress enacted at least part of only 44% of the regulatory proposals, the lowest presidential success rate of any of the four categories of policy.

In most cases, subjects of regulation are well aware of who they are and of the costs imposed by the regulation. At least they are more cognizant of their identity and of the burdens they bear than the beneficiaries of regulation are aware of the advantages derived from the legislation. The effect is a policy with concentrated costs and diffuse benefits, often resolved by the interplay of organized groups representing the targets of regulatory costs versus the entrepreneurial advocates of regulation.[47] Because the benefits are spread among members of a large group or even an entire population and will be enjoyed regardless of the participation of any single recipient, organizations to promote or support regulatory proposals are difficult to organize and maintain.[48] According to one senior official, the Carter administration learned this lesson while trying to enact its most important regulatory initiative, hospital cost containment:

> We spent weeks and months trying to organize groups on hospital cost containment, but all the people that we wanted to

47. Ibid., p. 370.
48. This point summarizes the classic argument developed by Mancur Olson in *The Logic of Collective Action: Public Goods and the Theory of Groups* (Cambridge, Mass.: Harvard University Press, 1965).

feel passionately about it were insulated from the problem by insurance. The other side was able to organize influential people in the communities, the doctors and so on, the movers and shakers. As you may recall, it was a very close vote. We lost by one vote. We were not able to overcome the other side's grass-roots lobbying.

Easiest to mobilize were those most directly affected by the regulation—the doctors, as well as the various health and hospital associations.[49] Presidents choosing to pursue regulation are likely to find themselves in a struggle to determine which faction will dominate the decision making in the legislative arena.

Redistributive and constituent policies introduce the kind of ambiguity that one might anticipate. The 27% of redistributive initiatives that were resolved by either presidential or opposition dominance constitute a level of conflict much lower than one would expect from policies of broad scope that bring together the incompatible interests of large classes of individuals. There seems to have been considerable room for compromise and, surprisingly, even opportunities for consensus. In fact, with 29% of the redistributive proposals accepted consensually by Congress, there was more consensus on redistributive issues in the sample than on any other sort.

Three explanations are possible. First, redistributive legislation is the most amorphous and inclusive type of policy. Very few of the proposals submitted by presidents between 1953 and 1984 constituted unmitigated redistribution.[50] Often legislation, such as the Model Cities bill in the Johnson years, included payoffs to dissuade the opposition or was distorted by legislative politics to reflect distributive outcomes.[51] Second, some of these proposals involved redistribution from the politically unorganized to those who dominate the institutions of government.[52] We have seen that some instances of consensus reflect the failure of potentially

49. Joseph A. Califano, Jr., *Governing America: An Insider's Report from the White House and the Cabinet* (New York: Simon and Schuster, 1981), pp. 144–145.

50. See Hayes, *Lobbyists and Legislators*, p. 33.

51. R. Douglas Arnold, *Congress and the Bureaucracy: A Theory of Influence* (New Haven: Yale University Press, 1979), chap. 8.

52. Ripley and Franklin, *Congress, the Bureaucracy, and Public Policy*, p. 25.

opposing groups to organize and gain political leverage. That concern is particularly pronounced in the area of redistributive policies, since the disadvantaged in society are least likely to have the ability to mount significant political challenges. All taxes, unless specifically intended to do something like regulate behavior, were treated as redistributive (see Appendix D). Certainly many tax proposals benefit business at the expense of individual taxpayers, especially those at the lower end of the income scale. It would not be altogether fatuous to view the 1981 Reagan-inspired tax cuts, particularly in combination with the budget cuts, as redistribution from the comparatively poorly organized constituencies of the least affluent in American society to the more fully mobilized citizens at the top. Third, even when programs are redistributive toward those with lower incomes, the cost implications are often diffuse enough to inhibit the development of potent opposition.[53] While many social welfare programs absorb fairly significant shares of the budget, except in times of budgetary crises those costs may be no more obvious than those of any other programs, including distributive ones.

As a final note, there is no distinctive pattern in the ways Congress acted on constituent programs. In fact, the distribution of congressional responses produced by the introduction of constituent policies matches almost exactly the distribution for the entire sample. There seems to be nothing about the content of those programs that inspires particular kinds of responses on the Hill. The typology of policies, therefore, has some but not universal utility for understanding presidential-congressional relations. Policies that seem to be relatively distinctive as distributive or regulatory issues contributed to the politics of how they were decided. This was much less the case for redistributive and constituent programs submitted by the president.[54]

53. Wilson, "The Politics of Regulation," p. 369.

54. One distinction among policies not discussed in this chapter but quite relevant to participants concerns the location of interest: whether a proposal is an "inside-the-beltway" or an "outside-the-beltway" issue. Some initiatives may attract little attention in the country as a whole, but still prove to be rather difficult to accomplish within the Washington establishment. Civil service reform during the Carter presidency, for example, was threatened by forces significant in Washington but less relevant elsewhere. According to a senior aide to President Carter: "It's likely that it didn't mean shit to the other members [of the House]. They can go

A Single Dimension

Several attributes of presidential proposals have been analyzed in this chapter. Each treatment of the initiatives has revealed a connection of one form or another between their characteristics and the manner in which Congress responded to them. The properties of the initiatives, to some extent the product of presidential strategic choices, have been useful for identifying the likelihood of each kind of congressional action, the instances when conflict is more prevalent than consensus, and the opportunities for compromise. It is possible that many of these attributes of proposals represent different ways of identifying a common underlying policy dimension that affects the politics of congressional action.

Although it is not possible to combine all of the various attributes in a simple way, one relatively straightforward question is worth pursuing. To what extent did programs of highest priority to the president involve large policy departures associated with major legislation drafted by the White House or special task forces and commissions? In other words, how much overlap is there among the most pronounced cases of these four sets of attributes?[55] The meshing of the categories is certainly not complete. For instance, apparently only 23% of the major bills were drafted in the White House. On the other hand, the bulk of White House–drafted proposals, most highest-priority issues, and the vast majority of initiatives involving a large change in policy were also associated with major bills.

Only 34% of the proposals in the sample did not involve at least one of these four indicators of an initiative's consequentiality. It would be appropriate to label these initiatives as the most peripheral and least consequential to the presidents and their administrations, as well as to the country. Of the remaining 186 proposals, only 8% possessed all four attributes. A third of them, however, incorporated at least three of the four characteristics.

---

back to their districts and sit in the barbershop and say they voted for something that allows the government to fire people who are incompetent, and everybody shakes their heads in agreement. But the people on the committee can't do that. Outside the beltway it was politically good. Inside it was tough to get."

55. The Lowi policy typology does not fit well with these other attributes. Roughly the same percentage of regulatory, redistributive, and constituent policies were associated with major legislation.

For purposes of analysis, those proposals falling into this latter category, 22% of the sample, will be treated as the issues of greatest consequence.

Discriminating among presidential proposals according to their overall level of consequence captures much of what has been discussed in this chapter. The least consequential initiatives, as presented in Table 5.3, were more than twice as likely to be denied active consideration by Congress than were those of the greatest consequence. Almost four of ten were ignored. Again, when it matters most, presidential agendas move in Congress. In addition, the most significant issues were much more likely to be settled through the most conflictive forms of congressional decision making. Six in ten were resolved that way, compared to 15% of the least consequential policies. When the most consequential legislation was granted active congressional consideration, three-quarters of the time resolution came in a public struggle in which either the president's coalition or its opposition suffered outright defeat. For both the most and least consequential initiatives, when a face-off between opposing factions transpired, presidents lost more times than they won. Presidential legislative success, however, occurred with the greatest frequency when it was the most important. Finally, almost a third of the least consequential proposals could be resolved with consensus, whereas that was true for only 7% of the most consequential, and therefore most difficult, issues. For a significant portion of the president's legislative agenda, congressional cooperation was the norm, if any action at all was possible.

Table 5.3 Congressional responses to presidential proposals and consequentiality of the initiatives

| Degree of consequentiality | N | Congressional response | | | | |
		Inaction	Opposition dominance	Compromise	Presidential dominance	Consensus
Most	67	16%	34%	15%	27%	7%
Intermediate	129	19%	21%	24%	8%	27%
Least	103	39%	11%	16%	4%	30%

Note: N = 299; chi square = 55.58; $p < .001$.
Source: See Appendixes C and D.

These patterns reaffirm the implications of the different methodologies applied to the study of presidential-congressional relations. They also speak to the different thematic approaches guiding analyses of the institutional relationship. The approaches that concentrate on the major issues, the most significant legislation, will find a relationship marked by considerable conflict and little in the way of harmonious accommodation. Here the concerns of presidency-centered scholars are all too clear. Quantitative approaches that include all presidential proposals, however, will uncover a more conciliatory pattern of interactions. But if they fail to take note of the distinctions among proposals having different characteristics, and most important, diverse consequences, they will overlook some of the factors that contribute to explaining how Congress responds to the president's agenda. They will also not be able to discover (ameliorating somewhat presidency-centered worries) that presidents have been most successful with those proposals that are neither the most nor the least consequential. Once again, in the case of the least significant initiatives, the issue is almost entirely one of agenda space. Seventy-eight percent of all defeats came via congressional inaction; 60% of the presidential successes were the product of consensus. Of those proposals in the middle of the consequence dimension, 59% passed in some form, with a considerable measure of consensus.

As one would expect, the biggest legislative battles have come on the issues of greatest consequence to the president and to the polity. Despite the extraordinary challenges to leadership that have surfaced in the more recent part of the postwar era, presidents have not fared so badly; they have secured some kind of legislative success on about half of these most significant initiatives. Modern presidents have been playing in a tandem-institutions arena, often with a considerable degree of cooperation from Congress, unquestionably shaping the legislature's agenda and even winning favorable congressional responses on some of the most challenging issues.

6. An Integrative Analysis

The two previous chapters have offered some insight into the specific links between the pure, malleable, and policy contexts of legislative consideration and the ways in which Congress responded to the domestic initiatives of presidents from Dwight Eisenhower to Ronald Reagan. But the results of this empirical exploration remain tentative and incomplete. The bivariate style of the preceding analysis is capable of leading to erroneous or, at the very least, incomplete conclusions. The world of presidential-congressional interactions is too complex to allow one to ascertain the independent effects of a particular feature of the legislative environment without taking into consideration the influence of all of the other factors that shape the collective choices of the president and Congress at any particular time. There has also been little opportunity so far to explore the exact character of the relationships between the institutional, political, economic, and policy properties and the style of congressional action. Rather than assuming that in each case the association between a contextual property and the congressional response is additive and linear, we may need to allow for the existence of interaction effects and, in some situations, to examine more complicated, nonlinear relationships.

Even more important, without integrating the various factors constituting the overall context in which legislative decisions were made about specific proposals, we cannot assess the context of legislative action or inaction as a fully developed pattern of forces shaping the responses of Congress to the president's initiatives. Throughout American history there have been occasions when the constellation of forces have seemed to align, narrowing to an extraordinary degree the institutional chasm imposed on the president and Congress by the Constitution. This century, for example, witnessed the confluence of the will of the Sixty-third Congress and Woodrow Wilson's programmatic designs; the receptivity to change of the Seventy-third Congress and FDR's New Deal call to action; the social welfare activism of the Eighty-ninth Congress and Lyndon Johnson's dream of a Great Society. During each of these periods, the political distance separating the legislature and the executive was attenuated, not just by one contextual factor but by many. The presumably unifying character of more robust political parties, acknowledged presidential electoral mandates, undivided government, popular support of the president, economic urgencies or opportunities, and public consensus all contributed to the tone of the institutional relationship. The tandem institutions became almost unitary.

At other times, indeed far more frequently, significantly more multifaceted contextual settings have surrounded the presidential-congressional relationship—with aspects that simultaneously favored unity in some respects and stimulated discord in others. Their impact, individually and collectively, can only be known in the aggregate. Consider the Carter and Reagan administrations. President Carter encountered a Congress controlled overwhelmingly by his own party and he at times enjoyed high levels of public approval. During his term the nation also experienced enormous economic dislocations and he witnessed ideological disagreements with many of his fellow partisans, as well as with various groups that made up part of the Democratic coalition. Ronald Reagan's GOP dominated only one chamber of Congress, but early on he benefited from a conservative majority in the House of Representatives and the perception of an electoral mandate. For Carter, the public perception was soon one of legislative conflict and failure; energy initiatives, plans to contain hospital costs, and proposed reforms in welfare and tax policy slid into a congressional quagmire. For Reagan, legislative conflict led to success, if only temporarily, as Congress, struggling all the way, accepted sweeping budget cuts and the kind of massive tax reductions it had publicly rejected prior to Reagan's arrival. Looking beyond the role of the individuals themselves, how are we to assess the significance and joint impact of the various properties constituting the pure, malleable, and policy contexts?

This chapter brings together the wide range of contextual attributes discussed in the preceding chapters, giving some weight to both their individual and their collective consequences.[1] Multivariate statistical techniques permit us to assess the independent effects of individual contextual properties by controlling for the presence of all the others. We can also investigate less straightforward relationships than we could with the bivariate analysis of the previous two chapters. Finally, we can achieve an integrative view of the entire context influencing congressional consideration of presidential proposals.

The analysis presented here continues the focus on two concerns. I have described Congress as responding to presidential initiatives through any one of five different ways of making collective decisions, and in a fairly rudimentary way I have made the argument that the likelihood of each kind of congressional response is affected by the status of various contextual properties. These legislative responses are linked, at least potentially, in some rather interesting ways. First, built into the derivation of the five possible congressional responses is the degree of manifest confrontation over legislative issues, so the responses can be ordered from those categories of legislative decisions that evidence the most cooperation to those that reveal the greatest conflict. This will be referred to as the conflict dimension. Second, from the tandem-institutions perspective, with its recognition of presidential agenda leadership, it is essential to interpret and evaluate the special role of the president in the American national legislative arena. However one wishes to portray the presidential-congressional relationship and the roles of each institution, in the end we always need a meaningful yardstick for evaluating the performance of the president. The five types of congressional responses also reflect to varying degrees the fulfillment of presidential preferences for legislative action. The presidential preference dimension has two stages: the choices that chief executives make about what kinds of initiatives to send to the Hill, and the decisions that Congress makes once the president's agenda has been articulated. The rest of this chapter examines with multivariate techniques the extent to which the conflict and presidential preference dimensions can be explained with reference to the integrated pure, malleable, and policy contexts of congressional action. The

1. Special thanks are due Stephen Ansolabehere and Erik Corwin for their contributions to the ideas and analysis presented in this chapter.

statistical technique used here, ordered probit analysis, is described in Appendix E.

Cooperation or Conflict?

Congressional responses to presidential initiatives offer empirical observations of various levels of cooperation and conflict. They can be arrayed, with minimal adjustments, along a conflict dimension to reflect a continuum that ranges from very low to very high. Four types of congressional responses to the president's initiatives are easy to locate on this conflict dimension. Occasions of consensus, when the president's initiatives passed intact without evidence of coherent opposition, clearly secure the lowest-conflict end of the scale. Cases of presidential dominance and opposition dominance, which differ only in whether the president's legislative coalition or the opposing coalition won or lost an open battle in committee or on the floor, rest together toward the highest-conflict extreme. In the middle is compromise, those instances in which the actual votes may have appeared consensual but where enough opposition or concern existed to prompt some retreat from the president's originally stated policy positions.

The fifth category of congressional response, inaction, needs refinement before being incorporated into the conflict dimension. Chapter 5 revealed that cases of inaction tend to be associated with two rather divergent styles of politics. Their differences hinge on the nature of the initiatives under congressional review. Inaction, the failure of the legislature to give meaningful consideration to a presidential initiative, requires a different interpretation when it occurs on a proposal associated with a program of low priority to the president than when it is the response to an issue of high priority. A substantial majority of lowest-priority initiatives (66%) either led to inaction or were settled by consensus. If they reached the active congressional agenda, there was little or no opposition. Undoubtedly these cases included the scores of proposals that presidents from Eisenhower to Reagan transmitted to Congress with relative insouciance. When Congress ignored these initiatives, it may well have been acceding to presidential identification of the issues least worthy of deliberate action in a crowded field. It would be inappropriate to portray this situation as Congress, or an opposition faction of Congress, in conflict with the chief executive. Inaction on lowest-priority issues, therefore, may be termed *passive inaction.* Since it does not evince overt opposition and reflects the priority presidents assign to their own programs, passive inaction joins with consensus at the low end of the conflict dimension.

On the other hand, for a controlling coalition in Congress to thwart an initiative of considerable interest to the president by not granting it any consideration at all represents the highest order of refutation. In a tandem-institutions setting in which almost 80% of such initiatives obtain active legislative consideration, inaction on proposals associated with programs of highest or medium priority to the president reflects motivated, strategic choice on the part of the administration's adversaries. These cases I therefore label *strategic inaction.* They are indicative of even greater conflict than the two types of dominance, where at least the agenda-setting prerogatives of the executive are recognized.

The conflict dimension, embracing this treatment of inaction, is therefore represented by a four-level ordinal variable:

Lowest conflict: 1. (30.1%) Consensus and passive inaction
                         2. (19.4%) Compromise
                         3. (31.4%) Dominance—presidential and opposition
Highest conflict: 4. (19.1%) Strategic inaction

Characterizing conflict in these terms demonstrates that for presidential initiatives introduced from 1953 to 1984, legislative cooperation and conflict struck a nearly equal balance. The general expectation is that the level of conflict during this period, and therefore the probabilities of the congressional responses captured by each of these categories of events, was influenced in a significant way by the combined pure, malleable, and policy context prevailing at the time each presidential initiative received consideration in Congress.

Before we proceed, it will be worthwhile to delineate which variables are to be included in the multivariate analysis of conflict and to elaborate on their most appropriate derivations. Recall that underlying each contextual property is its effect on empowering and increasing the number of natural allies of the president and those in each house who could be persuaded to join the president's position. Perhaps with the conflict dimension this should be stated as its complement: the most significant contextual effects are the ones that provide opportunities for the opposition to mobilize and incentives for its members to actively pursue their objections to the executive's initiatives.

The contextual factors creating or limiting venues for opposition are the institutional properties that compose the pure context of the political system. Here again three variables are employed (see Appendix D for a description of their construction). The first represents the degree of structural decentralization in Congress and the second portrays the elaboration of the interest-group community. Increases in either of these factors should contribute to conflict by increasing the opportunities for opponents of presidential initiatives to block action and by expanding the number of organized "interesteds" in the policy process. The third variable represents the strength of partisan ties among elected officials, established by voters in elections when they support congressional and presidential candidates of the same or different political parties. When the electorate votes for candidates of shared partisan affiliation for each branch, that may nurture an institutional partisan bond that reduces the level of conflict.

There are several dynamic political properties of the malleable context that also contribute to the quality of the presidential-congressional relationship. Elections produce three relevant results that can be fairly easily introduced in this analysis. First, the proportion of the two-party vote received by the president may shape the way members of each institution assess one another. Just as John Kennedy thought his slender majority denied him the resources to challenge opponents in Congress, a Johnson, Nixon, or Reagan enjoying the fruits of an impressive victory at the polls may have felt emboldened enough to confront congressional adversaries. Second, if the attractiveness of the president to the electorate contributes to the votes received by members of the president's party running as candidates for the House of Representatives, then this coattail effect may generate a sense of obligation on the part of the chief executive's fellow partisans, so that they seek to moderate conflict in the legislative arena. But diminished tensions among the president's fellow partisans may do little to temper the contrariness of those in the opposition party.

Elections also determine the distribution of seats in the House and Senate, establishing the partisan foundation on which all presidents have had to build their coalitions of the moment. If the president's party controls each chamber of the legislature, that should minimize the institutional conflict by granting natural allies more power and denying opponents theirs. Beyond that simple statement, however, the derivation of reasonable expectations is more complex. One might posit that the more seats held by the party of the president, the smaller the chances of legislative confrontations, since they increase the capacity of party leaders to dominate legislative deliberations at a variety of stages.

Opposition does not require title to many seats, however. It merely depends upon a faction's having the resources and willingness needed to state and pursue its antagonism to the president's program. That may entail a negative majority vote from an opposition party of diminished ranks or the concerted effort of only a few dedicated obstructionists using killer-amendment tactics in the House or filibusters in the Senate. Further, because of the changing dynamics of coalitions, as they expand in size one cannot begin with an a priori assumption of a linear relationship between seats held by the president's party and muted legislative conflict. Holding together expansive coalitions is often not as easy as maintaining smaller ones. We need to be able to both note when the president's party controlled Congress and provide a means for capturing nonlinear relationships between seats held and conflict. This can be accomplished by introducing a dummy variable into the probit analysis that represents the difference in levels of conflict between the cases when the president's party controlled each chamber and when it did not, and a quadratic function to fit a curvilinear relationship. The number of seats held by the president's party is used to estimate the basic relationship, and the number of seats squared captures the possible countervailing effects of extremely large partisan coalitions.

Another important attribute of the political context is popular support for the president, as measured by the Gallup poll. Several components are involved, each affecting the incentives faced by the president's natural allies, persuadables, and potentially activated opponents. Natural allies sense a strengthened bond to the president if public support is high, but they are unlikely to go into direct opposition, and therefore generate institutional conflict, if the president's popularity is low. On the other hand, members of the opposition party, a priori the most likely opponents, may be stimulated to actively block presidential initiatives when the president enjoys elevated public prestige, as long as other political forces have not sapped the opposition's political fortitude.[2] If the opposition controls Congress, this tendency provides a formula for even more intense institutional conflict, especially when high levels of public approval of the president's job performance also motivate the chief executive to press opponents on the Hill rather than to seek compromise. For the conflict dimension, therefore, one expects higher levels of public support of the president, and evidence that public approval has increased, to lead to more instances of conflict on the president's proposals. This pattern should be even more pronounced when the opposition party enjoys a majority in the House or the Senate.

Economic properties, the second part of the malleable context, should also affect the degree of legislative conflict. When societal resources are limited, as suggested by little growth in the Gross National Product or increases in the size of the federal deficit, as well as by high or increasing unemployment and inflation, it should be more difficult to accommodate all interests with divergent policy demands. Elevated unemployment rates signal economic disjunctions that may have a negative impact on government revenues and that focus attention on broad classes of inequality. An elevated inflation rate and evidence of a pattern of increasing inflation should also promote conflict by exacerbating concerns about resource constraints and stimulating disagreements over the appropriate programs to cut in the process of reducing aggregate demand generated by government expenditures.

Finally, we must consider the strategic choices presidents make about the proposals themselves that set the policy context. Some presidential initiatives during the period under study involved large policy departures and some represented efforts in entirely new policy areas. Further, more than 40% of the initiatives can be described as having been associated with major programs. The controversy that is inherent in innovations, or in significant and sizable programmatic changes, suggests that such initiatives invite disagreement, opposition, and conflict. On the other hand, a cooperative congressional response may be nurtured by two other attributes of proposals. If a large proportion of the public

2. Jon R. Bond and Richard Fleisher, "The Limits of Presidential Popularity as a Source of Influence in the U.S. House," *Legislative Studies Quarterly* 5 (February 1980): 75.

identifies a policy area as the most important problem facing the nation, officials in both the executive and legislative branches may seek to meet that concern with collaborative action. At the very least, forcing strategic inaction is a less viable option for opponents of the president. Specific events substantively related to the president's initiatives that occur after the introduction of legislation also may play a role. Sometimes events can be skillfully manipulated to mitigate conflict. Shipboard fires, for example, helped build a consensus in favor of Johnson's ocean transit safety initiatives in 1966.

The results generated by ordered probit analysis of the conflict dimension appear in Table 6.1. The vast majority of the variables have coefficients revealing the expected positive or negative association with legislative conflict. Several are statistically significant. In 44% of the cases the analysis correctly predicts the category of the conflict dimension that actually occurred. Much is not accounted for in this particular configuration of the contextual analysis, because of underspecification of the model, mismeasurement noise, and the intentional absence of factors that lie beyond the institutional, political, and economic setting of congressional action. Nevertheless, the variables selected to portray various aspects of the legislative context do influence significantly the extent of cooperation or conflict that appeared in congressional responses to the initiatives submitted by presidents from Eisenhower to Reagan.

The only statistically significant institutional variable measures the decentralization of authority in Congress, which contributed to increased legislative conflict on the executive's initiatives. Strengthened partisan linkages, though somewhat shy of significance, worked to decrease conflict and enhance cooperation. Although the effects are too small to achieve conventional levels of significance, and therefore one cannot have great confidence in the coefficient, the increased elaboration of the interest-group community is negatively correlated with conflict—an anomaly if true.

Among the political attributes of the malleable context, sizable electoral victories for the president and presidential popularity increased legislative conflict, whereas coattails produced no effect in the conflict analysis. The other measures of public support, trends in public approval and public support for the president when the opposition party controlled the House or the Senate,

Table 6.1   Ordered probit analysis of influence of contextual properties on level of conflict generated in Congress by introduction of presidential domestic initiatives

Contextual property	Coeffi-cient	Standard error	t-statistic
First threshold	0.589[a]	0.066	8.972
Second threshold	1.606[a]	0.116	13.886
Intercept	−20.326	29.356	−0.692
Pure context: institutional			
Decentralization of Congress	0.920[a]	0.428	2.151
Elaboration of interest groups	−0.861	0.719	−1.197
Electoral partisan links	−0.427	0.339	−1.257
Malleable context: dynamic political			
President's two-party vote	0.020	0.013	1.539
Presidential coattails	0.004	0.060	0.066
Intercept shift from House majority to minority	93.035[a]	52.541	1.771
House seats when minority	0.220	0.270	0.814
(House seats when minority)^2	−0.001	0.001	−0.961
House seats when majority	0.844[a]	0.322	2.617
(House seats when majority)^2	−0.002[a]	0.001	−2.678
Intercept shift from Senate majority to minority	−75.694	59.567	−1.271
Senate seats when minority	−0.883	1.311	−0.674
(Senate seats when minority)^2	0.013	0.016	0.785
Senate seats when majority	−2.990[a]	1.477	−2.024
(Senate seats when majority)^2	0.024[a]	0.011	2.106
Public approval of president	0.034[a]	0.014	2.388
Public approval—House minority	0.007	0.034	0.217
Public approval—Senate minority	−0.008	0.034	−0.250
Increase in public approval	−0.042	0.111	−0.375
Malleable context: economic			
Quarterly growth in GNP	−0.084	0.055	−1.533
Size of federal deficit	0.263[a]	0.105	2.507
Level of monthly unemployment	−0.288[a]	0.169	−1.708
Quarterly increase in unemployment	0.266[a]	0.161	1.656
Level of monthly inflation	0.080	0.082	0.977
Quarterly increase in inflation	0.248[a]	0.125	1.982
Policy context			
Large policy departure	0.155	0.155	0.999
New policy departure	0.281[a]	0.158	1.784
Importance of program	0.302[a]	0.111	2.728
Subsequent event	−0.334	0.489	−0.683
Most important problem	−0.008	0.006	−1.194
Number of cases:		298	
Log likelihood:		−371.35	
Percentage of cases correctly predicted:		44.0	

a. $p < .10$.

surprisingly show no additional influence during the period being studied. While control of the House of Representatives by the president's party minimized the amount of conflict, as expected, similar control of the Senate actually increased the level of conflict on the president's initiatives (the latter result would not be accepted as statistically significant).

The seats variables reveal curvilinear relationships when the president's partisans were in the majority in the House and the Senate, but no significant relationship when the party was in the minority. In the House, majorities with the president's party possessing 218 to about 270 seats marginally elevated legislative conflict, while possession of more than 270 seats substantially reduced the occurrence of conflict. In this case supermajorities served to squash opposition. The results for the Senate are a mirror image of the House. Slender majorities of 51 to 60 seats led to less confrontation, while majorities of more than 65 seats apparently induced conflict, if we control for all other contextual factors. This divergence between the House and Senate undoubtedly arises at least partially from the differences in the structure of the two chambers: the numbers of legislators involved, the degree of specialization and rigidity imposed by the rules of each house, and the institutional resources of the majority party leadership. Overwhelming majorities for the president's party in the House may have made opposition extremely difficult, since the more tightly controlled House offers fewer opportunities for single representatives to obstruct action. The Senate, however, with the filibuster, senatorial courtesy, and other provisions that grant considerable power to individual senators, provides the means for opposition at any time. Impressive majorities held by the president's party may have provided an incentive during this period for opponents to use these confrontational techniques, even opponents in the partisan fold of the president.

The economic properties of the malleable context prove to be quite important and for the most part consistent with expectations. Deficits produced conflict; growth in the GNP mitigated it. Inflation, especially a consistent rise in inflation, also begot conflict on the president's legislative agenda. On the other hand, once all of the other contextual factors are accounted for, high levels of unemployment were actually associated with more cooperative legislative action, contrary to the expectations generated in Chapter 4. If there was a sustained pattern of increasing unemployment, however, that instilled greater disharmony in the legislative arena. Perhaps it is during periods of rising or enduring unemployment that substantive conflicts over approaches become most pronounced, as the status quo represents failed policy. Merely going along with program authorizations and appropriations is not enough to forestall opposition.

Within the policy context, presidential proposals associated with major legislation that initiated new policy approaches created the greatest discord in Congress. As expected, large policy departures were associated with more legislative conflict, although the results are not statistically significant. Also not significant are the proportion of the public identifying the issue area as a most important problem and the occurrence of a related event; still, each coefficient is in the anticipated direction of decreased confrontation.

Incorporating nothing explicitly and very little implicitly about individual participants in the legislative process, including personal characteristics of the seven presidents and their unique amalgamation of traits and political skills, one is able to account for much of the cooperation or conflict in evidence when Presidents Eisenhower to Reagan submitted domestic legislative initiatives to Congress. Knowing something about the condition of major political institutions, the political position of the president and the opposition, the state of the economy, and the nature of the president's programs, we can say quite a bit about why Congress responded to the president by affirmation or condemnation, or by something in between. These patterns held true for the postwar period; they are likely to persist well into the future unless there are fundamental changes in the nature of American politics. Can the politics associated with presidential legislative preferences be understood in similar terms?

Presidential Preferences

The president is a uniquely placed legislative actor in the tandem-institutions setting, possessing more than any other individual the strategic resources needed to influence the process of legislative decision making. It is also the president who stands at the center of public expectations about what the government should and can do to address public issues.[3] Despite my argument in Chapter 1 that this focus on the president is overemphasized in the presidency-centered perspective, it is appropriate to judge the role of the president in legislative affairs and to assess congressional responses to presidential initiatives from the perspective of what presidents have sought to accomplish. To do so requires weaving a more complete understanding of the contextual setting in which Congress and the president interact; the ways Congress responds to the president's programs; and how the pure, malleable, and policy contexts influence whether or not Congress takes the kind of legislative action preferred by the president.

Chapter 2 presented argument and evidence in support of the proposition that the president's program is truly presidential. Rarely are there incentives for presidents to submit to Congress initiatives that run contrary to their own preferences. This line of reasoning, however, does not preclude the president and members of the executive establishment from choosing *among* presidential preferences and adjusting them in ways that are sensitive to the context of their congressional consideration. Within the range of possible alternatives that presidents might prefer is the potentially more limited collection of policies that they think are either politically possible or affordable with respect to their political capital. Part of what we witness as Congress responds to presidential initiatives, therefore, may be a reflection of the opportunities or constraints that presidents weigh as they survey the institutional, political, and economic landscape. The pure and malleable contexts of congressional action may matter less, and indicators of presidential performance may be difficult to gauge, because presidents have adjusted their particular selection of preferred proposals to match the setting in which they will be considered. They may choose to be bold, and to succeed as innovators, only when the opportunities are clear.

It is only after we have addressed these presidential choices at initiation that we can turn our attention to congressional responses. Investigating the issue of presidential preferences, therefore, requires a two-stage process centered on presidential

3. Theodore J. Lowi, *The Personal President: Power Invested, Promise Unfulfilled* (Ithaca, N.Y.: Cornell University Press, 1985), p. 51; and Jeffrey K. Tulis, *The Rhetorical Presidency* (Princeton: Princeton University Press, 1987).

innovation and "nested" models of congressional responses. The first stage examines the extent to which presidential innovation is influenced by the contextual contours of the political system at the time that the initiatives are introduced. Large-small and new-old dimensions of presidential initiatives are treated separately, with innovativeness comprising either large or new policy departures. The second stage explores the role of the pure, malleable, and remaining policy contexts in explaining congressional responses to presidential initiatives, conditional on whether what is introduced is a large or small policy departure and whether it represents a new policy area or action in an old policy domain. To be technically specific, the first-stage probit model considers contexts and presidential legislative innovation. Then for each of the four possible branches of presidential innovation—large, small, new, and old proposals—nested probit models evaluate the link between contexts and congressional action, given the strategic choices presidents make that define the major features of the policy context.

One can imagine three competing hypotheses concerning the innovativeness of presidential initiatives. One hypothesis is that whether the president submits large or new proposals has little to do with the circumstances of the political system, but much to do with factors that are reasonably independent of the context, at least as I have defined it. Two such factors are the campaign pledges of the president in the previous presidential election and precursor events that stimulate policy formulation.[4] An alternative hypothesis would discount the role of campaigns and events, and place emphasis on the strategic sensitivity of the president in selecting the form of proposals most suitable to the prevailing climate. To illustrate, I have noted earlier President Ford's prohibition on major policy departures as a result of the economic declines he faced during his years in office. Finally, one may hypothesize that both contexts and campaigns, along with events, play a role. Presidents have an agenda to move, the argument would be, but they temper it marginally according to what seems possible.

4. Campaigns are not entirely independent of other factors that help to shape the malleable context of the political system. Voter response to campaign issues and the existence of clear programmatic themes in campaign statements may contribute to the power of a president's perceived mandate.

What we find in the results of the probit analysis, presented in Table 6.2, is confirmation of the third hypothesis, but with a definite sense of the importance of campaigns and events. With respect to the amount of impact of the president's proposals, moving from cases when there were no relevant campaign references at all about the programmatic subject of the proposals to those with specific references during the campaign provides the most significant explanatory variable in the model. Thirty-nine percent of the proposals that involved any kind of campaign mention, specific or general, represented large proposals, compared to only 19% of those not referred to in the campaign. Precursor events, as one would expect with the size dimension, are not relevant, for there is nothing inherent in events that calls for either large or small policy departures. Some contextual variables are also significant. Strengthened partisan electoral linkages between Congress and the president facilitated the introduction of large proposals, the only institutional property to have a statistically significant effect.

The effects of the political and economic properties of the malleable context are not as obvious. The size of the president's vote in the previous election had no effect, and coattails were not a significant influence on this aspect of innovation. The basic public support variable for when the president's party controlled Congress is well below conventional levels of significance, but would endorse the idea that popular presidents felt emboldened and were more willing to attempt legislative innovations. The effects of public approval when the president's party was in the minority in both House and Senate are a little unusual, however. When the opposition party controlled the House, elevated public approval hindered innovation; but with an opposition majority in the Senate, it fostered innovation. Partisan coalitions in Congress also mattered independently, yet overall House and Senate effects are both divergent and puzzling, with the Senate again revealing the anomalies.

When presidents dealt with a House controlled by the opposition party, they were more reluctant to suggest large policy departures. Majorities of up to 260 seats actually led to more inhibition about introducing large proposals. With extraordinary majorities of 280 or more fellow partisans, however, the inclination to be bold increased. The Senate, following a now familiar pattern, instigated different presidential choices. Presidents facing a

Table 6.2 Ordered probit analysis of influence at time of introduction of contextual properties, campaign references, and precursor events on innovativeness of presidential initiatives

Contextual property	Large rather than small			New rather than old		
	Coefficient	Standard error	t-statistic	Coefficient	Standard error	t-statistic
Intercept	−16.121	39.385	−0.403	−22.086	39.100	−0.580
Pure context: institutional						
Decentralization of Congress	0.437	0.659	0.663	−0.896	0.686	−1.306
Elaboration of interest groups	0.000	1.047	0.000	2.719[a]	1.203	2.261
Electoral partisan links	0.967[a]	0.350	2.761	−0.085	0.395	−0.215
Malleable context: dynamic political						
President's two-party vote	−0.007	0.016	−0.444	−0.000	0.014	0.007
Presidential coattails	−0.121	0.116	−1.047	−0.370	0.088	−0.419
Intercept shift from House majority to minority	−134.695[a]	55.952	−2.407	42.967	51.582	0.833
House seats when minority	0.298	0.302	0.988	−0.257	0.299	−0.859
(House seats when minority)[2]	−0.001	0.001	−1.017	0.001	0.001	0.901
House seats when majority	−0.731[a]	0.349	−2.093	0.319	0.335	0.954
(House seats when majority)[2]	0.001[a]	0.001	2.072	−0.001	0.001	−1.032
Intercept shift from Senate majority to minority	113.257[a]	69.003	1.641	28.624	67.441	0.424
Senate seats when minority	−0.791	1.548	−0.511	−2.583	1.660	−1.557
(Senate seats when minority)[2]	0.009	0.019	0.478	0.031	0.020	1.528
Senate seats when majority	3.466[a]	1.746	1.986	−0.729	1.666	−0.438
(Senate seats when majority)[2]	−0.003[a]	0.014	−1.973	0.008	0.012	0.589
Public approval of president	0.015	0.012	1.198	0.010	0.011	0.934
Public approval—House minority	−0.112[a]	0.040	−2.816	−0.001	0.043	−0.022
Public approval—Senate minority	0.098[a]	0.044	2.218	−0.013	0.046	−0.290
Increase in public approval	0.065	0.184	0.352	0.261[a]	0.157	1.661
Malleable context: economic						
Quarterly growth in GNP	0.143[a]	0.078	1.846	−0.056	0.073	−0.768
Size of federal deficit	−0.252[a]	0.150	−1.685	−0.089	0.113	−0.789
Level of monthly inflation	0.221[a]	0.117	1.895	−0.138	0.122	−1.131
Quarterly increase in inflation	0.127	0.176	0.723	−0.099	0.161	−0.617
Level of monthly unemployment	0.087	0.197	0.443	−0.147	0.163	−0.902
Quarterly increase in unemployment	−0.200	0.181	−1.108	−0.035	0.174	−0.202
Policy context						
Campaign reference	0.700[a]	0.166	4.216	0.407[a]	0.176	2.291
Precursor event	−0.166	0.306	−0.541	0.475[a]	0.274	1.736
Most important problem	0.006	0.008	0.765	−0.005	0.009	−0.564
Number of cases:		298			298	
Log likelihood:		−134.94			−166.99	
Percentage of cases correctly predicted:		82.2			74.2	

a. $p < .10$.

majority opposition party in the Senate were more likely to take large initiatives, other things being equal, and when their party controlled the Senate, the possession of a greater number of seats led to less innovation. One has to keep in mind, of course, that when Presidents Eisenhower to Reagan were forming judgments about their programs and the congressional setting, they were having to make strategic calculations involving both houses simultaneously, taking into consideration many other contextual factors as well. They had to remain sensitive to the differing proportion of seats their party held in each chamber and the disparate structures and politics of the two houses. The unique combinations of these traits assessed by each president may have generated what appear to be anomalous results.

Economic properties mostly follow expected patterns, with large policy departures more likely when quarterly increases in the GNP indicated a growing economy. Large federal deficits limited such innovation. Contrary to what one would expect, these presidents introduced large policy proposals when inflation was high, perhaps even increasing. Some large-scale initiatives to combat inflation, such as Carter's hospital cost containment program, may be responsible, but relatively few proposals were of that nature.

The findings are somewhat different for the presidential decision concerning whether to introduce new policy departures rather than proposals that adjusted existing programs. Campaign references remain a most significant variable in the model explaining innovation. Precursor events may not have affected the size of initiatives, but they certainly contributed to new innovations. Among institutional properties, only the elaboration of the interest-group system had a significant effect, with a diverse group community having led to more new policy proposals. With the growing importance of public liaison activities, presidents— like members of Congress—may provide a conduit for new ideas emerging from interest-group activists. Somewhat short of statistical significance is the decentralization of power in Congress, the coefficient of which suggests a negative impact on new departures.

Political properties such as the electoral mandate, coattail effects, and level of public approval contribute little, although presidents with increasing popularity were apparently more willing to suggest new departures. Control of the House and

Senate by the president's party also did not matter, nor did the number of seats held by partisans of the president in either chamber. Because new policy departures need not demand much in the way of resources, economic factors played no real role. The only factor that comes anywhere close to statistical significance indicates that higher levels of monthly inflation inhibited this kind of innovation.

None of these results, for either the size or the newness components of presidential innovation, lead one to believe that the determinative forces rest in the pure or the malleable context of the legislative arena. Even partisan domination of Congress by the president's party did not provide definitive incentives for the president to innovate. A primary explanation of innovation lies in campaign commitments and events. Probit analysis permits this empirical interpretation to be reinforced by controlling for the vast set of factors that defined the pure and malleable contexts of presidential decision making at the time the initiatives were introduced. What remains to be seen is whether in the multivariate setting contextual properties affect congressional responses along the lines suggested by the results in Chapters 4 and 5. To examine this issue requires the derivation of a presidential preference dimension, ordering the responses of Congress according to what presidents would most like to see happen with their legislative initiatives.

Chief executives generally have a priori preferences for how Congress should react to their programs. One can examine the five basic ways Congress treats presidential initiatives, suggest a few reasonable assumptions about presidential preferences, and create an ordinal dependent variable that tracks along a presidential preference dimension. Two types of congressional responses are easy to place in such a continuum. The most inimical result for the president is to be publicly defeated, to suffer opposition dominance. At the other extreme is consensus, where the entire proposal passes without a political confrontation. The president's reputation is advanced without having to expend much political capital. Between these two poles of presidential preferences one can comfortably locate compromise and presidential dominance. While the former may require smaller expenditures of political capital, it entails sacrificing something of the proposal and does not grant the president the aura of legislative mastery. Presidential dominance, often achieved at some political cost, nevertheless represents total legislative success on that issue and builds the president's national image as a forceful and commanding leader in the Washington community. Inaction requires the kind of amendment introduced in the earlier discussion of conflict. Having Congress ignore issues of little interest to the president is much less disconcerting to the administration than having initiatives of high priority strategically avoided. Such strategic inaction is not as painful publicly as opposition dominance, but it is certainly less desirable than compromise. That leaves passive inaction, a relatively small category of proposals (6.4% of the total). It is decidedly more acceptable to the president than opposition dominance and strategic inaction, but one could not argue that is is better than compromise. That might suggest locating it between strategic inaction and compromise, but given the small number of cases and the advantage of limiting the number of categories in the dependent variable of presidential preferences, I have combined the cases of passive inaction with those of compromise.[5]

The presidential preference ordinal dependent variable thus has the following categories:

Lowest preference: 1. (20.4%) Opposition dominance
2. (19.1%) Strategic inaction
3. (25.8%) Compromise and passive inaction
4. (11.0%) Presidential dominance
Highest preference: 5. (23.7%) Consensus

In about 40% of the cases Congress from 1953 to 1986 responded to executive initiatives in ways entirely detrimental to the president's position, with either opposition dominance or strategic inaction. Otherwise presidents from Eisenhower to Reagan fared reasonably well. With this dimension now defined, we are ready to examine the impact of contextual factors on the congressional responses from the perspective of the kind of legislative action the president would prefer, and with sensitivity toward the opportunities presidents might have enjoyed to influence the pure and malleable contexts in which congressional decisions were made. The analysis, again, is conditional on the innovativeness of the president's initiatives.

5. There is no evidence in any of the analyses I performed that this categorization created distortion in the results.

The expectations associated with the role of each contextual property follow from the explanations presented in Chapters 4 and 5, except that now we must take into account the fluctuating influence of variables as the innovativeness of the president's initiatives changes.

For the institutional properties of the pure context, which invite the least presidential influence, congressional decentralization and a more complicated interest-group community should aggravate the challenge of constructing a policy consensus and provide more opportunities for opponents to block presidentially desired initiatives. Two possible exceptions are worth noting. First, there is some evidence in the literature on Congress that the decentralization of power in both the House and the Senate may facilitate the consideration and passage of new ideas that do not directly challenge existing jurisdictions.[6] The more autonomous subcommittees in the House, for example, may provide a means for overcoming the kind of opposition to new departures that was previously evident in the House as a result of the occasionally stultifying power of entrenched committee chairmen prior to the 1970s committee reforms. Second, because many interest groups comprise or represent the clientele of existing government programs, numerous presidential initiatives dealing with those programs may benefit from the presence of growing numbers of supportive groups and group representatives. The third institutional property, strengthening the partisan linkage joining members of Congress and the president, should favor the development of presidentially led coalitions, without any variation being evident across types of proposals.

Most of the dynamic political attributes of the malleable context, influenced to some degree by the president's own campaigning and by collective perceptions of the quality of presidential leadership, should expedite the crafting of legislative coalitions supportive of the president's position. The electoral mandate, presidential coattails, and public approval of the president's job performance are the wellspring of political capital available to the chief executive to entice the persuadables into

---

6. Bruce I. Oppenheimer, "Policy Effects of U.S. House Reform: Decentralization and the Capacity to Resolve Energy Issues," *Legislative Studies Quarterly* 5 (February 1980): 16; and David E. Price, *Who Makes the Laws?* (Cambridge, Mass.: Schenkman, 1972), pp. 319–320.

joining the administration's position. Previous scholarship, however, has demonstrated the ambiguous role of public support for the president. In Chapter 4, without controlling for other contextual factors, we saw presidents to be more successful when their level of public approval was higher rather than lower. Here we have an opportunity to hold constant the effects of other factors and to obtain a measure of the independent impact of public support. The last political variables included have to do with the strength of the president's party in Congress. Because members of the president's party provide the core of administration allies, their control of Congress should enhance the prospects of the president's agenda, as should increasing numbers of fellow partisans (whether or not they were in the majority). The relationship between party seats and presidential success may be more complicated than is implied by this simple statement, so the possibility of curvilinear relationships is once again introduced into the probit analysis.

The economic resource variables should help structure the politics associated with congressional responses in ways relevant to presidential preferences. Declining unemployment, receding inflation, healthy growth in the economy, and smaller federal deficits should all nurture the emergence of legislative agreements favorable to the president. High levels of inflation, however, probably complicate the politics of presidential-congressional relations and create problems for the chief executive. It seems logical, on the surface, to associate the same pattern with high levels of unemployment, but the previous analysis suggests that modern presidents have attained a unique leadership role on issues of unemployment. The more unemployment, the more all participants in the political process may turn to the president to set the agenda, unless an aggravated unemployment situation persists.

Since the strategic choices of the president are already incorporated in the nested models scheme, the policy context includes just two variables. One is the percentage of the public that identifies the policy area of the president's initiative as one involving the most important problem in the country. Public salience of issues should aid presidents both in getting the attention of Congress and in winning acceptance of their proposals. Events that transpire after the introduction of initiatives, but that have relevance for the policy being considered, probably focus congressional attention and accelerate legislative action.

The analysis is performed for each of the four types of policies associated with greater or lesser innovation. The results for both large and small policy departures appear in Table 6.3; those for both new and old policy departures are reported in Table 6.4. The analysis for each of the probit runs shows that the thresholds between the levels of the preference dimension as it has been defined are significantly different from one another, providing empirical evidence in support of the categorizations used to define the presidential preference dimension. The percentage of cases correctly predicted by the probit analyses ranges from 36% for the small proposals to 48% for the new initiatives. The size of the log-likelihood values indicates that the models, because of the inclusion of at least some of the variables, are unmistakably providing meaningful information about the variations in the presidential preference dimension.[7] And when we take into account the possible variations suggested above, most of the contextual variables have the anticipated relationships with presidential preferences or generate coefficients that are not statistically significant.

When presidents in the period of the study chose to introduce large departures in domestic policy, congressional action on those proposals was influenced most by the structure of the interest-group system (the elaboration of which hindered presidential coalition building) and the appearance of concrete events that reinforced the president's position. Of the other institutional variables, strengthened partisan electoral linkages seem ironically to have hurt presidents trying to enact large proposals, even though they stimulated presidents to introduce them. Perhaps the obvious presence of partisan bonds led presidents—Jimmy Carter, for instance—to misperceive the receptivity to such initiatives.

---

7. A chi-square test of the log-likelihood value can be used to ascertain whether the probit model, because of the inclusion of at least some of the variables, leads to a statistically significant improvement in explaining the variance of the dependent variable over simply knowing the overall distribution. The .01 level of significance is achieved if $-2 \times$ log likelihood $= 113$. In fact, for these two probit runs, the chi-square values range from 176.8 to greater than 600. The probit model that appears to have the weakest performance, assessing the role of context for large policy departures, is nevertheless statistically significant in these terms. Every probit model presented in this chapter easily attains at least the .01 level of significance.

Table 6.3   Ordered probit analysis of influence of contextual properties on presidential preference dimension for large and small policy departures

Contextual property	Large policy			Small policy		
	Coeffi-cient	Standard error	t-statistic	Coeffi-cient	Standard error	t-statistic
First threshold	0.574[a]	0.133	4.325	0.689[a]	0.073	9.614
Second threshold	4.458[a]	0.174	8.360	1.442[a]	0.051	28.295
Third threshold	2.416[a]	0.312	7.741	1.721[a]	0.060	28.295
Intercept	7.068	59.950	0.118	35.199	32.911	1.069
Pure context: institutional						
Decentralization of Congress	−0.062	0.693	−0.088	−0.102	0.314	−0.324
Elaboration of interest groups	−3.588[a]	1.605	−2.235	−0.344	0.557	−0.618
Electoral partisan links	−0.739[a]	0.437	−1.690	0.170	0.316	0.539
Malleable context: dynamic political						
President's two-party vote	−0.035	0.029	−1.207	−0.008	0.014	−0.570
Presidential coattails	−0.118	0.201	−0.587	0.121[a]	0.580	2.093
Intercept shift from House majority to minority	−64.525	113.901	−0.567	−71.544	45.194	−1.583
House seats when minority	0.409	0.545	0.749	−0.225	0.293	−0.768
(House seats when minority)^2	−0.001	0.001	−0.767	0.001	0.001	0.910
House seats when majority	−0.241	0.735	−0.328	−0.674[a]	0.289	−2.329
(House seats when majority)^2	0.001	0.001	0.364	0.001[a]	0.001	2.394
Intercept shift from Senate majority to minority	44.256	139.752	0.364	27.630	55.306	0.500
Senate seats when minority	−1.382	2.863	−0.430	1.382	1.432	0.966
(Senate seats when minority)^2	0.017	0.035	0.479	−0.018	0.014	−1.032
Senate seats when majority	1.136	3.351	0.393	1.831	1.334	1.372
(Senate seats when majority)^2	−0.015	0.026	−0.575	−0.015	0.010	−1.470
Public approval of president	−0.014	0.030	−0.486	−0.009	0.011	−0.764
Increase in public approval	−0.199	0.277	−0.718	0.003	0.119	0.021
Malleable context: economic						
Quarterly growth in GNP	0.007	0.144	0.050	0.078	0.067	1.153
Size of federal deficit	−0.208	0.242	−0.861	0.048	0.112	0.430
Level of monthly inflation	0.008	0.247	0.031	−0.060	0.089	−0.671
Quarterly increase in inflation	−0.035	0.332	−0.105	−0.195	0.145	−1.351
Level of monthly unemployment	0.201	0.303	0.664	0.111	0.150	0.735
Quarterly increase in unemployment	0.347	0.351	0.988	−0.054	0.185	−0.289
Policy context						
Subsequent event	1.360[a]	0.639	2.128	0.430	0.741	0.581
Most important problem	0.010	0.016	0.651	0.000	0.009	0.043
Number of cases:		71			227	
Log likelihood:		−88.40			−330.41	
Percentage of cases correctly predicted:		38.0			35.7	

[a] $p < .10$.

Table 6.4 Ordered probit analysis of influence of contextual properties on presidential preference dimension for new and old policy departures

Contextual property	New policy			Old policy		
	Coeffi-cient	Standard error	t-statistic	Coeffi-cient	Standard error	t-statistic
First threshold	0.932[a]	0.116	8.058	0.599[a]	0.076	7.881
Second threshold	1.403[a]	0.099	14.187	1.524[a]	0.060	25.327
Third threshold	1.968[a]	0.173	11.373	1.858[a]	0.073	25.524
Intercept	4.736	58.276	0.081	−9.478	34.754	−0.273
Pure context: institutional						
Decentralization of Congress	0.443	0.647	0.684	−1.222[a]	0.458	−2.671
Elaboration of interest groups	−2.762[a]	0.966	−2.859	1.816[a]	0.738	2.461
Electoral partisan links	−0.049	0.575	0.085	0.073	0.269	0.270
Malleable context: dynamic political						
President's two-party vote	−0.034[a]	0.020	−1.702	0.006	0.015	0.390
Presidential coattails	0.031	0.093	0.327	0.062	0.071	0.869
Intercept shift from House majority to minority	−266.745[a]	154.357	−1.728	−14.713	45.879	−0.321
House seats when minority	2.684[a]	1.531	1.753	−0.727[a]	0.297	−2.448
(House seats when minority)[2]	−0.007[a]	0.004	−1.742	0.002[a]	0.001	2.510
House seats when majority	−0.222	0.557	−0.399	−0.575[a]	0.285	−2.020
(House seats when majority)[2]	0.001	0.001	0.526	0.001[a]	0.001	1.978
Intercept shift from Senate majority to minority	147.750	149.562	0.988	55.604	58.574	0.949
Senate seats when minority	−5.869	4.861	−1.207	1.447	1.366	1.059
(Senate seats when minority)[2]	0.068	0.058	1.171	−0.017	0.017	−1.021
Senate seats when majority	1.150	2.429	0.473	2.716[a]	1.477	1.839
(Senate seats when majority)[2]	−0.013	0.019	−0.669	−0.021[a]	0.012	−1.822
Public approval of president	−0.066[a]	0.029	−2.262	0.016	0.012	1.377
Increase in public approval	0.409	0.272	1.505	−0.131	0.124	−1.061
Malleable context: economic						
Quarterly growth in GNP	0.090	0.139	0.649	0.071	0.064	1.109
Size of federal deficit	−0.002	0.177	−0.011	−0.150	0.118	−1.270
Level of monthly inflation	−0.210	0.201	−1.044	−0.033	0.079	−0.422
Quarterly increase in inflation	−0.163	0.260	−0.627	−0.057	0.161	−0.358
Level of monthly unemployment	0.051	0.326	0.157	0.188	0.158	1.192
Quarterly increase in unemployment	−0.070	0.306	−0.228	0.075	0.167	0.449
Policy context						
Subsequent event	1.352[a]	0.623	2.171	0.308	0.451	0.682
Most important problem	−0.034[a]	0.019	−1.827	0.007	0.009	0.759
Number of cases:	89			209		
Log likelihood:	−111.69			−330.24		
Percentage of cases correctly predicted:	48.3			37.3		

a. $p < .10$.

On the other hand, congressional fragmentation did not pose a problem. Let me emphasize that large proposals are not the same as comprehensive programs like Richard Nixon's Manpower Revenue Sharing, Jimmy Carter's National Energy Plan, or Ronald Reagan's 1981 Economic Recovery Program. Each of those programs was really a package of numerous proposals—some small, a few large, some new, many old. What made the decentralization of Congress significant for Carter's energy program, for example, was the sheer number and variation of the more than forty specific proposals that constituted the whole package and that required consideration in diverse committees and subcommittees representing a myriad of policy jurisdictions. Such dispersion led to the "new avenues for legislative obstructionism" examined by Bruce Oppenheimer.[8] The analysis presented here suggests that while Congress may have become a more challenging arena for comprehensive legislation, the decentralization of the Hill (other things being equal) did not thwart specific large policy departures suggested by the president.

According to the probit analysis presented in Table 6.3, none of the political or economic properties constituting the malleable context had a significant effect, not even the partisan composition of Congress. If some of these coefficients were in fact significant, the news would not have been good for the presidents under review, inasmuch as the electoral mandate, coattail, and public support variables are negatively correlated with presidential preferences, as are Senate seats. All of the economic variables had the expected effects; they are just not statistically significant. With all other factors controlled, congressional decision making on policies that have the largest social or budgetary impact do not seem to have been accomplished with serious reference to the state of the economy or the federal budget.[9]

The relative impotence of many of the variables in the contextual analysis for large proposals is not surprising, even within the tandem-institutions framework. One would not expect that for

8. Oppenheimer, "Policy Effects," p. 5.

9. The probit analysis of the large policy departures suffers from the relatively small number of cases, 71. With all of the variables that need to be included to define the context of congressional responses, this sample is not large enough to reduce the standard errors and offer confidence in the coefficients that are produced, if indeed the relationships are accurate representations of empirical reality.

the most significant presidential initiatives, members of Congress would be guided overwhelmingly by the institutional, political, and economic setting rather than by close deliberations among themselves and with participants in the executive branch. It is also in behalf of these proposals that presidents and their administrations made considerable efforts to influence members of Congress directly. Three-quarters of these initiatives were associated with programs of the highest priority to presidents and half were tied to policies the chief executive mentioned in at least one statement or address per month during the course of congressional consideration of the legislation. These are the proposals on which presidential effort, and the skills of individual presidents, should be most pronounced. It is no wonder that scholars examining case studies of major programs find legislative action to be somewhat divorced from contextual considerations. What presidents have actually done beyond the context of the issues will be investigated in the next chapter.

The story for small policy departures is quite different. All of the institutional factors had the expected effects, but none were statistically significant. Some political properties, however, were of importance. For these issues of lower salience to the Washington community, presidential coattails helped secure the presidentially preferred congressional responses, as did control of the House by the president's party. Particularly large majorities for the president's party in the House also aided the chief executive's position considerably. The number of seats held by the president's party in the Senate did not contribute any additional effect of which one can be statistically confident, even though there is some evidence that more seats helped marginally if the president's party was in the majority.

The state of the economy, while again not offering significant results, had some relevance. A healthy economy seems to have made it easier to pass the large number of small proposals sent to Congress, while increasing inflation limited the opportunities for success. Finally, the coefficient signs are as expected for the variables pertaining to most of the important problems and subsequent events, but they are not statistically significant.

This brings us to the analysis of new and old policy departures, reported in Table 6.4. The contextual analysis performs best for the new proposals, with several significant variables, despite the relatively small number of cases (89). While an expanded interest-group community apparently stimulated the introduction of more new presidential initiatives, it also increased the difficulty of enacting them. The recent growth in the complexity of the interest-group system brought with it the mobilization of new types of groups, which may have provided the basis for organized opposition to policies in areas that were previously more consensual.[10] On the political side, electoral mandates and the level of public approval of the president inhibited the achievement of presidential preferences when new policy departures were addressed by Congress. Opposition control of the House diminished the opportunities for presidential legislative success, as did an increase in the number of seats held by the president's party when it was in the minority. On new policy departures, as the president's party came close to the strength of the opposing party in the House, either the opposition became more obstinate or the president took more risks and showed a less compromising spirit. A trend of increasing public approval of the president also benefited the executive's position. Economic factors played the expected role or else no role at all, given the fact that none of the relevant coefficients reach conventional levels of statistical significance. Within the policy context, public identification of the issue area as one of high importance did not benefit new departures. In fact, success with new proposals came in areas where there was lower public salience. Events, however, had a strong impact. Not only did precursor events lead to the introduction of new policies, but subsequent events facilitated the passage of presidential initiatives that offered innovative departures.

Although many of the variables in the probit analysis of old proposals fail to reach conventional levels of significance, essentially all of them affected the presidential preference dimension in

10. Jeffrey M. Berry, Lobbying for the People (Princeton: Princeton University Press, 1977), and "Subgovernments, Issue Networks, and Political Conflict," in Remaking American Politics, ed. Richard Harris and Sidney Milkis (Boulder, Colo.: Westview Press, 1989), pp. 239–260; Christopher J. Boss, Pesticides and Politics: The Life Cycle of a Public Issue (Pittsburgh: University of Pittsburgh Press, 1987); Thomas L. Gais, Mark A. Peterson, and Jack L. Walker, "Interest Groups, Iron Triangles and Representative Institutions in American National Government," British Journal of Political Science 14 (April 1984): 161–185; and Kay Lehman Schlozman and John T. Tierney, Organized Interests and American Democracy (New York: Harper and Row, 1986).

the ways that were expected. Two of the institutional properties are particularly important. Because old policy departures proposed by the president involve changes in existing programs, for which there are firmly established jurisdictions, the decentralization of Congress since the early 1970s provided the means for opponents to block presidentially desired action. At the same time, the expanded group system apparently included more groups willing to support presidential initiatives in existing programmatic areas of interest to them. For old proposals, the basic ingredients of presidential political capital also made some difference, though not at a statistically significant level.

There is a positive association between presidentially preferred congressional action and the president's electoral mandate, presidential coattails, and level of public support of the president. Party control of either house of Congress did not make any statistically relevant difference, but there is some association between the number of seats held by the president's party and congressional action on old proposals. More seats of the president's party in an opposition-controlled House eventually benefited the president's coalition as it came close to the majority. Capture of an increasing number of House seats when the president's party already had a majority weakened the president's position. In a Senate dominated by the president's party, larger majorities helped the president's coalition. All of the economic properties show the expected relationships with presidentially preferred legislative responses, but again none of the variables are significant. The same is true of the two variables in the policy context.

To varying degrees, therefore, the factors that define the pure, malleable, and policy context of congressional action on the president's initiatives matter not only for understanding the level of cooperation or conflict in the legislative arena, but for explaining presidential success as well. No analysis of executive-legislative relations and presidential performance can begin without taking the different contexts into account. Presidents, of course, are often positioned to influence the various properties that define the contexts of congressional action. But how much influence or control have presidents from Eisenhower to Reagan had over the contextually based patterns evident in the probit analyses?

Other than indirectly prodding Congress into self-reflection, as Nixon did with the impoundment battle, a chief executive can do little to change the structure of Congress to the administration's advantage. President Reagan tried with some success to "defund the left" and generally restructure the interest-group system, but he failed to stem its growth and elaboration.[11] Some presidents have been able to strengthen the electoral base of their parties, and therefore one component of electoral partisan linkages, but there is little they can do directly to propel voters into more consistent partisan-based voting. In short, the three institutional properties included in this analysis are well beyond presidential control. Yet they have been found to be important stimulants of legislative conflict, and they influenced the legislative success of all but the small policy departures introduced by presidents from 1953 to 1984.

The political properties of the malleable context are more influenced by the behavior of individual presidents. They demonstrably affected the level of legislative discord during the Eisenhower to Reagan administrations, often by increasing conflict when presidents enjoyed a more propitious political status. In this respect the system of separate institutions sharing powers may be most dramatically different from the parliamentary experience. Electoral mandates and presidential popularity led to increased legislative confrontation, not cooperation. The level of conflict was mitigated when party congruence existed between the White House and the House of Representatives, and when the president's party majorities in the Senate increased somewhat or in the House grew immensely. Political properties of the malleable context also influenced the fulfillment of presidentially preferred congressional responses, but not always in predictable ways. A president would be hard pressed to define an optimal political setting for considering the administration's program, because the contextual effects varied so dramatically depending upon the nature of the issues involved.

Presidential actions affecting the state of the economy may also

11. Mark A. Peterson and Jack L. Walker, "Interest Group Responses to Partisan Change: The Impact of the Reagan Administration upon the National Interest Group System," in *Interest Group Politics*, 2nd ed., ed. Allan J. Cigler and Burdett A. Loomis (Washington, D.C.: CQ Press, 1986), pp. 162–182; and Harold Wolman and Fred Teitelbaum, "Interest Groups and the Reagan Presidency," in *The Reagan Presidency and the Governing of America*, ed. Lester L. Salamon and Michael S. Lund (Washington, D.C.: Urban Institute, 1984), pp. 297–329.

have some impact on the chief executive's programs. Growth in the GNP, low budget deficits or even surpluses, and low or decreasing inflation all attenuated institutional conflict and favored fulfillment of the president's policy preferences. But this pattern hardly suggests a clever political strategy for chief executives. Regardless of the consequences for their legislative programs, these conditions represent economic objectives pursued by all presidents, and all members of Congress, for the betterment of the nation. To paraphrase Charles Wilson, what is good for the nation is good for presidents. But because the health of the economy is well beyond the control of any single political actor, presidents during this period were unable to maintain the desired levels of affluence and productivity. Even the steady growth and low inflation of the middle part of the 1980s came at the expense of an enormous federal budget deficit. Presidents were often favored, as far as congressional action on their programs is concerned, by the existence of high unemployment. It seems unlikely that any chief executive would intentionally pursue a low-employment strategy in order to enhance the prospects of legislative success; so despite the opportunities for presidential influence, there is not much that presidents have done, or can do, to manipulate the contexts of congressional decision making to their benefit.

Even within the policy context there is little opportunity for premeditated presidential control. Consider the two factors included in the probit analyses of presidential preferences. Presidents certainly have tried, sometimes successfully, to promote the public salience of various issues. The public on occasion has come to identify major problems partially because presidents have succeeded as opinion leaders.[12] But there are few policy areas at any given moment that attract much attention from the public. For most presidential proposals to Congress since 1953, both the executive and the legislative branches operated in policy domains largely devoid of close public interest or inspection.

Presidents also demonstrated the capacity to use pertinent events to gain support for their programs. Passage of the Voting

12. Benjamin I. Page and Robert Y. Shapiro, "Presidential Leadership through Public Opinion," in The Presidency and Public Policy Making, ed. George C. Edwards III, Steven A. Shull, and Norman C. Thomas (Pittsburgh: University of Pittsburgh Press, 1985), pp. 22–36.

Rights Act of 1965 and gun control legislation in 1968, for instance, was certainly eased by Lyndon Johnson's knowing how to play to the incidents surrounding the civil rights marches in Selma, Alabama, in 1965 and the assassinations of Martin Luther King, Jr., and Robert Kennedy in 1968. These events could not have been manufactured from whole cloth, however. They had to happen, and as a result of forces beyond prediction and control.

The one aspect of context over which the seven presidents had the most definitive control is the kind of strategic decisions they made about the type of proposals to be submitted to Congress. The impact of the pure and malleable contexts of congressional action could conceivably be presidentially manipulated by sending up legislation likely to take advantage of the prevailing institutional, political, and economic forces. The conflict analysis showed, for example, that presidents from Eisenhower to Reagan could have reduced the incidence of legislative confrontations by submitting only those initiatives that constituted small policy departures, were linked to bills of minor significance, and were associated with established policy areas. It is doubtful that presidents would be willing to subject themselves to the gauntlet of the nominating process and the rigors of the election campaign if their legislative activity were going to be so constrained. To a considerable degree, in fact, presidential decisions about the nature of their policies were unaffected by such strategic concerns. To achieve what they wanted to achieve, these presidents often pressed ahead with their programmatic designs, seeing the responses of Congress to their initiatives influenced in meaningful ways by contextual forces largely independent of executive management.

7. Presidents, Choices, and Policy Leadership

One of the most frequently repeated anecdotes in Richard Neustadt's book *Presidential Power* is President Harry Truman's prediction about the discouragement likely to be felt by Dwight Eisenhower, should he be elected and attempt to issue a command. "He'll sit here," according to Truman, "and he'll say, 'Do this! Do that!' *And nothing will happen.* Poor Ike—it won't be like the Army. He'll find it very frustrating."[1] Truman, of course, was conveying his own sense of frustration, a sentiment undoubtedly shared by each of his successors. All new presidents assume office with a store of enthusiasm, ready to grasp the reins of power and guide the polity along the path of their choosing. Before long, however, each administration confronts the realities of power— or more precisely, the fundamental constraints on the use of presidential power. Those inhibitions exist in all realms of presidential action, from military decisions to administration policy, from personnel appointments to legislative relations with Congress. The preceding chapters have only reinforced the impression of a chief executive, functioning as chief legislator, bound by forces beyond the president's immediate control. It is time to ask, *Do individual presidents make a difference?*

Up to this point I have referred to "the president" in abstract terms, as a generic figure, almost a disembodied being, as though one resident of the White House were the same as the next. The level of abstraction has been purposeful, in order to generalize about the president as a continuing part of the enduring *institution* of the presidency. At the heart of this project is the intention to divine the patterns of presidential-congressional interactions

1. Richard E. Neustadt, *Presidential Power: The Politics of Leadership from FDR to Carter* (New York: Macmillan, 1980), p. 9.

that are evident regardless of the particular personalities of those resident in the tandem-institutions setting. It is not that the individuals are unimportant; in fact quite the opposite is the case. Real and very different individuals have served as president since 1953, bringing particular strengths and vulnerabilities to the office they held. But one of the main attributes of the tandem-institutions approach is the recognition that we cannot fully understand or appreciate the role of individuals in the institutional setting until we are able to give some measure to those factors that lie beyond the immediate boundaries of individual action. We require a kind of contextual baseline in order to draw meaningful conclusions about the contributions of individuals, even individuals as seemingly powerful as presidents of the United States. Without attention to the sometimes static, sometimes shifting milieu in which presidents must practice their leadership, "it is too easy to personalize the office and explain outcomes favorable to Presidents as due to the superior skill of a given President."[2] That is the typical deficiency of presidency-centered analyses. By starting from the perspective of the individual chief executive, these studies often lose touch with both the legitimacy of other players in the political system and the situational factors that define the challenges and opportunities of political leadership. They offer no yardstick for assessing what an individual president was able to accomplish, given the tenor of the times.

Each occupant of the White House, unquestionably, displays a unique set of responses to the situations that arise. Each action that is undertaken, each decision that is made, represents a partially reactive choice based to some extent on an assessment of the prevailing forces and a determination about how to both respond to and influence the contextual attributes shaping the political scene. Some of these presidential choices define the approaches administrations take to exploit the political resources afforded by the constellation of factors. Among the issues decided is the innovativeness of the president's program, discussed in the previous chapter. Other choices, either as the result of explicit strategic calculation or as the by-product of the actions they initiate, may bring about limited change in features of the institutional, polit-

2. Erwin C. Hargrove, *The Power of the Modern Presidency* (New York: Knopf, 1974), p. 209.

ical, or economic contexts of presidential leadership. My objective in this chapter is to examine the range of choices available to presidents in the modern era, and their effects, remaining sensitive to the link between the political environments presidents face and the opportunities they enjoy. I will look closely now at individual presidents, assessing the legislative performance of each president from Dwight Eisenhower to Ronald Reagan.

Do Individual Presidents Make a Difference?

Among the implicit precepts of systems founded on democratic principles "is the assumption that leaders do matter."[3] Since the time of George Washington, chief executives have been able to leave their individual imprints on the political and policy landscape. Periods of American history are even designated by the names of the presidents whose service in office marked an era's beginning and end. In the legislative domain, all chief executives have before them opportunities to shape the political arena in which their initiatives will be considered. By their actions, their failure to take action, and their responses to action-forcing events, presidents can realign the configuration of some factors that contribute to the political-economic context of their presidencies. They can make well-considered or ill-advised use of their political resources. They can reorient the organizational design of the Executive Office of the President. They can exhibit personal attributes consonant with or detrimental to the successful practice of political influence. In short, presidents can be leaders as well as constrained decision makers.

To be sure, it is often not easy to separate the individual from the context.[4] Were Ronald Reagan's convincing electoral victories, for example, the product of his own campaign skills, policy positions, and insight into the psyche of the American electorate? Or were they as much a rejection of Carter and Mondale, who came to symbolize, however inappropriately, an outworn mind-set of diminished expectations? Were the economic dislocations experienced during the Carter administration the consequence of an ill-

3. Valerie Bunce, *Do New Leaders Make a Difference? Executive Succession and Public Policy under Capitalism and Socialism* (Princeton: Princeton University Press, 1981), p. 3.

4. Ibid., p. 17.

prepared, inept leader? Or were they caused by a foreign oil cartel, serial droughts, and a worldwide economic downturn? Obviously some mix existed in each case, but the boundary between individual and contextual effects may not always be ascertainable. It remains vital, however, to understand the impact of context, no matter how it is produced, and the role of the individual, no matter how it is circumscribed.

Although their freedom of action is not unlimited, presidents have the opportunity to fashion their political choices in ways that enhance the likelihood of a favorable reception to their policy initiatives. First of all, they have some control over the scheduling, marketing, and substantive contours of the legislative programs they submit to Congress. One of the most important strategic decisions facing each administration is when to introduce particular features of the president's legislative agenda. New administrations, especially those unexpectedly thrust into office by the death or demise of their predecessors, may not develop their full effectiveness as policy-formulating enterprises until experience and early mistakes provide the pragmatic education necessary to temper the ignorance and lapses of judgment that plague new incumbents and their aides.[5] Some issues do not permit presidential discretion in timing. Unanticipated events, such as natural disasters or economic crises, may trigger unavoidable demands for presidential action. But with respect to most of the legislative agenda, presidents have considerable freedom to move their programs early or late in their administrations. Those who possess a confident sense of direction at the time of their inauguration and who can fully exploit the transition to the new administration will have greater success in overcoming the ensuing contextual constraints.[6]

Presidents must also make choices about legislative priorities. There are too many legislative issues to be processed without the benefit of some guidance. Presidents may want it all, but they cannot have it all. They and their staffs need to determine what is most essential. Sometimes that choice will be forced upon them by the course of events and the political realities. Sometimes legis-

5. The dangers that loom for new administrations are discussed by Richard Neustadt in *Presidential Power,* chap. 11.
6. James P. Pfiffner, *The Strategic Presidency: Hitting the Ground Running* (Chicago: Dorsey Press, 1988), esp. chaps. 1, 7.

lative priorities will require a president to concentrate on the most difficult legislation to enact. The easy bills do not require such concerted attention.

Related to both the timing and the priority of the legislative program is the size of the overall agenda presented by the White House. Even a small agenda formulated by a well-prepared executive policy team cannot be submitted in its entirety during any one moment in an administration. The more extensive the program, the longer the period over which its bulk must be spread. Any modern president is impelled to forge an agenda of dimensions far broader than can be handled personally by the president, or even by the White House establishment. As the magnitude of the agenda increases, the necessity of formally designating administration priorities becomes even more pronounced.

As all presidents come to understand, if they do not fully comprehend at first, there is only so much that Congress can handle at any given time. President Johnson, with his usual flare for colorful metaphors, described the strategic problem: "A congressman is like a whiskey drinker. You can put an awful lot of whiskey into a man if you just let him sip it. But if you try to force the whole bottle down his throat at one time, he will throw it up."[7] Because of the organizational limitations of the Hill and the need to generate support for major initiatives among the public, a senior adviser to Republican presidents commented that he "had a house rule . . . that you don't ever have more than five presidential proposals at a time, if you can avoid it." To the extent that presidents desire and seek a record of legislative success, presidents should practice some restraint, or at least discipline, in articulating their domestic policy ambitions.

Presidential agendas in this context have significance beyond the simple calculation of their overall size. Sometimes, as LBJ powerfully demonstrated, extremely ambitious, diverse, and sizable programmatic agendas can be guided through the legislative labyrinth. Other more limited agendas can be stymied. Each year Jimmy Carter submitted to Congress fewer domestic proposals than did John Kennedy, and the number of Kennedy's requests is dwarfed by comparison to Lyndon Johnson's prodigious legislative output. Nevertheless, Carter was perceived to have carelessly

7. Joseph A. Califano, Jr., *A Presidential Nation* (New York: W. W. Norton, 1975), p. 63.

overburdened Capitol Hill. His experience illustrates the importance of an agenda of size and form consonant with the particular institutional framework in which it is to be considered. President Carter had the misfortune to take up residence in the White House when the congressional agenda was already laden with pent-up Democratic legislation. Further, because of the issues Carter chose to pursue, and the manner in which he wished to approach them, the whole Congress did not get overloaded as much as parts of it did. By attempting comprehensive restructuring of federal energy policy, welfare, the tax system, health financing, and the like, Carter sent to Congress a good deal of legislation with provisions that required favorable review by two committees, Ways and Means in the House and Finance in the Senate. One of Carter's aides estimated rather expansively that 80% to 90% of the legislation required action by those committees. Two-thirds of the Carter initiatives in my sample that were tied to major legislation on which Carter expended the greatest effort fell under the jurisdiction of the Ways and Means Committee and the Finance Committee. Large agendas tend to invite problems. And large agendas directed extensively at so limited a number of bottlenecks invite disaster.

Presidents may enjoy some flexibility in deciding which substantive policy concerns to address in their proposals and in formulating the most advantageous legislative packages. If, for example, policy objectives can be fulfilled by either regulatory or nonregulatory approaches, choosing some form of nonregulatory procedure poses fewer threats to potential opponents and avoids the confrontational showdowns often associated with regulatory issues. Administrations can also choose to limit their ambitions by crafting legislative programs that promote smaller and less innovative expansions or changes in the role of government, eluding the legislative battles and possible defeats associated with legislative boldness. Frequently, however, these options are not available because institutional requirements, political pressures, or substantive problems dictate the need to pursue policies that are more contentious and difficult to accomplish.[8]

The packaging of initiatives allows the president to retain var-

8. Robert J. Spitzer, *The Presidency and Public Policy: The Four Arenas of Presidential Power* (University: University of Alabama Press, 1983), p. 156.

ious options. Although patriotism, Americana, and general good will cannot be wedded to every proposal that emanates from the White House, and concerns about the deliberation required to formulate sound public policy probably argues against it, presidents can try to invigorate their proposals politically by identifying them as, or cloaking them with, those kinds of valence issues. By making their initiatives seem to be less controversial options that invite instinctive approval, a president can hope to inspire an artificial consensus.[9] The pervasive view in the late 1980s that something must be done to fight drug abuse, and the resulting bandwagon—or more precisely, stampede—in Congress to enact responsive legislation offers one example.

Where neither the substantive direction can be changed nor the protection of valence issues employed, old-fashioned politicking remains a possibility. Members of Congress do not weigh presidential initiatives devoid of their own interests and concerns, many of which are independent of the president's policy objectives and therefore do not undermine the substantive core of the executive's proposals. The interests of senators and representatives can be accommodated in legislative fusions that incorporate a little horse-trading on issues peripheral to the president's position. It is possible to accomplish these trades in the postinitiation phase when negotiation, compromise, and logrolling begin; but they may also be anticipated and incorporated into the initial legislation. Presidents, therefore, can attempt to surmount some of the barriers imposed by the contexts of congressional action by the ways in which they choose, formulate, and present their policy proposals.

Most institutional features of American national government and politics are difficult to change within the scope of a single administration. Presidents do, however, enjoy considerable latitude in the realm of decisions about the arrangement and composition of the institutional entities most proximate to the Oval Office, such as the White House Office (WHO), the Office of Management and Budget (OMB), and the other agencies and offices within the larger organizational umbrella of the Executive Office of the President (EOP). Even though statutes dictate the necessity

9. Barbara J. Nelson, *Making an Issue of Child Abuse: Political Agenda Setting for Social Problems* (Chicago: University of Chicago Press, 1984), pp. 93–94.

of winning congressional approval of cabinet nominations and some nominations for positions in the EOP, there are relatively few restrictions on a president's design of the explicit and implicit organizational chart of the greater White House establishment. Even Congresses controlled by potentially hostile majorities have almost always yielded to the desires of the president on issues of staffing and appointments.

Short of the constitutional prohibition forbidding members of Congress from serving as executive officials and the persuasive force of tradition favoring certain kinds of occupational and constituency influences on the appointment of department secretaries, presidents have nearly complete freedom in selecting cabinet members and determining how to employ their cabinets as policy-making bodies. They may, as did President Eisenhower, view the cabinet as a collection of presidential advisers whose positions on various policy issues should be sought regularly in formal group meetings.[10] Or, recognizing the possible inappropriateness of having all department secretaries meet to discuss all issues, they may value the contributions of subgroupings of the cabinet organized around specific policy areas of direct interest to some secretaries. Reagan, for example, initially established an elaborate set of "cabinet councils" to provide the organizational setting in which the president's agenda would be formulated.[11] Or presidents may decide that the members of the cabinet represent too disparate a set of experiences and policy concerns to make them suitable as a collective decision-making body. They may prefer to emphasize the role of the cabinet members as independent managers of their departments, charged with the responsibility for conducting agency affairs consistent with presidential objectives.[12]

How a president ultimately decides to use the cabinet colors executive and congressional choices about the legislative program.

10. Fred I. Greenstein, *The Hidden-Hand Presidency: Eisenhower as Leader* (New York: Basic Books, 1982), pp. 113–115.

11. Interviews with aides to President Reagan; Dick Kirschten, "Policy Development Office: A Scaled-Down Operation," *National Journal*, April 25, 1981, p. 684, and "Reagan Sings of Cabinet Government, and Anderson Leads the Chorus," *National Journal*, May 9, 1981, pp. 824–827.

12. Theodore C. Sorensen, *Kennedy* (New York: Bantam, 1966), pp. 281–283.

A program that emerges from a consensus developed among members of the cabinet in formal sessions is likely to be different from proposals derived primarily under the leadership of a single secretary. The former may generate less controversial initiatives, providing the basis for securing relatively harmonious congressional approval. The latter may engender more dramatic and innovative approaches, with the potential for triggering opposition or excessive constituency influence.

Ever since the 1939 enactment of much of the Brownlow report, which created the Executive Office of the President, presidents have been able to determine the extent to which the Bureau of the Budget, reconstituted and renamed the Office of Management and Budget in 1970, functions as a direct arm of the presidency, and ultimately of the personal rather than the institutional presidency.[13] Eisenhower relied on the Budget Bureau as the main instrument for assembling his legislative program. It collected the budgetary and legislative proposals suggested by the departments, developed a "laundry list" of possibilities, then assessed their priorities with respect to Eisenhower's interests and objectives.[14] Central clearance evolved prior to the Eisenhower administration and remains significant to this day, but during the Eisenhower tenure it was the principal mechanism for crafting the president's program.[15] Other chief executives, such as Kennedy, chose to utilize officials of the Budget Bureau as more personal advisers, exploiting their expertise and institutional memories while integrating them as informal presidential assistants.[16] Under President Reagan the transformation of the OMB became complete. Because of the budgetary and regulatory nature of Reagan's agenda, the lack of aggressive programmatic advocacy from the White House Office of Policy Development, and the selection of

13. Larry Berman, *The Office of Management and Budget and the Presidency, 1921–1979* (Princeton: Princeton University Press, 1979), chaps. 1, 2.

14. Interview with an aide to President Eisenhower.

15. Richard E. Neustadt, "Presidency and Legislation: The Growth of Central Clearance," *American Political Science Review* 48 (September 1954): 641–671; Stephen J. Wayne, *The Legislative Presidency* (New York: Harper and Row, 1978), pp. 103–107; and interviews with aides to President Eisenhower. See also Berman, *The Office of Management and Budget*, pp. 50–52.

16. Berman, *The Office of Management and Budget*, pp. 67–104.

David Stockman as budget director, the OMB became, at least early on, the primary domestic policy organ of the Reagan presidency.[17] As with the choices made about the cabinet, different approaches to the use of the OMB can influence the character of presidential proposals and the legislative responses they engender. A presidential agenda built on central clearance is not likely to be as innovative and controversial as one generated with explicit White House input. An agenda controlled by a single powerful agency driven by an ethos of budgetary control and deregulation will probably remain relatively integrated and limited in scope.

In addition, presidents can make a variety of choices about how to structure the staff with which they work most closely—the officials often lodged in the West Wing directly above, below, and alongside the Oval Office itself. This core group can be organized in any way the president prefers, from a centralized, unitary structure, to a pluralistic array of quasi-equal advisers, to a managed system of multiple advocacy.[18] The first typically involves a hierarchical staff organization guided by a designated chief of staff, the pattern followed by President Eisenhower.[19] The second may be reflected in either a "collegial" or a "competitive" system, usually associated with what Roger Porter terms adhocracy. Under this system presidents serve as their own chief of staff, directing an assortment of generalists who bring diverse perspectives to the same issues; this was the approach Kennedy chose during his brief

17. Interviews with OMB officials and aides to President Reagan; Peter A. Benda and Charles H. Levine, "Reagan and the Bureaucracy: The Bequest, the Promise, and the Legacy," in *The Reagan Legacy: Promise and Performance,*" ed. Charles O. Jones (Chatham, N.J.: Chatham House, 1988), pp. 102–142; Fred I. Greenstein, "The Need for an Early Appraisal of the Reagan Presidency," in *The Reagan Presidency: An Early Assessment,* ed. Fred I. Greenstein (Baltimore: Johns Hopkins University Press, 1983), p. 17; and John H. Kessel, "The Structures of the Reagan White House," *American Journal of Political Science* 28 (May 1984): 246–251.

18. Alexander L. George, "The Case for Multiple Advocacy in Making Foreign Policy," *American Political Science Review* 66 (September 1972): 751–785; and Roger B. Porter, *Presidential Decision Making: The Economic Policy Board* (Cambridge: Cambridge University Press, 1980), esp. chap. 8, appendix.

19. Stephen Hess, *Organizing the Presidency* (Washington, D.C.: Brookings Institution, 1976), pp. 68–71; and Richard T. Johnson, *Managing the White House* (New York: Harper and Row, 1974).

administration.[20] The third may entail a more formally designated set of structures intended to ensure the consideration of disparate policy views.[21] Whichever arrangement is selected remains open to reassessment and change. Stephen Hess, for example, identifies the continuing organizational evolution of the Nixon White House, citing evidence of six phases over the six years of the administration.[22]

The choices about organization of the White House may be relevant to the kinds of congressional responses given presidential initiatives. The nonhierarchical, pluralistic approaches to staffing the presidency introduce into the policy development process a set of competing political forces possibly paralleling those found on the Hill. The political viability of presidential policy proposals may be enhanced by formulating them in an institutional context that requires the accommodation of interests that are likely also to be represented in the legislature. By contrast, if the ideological dispersion of the White House staff is so vast as to incorporate too many of the political divisions extant in the larger Washington community, as apparently was true of the Carter administration in at least some areas, then open, pluralistic advisory systems may defeat any attempt at coherence.[23]

The organizational choices open to presidents in actuality may not be as unrestricted as suggested in the previous discussion. With the modern presidency has come the creation of the president's own bureaucracy in the Executive Office of the President, concomitant with dramatic increases in the number of individuals working directly for the president and producing some of the same kinds of bureaucratic hurdles that characterize the rest of the executive establishment.[24] Near the start of the Eisenhower

20. Porter, *Presidential Decision Making*, pp. 231–235. Interviews with aides to President Kennedy; Hess, *Organizing the Presidency*, pp. 78–81; and Richard E. Neustadt, "Approaches to Staffing the Presidency, Notes on FDR and JFK," *American Political Science Review* 57 (December 1963): 855–863.

21. George, "The Case for Multiple Advocacy"; and Porter, *Presidential Decision Making*, chap. 8, pp. 241–252.

22. Hess, *Organizing the Presidency*, p. 112.

23. See John H. Kessel, "The Structures of the Carter White House," *American Journal of Political Science* 27 (August 1983): 433–439.

24. Thomas E. Cronin, *The State of the Presidency*, 2nd ed. (Boston: Little, Brown, 1980), pp. 243–247; Alfred De Grazia, "The Myth of the

administration, the White House Office alone employed 226 people; by 1971 the figure was 583, slightly higher than the 568 employed in 1987.[25] Much of the expansion came during the years of the Johnson presidency. An aide to President Kennedy illustrated the growth when he noted: "We had a very small White House staff. Only eighteen people . . . It didn't expand until the Johnson administration. Then my job was replaced by fourteen people." By the time Jimmy Carter took office, a potential presidential domestic proposal would be reviewed by the Office of Management and Budget, the Domestic Policy Staff, the Council of Economic Advisers, the Office of the Vice President, the Office of the Assistant to the President for Public Liaison, the Office of the Secretary to the Cabinet and Assistant to the President for Intergovernmental Affairs, the Office of Counsel to the President, and the offices of the Assistants to the President for Political Affairs and Personnel, Communications, and Congressional Liaison.[26]

In addition to decisions about the form and use of the presidential advisory system, a chief executive has to make the perhaps more important selections of individuals to fill positions in the

President," in The Presidency, ed. Aaron Wildavsky (Boston: Little, Brown, 1969), pp. 49–73; Hugh Heclo, "The Changing Presidential Office," in Politics and the Oval Office, ed. Arnold J. Meltsner (San Francisco: Institute for Contemporary Studies, 1981), pp. 161–183; Samuel Kernell, "The Creed and Reality of Modern White House Management," in Chief of Staff: Twenty-Five Years of Managing the Presidency, ed. Samuel Kernell and Samuel L. Popkin (Berkeley: University of California Press, 1986), pp. 198–203; and Terry M. Moe, "The Politicized Presidency," in The New Directions in American Politics, ed. John E. Chubb and Paul E. Peterson (Washington, D.C.: Brookings Institution, 1985), pp. 235–271.

25. The Eisenhower and 1971 figures are from Hargrove, The Power of the Modern Presidency, p. 80. The 1987 count is from Bradley H. Patterson, Jr., The Ring of Power: The White House Staff and Its Expanding Role in Government (New York: Basic Books, 1988), p. 339. These figures exclude a large number of executive office staff members, including those associated with the National Security Council. See John Hart, The Presidential Branch (New York: Pergamon Books, 1987), pp. 97–109, for different measures of size; and Kernell, "The Creed and Reality," p. 201, for changes in the budgeted and detailed White House Office staff from 1935 to 1985.

26. Paul C. Light, The President's Agenda: Domestic Policy Choice from Kennedy to Carter (Baltimore: Johns Hopkins University Press, 1982), p. 55.

administration. Interviews with Washington officials lead to the conclusion that to those who practice politics and to journalists who cover it, the key ingredient of understanding the processes and outcomes of policy making is the personalities of the participants and how well those personalities blend with one another. An OMB career official recounted the following story:

> Just before you came in, a guy called me and he told me about two major pieces of legislation. First they had been moving ahead and then they died off, and now they're on the front burner again because Phil Burton died. And he wasn't even on one of the subcommittees. But someone who is as obnoxious as Burton, and with so much influence, no one wants to buck him. So now there are things that come out off the back burner. You see this happen when a guy moves off a committee. So now things happen, and the legislation takes an entirely different turn. It revolves a lot around personality, the personality of who is a budget director or of the guy who runs things in the White House.

At least from the point of view of the participants, the success of the president's program may rest largely on the ability of White House aides and other appointed officials to handle the diverse group of individuals who populate Capitol Hill. How well that task is accomplished depends on two qualities of those people. One has to do with their skills and competency; the other concerns the compatibility of their personalities with those of the individuals with whom they must interact.

It is hardly novel to suggest that for members of the president's team to be effective, they must possess the appropriate skills, talents, and training needed to carry out their responsibilities. Presidents presumably make an effort to appoint individuals with suitable qualifications. What many of my informants alluded to in addition was a class of political skills uniquely important when operating in a professional context that includes Congress. One congressional staff member likened it to the importance of understanding the laws of physics in another situation.

> I once worked at a nursery, and we had to put in big trees; you know, the ones with the big balls [of soil]. You had to be in front of them only when they were sliding into the hole, so it's the same. When you had a two-ton or one-ton ball of dirt

about to go into the hole, you had to make quick adjustments. It's the same with legislation. At some point in the slide of legislation, whether it's in the committee, the Rules Committee, or on the floor, you have to make a quick jerk here and hold fast there.

Achieving those adjustments, knowing how and when to make them, requires legislative expertise among more individuals than just those on the congressional liaison staff.

Even if all of the players have the necessary expertise about the policy issues and the political process, there remains the question of compatibility. The congressional aide quoted above provided contrasting examples of individual rapport in the context of the House Committee on Ways and Means:

> If you take Carter and [Al] Ullman [chairman of Ways and Means at the time] and add in Frank Moore and [Bill] Cable, it was a disaster. If you take [Russell] Long [chairman of the Senate Finance Committee] and Carter, it was a disaster . . . [Reagan's] choice of [Ken] Duberstein [for liaison with the House] was exceptional from our point of view, and by our point of view, I mean as Democrats, as urban Northerners. [Dan] Rostenkowski [chairman of Ways and Means since 1981] is from Chicago, the chief counsel is from outside Boston, and then me. We're all east coast, urban-oriented Democrats. When you send us a good Brooklyn Jew who is familiar with bagels, and more familiar with bagels than, say, polo, and who has street smarts, as Ken certainly did, there is nothing in the textbook that catches this.

A president, however, cannot function as a "Dating Game" host, carefully matching the personality and background of each assistant and appointee with the range of character types that will be encountered in Congress in the course of forging and advocating the president's program. Once again, presidential decisions are not unconstrained; they are crafted in a setting of significant trade-offs. White House personnel selections must weigh the loyalty and campaign activities of longtime supporters, the conflicting demands of different groups within the president's electoral coalition, and the necessity of substantive talent.[27] However

27. Hess, *Organizing the Presidency*, pp. 161–166; and John H. Kessel, *Presidential Parties* (Homewood, Ill.: Dorsey Press, 1984), pp. 76–78.

these potentially divergent needs are addressed, the choices the president makes about whom to include in the administration will influence subsequent decisions about the proposals in the legislative program.

Perhaps as important as any decision made by the president is the style of politics and the approach to legislative influence to be used in support of the president's program. Every administration shows enormous diversity on this score, as legislative priorities are aligned with political resources, individual skills, and specific targets of persuasion. For each issue under consideration, overall strategies and specific tactics have to be formulated; these range from private, quiet lobbying to public, national campaigns; from "persuasion on the merits" to horse-trading; from group meetings with the congressional leadership to one-on-one sessions with members of Congress; from inside lobbying to interest-group mobilization; from soft diplomacy to ceaseless cajoling. While each administration practices the politics of persuasion using all of these techniques, general tendencies of individual presidencies can also be identified. No one knew, understood, or employed personal contact as effectively as Lyndon Johnson, the king of the head count, the telephone exchange, and the nose-to-nose encounter. Few have been as effective as Ronald Reagan, "the communicator-in-chief," in exploiting the media technology of their era to launch public campaigns in behalf of their legislative initiatives.[28] These tendencies emerge precisely because of the particular assemblage of political skills and deficiences embodied in each individual. Ford and Carter took to the national airwaves, but neither could master the medium of television as effectively as Kennedy and Reagan. Nixon invited representatives and senators to the Oval Office for private meetings, but had less skill than Johnson in securing commitments.

Finally, there are the large choices that presidents make about themselves, choices and orientations driven by their background and the experiences of their career and lifetime. They are decisions reflected in their character and personality. These decisions affect each president's capacity to understand and exploit the human element that rests at the heart of politics, to know when and how to cut a deal. "That's intuition, it's a judgment call.

28. Sidney Blumenthal, *The Permanent Campaign* (New York: Simon and Schuster, 1982), chap. 15.

That's what distinguishes a great leader from a middling and moderately successful one," said a senior adviser to LBJ. They are choices of life-style and perspective, which color the interactions of presidents with the political leaders they must cultivate as allies. Consider a congressional staff member's impression of the old-style politics of Lyndon Johnson and the moralism of Jimmy Carter:

Johnson and [Senate Minority Leader Everett] Dirksen would get together and drink until they were sloshed, and Johnson, when Dirksen was practically out, would get pledges out of him. Then Johnson would call him in the morning and tell him what he got out of him . . . The question is, do you have a Johnson and Dirksen getting stinking drunk over bourbon or do you have a Carter and [House Speaker Tip] O'Neill staring at each other over seltzer water and soda for an hour and a half?

So far I have laid out the choices that presidents can and must make, the potential for influencing congressional responses associated with their legislative initiatives, and the generic role of chief executives in the legislative process. Now we need to consider the decisions that specific incumbents made in the course of their administrations and speculate about the contributions of those choices to the legislative processes by which their domestic programs were enacted, modified, defeated, or ignored.

The Impact of Individual Presidencies

From the long list of options available to all presidents, each incumbent has made his own choices. To assess the significance of those decisions, we first need to examine how Congress reacted to the legislative programs of each chief executive. Table 7.1 analyzes the congressional responses to the sample of presidential proposals, broken down by administration from President Eisenhower through legislative action as late as June 1986 on the first-term initiatives of President Reagan. The distributions highlight the capacity of Congress to make decisions about presidential initiatives in vastly different ways from one presidency to the next. Dwight Eisenhower, Lyndon Johnson, and Ronald Reagan stand out as particularly successful presidents in getting Congress to move affirmatively on their initiatives. The first two, who were

Table 7.1   Presidential preference dimension of congressional responses
to initiatives of individual presidents from Eisenhower to
Reagan

President	N	Presidential preference dimension					
		Opposition dominance	Strategic inaction	Passive inaction	Compromise	Presidential dominance	Consensus
Eisenhower	48	17%	15%	2%	17%	19%	31%
Kennedy	45	18%	27%	7%	13%	11%	24%
Johnson	81	17%	7%	6%	21%	11%	37%
Nixon	39	13%	33%	8%	23%	5%	18%
Ford	16	38%	12%	12%	12%	6%	19%
Carter	48	31%	25%	10%	21%	2%	10%
Reagan	22	23%	23%	0%	27%	27%	0%

very different kinds of personalities and presidents, enjoyed much
consensus. Had John Kennedy's administration not ended so
abruptly with his assassination, it is conceivable that he would
have joined their ranks. If, for purposes of illustration, one drops
the 1963 proposals that Congress ignored (which may not have
had enough time for congressional consideration), strategic inaction on Kennedy's proposals drops to 12% and consensus rises
to 32%.

Reagan earns high marks for being able to dominate legislative
decision making when public struggles arose, but at the expense
of never achieving a consensus on the initiatives in this sample.
Jimmy Carter's program received the least favorable treatment,
suffering a good deal of opposition dominance. Opposition coalitions defeated almost as large a proportion of his domestic program as of Gerald Ford's, despite the dramatically different routes
the two presidents took to the Oval Office and the enormous difference in the number of seats held by their respective parties on
Capitol Hill. President Nixon saw a higher percentage of his initiatives ignored by Congress than any of the other presidents.
Fully a third were greeted by strategic inaction, when Congress
takes no serious action on initiatives of relatively high priority to
the president.

From the percentages in Table 7.1 can we therefore assert that
Presidents Carter and Nixon, along with Ford and perhaps Ken-
nedy, bungled their opportunities, while LBJ, Eisenhower, and
Reagan exemplified skillful political leadership? Would it be

appropriate to classify the former as failures and the latter as successes in the legislative domain on the basis of their individual performances in office? The simple distributions of congressional responses do not offer conclusive information. As has been argued throughout this book, each president, the apparently skilled and the seemingly inept, faced a set of circumstances a good deal beyond their control that fundamentally shaped the reactions of Congress to their initiatives. Furthermore, each president had different legislative ambitions and priorities, none of which are revealed in the table. What must concern us, then, is the performance of each president, given the specific pure, malleable, and policy contexts that each incumbent faced, as well as what each tried most earnestly to achieve.

The ordered probit analyses of presidential preferences reported in the previous chapter take into account the contextual baseline and offer one means for assessing the influence of individual presidents on congressional action. The probits did not include any variables that directly tap explicit efforts by individual presidents to influence the congressional responses to their programs. The predicted probabilities for each kind of congressional response generated by the probit models are therefore unencumbered by direct presidential action.[29] Any differences that exist between the predicted probability of each kind of congressional response and what actually happened in Congress to the initiatives of a particular president represent, at least to some extent, the contributions of presidential action. Such action reflects the range of choices made by individual presidents and their staffs, as well as their personal characteristics and skills.

Comparison of the aggregated predicted probabilities with the actual distributions of congressional responses offers some interesting insights into presidential-congressional relations from 1953 to 1986 and helps to evaluate the significance of the choices made by Presidents Eisenhower through Reagan. In the aggregate, the contexts of congressional responses predict rea-

29. The predicted probabilities, and thus percentages, for all types of proposals taken together were derived by combining the probabilities produced by the four presidential preference probit analyses of large, small, new, and old proposals. The probabilities from each probit were weighted according to the proportion of an individual president's legislative program comprising each type of policy.

sonably well the congressional decisions on the initiatives of these presidents. We have seen that the contextual probit models perform less well at predicting specific congressional responses to particular proposals. No matter what the predictions are for a specific case, the enormously complex forces of American politics, including random clashes of personalities over a single issue, make it possible for Congress to respond in any of the ways I have discussed. Despite this realization, overall predictions for each category of legislative response come quite close to the actual percentages. The idiosyncratic influences average out for the sample as a whole, quite frequently leading to empirical realization of the aggregate patterns expected from the probit analyses. The differences that do emerge are the subject of the rest of this chapter.

Dwight D. Eisenhower

We are left with two contradictory interpretations of Dwight Eisenhower's presidency. First, despite being matched against a Congress controlled by the opposing party for most of his administration, Eisenhower passed 67% of his initiatives—almost half of those successes coming from consensual congressional responses and nearly another third from victories over an organized opposition. Are these results an indication of real influence and control displayed by Eisenhower in his dealings with Congress? Do they reflect a president taking charge of the nation's domestic agenda?

Second, predictions from the contextual probit models show that Eisenhower's legislative performance was really about what one would expect from the pure and malleable contexts of the times, given the distribution of large and small, new and old proposals he submitted for legislative consideration. The high proportion of consensual legislative responses is almost exactly as expected based on the contextual analysis (the prediction was 32%). Eisenhower did win more public fights than the models predicted, achieving presidential dominance on 19% rather than 13% of his initiatives. He did particularly well with new policy departures, improving on the presidential-dominance prediction by 16 percentage points. Eisenhower, in fact, benefited from serving during a period reasonably favorable to the president's position. There was less institutional fragmentation, especially on the Hill.

It was still possible for the President to sit down with the House speaker and the Senate majority leader and for the three to strike reasonably binding legislative agreements. Each of his elections gave him significant public mandates, and at least until the 1958 Democratic congressional landslide the strength of the conservative coalition tended to mute the relevance of the Democratic margin in control of congressional seats. For the most part the economy remained healthy, especially with respect to the size of the federal deficit and inflation. Do we therefore have evidence not of a master legislative leader, but rather of a president who had the good fortune to serve when he did?

To address these questions, we need to develop a more elaborate sense of Eisenhower's legislative ambition and the extent to which he worked to gain favorable legislative responses to his initiatives. To assess any president's legislative performance, we need to know the extent to which that president offered a challenging legislative agenda and whether the successes came on the most important issues, the ones of highest priority to the administration. Further, to judge legislative performance and capabilities, we would like some measure of how hard and how fruitfully the president tried to influence congressional deliberations.

The percentage of Eisenhower's legislative initiatives that were particularly hard to pass, all other things being equal, place him about in the middle among the seven presidents. This is evident from the top of Table 7.2, which shows the percentage of each president's initiatives that were of the highest priority, associated with major bills, provided for large or new policy departures or both (the boldest form of legislation), and were regulatory in nature.

Eisenhower was extraordinarily successful at enacting these tough initiatives, passing 83% of the large proposals, 81% of the proposals associated with programs of the highest priority, and 80% of the initiatives tied to major legislation. No other president did as well. The second part of Table 7.2 reveals at least one source of Eisenhower's success, in addition to the favorable political environment in which he served. The only president to have a consistently less ambitious program as measured by the average number of tough proposals submitted each year was Gerald Ford, the president who faced the worst contextual circumstances of any in the sample. Eisenhower achieved much by limiting the targets of his interest and efforts.

Table 7.2   Legislative ambitiousness of individual presidents from
Eisenhower to Reagan

President	N	\ Highest priority	Major bill	Large	New	Large and new	Regu- latory
		\multicolumn{6}{c}{Attribute of ambitious legislative proposal}					

President	N	Highest priority	Major bill	Large	New	Large and new	Regu- latory
		\multicolumn{6}{c}{Percentage of president's proposals in sample}					
Eisenhower	48	44%	52%	25%	31%	10%	17%
Kennedy	45	58%	56%	22%	33%	11%	9%
Johnson	81	37%	41%	16%	35%	9%	16%
Nixon	39	54%	33%	31%	23%	15%	18%
Ford	16	31%	19%	19%	19%	0%	38%
Carter	48	60%	52%	25%	31%	17%	33%
Reagan	22	82%	73%	46%	23%	18%	9%
		\multicolumn{6}{c}{Average annual number of president's proposals in sample}					
Eisenhower	48	2.6	3.1	1.5	1.9	0.6	1.0
Kennedy	45	8.7	8.3	3.3	5.0	1.7	1.3
Johnson	81	6.0	6.6	2.6	5.6	1.4	2.6
Nixon	39	3.5	2.2	2.0	1.5	1.0	1.2
Ford	16	2.5	1.5	1.5	1.5	0.0	3.0
Carter	48	7.2	6.2	3.0	3.8	2.0	4.0
Reagan	22	4.5	4.0	2.5	1.2	1.0	0.5

There is some initial evidence that those efforts paid off. By restricting the size of his program and the number of his legislative priorities, Eisenhower was able to focus on a significant proportion of his initiatives. He gave extensive attention to the smallest number of proposals per year of any chief executive but, except for Reagan, a greater proportion of his initiatives registered high levels of presidential involvement compared to the other administrations. The general policy areas of 42% of the Eisenhower proposals were mentioned in at least one presidential statement a month, the highest percentage for any presidency other than Reagan's (which was dominated by the budget and tax cuts in 1981). When President Eisenhower took to television or radio in support of his limited number of initiatives, his success was overwhelming. For these proposals Congress passed *all* of what the president desired 82% of the time.

Despite all of this presidential lobbying, Eisenhower's activities apparently did not measurably advance his program beyond the

Table 7.3   Presidential legislative lobbying effort by individual presidents from Eisenhower to Reagan

| | Contextually controlled probit estimate of coefficient of presidential lobbying effort[a] | | | |
| | All proposals | | Large proposals[b] | |
President	Coeffi-cient	t-statistic	Coeffi-cient	t-statistic
Eisenhower	0.50	1.48	1.00	1.36
Kennedy	−0.02	−0.10	0.51[c]	1.71
Johnson	0.03	0.73	0.23[c]	3.65
Nixon	0.14	0.65	5.87[c]	2.61
Ford	—	—	—	—
Carter	−0.12	−1.58	−0.58[c]	−1.75
Reagan	0.08	1.36	−0.12	−0.60

a. The coefficients represent the independent effect for each president of monthly mentions by the president, controlling for institutional, political, economic, and policy contextual properties. Because the inclusion of each president is made possible by the introduction of dummy variables, and therefore not all presidents can be included in the analysis, Gerald Ford was excluded. The effect of monthly mentions during his administration serves as the baseline.

b. While inclusion of the presidential effort variables in the contextual analysis for all proposals did not enhance the predictive power of the probit model, their inclusion in the analysis for large proposals alone raised the percentage of cases correctly predicted from 41 to 59.

c. $p < .10$.

opportunities afforded by the auspicious circumstances of his administration. The independent effects of presidential lobbying effort, controlling for the pure, malleable, and strategic policy contexts, are presented in Table 7.3. The amount of public attention Eisenhower gave to his initiatives is positively related to favorable congressional action, but the effect is not statistically significant. The lack of significance holds true even for large policy departures, when one would expect the activities of a president to be of the greatest consequence. Eisenhower's presence failed to overpower the influence of the setting.

One might argue a more subtle point, however. Dwight Eisenhower displayed characteristics and made choices as president that contributed to an advantageous political and policy context. This reduced the need for him to demonstrate a more effective set of publicly recognized political skills. The traditional view of Eisenhower portrays him as essentially a political novice, devoid of enthusiasm for the political process and not well attuned to the means for achieving political ends. The revisionist literature of recent years, however, reveals a president who fully understood his strengths and the *perceptions* of his weaknesses, and who manipulated both to his political advantage.[30] Whichever view is accepted, Eisenhower's political orientation was not one of formulating and advocating dramatic innovations in the role of government, of pressing to the limit the possibility of leadership in public policy. According to Thomas Cronin, "His notion of policy leadership . . . was to move slowly, cautiously, and only after public opinion, Congress, or the courts had already taken a stand."[31] Although he held strong views about a handful of policy issues, remarked one of his advisers, in most areas of domestic policy he did not have definitive enough predispositions to wish to take the lead on them. These inhibitions were reflected in his limited legislative agenda.

Eisenhower's general cautiousness, and the small number of major policy challenges in his legislative program, may have contributed to one of the most significant phenomena of his tenure in office: the consistency and durability of his public support. The probit analyses presented in the previous chapter produced somewhat mystifying coefficients for public approval of the president, suggesting that it has little influence on congressional action on the president's program. Public approval of Eisenhower, though, may demonstrate the utility of looking beyond statistical correlations. Unlike those before and after him (other than Reagan in his second term), Eisenhower was able to maintain consistently high levels of public support. Over eight years fluctuations in his popularity fell within a 27 percentage-point range, compared to 45 and 51 points for Johnson and Carter respectively, each of whom served in office for considerably shorter periods. Further, during the eight years that Eisenhower occupied the White House, those approving of his job performance never constituted less than half of the public. It

30. See Greenstein, *The Hidden-Hand Presidency,* pp. 58–72; and Phillip G. Henderson, *Managing the Presidency: The Eisenhower Legacy—From Kennedy to Reagan* (Boulder, Colo.: Westview Press, 1988), pp. 29–32.

31. Cronin, *The State of the Presidency,* p. 271.

may be that a threshold effect surfaces. Changes in public approval may have little effect unless the president falls below the 50% level of support.[32] That possibility would account for the results in the multivariate analysis relative to Eisenhower's proposals: there was not enough variation in his public support to explain the differences in congressional responses. Finally, it seems clear that Eisenhower's level of popular support was so high and so consistent that congressional leaders had to take note. Rowland Evans and Robert Novak report that Lyndon Johnson, as the Democratic majority leader in the Senate, "measured the depth and permanence of Eisenhower's popularity beyond the Potomac and foresaw political disaster for any man who broke with the President."[33] Eisenhower himself was so intent on preserving his standing with the public that he rarely showed a willingness to exploit and perhaps expend this political resource to advance his positions on controversial issues.[34]

John F. Kennedy

The Kennedy administration, brief as it was, has long had the reputation of being more effective at advancing symbols than at moving its legislative program. Fewer than half of Kennedy's domestic initiatives were enacted even in part, a performance far below that of either his cautious Republican predecessor or his hyperactive Democratic successor. Remove the cases of inaction from the 1963 agenda, however, and Kennedy's success rate jumps to 65%, on a par with Eisenhower and Johnson. Even if a full four-year (or eight-year) administration had led to continued congressional avoidance or active defeat of many of the 1963 proposals that ended in inaction, Kennedy—had he lived—might have had greater success with his program than otherwise occurred. Indeed, the contextual probit analysis projected enactment of 63% of the Kennedy initiatives. Other than the significant underprediction of strategic inaction, primarily tied to the 1963 program, the predictions from the probit analysis track well with the actual aggregate congressional responses to the Kennedy

32. Light, The President's Agenda, p. 29.
33. Rowland Evans and Robert Novak, Lyndon B. Johnson: The Exercise of Power (New York: Signet, 1966), p. 184.
34. Samuel Kernell, Going Public: New Strategies of Presidential Leadership (Washington, D.C.: CQ Press, 1986), p. 186.

legislative program. The most significant variations occurred with large policy departures; there were more consensual congressional responses than anticipated by the model and proportionally fewer responses in the compromise and passive inaction categories.

As was the case with Eisenhower, context tells us much about how the legislature reacted to Kennedy's initiatives. But the similarity between the two presidents ends there. Kennedy and his aides were full of enthusiasm for launching an activist program.[35] Eisenhower had not been "too excited about the damn things that needed to be done," suggested a Kennedy adviser. "Kennedy wanted to get going. In addition, there were a number of people in the executive branch that Kennedy and his people knew who were brimming with new ideas." As president, Kennedy on occasion demonstrated a willingness to experiment with unusual programmatic initiatives, such as the proposal for a stimulative tax cut even during periods of deficit spending.[36] In three years he submitted almost as many proposals as Eisenhower had in eight years.

Additional facets of this activism are revealed in Table 7.2. An uncommonly large percentage of his initiatives were linked to legislation of highest priority to him and involved major legislation. About the same proportion of his legislative initiatives as Eisenhower's represented large policy departures or broke new ground, or were particularly bold. But his agenda was more expansive than Eisenhower's: based on the sample of proposals, Kennedy each year introduced more initiatives of high priority, tied to major legislation, and embracing large policy departures than any of the other presidents. Only Johnson submitted more new proposals each year. Only Carter offered more truly bold (both large and new) initiatives on an annual basis.

This activism at the initiation stage came despite the fact that President Kennedy recognized the limits of his political base. He needed little reminding of the narrowness of his electoral margin of victory. He was also aware that Congress remained largely in the grip of a conservative coalition probably hostile to many of his policy interests, and that being so much younger than most mem-

35. Arthur M. Schlesinger, *A Thousand Days: John F. Kennedy in the White House* (Greenwich, Conn.: Fawcett, 1965), p. 201.

36. Hugh S. Norton, *The Employment Act and the Council of Economic Advisers, 1946–1976* (Columbia: University of South Carolina Press, 1977), p. 166.

bers of Congress, especially committee chairmen, was hardly an advantage.[37] In spite of his television presence, Kennedy only rarely gave broadcast addresses that touched on the issue areas of his initiatives, turning to radio and television for this purpose less frequently than any of the other presidents. Some in the Kennedy coterie argue that JFK was waiting to press the most challenging issues on his agenda subsequent to the political boost he was anticipating from a victory in 1964 over Barry Goldwater, whom he thought likely to be the Republican nominee.[38]

Even with these constraints, having launched an extensive agenda, Kennedy undertook some efforts to get his proposals favorably considered. The average number of Kennedy proposals introduced each year and receiving at least one monthly presidential mention is matched only by the initiatives of his fellow Democrats, Lyndon Johnson and Jimmy Carter. These endeavors, however, had little impact on how Congress responded to Kennedy's program overall. Large policy departures present a rather different picture. Here Kennedy's public attentiveness seems to have mattered. The coefficient for presidential monthly mentions, reported in Table 7.3, is both positive and statistically significant. This fact is of some consequence, considering Kennedy's assertiveness in launching that type of initiative. His administration, it seems, succeeded with more than symbols.

Given the circumstances that John Kennedy confronted, and those he wished to face in the future, he arrived at several other decisions relevant to advancing his legislative interests. First, he assembled on his White House staff a group of individuals with at least a modicum of congressional experience and knowledge and, even more important, the capacity to learn and adapt. They were not as likely to stumble into the kind of political misjudgments that plagued future administrations. Second, in alliance with the congressional leadership, Kennedy participated in the successful maneuver that expanded the number of members serving on the House Rules Committee as a way to try to circumvent the historic role of the conservatives in blocking liberal legislation. Third, he was cautious in choosing the substantive areas of his domestic legislative agenda. Early in his term he avoided pushing serious civil rights legislation, afraid that the attempt would be

37. Sorensen, *Kennedy*, p. 345.
38. Ibid., p. 754.

futile and damaging to other priorities.[39] For the same reason, he delayed action on the tax cut proposal.[40] Fourth, according to Theodore Sorensen, his chief domestic adviser, Kennedy hoped to neutralize the Republican typecasting of Democrats as "big spenders" in order to retain some Republican support on the Hill and build a broader base among the public.[41] His initiatives included a relatively small proportion of regulatory issues and emphasized distributive proposals more than the other presidents included in the study. Because of Kennedy's assassination, of course, there is no way to ascertain the actual effects of, or motivations behind, the various legislative choices that he and his staff made. To some extent the by-then-experienced Kennedy staff and the articulated Kennedy agenda went on to contribute to the early successes of the Johnson administration.

Lyndon B. Johnson

If JFK was treading water waiting for better times, they arrived with the swearing in and subsequent election of Lyndon Johnson. During the Eighty-ninth Congress, Johnson enjoyed the most favorable institutional, political, and economic setting for domestic legislation of any president in the three decades being studied. The 1964 landslide over Goldwater gave him an impressive electoral mandate and undisputed coattails, with the congressional races in that election substantially fortifying the Democratic majority in the House. The economy was humming through a period of relatively noninflationary growth. It would not be until later in Johnson's administration that the course of the Vietnam War would sour relations with important members of Congress, dissipate popular support for the President, and threaten the vitality of the economy. Nor would the concerns about a weakening party system and the decentralization of power on Capitol Hill emerge until after Johnson's departure.

As one would expect, given these circumstances advantageous to the president's political position, the legislative proposals that Johnson introduced received generally favorable consideration on the Hill. Johnson experienced the least strategic inaction of Presi-

39. Ibid., pp. 474–476.
40. Edward S. Flash, Jr., *Economic Advice and Presidential Leadership* (New York: Columbia University Press, 1965), p. 246.
41. Sorensen, *Kennedy*, p. 463.

dents Eisenhower to Reagan (7%), relatively few of his proposals were defeated by opposing factions (17%), and almost 40% passed by consensus. Congress enacted 69% of LBJ's initiatives in some form; another 5% were pursued by the administration through nonlegislative channels. It would appear from the contextual analysis, however, that Johnson did not work magic on the Hill. This is not the stuff of legend. But Johnson did push auspicious circumstances for all they were worth, especially with respect to moving the agenda and dominating congressional action on his large policy proposals.

Two points deserve highlighting. Johnson's legislative successes came while serving up an enormous domestic agenda that resulted in "more power over domestic matters flow[ing] to the White House than during any other comparable time span in this century."[42] Johnson sent proposals to the Hill at an annual rate almost three times that of Eisenhower, accounting for 27% of all the specific domestic initiatives that presidents introduced from 1953 to 1984 (see Appendix C). Most of these proposals, however, required only incremental policy departures. With regard to the scope and innovativeness of individual proposals, Johnson was surpassed by both Kennedy and Carter. Only in the introduction of a higher percentage and a larger annual number of new proposals did Johnson's agenda lead the other six presidents (Table 7.2). Nevertheless, it remains a feat of no small proportion to get Congress to digest so voluminous a legislative program.

It should not be surprising that Johnson worked steadfastly to enact his program. He granted more extensive attention to a higher number of proposals in the sample per year than did the other presidents. When we control for the favorable effects of the contextual factors, Johnson's activities positively influenced congressional action on his program, though, as shown in Table 7.3, the relationship is not statistically significant. Like Kennedy, in the realm of large policy departures Johnson was particularly effective. Johnson also used public strategies effectively. He won public fights the two times he went on television with messages that were relevant to the sample of initiatives. Sixty-three percent of the time that he pursued a public strategy directed at specialized constituencies, the relevant proposals passed without modifications. It should also be remembered that

42. Califano, *A Presidential Nation*, p. 9.

neither of these indicators of presidential effort (the frequency with which proposals were mentioned by the president and the use of public strategies) registers the brand of activism at which Johnson was so skilled: counting noses and the private, incessant, pounding one-on-one encounters.[43] It is quite possible that Johnson was more adept at this form of lobbying than any other chief executive. Still, there is nothing in the analysis presented here to indicate that Johnson's skills were more important than the opportunities afforded by the institutional, political, and economical contexts of the period.

In a limited sense, therefore, the legislative achievement of the Johnson years was facilitated by the man in office. He knew not to squander opportunities. LBJ was the quintessential politician, a political enthusiast, an indefatigable, perhaps fanatical, player of the game.[44] He read the *Congressional Record* as though it were his hometown newspaper, noted Lawrence O'Brien.[45] As one aide, a holdover from the Kennedy administration, put it, "Johnson's idea of a big night was not going to the opera, it was sitting around having a couple of drinks with an old buddy, who happened to be the chairman of the Armed Services Committee." He offered an example of Johnson's political drive:

> He didn't want to pace himself, he wanted to get it all at once. I remember when he made that speech to a joint session of Congress on the voting rights bill in 1965. It was masterful, a great speech, real showmanship. Most of the time, that kind of thing is sent by a messenger, but here he was on TV. Back at the White House, we were celebrating, drinking, which is what you're supposed to do after that kind of thing. Well, Johnson turned to Larry O'Brien and said, "Larry, have you got the hearing set up yet?" He had just announced the thing on television, and he said to me, "Have you got a good editorial set up for tomorrow's papers?" I thought it, but I didn't say it, "Mr. President, it's eleven o'clock at night. Why

43. Terry Sullivan, "Head Counts, Expectations, and Presidential Coalitions in Congress," *American Journal of Political Science* 32 (August 1988): 567–589.

44. Joseph A. Califano, Jr., *Governing America: An Insider's Report from the White House and the Cabinet* (New York: Simon and Schuster, 1981), p. 41.

45. Lawrence F. O'Brien, *No Final Victories: A Life in Politics from John F. Kennedy to Watergate* (New York: Ballantine, 1974), p. 194.

don't we work on that tomorrow?" He just wanted to get things done right away.

Furthermore, he wanted to have things accomplished by what appeared to be a consensus. It is possible that Johnson saw everyone as a potential ally, at least until the end of his administration. While serving as the Senate's majority leader, he seemed to view even the Republicans across the aisle as part of his official field of operation.[46] This consensus-generating approach probably worked in the White House because of the particular timing of Johnson's early incumbency. LBJ held office at a time when the partisanly organized opposition had been demoralized and the country, on domestic matters, generally approved of an activist government. Explained one of his domestic assistants:

> It was a period of rising expectations. After years of . . . ferment in the labor unions and elsewhere, after years of ferment and no action under Eisenhower, when many things were passed and vetoed, and many ideas had no support in the executive branch, suddenly there came a president with a big majority, and there was the shock of the Kennedy assassination, and a repudiation of conservatism in the person of Goldwater. There was a feeling that now is the time to go and get things done.

So again there was a consonance between the drive of the particular leader in power and the context in which his administration served.

When it came to making choices about what policy role to play, therefore, Johnson was not shy. Instead of restricting his agenda in order to improve the chances of success, he chose to give it massive proportions and move it hard and fast. To keep the agenda innovative, he turned to establishing and almost institutionalizing outside task forces responsible for generating new ideas and approaches.[47] To sell his legislative initiatives, he not only relied on an experienced staff but functioned himself, con-

46. Harry McPherson, *A Political Education* (New York: Little, Brown, 1972), p. 69.

47. Hargrove, *The Power of the Modern Presidency*, p. 88; Norman C. Thomas and Harold L. Wolman, "Policy Formation in the Institutionalized Presidency: The Johnson Task Forces," in *The Presidential Advisory System*, ed. Thomas E. Cronin and Sanford D. Greenberg (New York: Harper and Row, 1969), pp. 124–143.

tended an aide, as the most knowledgeable and persuasive member of the congressional liaison team. He would use "the Treatment" and relentless telephoning, which Dirksen dubbed "the Texas Twist," to strengthen his congressional coalitions.[48] More fundamentally, he chose to concentrate his energies on developing legislation and passing it, rather than on weighing the cost of his programs, reflecting on their programmatic utility, or assessing the effectiveness of their implementation.[49] Sometimes his first concern may have been the benchmark of legislative success, not the substantive policy that would finally pass.[50]

The happy time did not last, however. Just as the persona of Johnson did so much to exploit the opportunities for legislative action provided by the advantageous circumstances of the first years of his administration, the decisions of the President concerning American involvement in Southeast Asia ultimately eroded his political base. The war in Vietnam became his personal war, the reason for his characterization as a "tragic figure."[51] The public had become less forgiving by the time of the 1966 congressional elections, manifested in the loss of forty-seven Democratic seats in the House, far more than the thirty-eight gained in 1964, and three seats in the Senate. The economy soured and the raging expenses of Vietnam and the Great Society necessitated Johnson's introduction and congressional enactment of a politically unpopular 10% tax surcharge to keep the federal deficit in line. Congress was no longer as affirming of the President's domestic agenda as it had been in the Eighty-ninth Congress.[52] One of Johnson's domestic policy advisers gave this summary of the atmosphere:

> There really was a gloom around the White House, a very negative attitude. As I said, there was Vietnam, and all the demonstrations, the riots in the streets, the Poor People's

48. Wilfred E. Binkley, *The Man in the White House: His Powers and Duties*, rev. ed. (New York: Harper Colophon Books, 1964), p. 153; and Evans and Novak, *Lyndon B. Johnson*.

49. Interview with a Bureau of the Budget official.

50. Interview with a congressional staff member.

51. Eric F. Goldman, *The Tragedy of Lyndon Johnson* (New York: Alfred A. Knopf, 1969), esp. pp. 509–531. See also Merle Miller, *Lyndon: An Oral Biography* (New York: C.P. Putnam's Sons, 1980), pp. 453–472; O'Brien, *No Final Victories*, pp. 191–199; and George E. Reedy, *The Twilight of the Presidency* (New York: Mentor, 1970), p. 72.

52. O'Brien, *No Final Victories*, p. 196.

Campaign on Washington. It was a pretty devastating couple of years. The political atmosphere was not one of a national consensus. There was the budget stuff, Vietnam, and the tax surcharge. Then a lot of people were physically worn out. There were not that many good people left, though Califano was there and he was good. Then, when the President announced [in March of 1968] that he was not going to run again—well, when the president announces that, that's sort of the end. Yes, people talked about the '64, '65 period, and how back then they were doing things more creatively . . . The first thing is that [after 1966] a lot of things just didn't move . . . First there were some people you didn't deal with, that you couldn't deal with. We couldn't work with [Eugene] McCarthy or with Bobby Kennedy, or even Teddy [Kennedy] . . . Even when they agreed with things there was not much cooperation. Of course, the Republicans were out for blood, though they supported Johnson on Vietnam. I remember people like Abe Ribicoff, who otherwise would have agreed with us on a lot of things, was carrying some kind of vengeance and you can't do much with that . . . A lot of things got stuck in committees, and we didn't have the relationship to work those things out.

For passing the president's program, the Johnson years in many respects embraced the best of times and the worst of times. Johnson could milk the former with his vast reservoir of legislative talent; he was condemned to endure the latter as the epiphenomenon of his Vietnam commitment.

Richard M. Nixon

With the inauguration of Richard Nixon, the institutional, political, and economic attributes of the pure and malleable contexts of presidential-congressional interactions completed the transition begun in the late Johnson years and became quite unfavorable to the president's legislative positions. Nixon entered office in 1968 on the slimmest of mandates, having garnered considerably less than a majority of the popular vote. While the election ensconced a Republican in the White House, the margin of Democratic control of the Congress remained essentially unchanged. On the economic front, inflation, in the form of stagflation, reigned instead of stable growth. After the lone surplus of 1969, the federal deficit began down the road of becoming a permanent fixture of American government. Abroad, the war in Indochina continued to poison relations among people at large and between members of their respective government institutions. And as the Nixon administration proceeded, many members of Congress, especially younger Democrats, successfully instigated organizational reforms, thereby increasing the complexity of the Congress as a partner in the policy-making process. With that kind of political environment, it is not at all startling that the Nixon administration would have special problems in trying to enact domestic legislation. Of the thirty-nine Nixon proposals in the sample, four of ten were ignored by the Hill and only 46% were passed in any favorable form. Consensus occurred less than a fifth of the time. These results are quite consistent with the predictions generated by the contextual probit analyses, except that Nixon drew less congressional attention than predicted. He experienced a third fewer occasions of opposition dominance and 50% more instances of strategic inaction than anticipated. He also enjoyed somewhat less frequent victories through presidential dominance.

Explanations for these general patterns, and for Nixon's not rising above the limits imposed by the contexts of the times, can be found in the political orientation of the man and the basic choices he made as president. Richard Nixon assumed office with his attention focused almost entirely on foreign affairs and with little interest in the domestic arena. It was his view that "this country could run itself domestically without a President. All you need is a competent Cabinet to run the country at home. You need a President for foreign policy."[53] If Evans and Novak are correct, the Nixon administration was sworn into office guided by no domestic theme except the amorphous plea "Bring Us Together Again," a slogan spotted by Nixon during the 1968 campaign when a little girl held up a poster that she had found on the ground.[54]

The absence of an organizing set of domestic principles meant that the administration was slow to assemble the components of

53. Rowland Evans, Jr., and Robert D. Novak, *Nixon in the White House: The Frustration of Power* (New York: Vintage Books, 1972), p. 11.

54. Ibid., p. 33.

its first series of legislative initiatives, forfeiting the benefits to be derived from swift action at the beginning of the term.[55] The fact that Nixon had few solid policy predispositions actually provided several notable opportunities for innovation. He was willing to support relatively novel ideas advocated by some of his advisers, such as the Family Assistance Plan, even if on the surface they ran counter to the presumed ideological position of a Republican administration.[56] The potential for successfully advocating such policy departures was countered, however, by other characteristics of the administration. Many of the proposals were so sweeping—family assistance, special revenue sharing, and the like—that they would have been difficult to pass under any conditions, but especially those that existed at the time. Although the President would support the proposals and transmit them to Congress, he sometimes lacked the level of interest necessary to maintain presidential pressure to sustain them. Despite a legislative agenda comparable in size to those of Eisenhower and Ford, and much smaller than those offered by any of the Democratic presidents, Nixon made extensive public reference to a smaller overall percentage and annual number of proposals than any of the other presidents in the sample, Republican or Democratic. And, rightly or wrongly, critics in the opposition charged that he was often unwilling to engage in the usual processes of bargaining associated with domestic politics.[57]

The avoidance of compromise with opponents on the Hill reflected Nixon's profound dislike of Congress, a sentiment shared by some of his staff. From the beginning of his administration Nixon chose to pursue a confrontational relationship with an institution that he felt was unlikely to heed his domestic agenda, limited though it was.[58] Further, despite the strong alliances he had with some members, he was by dint of character unable to put pressure on members of Congress to accept his position. A senior aide described a typical scene:

55. Light, *The President's Agenda*, pp. 44–45.

56. Daniel P. Moynihan, *The Politics of a Guaranteed Income: The Nixon Administration and the Family Assistance Plan* (New York: Vintage Books, 1973), pp. 72–76.

57. Walter F. Mondale, at the time a Democratic senator, presents such an accusation about the Family Assistance Plan in his book, *The Accountability of Power* (New York: David McKay, 1975), p. 83.

58. Hargrove, *The Power of the Modern Presidency*, p. 224.

It was very difficult for Nixon . . . to ask for a vote. It was almost personally impossible for him to make the sale. You would be sitting in there with him and he would lay out all the points, argue all the merits, and you would be sitting on the edge of your chair thinking to yourself, Say the sell-line! But then he would say, "I know you will do what is best," or "I hope you can be with us on this one, but I will understand if you can't." And with that, you have let them off the hook.

Some members of the White House staff were even more contemptuous of Congress, hardly willing to accept it as an equal branch of government.[59] Several began their duties with no previous Washington experience and, according to Robert Teeter, a long-time Republican operative, no sense of the relevant history:

I used to say that one of the biggest problems with the Nixon Administration was that he put a whole bunch of people in responsible positions who were bright, competent individuals, but who had absolutely nothing in their backgrounds or education or experience that gave them the perspective to have the jobs they had. I used to go to meetings at the White House, and I often got the feeling as I'd sit through the meetings . . . , "Jesus, I'm not sure any of these guys could pass History 101. They seem to have no perspective or background on what it is we're involved in here. *None.*"[60]

These qualities of the Nixon presidency were not likely to help smooth over differences with members of Congress. Finally, of course, the advent of Watergate, and all the events that the term has come to represent, fundamentally degraded the Nixon presidency and destroyed whatever political base Nixon had previously been able to maintain.

However accurate these general impressions of the presidential-congressional relationship during the Nixon administration may be, they miss some contrary evidence revealed by delving deeper into specific components of Nixon's legislative program. This

59. John Ehrlichman, *Witness to Power: The Nixon Years* (New York: Pocket Books, 1982), p. 181; and Evans and Novak, *Nixon in the White House*, p. 109.

60. Quoted in David S. Broder, *Changing of the Guard: Power and Leadership in America* (New York: Penguin Books, 1981), p. 419. Italics in original.

president may have presented a relatively sparse agenda to Congress, and he may have showered presidential attention on comparably few domestic initiatives, but he was not without his successes. While fewer than half of his proposals overall were enacted, 67% of the large policy departures initiated by Nixon were passed in some form. Even Lyndon Johnson could not get Congress to accept more than half of his large initiatives. Nixon himself seems to have had something to do with congressional enactment of these proposals. For those offerings associated with comments he made in television or radio broadcasts, Nixon had a 57% success rate.[61] Of the five proposals linked to occasions when Nixon delivered messages or spoke to specialized constituencies, four were enacted by Congress. The coefficients presented in Table 7.3 reinforce the point. The level of Nixon's activity had no significant effect on favorable congressional responses to his initiatives in general, but more presidential involvement did have a strongly significant positive impact on congressional acceptance of the large proposals of Nixon's program.

What we find in Richard Nixon is a president marked by contradictions. He entered office with little interest and not much direction on domestic policy issues, but was willing to launch innovative schemes. He distrusted Congress and was awkward in his interactions with its members, and largely ignored much of his own program. But when things did matter to Nixon, he was active in support of his initiatives and displayed considerable effectiveness in garnering favorable responses to the large policy departures he submitted to the Hill.

Gerald R. Ford

The president who endured the most challenging set of institutional, political, and economic circumstances was Gerald Ford. Everything detrimental to advancing the president's position during the Nixon administration grew increasingly troublesome during Ford's tenure. Ford enjoyed no popular mandate at all. In fact, as an appointed vice president who assumed the presidency without benefit of an election, his mandate was a negative one, carrying "the

61. Kernell notes that even though Nixon shunned press conferences, he made extensive use of prime-time television addresses to the American public and in this regard "dominated the medium" more than any earlier president. *Going Public*, p. 87.

stigma of illegitimacy."[62] Perceptions of his legitimacy among many were further eroded almost immediately by his decision to pardon Richard Nixon. Soon after that, Ford discovered he would have to work with a Congress composed of the lopsided Democratic majorities generated by the 1974 midterm election. Many on the Hill were already in a state of rebellion triggered by the excesses of Ford's predecessor.[63] To make matters even worse, the economy was in extreme disarray, with a deep recession, mounting deficits, and inflation unprecedented in the modern era.

The contextual probit analyses predicted that presidential defeats by opposition dominance would occur most frequently during the Ford administration (34%), and that is precisely what happened. Thirty-eight percent of the President's initiatives were defeated in such open confrontations. Indeed, there is little that occurred during the Ford years that cannot be contextually understood and explained. Only 37% of President Ford's proposals were passed by Congress, about what was expected given the circumstances experienced by the administration.

That Ford's program fared no worse under these most trying of situations, with less strategic inaction and more consensus than predicted, undoubtedly reflects his background and how he chose to approach the domestic policy arena. Like LBJ, he brought to the White House extensive knowledge of Congress—and perhaps more important, innumerable personal ties to various representatives and senators on both sides of the aisle. Several members of the White House staff commented that Ford was their most effective congressional liaison agent, knowing more about the Hill than anyone else in the Executive Office. He relied heavily on those close relationships to reinforce his position, fortified by a desire to avoid unnecessary confrontations in the interest, he said himself, of maintaining viable floating coalitions.

In addition, Ford made the explicit decision to limit the size and scope of his domestic agenda. Except in the realm of energy policy, he declared in the 1975 State of the Union address that there would be, as his aides put it, "no new starts." He is the only one of the seven presidents not to propose any of the most innovative initiatives, the conjunction of large and new policy depar-

---

62. Cronin, *The State of the Presidency*, p. 212.

63. James L. Sundquist, *The Decline and Resurgence of Congress* (Washington, D.C.: Brookings Institution, 1981).

tures (Table 7.2). Ford's legislative agenda was small and placed the least emphasis on high-priority issues, large or new policy departures, and major programs. Much of the agenda involved imposing budgetary restraints and blocking, by complementary use of the veto power, what he deemed to be undesirable legislation emanating from the Democratic Congress.[64] Had Ford for any reason wished to press a loaded domestic agenda, it is likely that the results would have been proportionally far less favorable. The only area in which he offered particularly difficult proposals was regulatory legislation. That agenda was probably propelled by the urgency of restricting energy consumption during the crisis of the mid-1970s, which required presidential action despite the inherent political hurdles.

Jimmy Carter

Whenever the discussion of American government turns to the legislative management of Jimmy Carter, he remains an object of derision, exemplifying a president unable to deal effectively with Congress and the Washington establishment. Certainly the figures in Table 7.1 underscore Carter's difficulties with the legislative branch. Here was a Democratic president leading sizable Democratic majorities on the Hill, and yet a third of his proposals in the sample were ignored, 31% were outright defeated, and for only one of the proposals was he able to lead a coalition that dominated congressional action. These are irrefutable signs of a presidency in serious trouble.

A full understanding of the Carter presidency and presidential-congressional interactions during that period, however, requires further dissection along three dimensions: the context of the times in which Carter served, the ambitions he had for his legislative program, and the degree of his effectiveness as a source of influence on Congress. From none of these perspectives does Carter emerge as a particularly efficacious leader. Nor is it apparent that his troubles were solely the consequence of political floundering.

In the aggregate, Carter did about as well with his initiatives as predicted by the contextual probit analyses. When we sum the predicted probabilities of each kind of congressional response, Carter should have had 39% of his initiatives decided by passive

64. Interview with aides to President Ford.

inaction, compromise, presidential dominance, or consensus. That actually occurred for 43% of his proposals. The predicted percentage for opposition dominance was 32%; the actual figure is 31%. The role of contextual constraints is emphasized by comparing the predicted probabilities for both Carter and Reagan with those for Lyndon Johnson, the most successful president in the sample. Carter confronted decidedly worse circumstances than Johnson. Whereas a third of Johnson's proposals would have been expected to be enacted by consensus, for Carter the prediction was 8%. While about one in ten of the Johnson initiatives should have been defeated by opposition dominance, the prediction for Carter was three times that. The differences are particularly pronounced for large and new policy departures. Even Ronald Reagan enjoyed marginally better contextual expectations than Carter. The Reagan program overall was expected to encounter a bit less strategic inaction and opposition dominance and slightly more presidential dominance and consensus. Like Ford, Carter was not serving during the most advantageous times.

The fact is that any president, even another Democrat, would have encountered problems during the period that Carter was in office, if the configuration of institutional, political, economic, and policy forces had been similar. Carter was elected by a narrow margin in 1976, denying him a clear mandate and the influence of congressional coattails. Carter also faced the same decentralization of congressional authority that Ford experienced, along with continued elaboration of the interest-group system. Jeff Fishel posits that "even a legislative horse trader as brilliant as Johnson would have had difficulty navigating the newly decentralized and factionalized institution that Congress had become."[65] In addition, the Democrats in Congress were not necessarily ideologically compatible with the orientation of the Carter administration. Shared partisan labels can bridge the institutional gap, but ideological cleavages reduce the willingness of members of Congress to go along with the president's position. From the perspective of those serving in the Carter White House, according to one of Carter's senior advisers, it was a problem that plagued the President from the start:

65. Jeff Fishel, *Presidents and Promises* (Washington, D.C.: CQ Press, 1985), p. 197. Nelson W. Polsby disagrees. *Consequences of Party Reform* (New York: Oxford University Press, 1983), p. 113.

Carter was really trying to move the center of gravity of his party, which is really defined by the party members in Congress, as they are the only continuing part of the government. If you looked at the public, they were already closer to Carter; but in dealing with Congress, which is the more public representation of the party, they were much farther away from Carter . . . And, of course, as everyone points out, when Carter came to Washington, when the administration came to Washington, it was facing a certain amount of skepticism. It was not necessarily hostility, but it fell somewhere between hostility and skepticism. Even within his own party, I heard people say this. It was almost as if they were waiting for the Visigoths to march into the capital from the swamps of south Georgia ready to loot and pillage and take away all of their privileges, their perks and cars, and their time-honored traditions.

Finally, as Carter's term progressed, the country experienced increasing economic difficulties, especially in the form of extraordinary rates of inflation.

The aggregate predictions for the success of Carter's legislative program, of course, hide some specific decisions that Carter made about the nature of this legislative agenda. As is evident from Table 7.2, Carter did not shy away from thrusting upon Congress and upon his fellow partisans a challenging domestic agenda. It emphasized major programs, large policy departures, new proposals, innovative proposals, and regulatory issues. All of these attributes invite legislative adversity even in the best of times. In addition, as noted earlier, Carter presented an agenda both substantively challenging and sizable. Rather than entering office with a well-defined but relatively constrained collection of policy goals, he started off by "inventorying the country's problems and determining what should be done about as many of them as possible."[66] Compared to presidents from Kennedy to Reagan, Carter fulfilled a higher percentage of his campaign commitments with actual proposals than did any of the others. But Carter was also the most dependent on Congress to enact his proposals, using administrative options less frequently.[67] His administration pro-

66. Jimmy Carter, *Keeping Faith: Memoirs of a President* (New York: Bantam Books, 1982), p. 66.
67. Fishel, *Presidents and Promises*, pp. 38, 41.

duced and introduced in the first year alone a wide variety of comprehensive legislative packages, including the National Energy Plan, Hospital Cost Containment, Labor Law Reform, and Welfare Reform—a call for legislative activism that probably went beyond the bounds of his mandate.[68]

Probably most important, Carter did not initially offer Congress an unambiguous indication of his priorities. Sixty percent of his proposals were sent to Congress in messages or statements that suggested in each case that they were of the highest priority to the administration. A member of Carter's White House staff made the following assessment: "In our first year one of the greatest problems was the absence of a legislative strategy. Each bill seemed to receive equal billing and Congress had no clue to what we wanted most." Looking back, another aide to Carter commented:

> There is something to be said for a president, and Reagan has done this with the economy, for finding one major item at the beginning of the term and getting it passed. Energy, I think, should have been ours. That's what we should have concentrated on. But we were dissipated on many other things. By the time we got to energy, we had already moved on many things, many of which I think were far less important.

In the second year of the term, the administration finally organized a Management Committee, under Vice President Mondale's direction, to identify the legislative priorities. By then, however, much of the momentum needed to pass legislation had already been lost.[69] At the same time, Speaker Tip O'Neill instructed his policy staff to meet with Carter's advisers in an effort to whittle down the active list of priority issues. They discovered, lamented one participant, that "it was a difficult process to keep going." Had President Carter from the beginning been able or willing to make some of these choices, he might have finished his term with a legislative record that surpassed the contextual expectations. Perhaps he even would have been reelected.

To suggest that Carter's problems with Congress rest substantially with these agenda decisions is a bit too simplistic. While the emphasis on large or new policy departures certainly diminished

68. Cronin, *The State of the Presidency*, p. 215.
69. Light, *The President's Agenda*, p. 158.

Carter's opportunities for success with the Hill, even an unambitious legislative program made up of small changes in existing programs (an unlikely option for a Democratic president following eight years of Republican presidents) would have been difficult to enact. The contextual predictions suggest that a program made up entirely of such initiatives would have resulted in rejection of more than half by either opposition dominance or strategic inaction, with an additional set ignored through passive inaction by Congress. That would have been true of only a quarter of such proposals if submitted during the Johnson administration. The contexts of congressional action would persist as a major handicap for Carter.

In addition, it may be that Carter's substantive policy problems were equally problems experienced by the Democrats in Congress. Fishel's defense of Carter continues with the assessment that "Carter was most successful precisely in those policy areas where Democrats, moderates, and others still agree; he was least successful in areas where the classic liberal/moderate/conservative continuum does not clarify the basic thrust of Democratic factional disagreement . . . *Carter failed where the majority party fails.*"[70]

It is undeniable, though, that President Carter did not bring with him a political background and the kind of government experience that would have helped him to overcome the challenges imposed by the institutional, political, and economic environment.[71] He had no domestic policy, national government, or communications experience of the sort that would have prepared him for the presidency.[72] He arrived in Washington knowing few members of Congress beyond those in the Georgia delegations to the House and Senate.[73] Finally, his approach to politics and policy making evidenced a disdain for the usual methods of reaching agreements. As a domestic policy adviser noted:

Carter wasn't a guy who would call up and chat. On major matters he would dutifully call people if told that was what

70. Fishel, *Presidents and Promises*, pp. 198, 200. Italics in original.

71. Charles O. Jones, *The Trusteeship Presidency: Jimmy Carter and the United States Congress* (Baton Rouge: Louisiana State University Press, 1988), chap. 2.

72. Kessel, *Presidential Parties*, p. 161.

73. Carter, *Keeping Faith*, p. 66.

was needed to get something passed. If you went and told Carter that to get something through he needed to call 150 members, he'd tell you to get the list, and he would sit down all night and call. He would then report back to us with what the members of Congress said. He was not very good at reading what they said. They would say, "Oh, yes, Mr. President, we support what you're trying to do," and that would just go against what we knew.

Although Carter recognized the necessity of forming alliances with influential members of the Washington establishment, he thought that could be achieved by simply doing "the best job possible."[74] As one of his aides declared in a 1979 speech, President Carter "would rather be right and President—but if he is ever pushed to a choice, there is no doubt in my mind about which he would pick." In other words, Carter chose to ignore the rather limited influence one can have on public policy by being right but forced from office. It was not easy for him to reconcile the trade-offs inherent in the goals that all elected officials must pursue, including the need to be elected in order to advance desirable public policy. To be reelected required establishing a record of some success, which in turn was predicated on working with influential competitors in the Washington community. Carter's predispositions aggravated the difficulty of the situation he faced and ultimately contributed to the election of a president who would advocate policies that Carter fundamentally opposed.

Also stemming from Carter's political orientation was a series of choices that dissipated his influence. Some were fairly minor decisions, such as the selling of the presidential yacht *Sequoia*, but even that decision denied him a much-appreciated milieu for maintaining effective relations with members of Congress.[75] Carter was perhaps most often criticized for some of the White House staff selections he made. A prime example involved the congressional liaison office. Selected to head that operation was

74. Ibid., p. 126. See also Betty Glad, *Jimmy Carter: In Search of the Great White House* (New York: W. W. Norton, 1980), esp. chap. 25; Jones, *The Trusteeship Presidency*, esp. chaps. 1, 4; and Lawrence E. Lynn, Jr., and David deF. Whitman, *The President as Policy Maker: Jimmy Carter and Welfare Reform* (Philadelphia: Temple University Press, 1981), esp. chap. 11.

75. Interviews with various informants both inside and outside the Carter administration.

Frank Moore, an individual with the requisite close connections to the President who eventually assembled a well-respected team of assistants, but who himself had no Washington or Hill experience. A Ford official told me that he had predicted disaster when Moore overruled his suggestion that Carter hire the best Democratic staff members from Capitol Hill. Moore replied, "We didn't have any trouble with the Georgia legislature, and Jimmy really wants to bring in his own team." The *perception* developed, however, that Moore was not managing the liaison functions well, and even though matters improved significantly after the first several months of the administration, the perception continued.[76] One senior adviser to Carter suggested to me that things would have changed dramatically had Carter been able to make the decision to replace Moore.

None of the Carter decisions in any of these realms helped him to overcome the obstacles he faced in seeking to move an ambitious program during trying times. The President became the victim of the situations he confronted rather than the resourceful tactician he needed to be to find his way clear. He put a considerable amount of effort behind his legislative program, publicly referring to 40% of his initiatives with considerable frequency, almost five proposals a year in the sample. Often Carter addressed the policy issues of his initiatives in national television broadcasts or in statements to specialized constituencies. None of these approaches worked. Whereas Eisenhower and Johnson had success rates of over 80% for the proposals to which they gave their highest efforts, and even Nixon's was 67%, Carter could get enacted a lowly 26% of his high-effort initiatives. Only Ford was less successful. When Carter turned to television, only 29% of his proposals passed; nonbroadcast addresses to specific groups generated 37% passage. Finally, the coefficients in Table 7.3 show a significant but *negative* relationship between Carter's efforts to pass his proposals and favorable congressional responses, even for large policy departures.

Given his approach to politics, Carter could not overcome the disadvantageous pull of the pure, malleable, and policy contexts of congressional action. Try as he might, his predicament only got worse. Jimmy Carter failed as a "chief legislator" not because only a third of his initiatives were enacted by Congress. Rather,

76. Interviews with aides to President Carter.

his shortcoming was his incapacity to rise to the occasion, to demonstrate effective personal leadership when it was most in demand.

Ronald Reagan

The Reagan administration invites equally careful analysis, since in the first term of the administration there were really two legislative presidencies. One is defined by the events of 1981, when Ronald Reagan launched an ambitious legislative program that included, by my count, 223 specific domestic proposals. That is an agenda comparable in size to those presented by earlier Democratic administrations. The vast majority of the proposals were the budget-cutting and tax-cutting provisions constituting Reagan's National Economic Recovery program and associated with the Omnibus Reconciliation Act (OBRA) and the Economic Recovery Tax Act (ERTA) of 1981. The second legislative presidency includes all Reagan proposals not related to OBRA and ERTA, but is characterized most fully by Reagan's program following his first year. After 1981 the Reagan legislative machine began to wind down. Only 44 initiatives were introduced in 1982, an agenda whose paucity rivals the first legislative agenda of Dwight Eisenhower. And in 1984 President Reagan announced only 28 specific initiatives.

The politics of the two legislative presidencies are quite dissimilar, although the differences can easily get submerged in the simple overviews of what happened to Reagan's initiatives. The contextual features of the time during which Reagan served matched the experiences of Jimmy Carter and Gerald Ford far more closely than they did those of Eisenhower, Kennedy, or Johnson. Against that background Reagan performed quite well in the legislative arena. He faced a House of Representatives controlled by the opposition party and tough economic circumstances, but still was able to get Congress to enact at least in part 54% of the proposals he submitted during his first term, suffering less outright defeat than the contextual probit analysis would have projected (23% of the cases, instead of 30%).

In order to understand Reagan's legislative success, and the institutional conflict that accompanied that achievement, we need to examine the differences between the 1981 legislative presidency of OBRA and ERTA and the one that followed. Of the eight proposals in the sample that formed part of the National Economic Recovery program, six were enacted—a success rate of 75%. Of the fourteen proposals from the second legislative presidency, only 43% passed Congress. The first legislative presidency was one of presidential dominance and no strategic inaction; the second was largely one of strategic inaction first (36%) and opposition dominance second (21%).[77] Although both legislative presidencies are part of Ronald Reagan's record, they are starkly different. Reagan was most effective at overcoming the contextual constraints and dominating congressional action when his proposals involved small policy changes or altered existing programs. In other words, success came when he proposed chipping away at the existing government establishment, activities represented by OBRA and ERTA. Congress typically ignored Reagan's ideas for new programs more than the contextual analysis would have predicted. Conservative innovation in the legislative arena, such as his scheme for urban enterprise zones—using tax credits to businesses to expand employment opportunities in poor neighborhoods—proved far more troublesome than incremental retrenchment.

Reagan entered office having defeated an incumbent president and at the same time having helped to elect many of his fellow partisans to Congress. More than sheer numbers were involved, however. He was the first Republican occupant of the White house since the initial term of Dwight Eisenhower to benefit from his party's control of at least one house of Congress. The new Republican majority in the Senate was eager to use its power to advance the interests of its standard-bearer. Many of the individuals I interviewed who served during the Nixon and Ford presidencies emphasized the extraordinary difference it would have made to the fortunes of their administrations if they had enjoyed a similar situation. By gaining 33 seats in the House of Representatives, the Republican minority in the House, in combination with conservative Democrats, also had the numbers to give Reagan a working philosophical majority. At least until the 1982 midterm election, therefore, President Reagan profited from a

77. During this period congressional support for the positions President Reagan announced on roll-call votes also declined. Reagan's success rate in 1981 was 82.4%, but it fell to 65.8% in 1984 and 43.5% in 1987. Chuck Alston, "Reagan's Support Index Up—But Not Much," *Congressional Quarterly Weekly Report*, November 19, 1988, pp. 3323–30.

political setting far superior to those that either Nixon or Ford encountered. Indeed, it would not be entirely unreasonable to argue that it was more advantageous than that which faced Jimmy Carter. Carter's election in 1976 brought neither the mandate of numbers nor the mandate of message, whereas Reagan's election was at least arguably clear on both. The unwieldly, frustrated Democratic majorities in Congress during the Carter administration displayed all of the incoherence and divisiveness that have come to characterize the party nationally. But congressional Republicans in 1981 came together forcefully to exploit the opportunities engendered by their rare simultaneous control of the White House and the Senate. Especially as long as the Reagan administration stuck to fiscal issues, it could hold together a reasonably coherent, economically conservative majority in each house.

The President's position was also assisted in the short run and on the specific issues of the first legislative presidency by two institutional features of Congress. First, the change in control of the Senate necessitated wholesale turnover in committee chairmanships and staffs. Whatever autonomous power bases had been established by Democratic committee and subcommittee chairs were effectively destroyed. Novice Republican senators were elevated to chairmanships, and scores of new faces replaced the committee and subcommittee staffs of the previous majority. Second, and far more important in that much of the President's 1981 legislative program involved budget cuts, the reconciliation provisions of the Budget and Impoundment Control Act of 1974, when exploited by the administration, gave Reagan a means for effectively sidestepping the institutional complexity of Congress. On budget issues Reagan was able to counter the adverse consequences of the institutional setting he had inherited; given the nature of his 1981 program, that made all the difference between legislative success and failure. There was no similar device to grant institutional protection to the initiatives of Reagan's second legislative presidency. These more subtle political and institutional features of the legislative setting were not captured in the probit contextual analyses, so the resulting predictions overestimate the constraints on presidential leadership that existed early in Reagan's administration.

Because of his political experience and background, as well as his personality, Ronald Reagan was also more inclined than

Jimmy Carter to make considered use of his personal political resources and skills. Even before the 1980 election, Reagan's years of campaigning for himself and other Republicans netted him a wide range of alliances with many members of Congress.[78] Once in office (with some exceptions), he proved willing and able to engage in the give-and-take of the political process. One of his aides, in fact, commented that he felt the President had been too willing to horse-trade in order to win approval of the major reductions in personal income tax rates embodied in the Economic Recovery Tax Act of 1981. Finally, of course, Reagan in 1981 demonstrated considerable skill in using the communications technology of the modern era. He was the first president since JFK to be completely at home in front of the cameras, and thus the first president to consummate the relationship between the media and politics at a time when nearly every American had access to a television set and most people obtained the bulk of their political information from TV news. Members of the White House staff viewed Reagan's capacity to communicate with the public as one of their greatest assets.

Assuredly it was an asset in 1981 for the economic program. President Reagan used specific prime-time television addresses and a triumphant appearance before a televised joint session of Congress, following his recovery from the March 30th assassination attempt, to focus public attention on his budget and tax proposals. Five of the seven relevant proposals in the sample were enacted (71%). The results for the second legislative presidency, however, were rather different. Only one of the five proposals associated with Reagan's television addresses was enacted (20%). These differences help to explain the variations in presidential effort and effectiveness. When we look at all of his proposals in the sample, Reagan put a tremendous amount of effort behind his program, mentioning issues relevant to 59% of the proposals in at least one public statement a month. The figure is only 36% for the initiatives of the second legislative presidency. The correlation between Reagan's efforts and legislative success for all of his proposals is modestly positive (gamma = .29), but the relationship disappears for the initiatives not associated with OBRA and ERTA (gamma = .04). As a result, the coefficient for presidential effort from the probit analysis, controlling for contextual factors, is pos-

78. Interview with an aide to President Reagan.

itive for all proposals but somewhat shy of statistical significance. The coefficient for large policy departures fails any test of statistical significance. It would be erroneous to judge either the Reagan administration or the proficiencies of Reagan himself on the basis of 1981 alone, however significant the events of that year.

Other choices made by Reagan undoubtedly affected the responses in Congress. Where President Carter's decisions about staff appointments and the domestic agenda may have aggravated the effects of an unfavorable political environment, many of Reagan's choices, at least in the first year, enhanced the benefits of a potentially advantageous one. Reagan seemed to avoid strict ideological tests in selecting his White House staff. He preferred instead to appoint those with considerable Washington experience or political savvy, including Max Friedersdorf as head of congressional liaison and James Baker as chief of staff.[79] To many of my informants, of even more import was the selection of Congressman David Stockman as director of the Office of Management and Budget. One of Reagan's aides suggested that it was fairly obvious that the domestic policy staff of the White House (the Office of Policy Development) would not be particularly effective, and Stockman realized that "after listening to these turkeys for a while, he knew that they couldn't last three days without him." A Republican with service in several administrations put it somewhat less disparagingly:

> You have to realize that in the Reagan administration there was a new personality, David Stockman. There had not been anyone like him in the Nixon or Ford administrations. [James] Lynn, budget director under Ford, and [Casper] Weinberger, who headed OMB under Nixon, came close, but they didn't have the same drives or the same familiarity with the budget details. I have worked with all of them, with Lynn and Weinberger . . . and Stockman . . . and Stockman knew more about the budget before coming in than the others did when they left OMB. He knew what would work. He had a clear understanding of his goals. He understood the process, knew the process. [George] Shultz, Weinberger, Lynn, they were all

79. The pragmatism did not rob the Reagan White House of fundamental ideological coherence, however. Kessel, "The Structures of the Reagan White House," p. 235.

good people and had the right instincts, and they knew what they wanted to do, but they didn't have the same depth of understanding of the process. Stockman also used the reconciliation process. It was a conscious decision during the transition . . . Stockman was also an attractive spokesman. He had the answers, the numbers. Nobody could stump him. He also had a supply of quips that were good for headlines, for making the news. He really sold the program. I think he was responsible for it.

It was Stockman, as a former member of Congress, who knew how to manipulate Congress' own budget procedures to the President's advantage. Friedersdorf, Baker, and others understood how to keep the agenda focused and how to fashion political discourse to the benefit of the administration. They skillfully implemented Reagan's decision to concentrate thematically the first-year legislative agenda. While pledging his commitment to the conservative social issues, during the initial year the President did little but press the economic recovery line. In messages, on television and radio, in conversation with members of Congress, Reagan emphasized the priority of the program that he was offering for economic recovery. A Republican official offered the following contrast between Reagan and Carter:

What you have to decide is, what do you want to do for the next four years, Mr. President? Carter would throw something up once a week. Nixon was more like once a month. Carter was a thrill a day. Reagan has decided, I think wisely, to concentrate on five or six issues, including deregulation, taxes, defense. You don't get a lot of messages on crime, immigration, and so on.

A congressional liaison official described Reagan as asking for what he could get during the honeymoon period, rather than either underestimating his political resources or overloading Congress.

The task of managing the legislative program became more difficult once the agenda moved away from the budget and tax issues of 1981. The changing political climate, particularly after the 1982 congressional elections, the substantive dispersion of Reagan's legislative agenda, and the absence of mechanisms like reconciliation to circumvent recent transformations of American institutions all led to a second legislative presidency for Reagan that is hard to distinguish from the experiences of his predecessors. The Democratic capture of the Senate in the 1986 election and the administration's loss of credibility in the wake of the Iran-contra affair reinforced the limits of Reagan's legislative leadership. But in addition all of these factors became less important to the President. The 1981 budget and tax victories created the aura of renewed presidential power, a reputation that would serve Reagan well in the later years. More to the point, the successes of 1981 left little for Reagan to accomplish legislatively. His major legislative priorities had been fulfilled. As the years went on, the administration placed increasing emphasis on the pursuit of policy goals through nonlegislative means. These included strict supervision by the OMB of government regulations, administrative procedures that brought statutory implementation in line with the President's objectives, and administrative and judicial appointments that would advance the interests of Reagan's philosophy of government well into the future.

I have presented the variety of choices open to presidents that can help or hinder the success of their legislative programs and their practice of presidential power. Yet the range of maneuvering on these choices is often quite limited. Eisenhower did not really choose a restricted agenda; it was rather a reflection of his basic orientation. Given the ideological perspective and traditions of the Democratic party, it would be difficult indeed for Democratic presidents to proffer legislative agendas as constrained as Eisenhower's. While it may have been feasible in Kennedy's day to have the president himself direct a small band of White House aides, with the present scope of government activity and the continual political demands a similar arrangement would scarcely prove efficacious today. It was not the intent of Richard Nixon and Jimmy Carter to be awkward and ineffective in the political give-and-take, any more than it could have been Johnson's decision to remain aloof from that which he enjoyed most. LBJ was good at conventional politics, or at least had an undeniable political presence, because that was his central interest. Had the politics of policy making required careful reflection, assimilation and interpretation of vast bodies of data, explicit itemization and weighting of substantive trade-offs, Johnson would have failed and Carter would have seemed phenomenally adept. As it turns out, effective policy making may benefit from those traits, but not the politics to enact the legislative programs. The latter falls into the purview of this study and therefore highlights Johnson's skills. Since the former does not, his limitations and Carter's strengths seem less pronounced. Still, they too must be added into the overall calculus of presidential power.

Presidents are never truly free to be the persons, and therefore the presidents, they choose, but the analysis presented here does suggest simple lessons and reinforce certain maxims about presidential leadership in the legislative arena. First, no matter how astute the politician, what we generally perceive as successful leadership requires a consonance between the politician and the setting. Lyndon Johnson showed us the possibilities inherent when activism is matched with opportunity. Gerald Ford revealed the necessity of discipline and equanimity in a world of oppressive constraints. Second, nothing an individual president can do breeds success like clear priorities. Eisenhower, Nixon, and Reagan, each in his own way, demonstrated the potential for obtaining favorable congressional action by carefully targeting their interests and efforts. Republicans, because of their philosophical predispositions, will always assimilate this lesson more easily than Democrats. Third, nothing fails quite so dramatically as ignoring the first two maxims. Judged by the scope of his commitments and the ambition of his legislative program, Jimmy Carter was in many ways a courageous president. Evaluated according to his willingness to take risks and work for his program, he should not be shortchanged. Any president serving when he did would have had trouble passing a program of such dimensions. But an essential measure of leadership ultimately has to be the capacity to prevail against the odds, and to know how to craft one's ambitions to fit the opportunities of the day. Jimmy Carter did not have the background, or the temperament, to learn that lesson soon enough.

8. Representative Institutions and Policy Making

Both the public and students of government have in recent years expressed growing apprehension about the capacity of the president, or anyone, to provide leadership in the bewildering institutional maze that is the modern American national polity. Each report of a beleaguered administration is a warning about the competence of the entire political system to surmount the domestic policy exigencies of the era, whether the stagflation of the early 1970s, the energy crisis later in that decade, or the budgetary conundrum of the 1980s. At times the country seems unable to find and implement solutions to the pressing problems faced by society. That failure more often than not is thought to reside in executive-legislative stalemate over the policy options advocated by the president.

To what extent is the health of our democratic system predicated on the wholesale acceptance of policy stances promulgated by the president? Must virtually all presidential policy initiatives be enacted for the political system to be judged effective? Should we endorse institutional or political reforms that would further centralize the entire domestic government in the hands of the executive? The answers to these questions cannot be an unqualified yes. As ever, the president and Congress, as separate institutions sharing power, have distinct roles that are both dependent and complementary. Members of both branches of government enjoy the same collective opportunities for Promethean policy advancement and face the same imperatives created by difficult times. That the modern era has become politically ever more demanding seems hardly debatable, but the consequent implications for improving the political process are far from obvious.

Assessing the presidential-congressional experiences of the current day requires an appreciation of the institutional relationship over the entire period that has been the subject of this study. It also invites a careful appraisal of the sources of increasing conflict in the political system, some of which have complicated the task of presidential legislative leadership and diminished the opportunities for presidential success. These concerns raise questions about the appropriate stature of the president and Congress in the contemporary context: their place, their design, their responsibilities. For many the answers are found in a reformist impulse, most often predicated on assumptions grounded in the necessity for presidential centrality in the American political system. The findings of this research offer the means for evaluating both the urgency and the value of many of the reforms intended to mitigate the confusion seemingly inherent in national policy making.

Inextricably linked to the issue of making American government "work better" is the contemplation of what "work" means in the American democratic context. Government in the United States rests as a balance between two contending values of governance, securing the accoutrements of effective action and guaranteeing the presence of representative deliberation. It is against that potential trade-off that I consider the roles of the presidency and Congress, their current status, and the suitability of various reforms. To the extent that any reformist ideas are attractive, they are those that would invigorate governing coalitions without impairing the channels of representation. More important than any structural reform, however, is the need to sharpen political discourse on the issues of the day. It is in that context, within the persistent realities of the tandem-institutions setting, that the vital prescriptive contribution of the presidency can be found. As a singularly empowered political leader, the president should emphasize the institutional responsibilities associated with being an agenda focuser, clarifying the terms of political debate and introducing viable policy alternatives to the agenda for active consideration.

The State of Presidential-Congressional Relations

Normative evaluations of any political system are easily sidetracked, if not distorted, by impressions and conclusions derived from an incomplete measure of the empirical realities of the interactions among political institutions and participants. Impressions of reality can, in turn, be confused if the observation of political behavior has as its starting point a theoretical perspective that denies the complexity and subtlety of genuine politics. The design of this study, from the derivation of the guiding thematic perspective to the method of analysis, has as one of its objectives development of the capacity to arrive at more precise normative judgments about presidential-congressional interactions, what each institution contributes to the process and what conditions their relationship.

In examining the derivation and congressional resolution of the president's legislative program, we focus on one of the most significant facets of the institutional relationship. A deductive argument about White House strategic capabilities and an empirical analysis of interviews with members of the White House and Capitol Hill establishments support the conclusion that presidents generate legislative programs comprising their policy preferences. Ongoing White House consultation with members of Congress, even anticipation of their future reactions, typically does not dilute the executive's agenda. Presidential programs remain presidential. When choosing among their policy preferences and deciding on the innovativeness of their initiatives, chief executives are somewhat influenced by their assessments of the political environment in Congress and the health of the economy. Yet the innovativeness of presidential programs is demonstrably the product of their preferences, their campaign references, and substantively relevant events.

A typically cited measure of the viability of the American political system is the ability of presidents to get Congress to enact their legislative proposals once they have been announced. There is no preexisting normative baseline, however, from which we can draw conclusions about either the absolute effectiveness of presidents or the relevance of particular levels of presidential success to a healthy political order. We know from numerous case studies that a chief executive can rarely obtain presidential objectives through the issuing of commands, needing instead to engage other influential actors in the system in a process of bargaining and persuasion.[1] Previous quantitative studies have suggested that only a minority of the initiatives suggested by modern chief executives have survived the legislative gauntlet. Given the fact that

1. Richard E. Neustadt, *Presidential Power: The Politics of Leadership from FDR to Carter* (New York: Macmillan, 1980).

the president is now acknowledged to bear the greatest responsibility for providing policy leadership, these bits of information could raise serious doubts about the coherence of the policy-making process.

The results of my own research indicate that such a conclusion would be overly pessimistic. Case studies tend to dwell on the most controversial legislative issues and exaggerate the overall contentiousness in the legislative arena. The Congressional Quarterly measures that furnish the material for many quantitative studies fail to take into account the amount of time it takes to pass legislation; indeed, the amount of time it often *should* take to promote policy proposals to the status of law. Tracing the life of presidential initiatives during each administration reveals that well over half are enacted in some form. Of the presidents since 1953, Lyndon Johnson was the most successful, gaining passage of 68% of his specific proposals, and almost half of those without any amendment.

The difficulties encountered by individual presidents within the period of their administration may also overstate the degree to which the presidency as an institution is circumvented in the long term by programmatic adversaries in the legislature. Some initiatives introduced by one president go on to be enacted under the leadership of another. President Johnson offered the original plan to reorganize the post office and remove it from the Cabinet; this program became a key part—a successful one—of the early Nixon agenda. He also introduced public financing for presidential campaigns, later enacted in the wake of the Watergate scandal. Many of the provisions in Gerald Ford's energy policy found their way into the statute books as a result of congressional action on Jimmy Carter's National Energy Plan.

It is true that presidents from Eisenhower to Reagan had trouble winning approval of the more controversial aspects of their legislative programs. A majority of these tough issues were decided by the most publicly confrontational forms of congressional action, and barely half were finally enacted with or without amendment. Only 40% of the most innovative presidential initiatives (those involving large and new departures in government activity) were passed. Perhaps the political system should furnish better opportunities for presidents to prevail on these difficult issues, but that is not an unassailable proposition. One must first inquire whether our presidents, or the political system as a whole, have really fared so poorly according to these results, especially when they are evaluated in light of the turmoil associated with much of the postwar period. From 1953 to 1986 Congress enacted a majority of the domestic presidential proposals linked to major legislation despite twenty years in which the country endured partisanly divided government, the trauma of the Vietnam War, the inflamed passions of urban turbulence, the frustrations of economic stagflation, and the creedal shame of Watergate. One may ask in addition whether bold and dramatic policy innovations should be easily accepted, even in times of consensus and tranquility. Many individuals whom I interviewed, including those who participated directly in the Johnson administration, commented on the costs imposed on the policy-making process by the torrent of legislation that LBJ submitted and enacted as part of the Great Society. It is not that the programs, either standing alone or considered together, constituted an improper course of government action. That issue is the proper subject of ideological debate. Rather, the initiatives came so fast, and the prodding from the President was so strong, that there was little time and few institutional opportunities to reflect carefully on the possible unanticipated consequences of their implementation and their eventual budgetary impact. In one case the formula for a domestic program, reported an EOP official, was decided at two in the morning by Wilbur Cohen as he spoke to Joe Califano on the phone, the latter having just awakened him. Cohen's only time to contemplate the final decision was the few minutes it took him to find his slippers. Other programmatic issues were decided by exhaustion during late night–early morning sessions in Califano's office. Johnson wanted answers on his desk, without delay.

Similar difficulties plagued the most recognized achievements of the Reagan administration. It would be reasonable to assume that few members of Congress, when they voted on the legislation, actually knew the details encapsulated in the budget resolution (OBRA) and tax-cut package (ERTA) enacted in 1981, even in the areas of their own expertise. The $100 billion tax increase that emerged from Congress the very next year, the Tax Equity and Fiscal Responsibility Act, suggests that they did not. It is not altogether obvious that the abstemious manner in which Congress has sometimes responded to a president's legislative program constitutes an unmistakable indicator of system failure.

Ascertaining *why* Congress responds to the president's legislative program in particular ways is as meaningful as determining *how* Congress responds. To the extent that conflict between the two institutions occurs, it is necessary to know the sources of the confrontations, some of which end in rejection of the president's program. We need to understand the significance of forces largely beyond presidential control and of factors associated with the personal traits of presidents and other participants in the process. The influence of the individual must be distinguished from the coercion of the environment.

The settings in which the Congress assesses and responds to presidential initiatives vary enormously. Even the institutional arrangements of government and the political system—what I have termed the pure context of congressional decision making—are not static. It is now evident that the decentralization of authority in Congress begun in the early 1970s elevates the level of institutional discord and encumbers a president seeking to form winning coalitions for initiatives affecting already existing programs. The much-elaborated interest-group system works to the disadvantage of the president's position, except when the initiatives pertain to established programs.

Aspects of the malleable context of legislative action, open to some presidential influence, also have an impact on domestic policy decisions. Several dynamic political properties of the system influence congressional responses in a variety of ways. The probability of legislative confrontations rises when presidents are invigorated by having won a large majority in the previous election or when they are enjoying high levels of support among the public. Control of the House of Representatives by the opposition party also invites confrontation. Presidential legislative success is generally aided when the president's party has a majority in the House and in some instances when there is evidence that presidential coattails contributed to the election of members of Congress. The patterns for the Senate are more ambiguous. The second set of factors constituting the malleable context, properties measuring the health of the economy, are of importance too. Indicators of resource scarcity, such as slow or no growth in the Gross National Product, large budget deficits, and inflation, lead to more legislative conflict. A president's program also seems to be less likely to win favorable action during periods of economic scarcity and dislocation.

The policy context of congressional action plays an additional role. Presidential proposals diverge in the amount of impact they have on the budget or, more generally, on the political-economic system. The initiatives enjoying different levels of presidential priority attract variable amounts of lobbying effort from presidents and their aides. Further, the substance of policy initiatives triggers different kinds of politics. In general, the most consequential proposals generate the greatest legislative conflict and are the most troublesome to enact. But they almost always draw the serious attention of Congress. The least consequential initiatives invite relatively little notice and are often ignored by the Hill; but once considered, they are as likely as not to be accepted by consensus.

Examining the pure, malleable, and policy contexts of congressional responses to presidential initiatives ultimately provides an opportunity to explore the role of the person in legislative politics, to assess the influence of individual presidents and their administrations on congressional deliberation. Presidents differ, of course, in their talents and orientations, and in the range of choices they make to advance their legislative programs. When we control for the influence of contextual factors, in addition to measures of presidential programmatic ambitions and effort, the analysis of presidential legislative performance reveals that many assessments of individual presidents demand reevaluation.

Little about any of the presidents from Dwight Eisenhower to Ronald Reagan can be understood without reference to the times in which they served. In the aggregate, the responses of Congress to each president's policy agenda conform quite closely to the expectations prompted by an examination of institutional, political, and economic contexts. Nor can the individuality of each president be ignored. Eisenhower not only served during favorable times, but he also submitted a more restrained and judicious program than many of his successors. Lyndon Johnson, riding the crest of the Eighty-ninth Congress, exploited the contextual opportunities to the fullest. While Nixon experienced enormous conflict with Congress and had trouble with much of his legislative program, he actually fared quite well on those items that really mattered to him. Ford, facing deleterious institutional, political, and economic circumstances, had the good sense to proceed within the known constraints without making them worse. The troubles of the Carter administration had deep roots in the contexts of congressional deliberations on his proposals, but the ambitiousness of his legislative program demonstrated little willingness on his part to live within his means. Ronald Reagan won definitive victories in 1981 on budget and tax cuts, slightly outperforming the contextually based expectations. But his successes came at the expense of tremendous institutional conflict. They were also not repeated once the agenda shifted from the economic recovery initiatives of the first year of his administration.

There is no question that the successes and failures of each of these presidencies were tied to forces beyond the manipulation of the individual incumbents. Yet there was room for maneuver and personal impact, if leadership skills were artfully applied. Each of these general impressions has important normative implications, especially as we turn to the later years of the period being studied.

Emerging Problems for Presidential Legislative Leadership

There is reason, therefore, to concede some optimism about the practicability of the relationship between the president and Congress on legislative issues, at least if one remains attentive to the broad sweep of experiences from the early 1950s to the present. Concentration on the more immediate past, however, introduces reservations about the continued viability of presidential coalitions in Congress. Both Gerald Ford and Jimmy Carter had difficulty inspiring Congress to pass more than a third of their initiatives, a record of legislative performance well below that of their predecessors, even that of Richard Nixon. Conflict also came to dominate congressional action, with opposition and presidential dominance combining with strategic inaction to account for well over half of congressional responses to their initiatives. By the time of Ronald Reagan's first term, consensual legislative responses had disappeared altogether, at least within this sample. Confrontation became the standard. For all the conflict, the events of 1981 brought a temporary respite to concerns about the "imperiled" presidency. Reagan's first-year manipulation of the legislative agenda called up a recrudescent image of the president as chief legislator. One journalist, commenting on the aura generated at the time, told the following story:

> I was out having drinks with a guy who's a friend of Mondale's, and one thing he said is how the Reagan adminis-

tration has really shattered the myth that the presidency is powerless to do anything. After the Vietnam era and the Watergate era, there's still plenty of juice in that place.

But that speaks to the first legislative presidency of the Reagan administration, not the second.

Once the grand legislative achievements of Reagan's economic recovery program receded from the contemporary agenda, the administration's success with Congress, and the extent of institutional conflict, mimicked the patterns of recent memory. President Reagan witnessed one budget after another being declared dead on arrival by members of Congress on both sides of the aisle. Budget making became a game of executive-legislative cat and mouse, with posed and sometimes realized threats to temporarily shut down the government. Rather than enacting the thirteen regular appropriations bills traditionally used to establish annual federal expenditures, public spending was routinely authorized by continuing resolutions.[2]

The evidence of diminished presidential influence in Congress has less to do with any plausible scenario of declining presidential talent than with extensive contemporary changes in the institutional, political, economic, and policy contexts of American politics. Although many of the contextual attributes addressed in this book do not divulge any manifest secular trend, the transformations of several in the 1970s and 1980s regularly contributed to intensified conflict in the political system and, at least for some types of issues, increased for everyone the difficulty of forging successful legislative coalitions.

The consequences of the institutional evolution of American politics are all of a piece. With the exception of a few countervailing reforms that strengthened the bargaining influence of the House leadership (such as bringing the Rules Committee and committee assignment responsibilities more into the leadership's domain, and the emergent centrality of floor activity in the 1980s), most of the changes in Congress implemented since 1971 have granted more individuals increased autonomous power. Veto points have expanded concomitantly with access points. Although presidential coattails appear to have retained some currency, in general members of Congress are now more

2. Joe White, "The Continuing Resolution: A Crazy Way to Govern?" *Brookings Review* 6 (Summer 1988): 28–35.

isolated from the vicissitudes of presidential politics and enjoy enhanced freedom to pursue individualized policy making. These characteristics of the modern Congress do not always interfere with the pursuit of presidential priorities, but they certainly do not reinforce the perspective of the president in the legislative domain.

The effects of the transfigured congressional establishment are amplified by two other major changes in the institutional setting of American politics. Progressive shifts in both the party and the interest-group systems since the early 1960s have encumbered the political process even further, some would argue, by expanding the range of policy demands, heightening political discord, and weakening the integrative capabilities of partisan coalitions. The resulting "riot of pluralism" threatens to overload the political system with competing and sometimes antithetical group demands that resist coherent executive management.[3] There is little doubt that the emergence of newly organized groups, giving voice in the 1960s and 1970s to constituencies without previous organizational representation, has complicated policy making and reduced political comity by expanding the "scope of conflict," to use E. E. Schattschneider's oft-repeated phraseology.[4] The politics that previously masqueraded as consensus in certain policy domains became combative once a few elements of the opposition gained the resources of agency. What happened in policy arenas occurred in political parties as well, especially as changes in the presidential nominating process after the post-1968 rules reforms in the Democratic party accented the factionalism rather than the shared commitments of the party.[5] Jimmy Carter remarked to me that the ensuing political chaos, as it is commonly perceived, poses a threat to the national interest by fragmenting the national pur-

3. The quotation is from Andrew Shonfield, *Modern Capitalism: The Changing Balance of Public and Private Power* (New York: Oxford University Press, 1969), p. 336. The overload thesis is most starkly presented in Samuel P. Huntington, "The Democratic Distemper," *Public Interest* 14 (Fall 1975): 9–38.

4. E. E. Schattschneider, *The Semisovereign People: A Realist's View of Democracy in America* (Hinsdale, Ill.: Dryden Press, 1975), p. 20.

5. Nelson W. Polsby, *The Consequences of Party Reform* (New York: Oxford Unversity Press, 1983); and Austin Ranney, *Curing the Mischiefs of Faction: Party Reform in America* (Berkeley: University of California Press, 1975).

pose and inhibiting the ability of governmental leaders, particularly the president, to nurture a basic consensus on the most urgent issues.

The languishing condition of the economy in the 1970s exacerbated the potential for conflict created by the institutional fragmentation of the period. The most concrete manifestation of confrontation involved the budget and impoundment wars between President Nixon and the Democratic majorities in Congress, but the resource scarcity of the 1970s and beyond colored institutional politics in general, often by simply dominating the policy agenda.[6] Devoid of the "fiscal dividend" of the booming sixties, and implicitly the relatively stable fifties, there was no longer the fiscal "increment" by which accommodation could be purchased with expanding federal revenues.[7] Economic conditions naturally fluctuate within presidential administrations, but stagflation and the three recessions of the 1970s made things decidedly more difficult then for the President than they had been before. So did the rise in inflation and interest rates at the end of the decade, followed by the severe recession of 1982. As long as the unprecedented budget deficits of the Reagan years persist, measured in the way that deficits are commonly calculated, even a healthier economy as indicated by other measures will do little to mitigate perceived resource scarcity.

Related to the economic uncertainties is the final contextual change that has become most pronounced in the second half of the period under study. Despite the availability of some strategic choices by the president, the policy mix of both proposed and enacted programs was dramatically transformed. Joseph Califano put it most directly:

> When John Kennedy and Lyndon Johnson took charge of the executive branch, the federal government was not involved in manpower training programs; social security did not include medicare; less than $2 billion was being spent on health and education programs; defense expenditures represented some 60 percent of the budget; there was no antipoverty program;

6. Allen Schick, "The Distributive Congress," in *Making Economic Policy in Congress*, ed. Allen Schick (Washington, D.C.: American Enterprise Institute, 1983), p. 259.

7. Allen Schick, *Congress and Money: Budgeting, Spending, and Taxing* (Washington, D.C.: Urban Institute, 1980), pp. 23–30.

the environment was a matter of concern to a few professors and perhaps those students entranced by Thoreau.[8]

As the proportion of the budget and the GNP absorbed by defense expenditures declined, a trend later reversed by the Reagan administration, the range of domestic programs was enlarged both in breadth of activities and in absolute size of the federal commitment to each. Some of the proliferation of the federal domain incorporated dramatic innovations and new approaches. Much resulted from fairly large-scale increases in the funds allocated to existing programs. Each process entailed some of the trickier politics associated with the most consequential proposals examined in this book. The establishment of new, relatively bold programs often creates difficulties later when adjustments proposed in subsequent years must survive the review given them by participants in established policy communities. As Lawrence Brown puts it, U.S. policy making has moved from an era of "breakthrough" agendas to one of "rationalizing politics," no matter which party controls the lead institutions of government. Ronald Reagan notwithstanding, leaders in both political parties have developed a "regard for complexity," but that may have come at the expense of the convictions needed to mobilize both the public and its political protagonists.[9]

The ways in which presidential priorities are addressed and administration lobbying efforts are extended also may have instigated a nascent and perhaps more difficult politics. There is growing concern about the old refined strategy of "going public." If Samuel Kernell is correct in suggesting that going public solidifies positions and reduces the flexibility required for effective bargaining at the margins, then more leverage gained for the president through television and specialized public strategies may well generate more coalitional conflict.[10]

These shifts in the politics of policies are perhaps only symptomatic of more generic transitions evident in this and other

8. Joseph A. Califano, Jr., *Governing America: An Insider's Report from the White House and the Cabinet* (New York: Simon and Schuster, 1981), p. 13.

9. Lawrence D. Brown, *New Policies, New Politics: Government's Response to Government's Growth* (Washington, D.C.: Brookings Institution, 1983), pp. 66–67.

10. Samuel Kernell, *Going Public: New Strategies of Presidential Leadership* (Washington, D.C.: CQ Press, 1986), p. 218.

political systems. Contemporary government generates policy choices that are often extremely challenging to enact. These programs do not distribute benefits to a receptive public, but rather demand of the public new behavior and collective restraint. Paul Light calls these issues—the need to regulate energy consumption, to control inflation, to harness the federal deficit—"constituentless."[11] They may among them constitute the national interest, if it could be defined, but few organized interests support them and, in the aggregate, whole segments of the population lie in opposition. As a result, "the search for acceptable alternatives has become more difficult . . . , [and] the kinds of programs that can survive the legislative process are increasingly limited."[12]

Put more broadly, these issues engender what economist Lester Thurow identifies as "the zero-sum society," which appeared in full flower at the end of the 1970s. Under its tenets the basic problems confronting the society can no longer be resolved without requiring that the costs of solutions be explicitly borne by one group or another.[13] From one perspective the United States has reached a plateau of postindustrialization in which mature economic development, combined with the recent mobilization of myriad new groups and enhanced citizen sensitivity to externalities, has led to struggles over the state provision of collective goods.[14] Presidents Eisenhower, Kennedy, and Johnson would have found this a strange and discouraging environment in which to practice the art of political leadership; for presidents since then, and for Congress as well, it has been the stuff of daily existence. The subsequent frustration leads naturally to reformist pleas that something be done.

The Reformist Impulse

Proposals to redirect the American political system, to endow it with invigorated policy coherence, range across the board. Some

11. Paul C. Light, *The President's Agenda: Domestic Policy Choice from Kennedy to Carter* (Baltimore: Johns Hopkins University Press, 1982), pp. 215–217.

12. Ibid., p. 105.

13. Lester C. Thurow, *The Zero-Sum Society: Distribution and the Possibilities for Economic Change* (New York: Basic Books, 1980), esp. p. 10.

14. Roger Benjamin, *The Limits of Politics: Collective Goods and Political Change in Postindustrial Societies* (Chicago: University of Chicago Press, 1980), esp. chaps. 1–3.

seek to penetrate not the written constitutional structure of American government, but rather the traditions, norms, and practices that have come to define the "unwritten constitution" of the United States.[15] Others speak more directly to the established framework of American national government, addressing the concern that, in Walter Lippmann's words, "the anatomy of our politics does not correspond to the anatomy of our life."[16] A few, such as the single six-year term for presidents advocated by President Carter, would require relatively modest changes in the formal design of the government. Others would necessitate radical transformations in the way the government is organized; an example is Charles Hardin's plan for a new constitutional order assimilating the essential elements of parliamentary democracy.[17] Each is some sort of attempt to ameliorate the problem at the heart of Lloyd Cutler's admonition about the current state of American national government:

> A particular shortcoming in need of remedy is the structural inability of our government to propose, legislate and administer a balanced program for governing. In parliamentary terms, one might say that under the U.S. Constitution it is not now feasible to "form a Government." The separation of powers between the legislative and executive branches, whatever its merits in 1793, has become a structure that almost guarantees stalemate today.[18]

The lament is not new, only newly experienced by each individual. James Bryce expressed it a century ago when he noted that "there is an excessive friction in the American system, a waste of force in the strife of various bodies and persons created to check and balance one another." It is "only when a distinct majority of the people are so clearly of one mind," Bryce continued, that the

15. Don K. Price, *America's Unwritten Constitution: Science, Religion, and Political Responsibility* (Cambridge, Mass.: Harvard University Press, 1985), p. 9.

16. Walter Lippmann, *Drift and Mastery* (Englewood Cliffs, N.J.: Prentice-Hall, 1961), p. 96.

17. Charles M. Hardin, *Presidential Power and Accountability: Toward a New Constitution* (Chicago: University of Chicago Press, 1974).

18. Lloyd N. Cutler, "To Form a Government," *Foreign Affairs* 59 (Fall 1980): 126–127.

American government affords concerted action.[19] Such is the indictment of the reformer.

Each suggestion for reform reflects an underlying set of assumptions about the shortcomings of American representative democracy and the appropriate role of national governing institutions, especially the presidency. Essentially the assumptions I attached to the presidency-centered perspective of American politics, they ultimately rest on the assertion that of all the possible sources of government authority, only the president can and does represent the national interest. Elected by a constituency comprising the entire electorate, the chief executive need not distort policies serving the best interests of the country by succumbing to the parochial concerns of individual states or localities. The president is nevertheless thwarted in the pursuit of national goals by the reinforcement of regional and constituency provincialism in Congress, aggravated by the enfeeblement of the party system and the proliferation of vocal special interests. The national interest, therefore, requires reforms in practice and structure to permit the atavism of a style of presidential leadership in which the chief executive has more authority not only in setting the nation's policy agenda, but also in implementing it.[20]

A different philosophical perspective guides the reformers who advocate a kind of change rather contrary to those suggested above. Their premises have inspired the institutional modifications that open the system to a wider spectrum of interests, such as the more "democratic" party nominating procedures that are the very targets of those who desire increased centralization. Advocates of invigorated democratic procedures will continue to urge reforms that favor a broadening of the participatory base—in nominations, in congressional and administrative proceedings, and in nongovernmental political arenas such as the workplace.

These two competing sets of political assumptions confront each other as part of a fundamental dilemma. Any democratic society must weigh in the balance the potential trade-off between, first, enabling its governmental institutions to design and implement with reasonable effectiveness the public policies needed to

19. James Bryce, *The American Commonwealth*, 3rd ed. (New York: Macmillan, 1899), vol. 1, p. 302.

20. For one of the most inclusive analyses of reform, see James L. Sundquist, *Constitutional Reform and Effective Government* (Washington, D.C.: Brookings Institution, 1986).

address important issues and, second, imbuing its governmental procedures with the mechanisms required to ensure the representation of legitimate but disparate interests and claims. The fundamental question is how to craft a government that is both effective and responsive, since the absence of either feature would be debilitating to the political system. A state formulating and administering programs that meet standards of efficiency and effectiveness by ignoring or thwarting interests of the polity other than the traditional ones violates the basic democratic tenets of the polity. Yet a government that is unable to handle the problems most threatening to the country loses its legitimacy and fails to accomplish the primary tasks of organized society.

Whichever proposed reforms are addressed, one needs to evaluate both the empirical reality of the problems they target and the political viability of the changes they suggest. As an example, the research reported in this book bolsters the argument that the decentralization of Congress has, ceteris paribus, complicated the business of policy making. But since the design of Congress ultimately rests on the incentives that representatives and senators perceive with respect to advancing their own interests, the decentralization of Congress is not likely to be reversed in a measurable way unless the members themselves become seriously frustrated with the consequences of institutional paralysis, real or imagined.[21] So far those frustrations have facilitated the acceptance of flexible, ad hoc approaches to overcoming the fragmentation of authority, but they have not stimulated a redesign of the institution. Members of Congress have willingly participated in commissions and backroom strategies to secure a compromise on social security reform.[22] They have gone along with continuing resolutions and automatic enforcement mechanisms to discipline the budget.[23] They have been willing to leave more issues to the discretion of the floor. But

21. Lawrence C. Dodd, "A Theory of Congressional Cycles: Solving the Puzzle of Change," in *Congress and Policy Change*, ed. Gerald C. Wright, Jr., Leroy N. Reiselbach, and Lawrence C. Dodd (New York: Agathon Press, 1986), pp. 3–44.

22. Paul C. Light, *Artful Work: The Politics of Social Security Reform* (New York: Random House, 1985), esp. chaps. 12, 15.

23. John F. Hoadley, "Easy Riders: Gramm-Rudman-Hollings and the Legislative Fast Track," *PS: Political Science and Politics* 19 (Winter 1986): 30–36; and White, "The Continuing Resolution."

they have not favored a streamlining of their institution's structure and procedures.[24] Not yet.

Some reforms suggest roads to institutional regeneration that
do not directly involve either the president or Congress, but do
impinge upon the quality of their relationship. They are directed
at healing what is perceived to be the anemia of the party system
and the excessive fragmentation of the group system. Whereas
parties are seen as the only institutional means for bridging the
constitutional gap between the president and Congress, interest
groups are censured as spoilers, pressuring members of Congress
to protect their individual interests at the expense of the common
good. To meet this challenge, some would suggest reforming the
party system by revitalizing party organizations and instilling in
them greater policy coherence and responsibility. Interest groups,
they would say, should be contained by having parties supplant
them as articulators of political interests and by substituting
public financing for the campaign funds contributed by political
action committees (PACs).

Assessing parties, interest groups, and the most appropriate
methods of dealing with them, however, requires a more subtle
prescriptive approach. First, there is the implication that both parties and interest groups can be changed by direct action, that a
particular party and group system can be imposed on society.
That was the assumption behind the proposal for a "more responsible two-party system" sponsored by the American Political Science Association in the 1950s.[25] Parties and groups, however, are
concurrent products of societal forces, not an arbitrary creation.[26]
From the beginning of the republic they have reflected cleavages
inherent in the political system. Second, there is evidence that
both the party and the group systems are moving in a direction
conducive to enhanced cohesion in the political system, in as well

24. Roger H. Davidson and Walter J. Oleszek, *Congress against Itself*
(Bloomington: Indiana University Press, 1977).

25. "Toward a More Responsible Two-Party System" (Report of the
Committee on Political Parties), *American Political Science Review* (Sup-
plement) 44 (1950).

26. Mark A. Peterson and Jack L. Walker, "Interest Group Responses
to Partisan Change: The Impact of the Reagan Administration upon the
National Interest Group System," *Interest Group Politics*, 2nd ed., ed.
Allan J. Cigler and Burdett A. Loomis (Washington, D.C.: CQ Press,
1986), pp. 162–182.

as out of government. Because parties and interest organizations simultaneously reflect trends in society at large, they have the potential of working together rather than as mutually exclusive mechanisms for organizing political demands. In the last decade the national party organizations, especially that of the Republicans, have demonstrated increasing vitality. As instruments for raising and channeling funds, educating candidates, and directing media campaigns, the parties have begun to reclaim their place in the electoral process. Further, if the last few years offer any clues, the parties in government, including members of Congress, have developed intimations of the programmatic coherence longed for by the advocates of a responsible party system.

Ironically, the major party reforms that have actually been planned and systematically implemented (in the nominating process by which the two major parties select their standard-bearers for the presidential race) sprang from the participatory reformist impulse and enhanced the porousness of the parties rather than their coherence. Given the centrality of these reforms to perceptions of the responsiveness of American political institutions, it would be untenable to suggest anything approximating the elimination of primaries as a means for choosing the delegates to the national conventions. It is also difficult to argue that the system in place before the expansion of the primary system yielded presidents or alternative candidates of appreciably higher quality.

Just as it is important to guard against diminishing the responsiveness of government institutions by relying on excessive centralization, however, it is essential to preserve the legitimacy of the electoral process by ensuring that it contributes to governability. That can be accomplished by maintaining the procedures adopted by the Democratic party for the 1984 election. Saving a block of delegate seats at the convention for members of Congress (and other party officials), the "superdelegates," furnishes an incentive for the candidates of the party to familiarize themselves with some of the individuals with whom they will have to work if elected. It supplies the incentive for outsider candidates such as Jimmy Carter to meet officials other than those in their own state congressional delegations prior to assuming office. The number of delegate positions assigned to representatives and senators is far too small to permit any serious candidate to ignore the primaries and the electorate of the party, but it contributes to joining the party of elections with the party of governance.

The dilemma of democratic government is particularly pronounced in a nation as large, as diverse, and as populated with organized interests as the United States. With the increased educational sophistication of the public and the related potential for mobilizing large numbers of political activists, the challenge has become even greater. New interest organizations are joining the process as rapidly as ever.[27] The remedy for tempering a growing number of group demands is not to harken back to bygone days by trying to subvert the group voices made prominent in recent decades. They are not likely to slip away quietly in the night, nor is it desirable that they should. The demands springing from groups well organized early in our history—largely agricultural, business, and commercial interests—have claims on the system that are no more certifiably legitimate than those of the more recently articulated interests. Muting new interest groups would require the kind of state activity that is anathema to representative government.[28] The burden on the political process and its leaders is to accommodate the diversity of interests while simultaneously inspiring the level of social cohesion necessary for the government to fulfill its obligations. That too is a predominant responsibility of the tandem-institutions system comprising the president and Congress. Although interest organizations are often formed in response to specific kinds of issues or occupational needs, like the parties they reveal a certain degree of ideological coherence. Even political action committees are usually not lone operators in the political process. Quite often the PACs move in packs, reflecting philosophical cleavages similar to those of the political parties. There is even some evidence that PAC strategists are accepting cues from each party's congressional campaign committees in deciding which candidates to support, providing at least one small bridge toward greater partisan cohesion among interest groups.[29]

Instead of substantial reform of the party and group systems,

27. Kay Lehman Schlozman and John T. Tierney, *Organized Interests and American Democracy* (New York: Harper and Row, 1986), chap. 4; and Jack L. Walker, "The Origins and Maintenance of Interest Groups in America," *American Political Science Review* 77 (June 1983): 390–406.

28. Robert A. Dahl, *Dilemmas of Pluralist Democracy: Autonomy vs. Control* (New Haven: Yale University Press, 1982), pp. 38, 67.

29. Alan Ehrenhalt, "Political Parties: A Renaissance of Power?" *Congressional Quarterly Weekly Report*, October 26, 1985, p. 2187.

the effects of which can be wildly unpredictable, the real need is for more effective use of the partisan and group resources already available to political leaders. The overlapping programmatic coherence among the parties, interest groups, and PACs provides the basis for forming coalitions in support of various legislative approaches. The evolution of the public liaison function in the White House during the period of this study from an informal effort at communication to a full-fledged office with advocacy responsibilities indicates one institutional response to the new politics. In the Carter administration, for instance, Anne Wexler ran the Office of Public Liaison (OPL) as one arm of the effort to lobby Congress in favor of administration positions. The OPL also brought various interest groups into the policy development process. Because of their opportunity to influence the budget as it was being developed, the group representatives developed a mutual commitment to support the final product, notwithstanding the compromises and requirements for individual sacrifices.[30] One aspect of the legislative success story for Ronald Reagan in 1981 was the coordination by the White House of grass-roots activities engaged in by sympathetic groups. Elsewhere I have used the term "liaison as governing party" to describe White House public liaison strategies that emphasize advocacy of the president's policy program.[31] Without the need for legal reforms, continued pursuit of this approach could contribute to coalition building by the president.

Constitutional Reform

Until there is verification that the president and Congress as tandem institutions are able to come to grips with the major issues of coming years, many individuals will remain unsatisfied with the previous discussion, which has mixed a cautionary approach to reform with residual optimism about current institutional arrangements. There have been several changes in the institutional and political setting that seem conducive to establishing more broad-based coalitions in the government; nonetheless, the

30. Interviews with aides to President Carter.
31. Mark A. Peterson, "Interest Groups and the Reagan White House: For Whom the Doorbell Tolls," paper presented at the annual meeting of the American Political Science Association, Washington, D.C., August 1986, pp. 7–12.

prevailing forces of the institutionally, politically, and economically defined contexts of legislative policy making may overwhelm the marginal impact of any one of these changes. Regardless of the willingness of Congress and the president to conduct government by commission, regardless of how nominees are selected and who is ultimately victorious in the race for the presidency, and regardless of evolving cohesion in the party and group systems, the general structure of political institutions, the thrust of dynamic political forces, and the condition of the economy have all in recent years limited the opportunities for presidential leadership. The call for a major restructuring of the national government therefore continues in some quarters.

When we consider the prospect of extensively reforming the institutions of American government, of adjusting its constitutional foundation, two questions are involved. First, is there hard evidence that such reforms are needed? I for one remain skeptical. And second, if some advantage could be derived from implementing various reforms, which ones would they be? Once again, the thematic perspective and the empirical results of the present research offer some guidance in trying to resolve these questions, while still maintaining the balance between the effectiveness and the responsiveness of government.

Rather than tolerating the relatively loose cohesion generated by extraconstitutional institutions and political associations, those who suggest that we discard the current constitutional provisions for separate branches of government and replace them with the arrangements for a parliamentary system seek to establish well-defined governing coalitions of unquestioned prerogative. The idea is to grant greater endurance to the political result of each election by replacing a "system [that] proceeds through a succession of ad hoc legislative majorities" with one that provides for "a longer lasting majority that empowers a strong decision-making authority to act until removed."[32]

Whatever the merits of such reforms, they are fodder for debate rather than serious consideration in the theater of American politics. As President Carter reflected, "That's a radical change in our government structure that the people of our country would never accept. To say that Canada or Great Britain has a better system

32. Charles E. Lindblom, *Politics and Markets: The World's Political-Economic Systems* (New York: Basic Books, 1977), p. 321.

than ours would be a blow to American pride." Perhaps more to the point, parliamentary systems have not proved to be more adept at solving the dilemmas of the modern age. They can be as prone to parochialism, fragmentation, and logrolling as the American system, although each is promoted in different parts of the government.[33] Political discord and polarization often are even more rampant. Let us therefore consider institutional reforms that would require less dramatic constitutional change but nevertheless foster government cohesiveness.

The central objective of reform should be to build into the system incentives that facilitate congruence between the dominant electoral coalitions responsible for sending members of Congress to Capitol Hill and the president to the White House. It should nurture the sort of governing coalition needed to produce majorities in the legislative arena. Politics is to be accentuated, reinforcing the political glue that binds disparate segments of the government. The links are to be invigorated, not by casting Congress as a diffident rubber stamp for presidential initiatives, but by electorally aligning the two institutions in a manner that does not thwart the capacity of Congress to make representation meaningful in the deliberative process. Correlating the forces affecting congressional elections with those buffeting the president would not pose a threat to the kind of institutional autonomy of Congress that is required if the legislature is to continue serving as an originator of ideas, an appraiser of legislation, and a promoter of oversight of the executive branch.

On these grounds one proposed reform can be fairly easily rejected: the single six-year term for the president. The concept per se is not without merit. Some legislative initiatives do take a long time to be enacted, even to be formally considered by Congress. Legislative delays, combined with the necessity for electioneering, diminish the four years of the current term to a much briefer period of actual governing. The one-term limit is advocated to prevent incumbents from becoming preoccupied with reelection and to allow them to introduce initiatives and make other policy choices, Jimmy Carter suggested, without the taint of partisan political motivations. One can appreciate the frustration of a chief executive experiencing the time pressures of a four-year

33. R. Kent Weaver, "Are Parliamentary Systems Better?" *Brookings Review* 3 (Summer 1985): 19–22.

term and suffering the charges of partisan manipulation; still, neither argument is compelling. While approximately 8% of the proposals in this study tied to major legislative packages required more than two years to receive final congressional action, half were given active consideration within eight months. The other initiatives in the sample reflected similar patterns. Some of the proposals were defeated, and a six-year term would afford each administration an extended opportunity to try to reverse its losses, but it is not clear that the impact would be dramatic. And it would come at the cost of distancing the presidency from elections and electoral mandates, the principal means for ensuring political accountability.

Second, and far more important, the idea of restricting presidents to one term assumes that the presidency can be treated as a nonpolitical institution, that a chief executive can purvey political leadership without practicing politics. Nothing in this or any other research, however, supports the notion that the president's policy positions would be advanced, or productive presidential-congressional relations would be promoted, by diminishing politics in the Oval Office. To the contrary, Thomas Cronin suggests that "the proposed divorce between the presidency and politics presupposes a significantly different kind of political system from that of the United States, which is glued together largely by ambiguity, compromise, and the extensive sharing of powers. In light of the requisites of democracy, the presidency must be a highly political office, and the president an expert practitioner of the art of politics."[34] As FDR aide Thomas Corcoran is purported to have said, "It is impossible to take politics out of politics."

If anything, it would be reasonable to argue that the existing two-term limit dictated by the Twenty-second Amendment to the Constitution should be repealed. Past elections and the prospect of future campaigns help to place the president and the Congress on common ground. Prohibiting an incumbent from seeking reelection undermines the president's political stature by denying the opportunity to help orient the subsequent governing coalition, and hence to influence the future of members of Congress. The political significance of Congress is attenuated by requiring it to manage political forces of electoral import that the president

34. Thomas E. Cronin, *The State of the Presidency*, 2nd ed. (Boston: Little, Brown, 1980), p. 356.

can ignore. A president is allowed to maintain the popular image of commanding the high ground while members of Congress must continue to respond to the "baser" incentives of remaining in office. Such divergent motivations are unlikely to produce accord.

Rather than changing the duration of only the president's term in office, we can justifiably argue that representatives, senators, and the president should be placed on coterminous electoral cycles, probably four years in length. As this study confirms, the current system with two-year House terms, six-year Senate terms, and four-year presidential terms sets into motion an array of political forces that does anything but bring the executive and legislative branches together. Having to seek reelection every two years, members of the House of Representatives have little time to devote to policy development and issues of governance without constant worry about the electoral implications. Campaigning itself absorbs large amounts of a member's time and energy that could otherwise be focused on legislative issues. More important, the scheduling of midterm elections, especially for House seats, means that during a single term a president actually has to work with two different Congresses. Since in the modern era the party of the president almost inevitably loses seats in the House, the second Congress tends to be far more belligerent. The post-midterm phenomenon has serious implications for presidential-congressional interactions. Of the presidential initiatives in the sample, 56% of those that were settled in the first year of post-midterm Congress were either ignored or defeated.

The current electoral cycle, therefore, exacerbates the potential for institutional conflict and creates an atmosphere conducive to stalemate in the policy-making process. It is the presence of midterm elections that shortens the period available in the president's four-year term for program development and enactment, forcing administrations to move their agendas early and fast, perhaps without giving their initiatives the optimal level of substantive review. The existing electoral routine strengthens no part of the policy-making system. It may assist some factions in the Congress seeking to block legislation, but it does not allow participants in either branch to strengthen their role in the production and enactment of policy initiatives.

Elections should both convey popular sentiments and provide programmatically relevant cues to the entire government about the political direction of the polity, lending some coherence to the development and consideration of legislation. While I have argued that presidents should not be anointed the sole protectors of the national interest, the fact of their installation by a national electorate suggests that presidential electoral mandates should have some significance in organizing the country's agenda.

Electing the president and members of Congress simultaneously for terms of equal length would have several salient effects. First, it would permit participants in both the executive and the legislative establishments to spend more time practicing the politics of governance instead of electioneering. As the issues grow more complex and the legislation being reviewed becomes broader in scope, it is vital to create longer periods during which legislative factions can engage one another and maneuver without direct reference to campaigning. Longer terms may also be compatible with proposals to make reauthorization and budgetary decisions less frequent, perhaps on a biennial basis.[35] Stronger incentives for compromise and less grandstanding may also be possible under these conditions. Second, reforming the electoral process in this way would eliminate the potential for the post-midterm election stalemate. While the frequent election of members of the House arguably reinforces their proximity to the electorate, in this age of mass communication and easy transportation such frequent elections are both unnecessary and detrimental to establishing coherence in the policy-making process. Third, coterminous terms would increase the overlap between the majority electoral coalition and the dominant governing coalition by subjecting all officeholders to the same set of national forces.

It is equally important to point out what changes in the electoral cycle would not do. Without a dramatic shift in voter attitudes, the subjugation of regional and local differences, or the introduction of a very different, nonfederal system of government, placing the president and Congress on the same electoral cycle would not prevent the occurrence of divided government. As long as ballots can be split (and from the electorate's point of view there remain reasons to do so), the country will experience times of divided party control.[36] I also do not view these reforms as paving the way to

35. Alice M. Rivlin, "The Need for a Better Budget Process," *Brookings Review* 4 (Summer 1986): 3–10.

36. See, for example, Morris P. Fiorina, "The Reagan Years: Turning to the Right or Groping for the Middle," in *The Resurgence of Conservatism in Anglo-American Democracies*, ed. Barry Cooper, Allan Kornberg, and William Mishler (Durham, N.C.: Duke University Press, 1988).

complete presidential dominance of legislative responsibilities. Even now all members of the House must share the ballot with the president in every other election. The research on coattail effects has not concluded that most members are electorally bound to the leader of the ticket. In addition, if presidents are not constrained by the Twenty-second Amendment or the effects of midterm elections, they may be motivated to work more closely with members of Congress in an effort to build more durable coalitions, especially with all members of the coalition facing reelection at the same time. Members of Congress would retain enough independence to make this an interactive game.

No matter what changes in the political system are being considered, one has to be careful about advocating reform, given what the unintended consequences may be. The need for caution is nowhere better demonstrated than by the effects on politics and policy making resulting from the transformations of the congressional committee system during the 1970s, the new procedures introduced by the Budget and Impoundment Control Act of 1974, and the changes in the Democratic party's rules for selecting its presidential nominee. The revolt against the committee chairmen in the House was launched to make the committee system more responsive to the desires of Congress as a whole and to allow the institution to respond to the exigencies of the modern era. Few anticipated the stalemate effect of introducing even more committee baronies in the subcommittees, different only because they were new and changed the distribution of beneficiaries. The reconciliation provision of the Budget Act was designed to help shield Congress from executive intrusions by bringing order to its budget making. Ronald Reagan, however, in 1981 transformed it into an instrument of presidential leverage. Whatever was structurally intended by the democratizing reforms in the nominating process of the Democratic party, few expected the mushrooming of primaries and the repeated inability of the party to select a nationally viable candidate.

Final Reflections

A major theme of this book is that none of the reforms proposed for the American political system are as urgent as they might seem. By adjusting both the way in which we think about the president and the Congress—viewing them as tandem institutions, with all that the term embodies—and the way in which we gather empirical information about them—merging, in a sense, the case-study and quantitative approaches—it becomes evident that conflict and confrontation, presidential failure and legislative stalemate, are but one part of the picture, representing only a subset of the possible avenues of institutional interaction. Presidents serving since 1953 have been more successful legislatively than previously believed, although the trials of the last few presidencies cannot be ignored. Examining the diverse ways in which legislative issues are decided has revealed more harmony in the system than is apparent from previous research on the same period. The process of policy making by the American national government is so complex that assumptions, analyses, and reforms confined to only one aspect of the presidential-congressional legislative relationship are insufficient. The salutary impact of electing to the presidency individuals of undisputed talent will be limited by the considerable role of the institutional, political, and economic contexts in shaping the relations of those executives with the Hill. The consequence of modifying one aspect of the institutional setting will be minimized by the significance of other factors defining the structure and dynamics of the political environment. At the same time, reconstituting the policy-making process without recruiting politically savvy presidents will translate into lost opportunities for policy leadership.

Because of the complexity inherent in policy making at the national level, and because of the need to balance effective leadership against responsive government, we must take great care in assigning appropriate roles to the president and Congress. This caution is all the more valid as institutional and economic conditions, and the emerging policy agenda, conspire to make politics both more difficult and more necessary. Capitol Hill has always been the focal point for representation in the political system, reflecting among its members and procedures multiple points of access to innumerable points of view. Congress provides the setting into which representatives of business can inject their concerns about the harebrained schemes of a liberal administration. It supplies the platform on which defenders of the poor can express their shock at the inhumanity embodied in a conservative administration's budget. For that access to be meaningful, Congress must play a significant part in the development and evaluation of public policy. It must contribute to the nation's agenda issues otherwise ignored. It must have the capacity to judge and make decisions about legislative schemes as they affect all segments of society. Both Congress and the president must be disciplined enough to deliberate the issues of the day with a more cogent recognition of trade-offs and incongruities.

A president cannot, and should not, do everything. Nor should the members of the administration. They cannot generate every idea, study every proposal, run every agency, evaluate every program. Far too great a burden has been thrust upon the presidency in both popular and scholarly expectations. Unless there is a radical transformation in American government, both presidents and the public must learn to recognize Congress as the executive's legislative partner.

Even if that recognition takes place, presidents, by virtue of their national constituency, their prominence in the media, and their centrality in the popular imagination, will continue to rest atop the mountain of apparent confusion that often characterizes American politics. They should exploit the vantage point of their lofty position to bring coherence to policy making by functioning as agenda *focusers.* Electoral mandates, no matter how slim, afford them the occasion to enunciate the major issues that will occupy the agenda of the government's various institutions. Their actions will not resonate as complete presidential victories. Ideas for the nation's agenda will have originated in Congress and elsewhere in the nation. The variegated institutional, political, economic, and policy constraints reviewed here will prevent presidents from continuously building winning coalitions in Congress. But rather than attempting to be the government and the repository of solutions for all problems, presidents should identify the problems, challenge others to respond, and work with other participants in the process to craft possible policy solutions.

Finally, presidents should use their constrained but unique leadership position to ennoble modern politics, to light the lantern of political reflection and inspiration, always knowing that their promises and actions must be lodged firmly within the boundaries of the possible. The style of recent presidential campaigns has not elevated our expectations on this score. The Hollywood-derived "read my lips, no new taxes" 1988 campaign theme of President George Bush ran exactly counter to the requirement of enlightened political debate. So did the "competency, not ideology" theme of his Democratic challenger, Michael Dukakis. Presidential leadership is a matter of both competence and ideology. It requires competence in managing the resources of the presidency in a tandem-institutions world, but it also demands motivation by an ideological perspective, debated and judged in the electoral process, that gives direction to the actions of government.

Appendixes
Index

Appendix A. The Sample of Informants

Some of the analysis presented in this book, especially in Chapter 2, is based on interviews with individuals who served in the Executive Office of the President or on Capitol Hill sometime during the period 1953 to 1986. In addition, several prominent Washington journalists who cover the White House and Congress were interviewed to secure a different perspective. No attempt was made to select a representative sample of respondents from either the EOP or Capitol Hill. Rather, the goal was to develop a sample composed of informed observers who could comment knowledgeably about presidential-congressional relations as witnessed from their particular (often multiple) vantage points.[1]

In the case of administration figures, I sought to talk with individuals representing a variety of offices in the EOP, including domestic policy, congressional liaison, public liaison, the president's personal staff, the Council of Economic Advisers, and the Office of Management and Budget. Most likely to be contacted were those who (a) held senior positions in charge of major offices, (b) had experience in a variety of White House posts or in more than one administration, or (c) enjoyed a reputation for influence beyond the implications of their formal titles. The informants from Capitol Hill were selected on the basis of recommendations made by students of Congress, or because of their positions with respect to committee staffs or the majority and minority leaderships of each house.

Table A.1 shows the percentage of individuals contacted who agreed to be interviewed and summarizes the informants by the

1. For a general discussion of informants as used here, see Lawrence B. Mohr, "The Concept of Organizational Goal," *American Political Science Review* 67 (June 1973): 478.

Appendix Table A.1   The most senior positions held by the two major
types of informants through 1986

Executive Office of the President		Capitol Hill	
Most senior position[a]	Number of individuals	Most senior position[a]	Number of individuals
President of the United States	2	Member of Congress	5
Counselor, counsel, assistant to the president	30	Aide to member of Congress	11
Deputy counselor, deputy counsel, deputy assistant to the president	15	Majority/minority committee staff director or counsel	13
Special counsel, special assistant to the president	3	Other committee staff	4
OMB/CEA[b]— political appointee	12	[Leadership aide][c]	[10]
OMB—senior career official	5		
Interviews as percentage of those contacted:	74		78
Total number of informants:[d]	67		33

a. Each informant is categorized by the contemporary equivalent of his or her position. For example, a special assistant to the president serving in the Johnson administration would be equivalent to an assistant to the president in the current White House. Many of the informants held several posts at different ranks; listed here are their most senior positions. More than a third of the executive officials also served in Congress in a variety of capacities.

b. OMB = Office of Management and Budget; CEA = Council of Economic Advisers.

c. The ten aides who worked for a member of the leadership of either party are also included in the other categories.

d. The total number of informants, with the inclusion of 9 journalists, is 109. Overall, interviews were granted by 76% of the individuals contacted.

Appendix Table A.2   Characteristics of the interviews

Type of informant	Mean interview length (minutes)	Range of interview length (minutes)	Mean number of interruptions
In Executive Office of the President[a]	51[b]	18–122	1.0[b]
From Capitol Hill	48	25–85	1.2
Journalist	50	30–70	1.0
All informants	50	18–122	1.0

a. Not included are the interviews with Jimmy Carter and Gerald Ford, which averaged 30 minutes in length. Also not included is the response from one informant in EOP who did not have time to provide an interview, but who instead responded in writing to a specially tailored questionnaire.

b. Thirteen of the interviews with informants from EOP were conducted by telephone rather than in person. They tended to be shorter (an average of 43 minutes compared to 53 minutes), but they were also less likely to be interrupted (an average of 0.4 compared to 1.1 interruptions). No deficiencies were apparent in the telephone interviews compared to the face-to-face interviews, a pattern consistent with the findings reported in Paul C. Light, "Interviewing the President's Staff: A Comparison of Telephone and Face-to-Face Techniques," *Presidential Studies Quarterly* 12 (Summer 1982): 428–433.

most senior position held in their respective institutions through 1986. It should be noted that 37% of the informants selected from the Executive Office of the President had also served in some capacity on Capitol Hill, and 33% of the Capitol Hill informants at some time had had agency or departmental appointments. Table A.2 recapitulates the length of the interviews and the frequency of the interruptions.

Appendix B. Previous Quantitative Research

The behavioral revolution that swept the discipline of political science in the 1960s and 1970s not only created new expertise in such areas as election studies, but also nurtured a core of scholars equipped with both the quantitative instruments of behavioral analysis and a substantive interest in the presidency, including its relationship with Congress. Until the emergence of this methodological approach, examination of the presidency and its institutional relationships had been generally accomplished through case studies and concentration on single administrations.[1] The consequence was an "overdramatization" of the presidential role and a failure to elicit broad, testable generalizations. Indeed, it was presumed that generalizations involving as personal an office as the presidency were not possible.[2] The new wave of scholars contended that meaningful generalizations about the presidency *could* be generated, but only by employing "the theory and methods of behavioral political science."[3] These two methodologies together dominate the contemporary discipline of presidential-congressional studies. Each, however, is burdened with its own set of constraints, limitations, and distor-

1. Thomas E. Cronin, *The State of the Presidency*, 2nd ed. (Boston: Little, Brown, 1980), p. 93.
2. Ibid.; James MacGregor Burns, *Presidential Government: The Crucible of Leadership* (Boston: Houghton Mifflin, 1973), p. 151; and Paul C. Light, *The President's Agenda: Domestic Choice from Kennedy to Carter* (Baltimore: Johns Hopkins University Press, 1982), p. 7.
3. George C. Edwards III, *Presidential Influence in Congress* (San Francisco: W. H. Freeman, 1980), p. 206. For a sharply stated argument in support of quantitative work on the presidency, see Dean Keith Simonton, *Why Presidents Succeed: A Political Psychology of Leadership* (New Haven: Yale University Press, 1987), esp. pp. 4–6.

tions. The liabilities of the case study approach have been fully explored elsewhere. I concentrate here on the problems introduced by the now-abundant quantitative analyses of the presidency.

To exploit quantitative methods requires the acquisition of rather large amounts of data reflecting the behavioral patterns of, in this case, the presidential-congressional relationship. Given the unique nature of the White House establishment, its isolation and its secrecy, scholars have great difficulty obtaining such data. Unlike Congress, in the executive there are not multitudinous public roll-call votes to analyze. Still, presidents engage in behavior that translates into observable facts: appointments are made, decisions are reached, executive orders are issued, positions are taken, and legislative proposals are submitted. In the search for numerical data, quantitative scholars came across two measures reflecting the last two categories of activity, both published by Congressional Quarterly: the Presidential Support Scores and the Presidential Boxscores. Each stretched over a lengthy period of time, bridged several administrations, encompassed all policy domains—and *each was available.*

As a result, a great deal of quantitative analysis has been performed treating the Support Scores or Boxscores as dependent variables.[4] But these measures, for many of the issues to which they are applied, do not constitute viable sources of data. Their deficiencies are rather glaring, a fact acknowledged by numerous scholars, including those who have used them.[5] Consider the Sup-

4. See, as examples, George C. Edwards III, *Presidential Influence in Congress,* and *At the Margins: Presidential Leadership of Congress* (New Haven: Yale University Press, 1989); Richard Fleisher and Jon Bond, "Assessing Presidential Support in the House: Lessons from Reagan and Carter," *Journal of Politics* 45 (August 1983): 745–758; Lance T. LeLoup and Steven A. Shull, "Dimensions of Presidential Policy Making," in *The Presidency: Studies in Public Policy,* ed. Steven A. Shull and Lance T. LeLoup (Brunswick, Ohio: King's Court Communications, 1979); and Steven A. Shull, *Domestic Policy Formation: Presidential-Congressional Partnership?* (Westport, Conn.: Greenwood Press, 1983).

5. For example, Cronin, *The State of the Presidency,* p. 170; Edwards, *Presidential Influence in Congress,* pp. 14–15; Gary King and Lyn Ragsdale, *The Elusive Executive: Discovering Statistical Patterns in the Presidency* (Washington, D.C.: CQ Press, 1988), pp. 48–49; Paul C. Light, "Passing Nonincremental Policy: Presidential Influence in Congress, Kennedy to Carter," *Congress and the Presidency* 9 (Winter 1981–82):

port Scores. It is exceedingly difficult to know precisely what they measure. They indicate the annual percentage of congressional roll-call votes on which a member of Congress, groups of members, or the Congress collectively supported the announced position of the chief executive. What are the problems? We do not know the nature of the president's position—whether it is intensely or superficially held, whether the legislation linked to it is part of the executive's legislative program, or whether it is chosen strategically to enhance the perception of support.[6] The Support Scores do not include legislation that fails to reach the floor (defeats in committee, for instance), voice votes, or (from earlier years) unrecorded teller votes. We also do not know anything about the importance of the issues lying behind the votes. Significant pieces of legislation might automatically be given more weight because they are more likely to involve several roll-call votes—on amendments, on rules in the House—but repetitious votes may represent more the filibuster-like behavior of an obstreperous member with a personal qualm than the dimension of national policy significance. At best, the Support Scores provide data at the level of the individual member that can be employed to investigate the extent to which the behavior of members of Congress, *specific to recorded votes,* is influenced by presidential lobbying efforts and other factors.[7] At the macro level, the data reveal

65; David M. Olson, "Success and Content in Presidential Roll Calls: The First Three Years of the Reagan Administration," *Presidential Studies Quarterly* 15 (Summer 1985): 602–610; Douglas Rivers and Nancy Rose, "Passing the President's Program: Public Opinion and Presidential Influence in Congress," *American Journal of Political Science* 29 (May 1985): 190; Shull, *Domestic Policy Formation,* pp. 195–197; Lee Sigelman, "Reassessing the 'Two Presidencies' Thesis," *Journal of Politics* 41 (November 1979): 1198; and Stephen J. Wayne, *The Legislative Presidency* (New York: Harper and Row, 1978): 168–171.

6. Shull, *Domestic Policy Formation,* p. 115.

7. George C. Edwards III, "Quantitative Analysis," in *Studying the Presidency,* ed. George C. Edwards III and Stephen J. Wayne (Knoxville: University of Tennessee Press, 1983), pp. 112–115. A more satisfying approach to studying presidential influence on congressional voting has been taken by Cary Covington and Terry Sullivan. The advantage of Office of Congressional Relations listings of important legislation over Support Scores is discussed in Cary R. Covington, "Congressional Support for the President: The View from the Kennedy/Johnson White House," *Journal of Politics* 48 (August 1986): 717–728. Sullivan studies

little about the president's domestic legislative *program*.[8] President Carter noted that his overall Congressional Quarterly Presidential Support Score of over 75% approximated that of Johnson, "the masterful congressional manipulator," which registered at 82%.[9] Whatever the reasons for this similarity of percentages, it would be difficult to maintain that the legislative performance of the two administrations can be so favorably compared.

The Presidential Boxscores share many of the difficulties evident with the Support Scores, and in fact the problems are even more severe. Between 1953 and 1975, with the procedure revised in 1954, Congressional Quarterly (CQ) surveyed the *Weekly Compilation of Presidential Documents* or its equivalents to locate specific legislative proposals suggested explicitly by the president (not other administration officials) in various addresses, messages, statements, and speeches for each calendar year. By examining the legislative record, CQ determined whether the president's proposal had been enacted during the same calendar year, and then reported an aggregate score indicating the percentage of proposals successfully acted on by Congress. For example, 69% of the specific proposals offered by President Johnson in 1965 passed into law in reasonably intact form by the end of that year.[10]

Like the Support Scores, however, the Boxscores do not include any weighting that reflects the importance or presidential priority of each proposal.[11] Requesting the expansion of a national park in

---

the effects of direct administration lobbying by also using data recorded by the Office of Congressional Relations. "Headcounts, Expectations, and Presidential Coalitions in Congress," *American Journal of Political Science* 32 (August 1988): 567–589. In the data employed by Covington and Sullivan there is little ambiguity about the importance of specific legislation to the administration and the level of presidential attention. Unfortunately, such data are available for few administrations.

8. Light, *The President's Agenda*, p. 65.

9. Jimmy Carter, *Keeping Faith: Memoirs of a President* (New York: Bantam Books, 1982), p. 88.

10. *Congressional Quarterly Almanac, 1965* (Washington, D.C.: Congressional Quarterly, 1966), p. 97.

11. Shull argues that the weightings are reflected in the tendency for more significant programs to include several component parts, and therefore multiple proposals. *Domestic Policy Formation*, p. 196. That characterization is at best a *tendency*, and one that remains hidden in the aggregate data. Furthermore, it is somewhat sensitive to the form in which particular presidents choose to present their proposals and legislation.

Wyoming or establishing a million-dollar federal agency is equivalent to proposing passage of the Voting Rights Act of 1965. More important, because the Boxscores are annual aggregate figures, all of the explanatory variables in a data set must also be annual values. George Edwards notes that these annual aggregates make it impossible to draw causal inferences about the behavior of individual members of Congress.[12] They also suffer from attempting to explain specific temporal events with data that generally lose that level of precision by averaging values for an entire year. There is the potential that annual averages in both the dependent and independent variables hide significant fluctuations through the course of the year, and as a result fail to capture accurately the circumstances associated with any actual period during which Congress acted on presidential initiatives. The threat to the validity of analyses using the aggregate scores was a prime factor in CQ's decision to drop the Boxscores after 1975.[13]

Finally, from the perspective of presidential success in Congress, the basic structure of the Boxscores is flawed. Legislative success or failure should not be considered within the confines of a single calendar year. Paul Light points out: "The boxscore must be sensitive to the amount of time needed to pass presidential priorities. If a bill is introduced in the first year of the President's term, and is passed in the fourth year, it should still be counted as a success for a first year proposal."[14] For example, each year from 1953 to 1959 President Eisenhower proposed granting statehood for Hawaii. Congress finally responded favorably in 1959. The CQ Boxscore would calibrate that proposal as six years of "failure" and one year of "success." What fundamentally mattered to Eisenhower was the granting of statehood during his administration, so undoubtedly he would have viewed the proposal as a successful legislative effort.

The calendar year constraint is of considerable substantive significance. I describe in Appendix C how I selected for analysis a random sample of 299 specific legislative proposals, all in the domestic realm, suggested by Presidents Eisenhower to Reagan from 1953 to 1984. When there was final congressional action of

12. Edwards, "Quantitative Analysis," p. 112.
13. From a conversation with Alan Ehrenhalt, political editor at Congressional Quarterly.
14. Light, "Passing Nonincremental Policy," p. 66.

some kind on these proposals, it took an average of more than nine months, suggesting that consideration of a large number of the presidential initiatives overlaps into at least a second year, a second congressional session, and perhaps an entirely new Congress.

Consider what happens to measures of "success" when the time constraints are eliminated. The CQ Boxscore for all domestic proposals identified by CQ from 1953 to 1975 yielded an overall presidential success rate of 43%.[15] Application of the rules followed by Congressional Quarterly to the 224 proposals in my sample of 299 that were introduced from 1953 to 1975 results in a similar overall success rate, 46%. If one traces the legislative history of each proposal, however, and examines the congressional responses secured throughout the period of each president's administration, then fully 58% of the proposals in the sample introduced from 1953 to 1975 received favorable congressional consideration. This increases the aggregate "success rate" of presidents by more than a quarter. If policy achieved with nonlegislative methods is included—for example, unilateral administrative action by the executive—the percentage of policy "successes" rises to 60% for this part of the sample. The effects for individual presidents of breaking the calendar year constraint are equally dramatic: the percentage for Richard Nixon jumps from 28% to 46%, John Kennedy goes from 38% to 49%, and Lyndon Johnson climbs from 60% to 69% (73% if instances of unilateral administrative action are added).

Yet it is the CQ Boxscores that are reported in textbooks on the presidency and that shape the perception that modern chief executives have witnessed congressional passage of less than half their initiatives.[16] Instead, it should be clearly understood that well over half of presidential initiatives received some kind of favorable action—a fact that says something about both presidential performance and the nature of the relationship between the executive and legislative branches.

The validity of using the Support Scores and Boxscores to examine executive-legislative interactions, at least in terms of the

15. LeLoup and Shull, "Dimensions of Presidential Policy Making," pp. 9, 16.
16. Richard M. Pious, The American Presidency (New York: Basic Books, 1979), p. 179; and Shull, Domestic Policy Formation, p. 111.

president's legislative program, is highly suspect. Nevertheless, such analyses continue to be performed. The matter is even more troubling when one realizes that the Boxscores have not been calculated for one period of great importance: the Carter and Reagan administrations. In other words, those wishing to apply quantitative techniques to study the interactions between the president and Congress on the president's legislative program have had to ignore the two most recently completed administrations, and therefore those most relevant to both contemporary and future relations between the two institutions. These presidencies were not mere extensions of those that preceded them. The Carter administration witnessed a majority party president unable to enjoy the full benefits of a Congress controlled by his own partisans. His presidency also demonstrated the difficulties of attempting to move a complex and controversial agenda. President Reagan, on the other hand, created the impression of strong presidential leadership and the reality of substantial change in the programmatic direction of the federal government. No model of the modern presidency can be complete without giving consideration to the period since 1975. One means for extending the number of administrations has been to shift from using the Boxscores to analyzing the Support Scores; but again, the latter do not measure activity on the president's legislative program.

Skilled analysts persist in using these measures because they are the "only systematic data *that are available.*"[17] They have carried us some distance in understanding an institutional relationship that had previously been appreciated only in light of detailed case studies, but the deficiencies are now too apparent to continue past practices. If adequate information is not already available, then the responsibility of new scholarship is to develop research designs to produce superior data. This book is devoted in part to arguing the case for a refined methodological approach and demonstrating the utility of that approach for analyzing significant issues of presidential-congressional governance.

17. The quotation is from Edwards, *Presidential Influence in Congress,* p. 51, emphasis added; see also Shull, *Domestic Policy Formation,* p. 59.

Appendix C. The Methodological Approach

Despite their ultimate failings (discussed in Appendix B), the CQ Presidential Boxscores have one tremendous virtue. In order to derive the annual success scores, the staff of Congressional Quarterly identified every specific proposal made by the president in a calendar year that involved legislation in the foreign and domestic policy arenas. Accompanying each score is the itemized list of these proposals. For 1953 to 1975, therefore, much had already been done in the way of developing a population of presidential initiatives from which a sample could be chosen. To accomplish the objectives of this research, however, I had to make several adjustments, amendments, and additions to the list furnished by CQ.

The first task involved deleting those proposals that lay beyond the confines of domestic policy. The boundary between domestic and foreign issues is certainly not unambiguous. I made the choice to exclude those policy concerns that tended to originate outside this country. All foreign, defense, and military matters were excluded except for veterans affairs, which resemble the traditional social welfare issues. I also omitted proposals dealing with refugees and immigration, as well as trade, tariffs, and foreign aid. The confluence of national economic interests in an increasingly integrated world economic system highlights the growing entanglement of domestic and international affairs. One need only recall the politics associated with the Carter administration's grain embargo against the Soviet Union to acknowledge the interdependence of domestic pressures and choices in foreign policy. While each of the excluded policies could not have been decided without a reference to the domestic scene, the basic problems involved in each originated in the military, economic, cultural, or political positions of other countries. That distinguishes them from rivers and harbors projects, transportation systems, education, nutritional aid for the poor, and the like.[1]

When compiling the inventory of presidential initiatives, Congressional Quarterly treated each calendar year as an independent period without reference to the past. Each proposal that CQ identified was included, whether or not essentially the same proposal had been offered in previous years by the same president. In addition, the Boxscore for any one year does not reflect congressional action in the year on initiatives submitted in a prior period that did not receive explicit presidential reference in the year of the Boxscore. In the present study each initiative is treated as a single proposal, no matter how many times it was mentioned by the same president. My purpose is to evaluate the legislative life of each proposal, from the time of its public announcement or introduction to the time when it gained final resolution during an administration. The overall population of proposals assembled by CQ, therefore, was amended by omitting the repetitions of initiatives made within the same administration.

The dropping of duplications was usually quite straightforward. Many times presidents restate in a new message the proposal originally propounded in an earlier announcement. Sometimes they indicate specifically their wish that Congress take up consideration of proposals from a previous year. There were a few occasions, however, when subsequent mentions of an initiative reflected substantive changes. If the basic structure of the proposal remained the same, I treated the later versions as repetitions that provided evidence of presidential bidding in the process of trying to reach a compromise. The marginal changes indicated the willingness of the chief executive to move in the direction of a more accommodating position. If the more recent mention of an initiative involved a clearly different approach, however, it was counted as a new proposal, with the previous initiatives generally

1. An additional policy area had to be excluded from the study: proposals pertaining to the administration of the District of Columbia prior to home rule. Until the Nixon administration the president and Congress bore responsibility for the basic governance of the nation's capital, and some of the initiatives in each president's program involved issues of local legislation and administration. Since my focus was on national policy, the proposals directed at the District were not included unless they were associated with concerns of national import, such as civil rights.

ending in inaction or opposition dominance. The exceptions often involved issues dealing with the budget and appropriations. If the president proposed a specific level of appropriations for a program in a certain fiscal year, then the life of that proposal was limited to the relevant year and equivalent efforts in future years were considered new proposals.

The final adjustments I made in the CQ pool of initiatives entailed an effort to introduce greater consistency in the definition of specific proposals throughout the almost thirty-year period.[2] First, CQ reported that a somewhat different process was used for identifying the initiatives in 1954 and later years than had been applied to 1953. I therefore compiled a new list of initiatives for 1953, employing the upgraded guidelines followed by CQ after 1953. Second, sometimes similar situations received disparate treatments by CQ. In one year, for example, a presidential message requesting the development of several national parks might be classified as a single proposal, while in another year an analogous message might be broken into separate proposals for each park. When those circumstances arose, I revised the listing of initiatives to conform to the latter procedure. Similar adjustments were made whenever I discovered inconsistencies attributable to the procedures followed by Congressional Quarterly.

After 1975, however, neither the Presidential Boxscores nor a detailed listing of proposals was supplied by CQ. To bring the population of presidentially initiated legislation up through the first term of the Reagan administration, therefore, required constructing from scratch the complete set of proposals for 1976 to 1984. To accomplish that task, I reviewed the more than twenty thousand pages of the *Public Papers of the President* or the *Weekly Compilation of Presidential Documents* published for the Ford, Carter, and Reagan administrations during that period.[3] Guided by the procedures described in the CQ *Almanac* and those

2. Some inconsistencies in the CQ lists derive from variations in the way presidents present their programs, and these differences may reflect presidential legislative strategies. Such inconsistencies, which cannot be corrected, pose some threat to any analysis of the president's overall program. See Gary King and Lyn Ragsdale, *The Elusive Executive: Discovering Statistical Patterns in the Presidency* (Washington, D.C.: CQ Press, 1988), pp. 48–49.

3. Proposals made by President Reagan in years after 1984 were not included because of the need to ensure that enough time had elapsed to

that I developed to amend the CQ lists, I identified the specific domestic legislative proposals suggested by each president during that period.[4]

President Reagan in 1981 introduced some special problems. By everyone's reckoning, his legislative program was largely embodied in the February 1981 announcement concerning reductions in fiscal 1981 outlays and in the revisions he proposed in March 1981 for the fiscal 1982 budget. Both sets of proposals were mentioned often in his various speeches and addresses, although the specific changes were not. Because the cuts were not generally given explicit mention in Reagan's messages, a strict adherence to CQ's procedures would result in their not being included in the President's legislative program. But given the preeminence of the budget reductions in the President's economic program, the fact that he did refer to them as a body of specific requests ("the 200 additional proposals") suggested that conceptual consistency required their inclusion in the population of proposals.

These various adjustments, amendments, and selection procedures yielded a population of 5,069 new domestic legislative proposals initiated from 1953 to 1984. From this population a sample of 299 proposals was selected, chosen randomly and stratified by year. This selection procedure yielded a sample that reflected the rhythm of presidential legislative initiation exhibited during the period under study. Appendix Table C.1 reports by administration the number of new domestic initiatives and the number included in the sample.

Once the sample of presidential initiatives was selected, an extensive legislative history was generated for each proposal. Most of the information was acquired from issues of the annual Congressional Quarterly *Almanac* and the *Weekly Report*, but these were often supplemented with the *National Journal*, the *Public Papers of the President* (also used to assess presidential priorities), the *United States Statutes at Large*, the *Commerce Clearing House (CCH) Index*, committee reports, and secondary literature. Given the number of proposals involved, these legisla-

---

permit congressional action on the president's initiatives before the analysis was begun.

4. A typical statement of the CQ selection rules is presented in *Congressional Quarterly Almanac, 1960* (Washington, D.C.: Congressional Quarterly, 1961), p. 93.

Appendix Table C.1   Presidential domestic legislative proposals and the sample selected for study, by president, from 1953 to 1984

President	Total new proposals	Annual mean	Number in sample
Eisenhower	816	102	48
Kennedy	752	251	45
Johnson	1,369	274	81
Nixon	669	120	39
Ford	277	115	16
Carter	812	203	48
Reagan, through 1984	374	94	22
Total	5,069	158	299

tive histories obviously could not be detailed, blow-by-blow case studies, but enough information was accumulated to make judgments about the timing of action, the decision-making processes in Congress, and the nature of the proposals themselves.

With the background information collected, the task became one of categorizing the proposals according to the congressional responses they engendered. Sometimes the coding was obvious; other times difficult judgments were required. First, I determined whether any legislation passed during the administration fulfilled at least part of the president's proposal. If not, then the proposal became a candidate for inaction or opposition dominance. When legislation had been enacted that very closely or perfectly resembled the president's request, the proposal became a candidate for consensus or presidential dominance. Finally, if some meaningful part, but nowhere near all, of the president's request was enacted, the proposal was coded as a case of compromise.

To distinguish between inaction and opposition dominance, I looked at additional questions. First, I ascertained whether any votes had been taken that pertained to the proposal. If there had been a vote, in committee or on the floor of either house, and the result was defeat of the legislation, or if the initiative was blocked by the actuality or threat of a filibuster or other parliamentary considerations, the proposal became a candidate for opposition dominance. If there was no evidence that the proposal received anything more than consideration at a committee or subcommittee hearing, then it became a candidate for inaction. Many proposals were literally ignored. If the administration appeared to use some form of administrative or legal action to accomplish some part of the request, that information was noted.

A similar procedure was followed to distinguish between consensus and presidential dominance. If the votes for passage did not suggest any organized opposition (that is, majorities of both parties favored the legislation, as well as northern and southern Democrats, and no other relatively defined factions were apparent from the record), then the proposal was coded as a case of consensus. On the other hand, if the votes indicated that there was organized opposition, or if other parts of the legislative record indicated that passage of the legislation required the defeat of organized opponents, the proposal was coded as a case of presidential dominance.

When there were ambiguities, I tried to make decisions that conformed as closely as possible to the underlying concepts of the coding scheme. For example, there were often votes on entire bills, but not on specific proposals. Sometimes the votes on whole bills had to be used; but whenever possible the coding was based on action that pertained directly to the specific proposals.

The individual characteristics of the proposals themselves constituted a second body of information, permitting distinctions to be drawn among the various kinds of initiatives.

Finally, in order to examine the influence on congressional responses of the context in which proposals were being considered, data for 1953 through June 1986 were collected relative to the several properties that together make up the institutional, political, and economic settings in existence at the time decisions were made about each proposal. The relevant variables designed to represent these contextual attributes are described in Appendix D.

Let me emphasize again one methodological note. Unlike the situations in previous studies in which aggregate data have been used, all of the attributes examined in this research are characterized by values as relevant as possible to the actual times when proposals were being considered. The level of public approval of the president's job performance, for example, is not measured as an annual average, but rather at the level that was actually reported prior to action on the president's initiative. There is, of course, considerable variation in the timeliness of the properties being studied. Presidential popularity, inflation, and unemployment are usually reported on a monthly basis. Changes in the GNP are announced each quarter. The size of congressional staffs can be calculated for each year. The biannual election cycle means that the number of seats in the Congress controlled by the president's party fluctuates every two years, except for vacancies created by deaths or retirements and the consequent replacement of members. Presidential elections occur only once in four years, so whatever mandate is produced has to be applied to an entire term, even though the effects are known to wane.

Appendix D. Explanatory Variables

The following variables are used in the analysis of congressional responses to presidential initiatives, as presented in Chapters 3 through 7. This appendix describes the derivation of those variables and the sources of the data used to construct them.

Pure Context: Institutional Variables

Level of Congressional Decentralization

An index constructed by standardizing the sum of four standardized variables: the number of committees and subcommittees in Congress, the number of committee and subcommittee staff in Congress, and the percentages of representatives and senators having served six years or less in Congress. The index was calculated for each calendar year and ranges from -1.21 to 2.18, with a mean of -0.06. When used as an ordinal variable, "lowest" decentralization is less than or equal to -0.65; "intermediate" is greater than -0.65 and less than -0.23; and "highest" is greater than or equal to -0.23. The divisions separate the sample roughly into thirds at natural breaks in the distribution.

Sources of data: Charles B. Brownson, ed., *Congressional Staff Directory* (New York: Bobbs-Merrill, various years); Norman J. Ornstein, Thomas E. Mann, and Michael J. Malbin, *Vital Statistics on Congress, 1987–1988* (Washington, D.C.: American Enterprise Institute, 1987); *Congressional Quarterly Almanac, 1957* (Washington, D.C.: Congressional Quarterly, 1958); Judy Schneider, "Congressional Staffing, 1947–1978," Congressional Research Service, August 24, 1979, reprinted in U.S. Congress, House Select Committee on Committees, *Final Report*, April 1, 1980.

Implementation of Budget and Impoundment Control Act

The Budget and Impoundment Control Act was enacted in 1974, but its provisions did not become fully operational until congressional action in 1975 on the fiscal 1976 budget.

Strength of Public Attachment to Political Parties

The inverse of a variable constructed by standardizing the sum of three standardized variables: the percentage of the public claiming to be independents, the percentage of voters who in the most recent House election deviated from their party affiliation, and the percentage of voters who reported having voted for presidential candidates of different parties in a series of elections. The index, calculated for four-year periods, ranges from −1.24 to 1.51, with a mean of −0.007. When used as an ordinal variable, "weaker public partisan attachments" are less than or equal to −0.76, "medium" are greater than −0.76 and less than 0.77, and "stronger" are greater than or equal to 0.77. The divisions separate the sample roughly into thirds at natural breaks in the distribution.

Sources of data: Herbert B. Asher, *Presidential Elections and American Politics*, 3rd ed. (Homewood, Ill.: Dorsey Press, 1984), p. 32; Morris P. Fiorina, "The Presidency and the Contemporary Electoral System," in *The Presidency and the Political System*, ed. Michael Nelson (Washington, D.C.: CQ Press, 1984), pp. 204–226; Warren E. Miller, Arthur H. Miller, and Edward J. Schneider, *American Election Studies Data Sourcebook, 1952–1978* (Cambridge, Mass.: Harvard University Press, 1980), p. 383; and data from the National Election Study, 1952, 1954, 1982, and 1984, Center for Political Studies, University of Michigan, supplied by the ICPSR.

Strength of Partisan Linkages among Elected Officials

The inverse of a variable constructed by standardizing the sum of three standardized variables: the percentage of House districts in the previous election carried by House and presidential candidates of different parties, the percentage of voters in the previous election who reported voting for House and presidential candidates of different parties, and the percentage of voters who reported voting for senatorial and presidential candidates of different parties. The

index was calculated for four-year periods and ranges from −1.57 to
1.44 with a mean of 0.18. When used as an ordinal variable,
"weaker partisan linkages" are less than or equal to −0.3,
"medium" are greater than −0.3 and less than 0.52, and "stronger"
are greater than or equal to 0.52. The divisions separate the sample
roughly into thirds at natural breaks in the distribution.

Sources of data: Warren E. Miller, Arthur H. Miller, and Edward
J. Schneider, *American Election Studies Data Sourcebook,
1952–1978* (Cambridge, Mass.: Harvard University Press, 1980),
pp. 386, 388; Norman J. Ornstein, Thomas E. Mann, and Michael
J. Malbin, *Vital Statistics on Congress, 1987–1988* (Washington,
D.C.: American Enterprise Institute, 1987), pp. 17–19; and data
from the National Election Study, 1980 and 1984, Center for
Political Studies, University of Michigan, supplied by the ICPSR.

Degree of Elaboration of Interest Group System

An index constructed by standardizing the sum of three standardized variables: the cumulative number of lobby registrations
recorded with the Clerk of the House, the growth in the number
of national voluntary membership associations, and the total
number of political action committees. The cumulative number
of lobby registrations was calculated by adding the new registrations of each year to the previous total, which was discounted by
an arbitrary 10% to compensate for inactive and multiple-lobby
representatives. The growth in the number of voluntary associations was based on the differences in dates of origin reported by
groups in a 1985 survey of associations, adjusted to compensate
for an estimated 4.6% mortality rate over each five-year period.
The index, calculated for each calendar year, ranges from −1.0 to
2.12, with a mean of −0.19. When used as an ordinal variable, a
"less complex" interest group system is less than or equal to
−0.72; "intermediate" is greater than −0.72 to less than −0.14,
and "more complex" is greater than or equal to −0.14. The divisions separate the sample roughly into thirds at natural breaks in
the distribution.

Sources of data on lobby registrations: *Congress and the Nation,*
vol. 2, *1965–1968* (Washington, D.C.: Congressional Quarterly
Service, 1969), p. 925; vol. 3, p. 477; and *Congressional Quarterly
Almanac,* 1975–1986 issues. On voluntary associations, see the
1985 survey by Jack L. Walker, Institute of Public Policy Studies,

University of Michigan. For a discussion of the mortality rate, see Mark A. Peterson and Jack L. Walker, "Interest Group Responses to Partisan Change: The Impact of the Reagan Administration on the National Interest Group System," in *Interest Group Politics*, 2nd ed., ed. Allan J. Cigler and Burdett A. Loomis (Washington, D.C.: CQ Press, 1986), p. 165. On political action committees: Larry J. Sabato, *PAC Power: Inside the World of Political Action Committees* (New York: W. W. Norton, 1985), pp. 12–13; *Congressional Quarterly Almanac*, 1953–1971 issues; and Federal Election Commission, *Record* 11 (March 1985): 6; 12 (March 1986): 6; 13 (February 1987): 10.

Malleable Context: Dynamic Political Variables

Period of the Administration

The categories representing the period within the administration are nearly synonymous with the year within the presidential term. First and second terms were aggregated. The categories are "honeymoon/first year," "midterm election," "post-midterm election year," and "presidential election year." Special consideration had to be given to the Johnson and Ford administrations because of the unusual circumstances that initiated them. For Johnson, the end of 1963 and all of 1965 were treated as "honeymoon/first year" periods, with 1964 constituting a presidential election year. Ford's "honeymoon" was defined as lasting until the pardon of former President Nixon on September 8, 1974, and the remainder of 1974 was treated as a midterm election year.

President's Percentage of the Two-Party Vote in the Previous Presidential Election

The actual percentage of the two-party vote received by the president. When used as an ordinal variable, the categories are "less than a majority," "51% to 60%," and "61% or more."

Estimated Coattail Effects on House Voting (1956–1980)

The predicted percentage-point increase in voting for House candidates of the president's party created by the inclusion of presidential candidate evaluations in voter decisions, calculated by

Randall L. Calvert and John A. Ferejohn using data from the National Election Studies. "Coattail Voting in Recent Presidential Elections," *American Political Science Review* 77 (June 1983), table 2, p. 415. When used as an ordinal variable, the categories are "none," "up to 5 percentage points," and "more than 5 percentage points."

Difference between President's Popular Vote Percentage and Percentage of the Vote Received by House Candidates of the President's Party

The actual percentage-point difference between the president's two-party vote and the two-party vote received by House candidates of the president's party. When used as an ordinal variable, the categories are "president ran behind," "president ran up to 5 points ahead," and "president ran more than 5 points ahead."

Sources of data: Norman J. Ornstein, Thomas E. Mann, and Michael J. Malbin, eds., *Vital Statistics on Congress, 1982* (Washington, D.C.: American Enterprise Institute, 1982); and Bureau of the Census, *Statistical Abstract of the United States, 1986*, 106th ed. (Washington, D.C.: G.P.O., 1980), p. 245.

Percentage of Seats Controlled by the President's Party in the House of Representatives

The actual percentage of seats held by the president's party in each year. When used as an ordinal variable, the categories are "less than a majority," "51% to 60%," and "61% or more," the latter being a supermajority.

Percentage of Seats Controlled by the President's Party in the Senate

Same procedure as with the House. The ordinal middle category, however, is "50% to 60%," because the vice president can cast the tie-breaking vote in favor of the president's party.

Percentage of the Public Approving of the President's Job Performance

Measured in the month prior to final action by Congress, using the figures reported by the Gallup poll. If no polls were reported then, data were taken from the most recent month with a reported poll. When used as an ordinal variable, categories are "40% or less," "41% to 49%," "50% to 60%," and "61% or more."

Sources of data: Everett C. Ladd, "Public Opinion: Questions at the Quinquenniel," *Public Opinion* (April/May): 32, 40; *The Gallup Poll, Public Opinion 1935–1971*, vols. 2 and 3 (New York: Random House, 1972); *Public Opinion* (February/March 1986); and *Gallup Report* (May 1986).

Level and Trend in Public Approval of the President's Job Performance

Combines the absolute level of support for the president and the trend in support over the previous quarter. A high level of support is defined as approval of the president's performance by 61% or more of the public; intermediate support is 40% to 60%, and low support is defined as less than 40%. A constant or rising trend in support means that over the previous quarter the president's support was either constant or fluctuating without a pattern, or that it rose by more than 4 percentage points. A constant or falling trend means that the president's support was constant or fluctuating, or that it fell by more than 4 percentage points. All other cases are "mixed."

Malleable Context: Economic Variables

Quarterly Changes in the Real Gross National Product

Change in the log of the GNP for the quarter prior to final congressional action from the log of the GNP for the quarter one year before. The values range from −3.1% to 7.8%. When used as an ordinal variable, the categories are "decline or no change," "up to 5% growth," and "more than 5% growth."

Source: Citibase data provided by Nathaniel Beck.

Size of the Federal Budget Deficit

Calculated as a percentage of the Gross National Product for each calendar year using deficit and GNP figures from the National Income and Products Accounts (NIPA). When used as an ordinal variable, categories are "surplus or balanced budget," "less than 2% of GNP," "2% or more of GNP."

Sources: Herbert Stein, *Presidential Economics: The Making of Economic Policy from Roosevelt to Reagan and Beyond* (New York: Simon and Schuster, 1984), p. 381. The deficit for 1983–1986 is calculated from figures provided over the telephone by the Department of Commerce.

Monthly Unemployment Rate

Measured in the month prior to final action by Congress on the president's proposal. The figures range from 2.9% to 10.7%. When used as an ordinal variable, categories are "less than 5%," "between 5% and 7%," and "7% or more."

Source: Citibase data provided by Nathaniel Beck.

Trend in Monthly Unemployment Rate

Defined as a rise or a decline of more than 0.2 percentage point during the quarter prior to congressional action. Smaller overall changes are defined as constant or fluctuating.

Level of Monthly Inflation

Calculated as the change in the log of the Consumer Price Index (CPI) for the month prior to final congressional action on a presidential proposal from the log of the CPI for the same month one year before.

Source: Citibase data provided by Nathaniel Beck.

Trend in Monthly Inflation

Inflation skyrocketed in the period from 1953 to the early 1980s. Until the late 1960s the country was accustomed to annual inflation rates of less than 2%, and sometimes less than 1%. The 1970s witnessed annual inflation rates as high as 13.5%. The American public and elected officials are now accustomed to, and view favorably, inflation rates of less than 5% a year. A significant change in the inflation rate in 1956, therefore, would scarcely be measurable in the context of 1980. And changes in the rate that would be significant for the late 1970s would overwhelm all of the fluctuations in the 1950s, giving the appearance of no discernible change in prices. Trends in inflation, therefore, are treated as discernible changes of any size over the previous quarter.

Strategic Policy Context

Innovativeness of the President's Proposals

Categorized using John Campbell's scheme involving size of impact (large-small) and nature of approach (new-old). The former involves a judgment about the budgetary or societal impact of the proposal; the latter poses the question raised by Paul Light, "Did the [proposal] involve a new departure in domestic policy or a modification of a past initiative [or existing program]?" Categories are "large/new," "large/old," "small/new," and "small/old." The coding rules are not precise, but in most cases there was little ambiguity. Deciding what constituted a large policy departure, however, was more troublesome. Light defines large programs (using entire bills) in the same way that I have characterized major legislation, using the Congressional Quarterly Legislative Boxscores. But not all legislation appearing in the Legislative Boxscores could be considered large, and some programs not included in the Boxscores should be viewed as large. Nor can one rely on dollar figures, since some proposals (such as civil rights legislation) have significance well beyond their budgetary impact. See John Creighton Campbell, "The Old People Boom and Japanese Policy Making," *Journal of Japanese Studies* 5 (Summer 1979): 321–357; and Paul C. Light, "Passing Nonincremental Policy: Presidential Influence in Congress, Kennedy to Carter," *Congress and the Presidency* 9 (Winter 1981–82): 65.

Importance of the Overall Program of Which the President's Proposal was a Part

Determined largely by the appearance of the legislation in several specialized sources. If for any year during which it was under consideration the bill or program of which the proposal was a part appeared in the CQ Congressional or Legislative Boxscore (which identifies the most significant legislative issues considered by Congress each year), then the legislation was considered of major importance. If there was no indication that the legislation was significant—no mention in the Congressional Boxscore, no article in the CQ *Almanac* or *National Journal*, no other similar reference—then the legislation is treated as of minor importance. Intermediate importance indicates that the program or bill received some specific treatment in the CQ *Almanac*, *National Journal*, and perhaps other sources. Since the Congressional Boxscore was not available for all years, a judgment sometimes had to be made based on an appraisal of the program. It should be noted that "major" legislation is not the same thing as controversial or newsworthy legislation. Of the proposals linked to major legislation, 41% passed by compromise or consensus and 14% received no congressional action at all.

Effect of the President's Proposal on the Status Quo

Proposals that preserve the status quo include reauthorizations that did not change existing statutes and positions taken by the president against the introduction of new legislation, such as executive opposition to calls for new taxes in a particular year. Changes in the status quo are the opposite. Only 12 of the 299 proposals sought to preserve the status quo. The distinction was suggested by Thomas Schwartz.

Requirement of the Proposal for Congressional Action

Proposals that do not require congressional action include some reorganization plans and presidential positions opposed to new legislation. Only 7 of the 299 proposals did not require congressional action.

Presidential Priority of the Proposal

Legislation is considered to be of "highest presidential priority" if it was presented in a presidential message to Congress specific to the policy area of the program, in a letter to the speaker of the House or the president of the Senate, or in an address to either a joint session of Congress or a television audience. A "medium priority" program is one that did not receive any of the above treatment, but that appeared in the State of the Union address, the budget or economic message, or a letter to members of Congress other than the speaker of the House or president of the Senate. "Lowest priority" legislation involves presentation in none of these forums.

Mean Total Presidential References

The average number of messages, statements, or other settings in which the president made specific or general references to the program during the period that the legislation was under consideration by Congress.

Sources: *Public Papers of the Presidents of the United States* and *Weekly Compilation of Presidential Documents.*

Mean Monthly Presidential References

The total number of presidential references divided by the total number of months that the proposal was under consideration by Congress, which is defined as the number of months between the date legislation was introduced (if there was an administration bill) or the date of the president's statement announcing the proposal (if there was not an administration bill), and the date of the president's last day in office.

Form of the Legislation of Which the President's Proposal Was a Part

Involves four different ways in which the legislation may have been produced. "White House drafted" proposals include initiatives that appeared, based on a reading of the CQ *Almanac* and the *National Journal,* to have been produced largely in the White House, by other agencies in the Executive Office of the President, or by task forces and commissions. "Agency or departmentally drafted" proposals are those that appeared to have been produced in an agency or cabinet department, but that at some point received explicit presidential endorsement in a message to Congress or other presidential statement. "Proposals on the Hill" refer to instances in which the president appeared to have assimilated as part of the presidential program an initiative already existing in Congress, without offering an executive version of the bill. Finally, there are a few proposals that were made by the president in some form but did not appear to involve an actual draft of legislation.

Percentage of the Public Identifying the Policy Area of the President's Proposal as the Most Important Problem Facing the Nation

Based on responses to the question frequently asked by the Gallup poll, "What do you think is the most important problem facing this country today?" The question was included in Gallup polls on eighty-five occasions from March 1954 to October 1985. There was often a period of several months between the date of congressional action on an initiative and the date of the survey, so the results from the poll conducted closest in time to congressional action were used. One might be concerned that the salience of issues merely reflects public attention to coverage of the struggle between the president and factions in Congress. Of the fourteen proposals in which 50% or more of the public identified the policy areas as constituting major problems for the country, however, three of the surveys occurred in the same month as congressional action, ten surveys entered the field *before* congressional action, and only one was administered afterward.

Source: *Gallup Report,* 1954–1985 issues.

Frequency with Which the President Used Strategies Associated with "Going Public"

Strategies for each proposal are identified according to the kinds of presidential statements that made either specific reference to the proposal itself or general reference to the overall program, bill, or policy area of the proposal. One strategy was the use of television or radio addresses, excluding routine speeches such as delivery of the State of the Union address before a joint session of Congress. Another strategy employed special-constituency messages, such as presidential statements to interest-group leaders, town meetings, interviews with local media, and other public presidential statements not directed toward a national broadcast audience. The category of "no public strategy" includes none of the references mentioned above.

Sources: *Public Papers of the Presidents of the United States* and *Weekly Compilation of Presidential Documents.*

Appropriateness of Conditions for Employing a Public Strategy

Conditions "favorable for using public strategies" are defined as occurring when the president's job performance was approved of by 50% or more of the public and any percentage of the public had identified the policy area as the most important problem facing the nation. Conditions "not favorable for using public strategies" are defined as occurring when the president's job performance was approved of by less than 50% of the public and none of the public had identified the policy area as the most important problem facing the nation. Other conditions are "mixed."

Occurrence of Events Associated with the President's Proposal

The occurrence of an event includes an incident that led directly to initiation of the president's proposal, such as the earthquake that struck the state of Alaska in 1964, or an event that happened after introduction of the proposal that was related to the policy being pursued by the president, such as the assassination of Senator Robert Kennedy while Congress was considering President Johnson's gun control legislation.

Type of Policy Represented by the President's Proposal

Categorization of the president's proposals into distributive, regulatory, redistributive, and constituent policies is based on the procedures explained in Robert J. Spitzer, "Presidential Policy Determinism: How Policies Frame Congressional Responses to the President's Legislative Program," *Presidential Studies Quarterly* 13 (Fall 1983): appendix A, pp. 569–570.

Consequentiality of the President's Proposal

Determined by whether the proposal possessed the following characteristics: it was associated with major legislation; the program was of highest priority to the president; it was a large policy departure; and the legislation appeared to have been drafted by the White House, task forces, or special commissions. The "most consequential" proposals had at least three of these attributes; the "least consequential" had none; and those of "intermediate consequence" had one or two.

Appendix E. Multivariate Analysis

The introduction of multivariate statistical techniques to examine congressional responses to presidential initiatives invites a brief discussion about the character of the "dependent variables" associated with the conflict and presidential preference dimensions. Standard forms of multivariate analysis, where a linear relationship is hypothesized to exist between the set of independent or explanatory variables and the dependent variable, require that the dependent variable adhere to certain specifications. It must be measured as an interval scale, so that the categories of the variable are explicitly and conceptually equidistant from one another and the interpretation of a one-unit change in the value of the dependent variable is the same throughout the range of its scale. Predictions of the dependent variable generated by the analysis must also fall within the range of values that are empirically possible. If the lowest actual value is zero, there can be no meaningful prediction of negative values. None of these conditions holds for the conflict dimension or the presidential preference dimension constructed and examined in Chapter 6.

For each dimension, I assume an *underlying* interval scale that is not explicitly measured but that is reflected in the form of congressional action taken on the president's proposals. The five types of congressional responses represent discrete categories of events, with each category displaying similar collective behavioral characteristics. Since they reflect the underlying interval dimension, these categories can also be placed along an ordinal scale. For example, we can compare two congressional responses and know that one reveals more conflict than the other, but we cannot measure precisely how much more. Because of the process of grouping, which is necessitated by the nature of the information involved, individual cases are not assigned to precise positions on the underlying interval scale.

A simple hypothetical example will clarify the matter. Suppose that we have a dependent variable indicating the heights of individuals, but the available information only allows us to classify each person as "short," "of medium height," or "tall," coded 1, 2, and 3 respectively. Suppose further that we have a sample of ten individuals, X_1 to X_{10}, three of whom are short, four who are of medium height, and three of whom are tall:

X_1	X_2	X_3	X_4	X_5	X_6	X_7	X_8	X_9	X_{10}
1. SHORT			2. OF MEDIUM HEIGHT				3. TALL		

While the height variable is appropriately ordinal, it does not capture the true position of the individuals along the scale. Individual X_7 is treated as one unit taller than X_1, and X_4 is also treated as one unit taller than X_3, even though the actual difference in height is obviously greater for the first pair. Statistical techniques such as regression analysis, with the three-level height scale used as a dependent variable, suffer from the lost measure of true variation among the cases. As a result, the variance of residuals produced by the analysis is heteroskedastic, violating one of the most important assumptions of the regression model.[1] The analysis is also likely to underestimate the impact of the independent variables introduced to explain the variations in the dependent variable.[2]

In addition, as a "variance model" regression analysis is most appropriate for situations when the hypothesized relationships between the dependent and explanatory variables are of the sort where a unit change measured in an explanatory variable produces a specific measurable change in the dependent variable.[3] I have argued in the case of congressional responses to presidential initiatives, however, that the influence of the various properties of the pure, malleable, and policy contexts is probabilistic. Anything

1. John H. Aldrich and Forrest D. Nelson, *Linear Probability, Logit, and Probit Models* (Beverly Hills, Calif.: Sage Publications, 1984), pp. 27–28; and Richard D. McKelvey and William Zavoina, "A Statistical Model for the Analysis of Ordinal Level Dependent Variables," *Journal of Mathematical Sociology* 4 (1974): 104–105.

2. Aldrich and Nelson, *Linear Probability*, p. 29.

3. Lawrence B. Mohr, *Explaining Organizational Behavior* (San Francisco: Jossey-Bass, 1982), pp. 37–44.

can happen at any time, and often does; but changes in the configuration of contextual properties produce changes in the probabilities of any particular kind of congressional response. Therefore, the appropriate multivariate technique for this analysis is one that both incorporates the notion of the underlying interval dimension and explicitly suits probabilistic relationships.

Ordered multinormal probit analysis satisfies these requirements.[4] First, both dichotomous and polytomous probit routines interpret the dependent variable as one (in the former case) or more (in the latter case) discrete probabilistic events that either occur or do not occur. Changes in the explanatory variables produce changes in the predicted probabilities that these events will transpire. Second, the ordered probit model interprets a polytomous dependent variable as an ordinal array of grouped responses or events that reflects a hypothesized and unmeasured underlying interval scale. It uses "maximum likelihood estimation" techniques to identify the parameter values that would be the most likely to generate the observed distribution of the dependent variable given the assumed underlying dimension, the configuration of values for the explanatory variables in the data set, and the basic assumption of linearity in the relationships between the underlying dependent variable and the explanatory variables. Third, ordered probit statistical routines produce several kinds of information that aid in understanding the relationship between the explanatory variables, both individually and collectively, and the dimension to be explained. Variable coefficients are similar to the coefficients produced in regression analysis, estimating the direction and strength of the relationship between the explanatory variables and *the underlying interval dimension* of the dependent variable. Calculated standard errors allow one to test whether the coefficients are statistically different from zero for the sample. The analysis also generates, for each case, the predicted probabilities of each category of event identified in the dependent variable. Among other things, these estimated probabilities allow the model to predict which event of the dependent variable is most likely to occur for each case; it is possible, therefore, to derive a summary statement on how many of the cases in the data set are predicted correctly. For these reasons ordered

4. The underlying but not explicitly measured interval variable is assumed to be normally distributed.

multinormal probit analysis is the statistical instrument used in Chapter 6 to conduct a multivariate analysis of the presidential-congressional relationship with regard to the president's domestic legislative initiatives, first with reference to cooperation and conflict, and then with attention to presidentially preferred legislative action.[5]

Despite the advantages of the multivariate approach, a few qualifications need to be addressed. The analysis is complicated by the nature of the data constituting the sample of presidential proposals. The sample creates two limitations for the research. First, because the institutional properties of the pure context all have a strong time dimension—the institutional changes have paralleled one another from 1953 to the present—the level of multicollinearity among the variables representing institutional change is high enough to pose difficulties for multivariate techniques. Because, at the same time that Congress has become decentralized, the parties have weakened and the interest-group community has become more complicated, any statistical technique is hard pressed to identify the independent effects of each of these changes.[6] Second, even with 299 proposals in the sample of presidential initiatives, there are not enough cases to calibrate as effectively as one would like the impact of all the factors discussed in Chapters 4 and 5. There simply are too few cases to permit all the different combinations across explanatory variables that would be necessary to fully explain the variation in the ways in which Congress has responded to the president's proposals.[7] In addition, of course, even with the broad range of contextual properties that I have discussed in this book, many relevant attributes have been left out because of the impossibility of carefully measuring them.

5. The ordered probit analysis was accomplished using SST (Statistical Software Tools), a statistical package for personal computers created by Jeffrey A. Dubin and R. Douglas Rivers, version 1.1, copyright March 1987.

6. Eric A. Hanushek and John E. Jackson, *Statistical Methods for Social Scientists* (New York: Academic Press, 1977), p. 87.

7. Ibid., p. 90.

Index

4.00